THE BERLITZ SELF-TEACHER:
HEBREW

THE BERLITZ
SELF-TEACHER:
HEBREW

BY THE EDITORIAL STAFF OF
BERLITZ PUBLICATIONS, INC.

GROSSET & DUNLAP

PUBLISHERS   NEW YORK

INTRODUCTION

In presenting the BERLITZ SELF-TEACHER: HEBREW to the public, the Berlitz Schools are proud to take part in a linguistic movement that has brought Hebrew back from the status of a dead language to that of a very live one of constantly increasing importance.

Fifty years ago Hebrew was in the domain of theological and linguistic scholars; now it is the living tool in education, commerce, government and day-to-day life of a young and vigorous nation. It is indicative of the increasing importance of the language that this should be the eighth of the Berlitz Self-Teacher series, heretofore published only in the traditionally important world languages of French, Spanish, German, Italian, Russian, Portuguese and English.

In presenting BERLITZ SELF-TEACHER: HEBREW we have endeavored to select a modern, up-to-date vocabulary which the traveler will find of immediate use upon his arrival in Israel. At the same time, we have not neglected the basic grammar of Hebrew which we have presented through usable and concrete examples. If some of these grammatical concepts seem completely different from those familiar to the student in his own language, he should be more than compensated by the realization that he is using the same vocabulary and the same

v

construction used by Moses, Solomon, David and the other great kings, prophets, and lawmakers of Hebrew history. For Hebrew, though in a sense the youngest language, is really the most ancient in current use, and if a student of today could travel backward in time, he would not have much difficulty making himself understood at the court of King Solomon, with the possible exception of some words like "airplane" (aviron), "passport" (darkon), or "taxi" (monit).

We have employed our own phonetic system in this book, written directly under the Hebrew letters. Thus, "airplane" is rendered by *ah-vee*-ROHN with the stress on the last syllable. But although this will give you the closest approximate pronunciation, nothing can take the place of listening to a native speaker's rendition of the word. We urge you, moreover, to read aloud and constantly to practice the lessons and questions (the answers to which are in the back of the book) with your Hebrew-speaking friends. If you have difficulty on any point, drop in at the nearest Berlitz School. We shall be glad to help you!

The authors wish to express their appreciation to Mr. Moshe Jahrblum, Hebrew educator and writer, and teacher with the Israeli Ministry of Education, for his valuable assistance in the preparation of this book.

R. S-D.
C. F. B.

THE HEBREW ALPHABET

When people say that Hebrew is written backward, they are completely in error. This system goes back to the dawn of history when all alphabetical languages were written from *right* to *left*, so it is really English, not Hebrew, that is written "backward."

Remember, when you start the first lesson, that every Hebrew word or sentence is read in the exact reverse order of English. In order to get used to this idea, read the following twenty-two letters of the Hebrew alphabet. We have added after each one the phonetic rendition of its name. The syllables in capital letters are stressed.

START HERE ⟶

(DAH-*let*) ד	(GHEE-*mel*) ג	(*beht*) ב	(AH-*lef*) א ⟵
(*het*) ח	(ZIGH-*yin*) ז	(*vahv*) ו	(*heh*) ה
(LAH-*med*) ל	(*kahf*) כ	(*yood*) י	(*tet*) ט
(EYE-*yin*) ע	(SAH-*mekh*) ס	(*noon*) נ	(*mem*) מ
(*rehsh*) ר	(*koof*) ק	(TSAH-*dee*) צ	(*peh*) פ
	(*tahv*) ת	(*sheen*) ש	

To these we can add four alternative forms as follows:

START HERE ⟶

(*seen*) ש	(*feh*) פ	(*hahf*) כ	(*veht*) ב ⟵

In these last four forms, the only difference in writing is that the dot has been either dropped or displaced.

These letters correspond generally to English letters, the Ahlef to A, Beht to B, Dahlet to D, etc.

But, the student may ask, what about the vowels? Is Hebrew *all* consonants?

Far from it. Hebrew has evolved an ingenious system of dots and marks, placed under the letters, to indicate the vowel that follows the consonant. These dots, called "nikkud", represent long and short vowel sounds. There is a long and a short nikkud for each vowel sound: ah, eh, ee, oh, oo. The nikkud for the short sounds are ־ ־ ⋅ ⋅ ⋅ ׀ Therefore בַ (*beht*) would read bah, beh, bee, boh or boo, if the nikkud were written בַ בֶ בִ בֹ בֻ respectively. This first group of five are called the short vowels.

There is still another set corresponding exactly but representing longer sounds. They are written, using בּ (*beht*) as an example, as follows: בָ(*bah*) בֵ (*beh*) בִי (*bee*) בּוֹ (*boh*) בּוּ (*boo*). As you see, the long sound of ah has the same symbol as the short symbol of oh.

You will notice that the *long* sounds are not always written *under* the letter, but may be written to the left, even using a completely separate letter as a nikkud or vowel. This may seem confusing, but it has been established by many centuries of use. Don't think that English is not confusing too, with its different sounds for the same letters! In basing its spelling on consonants, Hebrew, although coming to us from antiquity, bears a resemblance to modern shorthand. At any rate, usage has largely discarded the nikkud. We have used them only through the tenth lesson to make your initial reading guess-free.

Now that you have a nodding acquaintance with the alphabet and the nikkud, let us see how some common Hebrew words are written.

Take a word like "pen" for instance, which is pronounced "eht" and written (from right to left) עֵט or "Saturday" (*Shah*-ВАНТ) written שַׁבָּת . Notice that the latter word uses one short and one long vowel. You will get used to these nikkud through practice and association.

There is one more vowel sound represented by two dots ":" and pronounced like a very short "eh" if it occurs at the beginning or in the middle of a word after a long vowel. In fact it hardly has a sound of its own and in our phonetic transliteration we have indicated it as an apostrophe. If it occurs with ה ח ע א , it must be reinforced by ָ ֳ or ֱ to obtain the corresponding vowel sound. In this way we can obtain such combinations as חָ, הֶ, אֱ which have the sounds of hah, heh and oh.

One thing more: the same letter can never be written twice consecutively in Hebrew. So a small dot is added immediately after the letter to double it.

Now you have the information essential to enable you to cope with the Hebrew text yourself. In order to help you even more, we have written our phonetic transliteration, sentence by sentence, under the Hebrew text. *Remember to read the Hebrew from right to left!* Now turn to the first lesson and מזל טוב ! (Good luck!).

RECITE THE ALPHABET! Here are the letters of the Hebrew alphabet with the pronunciation of their names and their approximate phonetic equivalents in English:

HEBREW LETTER	NAME OF THE LETTER	PHONETIC EQUIVALENT
א	AH-*lef*	ah
ב	*beht*	b
ג	GHEE-*mel*	gh
ד	DAH-*let*	d
ה	*heh*	h
ו	*vahv*	v
ז	ZIGH-*yin*	z
ח	*het*	kh
ט	*tet*	t
י	*yood*	y
כ	*kahf*	k
ל	LAH-*med*	l
מ	*mem*	m
נ	*noon*	n
ס	SAH-*mekh*	s
ע	EYE-*yin*	ah
פ	*peh*	p
צ	TSAH-*dee*	ts
ק	*koof*	k
ר	*rehsh*	r
ש	*sheen*	sh
ת	*tahv*	t

and the alternative letters:

ב	*veht*	v
כ	*hahf*	kh
פ	*feh*	f
ש	*seen*	s

Five letters have a different shape when they occur at the end of a word:

The final	כ	or	כ	is written	ך
The final	מ			is written	ם
The final	נ			is written	ן
The final	פ	or	פ	is written	ף
The final	צ			is written	ץ

מַה זֶה?

Mah zeh?

What is this?

נְיָר	סֵפֶר	עִפָּרוֹן
n'yahr	SEH-*fer*	*Ee-pah-*ROHN
paper	book	pencil

מַפְתֵּחַ	קוּפְסָה	עֵט
*mahf-*TEH-*akh*	*koof-*SAH	*eht*
key	box	pen

הַזֶה עִפָּרוֹן?	כֵּן, זֶה עִפָּרוֹן.
*Hah-*ZEH *ee-pah-*ROHN?	*Kehn, zeh ee-pah-*ROHN.
Is this a pencil?	Yes, this is a pencil.

הַזֹאת קוּפְסָה?	כֵּן, זֹאת קוּפְסָה.
*Hah-*ZOHT *koof-*SAH?	*Kehn, zoht koof-*SAH.
Is this a box?	Yes, this is a box.

1

הַזֶה עֵט?

Hah-ZEH eht?
Is this a pen?

לֹא, זֶה לֹא עֵט, זֶה סֵפֶר.

Lo, zeh lo eht, zeh SEH-fer.
No, this is not a pen, this is a book.

WATCH OUT FOR THE GENDER: There are two genders in Hebrew, masculine and feminine. Of the six words we have already seen, all are masculine except קוּפְסָה (*koof-SAH*). You can usually recognize feminine nouns by watching for the ending in ﬞﬞה (*ah*) or ת (*t*). Moreover, the words "zeh" and "zoht" both meaning "this" are used for masculine and feminine nouns respectively.

כִּסֵא	שֻׁלְחָן	מְנוֹרָה
kis-SEH	*shool-HAHN*	*m'noh-RAH*
chair	table	lamp

הַזֹאת מְנוֹרָה?

Hah-ZOHT m'noh-RAH?
Is this a lamp?

לֹא, זֹאת לֹא מְנוֹרָה, זֶה שֻׁלְחָן.

Lo, zoht lo m'noh-RAH, zeh shool-HAHN.
No, this is not a lamp; it is a table.

NOTE TO STUDENT: ה (*Hah*), as used above, is simply an interrogative particle, the only function of which is to make the sentence a question. There is another ה (*Hah*), meaning "the". The interrogation can also be expressed by a simple rising inflection of the voice, as in English, without the use of the interrogative particle.

NEGATIVE FORM OF VERBS

There is a special negative form in Hebrew, which will be explained later, when you learn some verbs. In sentences where *no* verb is used, the repetition of the word לֹא (*lo*), as shown above, supplies a colloquially acceptable and easy negative. Example: לֹא, זֶה לֹא סֵפֶר (*Lo, zeh lo SEH-fer*) "No, it is not a book".

HELPFUL HINT: The present tense forms of "to be" ("am", "is", and "are") are not used in Hebrew. They are implied. For example:

זאת קופסה   (*Zoht koof-*SAH). "This is a box".

זאת הקופסה   (*Zoht hah-koof-*SAH). "This is the box".

דֶלֶת	חַלוֹן	תְּמוּנָה
DEH-*let*	*hah-*LOHN	*t'moo-*NAH
door	window	picture

רִצְפָּה	תִּקְרָה	קִיר
*ritz-*PAH	*teek-*RAH	*keer*
floor	ceiling	wall

מַה זֶה?   זֶה קִיר, זֹאת דֶלֶת, זֹאת תְּמוּנָה וְכוּ'

Mah zeh?   *Zeh keer, zoht* DEH-*let, zoht t'moo-*NAH*, weh-*HOO.
What is this?   This is a wall, a door, a picture, etc.

אֶחָד	שְׁנַיִם	שְׁלוֹשָׁה	אַרְבָּעָה	חֲמִשָׁה
*eh-*HAHD	*sh'*NAH-*yim*	*sh'loh-*SHAH	*ahr-bah-*AH	*hah-mee-*SHAH
1	2	3	4	5

טוֹב מְאֹד	זֶה הַכֹּל	שָׁלוֹם
*Tov meh-*OHD!	*Zeh hah-*KOHL!	*Shah-*LOHM!
Very good!	That is all!	Good-bye!

NOTE ON GREETINGS: שָׁלוֹם (*shah-*LOHM) meaning "peace" is used at any time of the day to express "Hello!", "good morning", "good evening", or "good-bye", etc. It more than compensates for its lack of variety by the sincerity of its message.

THINKING IN HEBREW

Now, on the basis of your study of the first lesson, read the following questions along in Hebrew and answer them yourself in reference to the pictures alongside the questions. Check your answers in the key beginning on page 278.

1. הֲזֶה סֵפֶר ?
   (*Hah-*ZEH SEH-*fer?*)

2. הֲזֶה עִפָּרוֹן ?
   (*Hah-*ZEH *ee-pah-*ROHN?)

3. הֲזֶה שׁוּלְחָן ?
   (*Hah-*ZEH *shool-*HAHN?)

4. מַה זֶה ?
   (*Mah zeh?*)

5. הֲזֹאת קוּפְסָה ?
   (*Hah-*ZOHT *koof-*SAH?)

6. הֲזֶה חַלוֹן ?
   (*Hah-*ZEH *hah-*LOHN?)

7. הֲזֹאת דֶלֶת ?
   (*Hah-*ZOHT DEH-*let?*)

8. מַה זֹאת ?
   (*Mah zoht?*)

9. הֲזֶה מַפְתֵּחַ ?
   (*Hah-zeh mahf-*TEH-*akh?*)

10. הֲזֶה כִּסֵּא ?
    (*Hah-*ZEH *kis-*SEH?)

11. הֲזֹאת מְנוֹרָה ?
    (*Hah-*ZOHT *m'noh-*RAH?)

12. מַה זֶה ?
    (*Mah zeh?*)

13.   הֲזֶה עִפָּרוֹן?
(Hah-ZEH ee-pah-ROHN?)

14.   הֲזֹאת קוּפְסָה?
(Hah-ZOHT koof-SAH?)

15.   הֲזֶה מַפְתֵּחַ?
(Hah-ZEH mahf-TEH-akh?)

16.   מַה זֶה?
(Mah zeh?)

17.   הֲזֶה שֻׁלְחָן?
(Hah-ZEH shool-HAHN?)

18.   הֲזֶה כִּסֵּא?
(Hah-ZEH kis-SEH?)

19.   הֲזֹאת דָלֶת?
(Hah-ZOHT DEH-let?)

20.   מַה זֶה?
(Mah zeh?)

שִׁעוּר 2

הַבְּגָדִים

*Hah-b'gah-*DEEM

Clothing

מָעִיל	זֶה כּוֹבַע	מַה זֶה?
*meh-*EEL	*Zeh* KOH-*vah.*	*Mah zeh?*
coat	This is a hat	What is this?

אַרְנָק	כִּיס	חֲלִיפָה	צַוָּארוֹן
*ahr-*NAHK	*kiss*	*hah-lee-*FAH	*tsah-vah-*ROHN
purse	pocket	suit	collar

נַעַל	כּוּתֹנֶת	מַה זֹאת?
NAH-*ahl*	*koo-*TOH-*net*	*Mah zoht?*
shoe	shirt	What is this?

GENDER AGAIN: The reason the teacher says here
מַה זֹאת? (*Mah zoht?*) instead of מַה זֶה? (*Mah zeh?*)
is that the objects he is pointing to are feminine.

6

עֲנִיבָה	שִׂמְלָה	מִטְפַּחַת
ah-nee-VAH	*seem-LAH*	*meet-PAH-haht*
tie	dress	handkerchief

הֲזֶה מְעִיל?	לֹא, זֶה לֹא מְעִיל, זֹאת חֲלִיפָה.
Hah-ZEH meh-EEL?	*Lo, zeh lo meh-EEL, zoht hah-lee-FAH.*
Is this a coat?	No, this is not a coat, this is a suit.

הֲזֶה כּוֹבַע, אוֹ צַוָּארוֹן?	זֶה צַוָּארוֹן.
Hah-ZEH KOH-vah, oh tsah-vah-ROHN?	*Zeh tsah-vah-ROHN.*
Is this a hat or a collar?	It is a collar.

הֲזֹאת עֲנִיבָה, אוֹ מִטְפַּחַת?

Hah-ZOHT ah-nee-VAH, oh meet-PAH-haht?
Is this a tie or a handkerchief?

לֹא, זֹאת לֹא עֲנִיבָה, אַף לֹא מִטְפַּחַת, זֹאת כְּפָפָה.

Lo, zoht lo ah-nee-VAH, aff lo meet-PAH-haht, zoht kfah-FAH.
No, this is not a tie, nor a handkerchief; this is a glove.

WATCH OUT: There is no word for "neither". There-fore the expression "also not" אַף לֹא (*aff lo*) is used in its place.

הֲזֹאת שִׂמְלָה, אוֹ מְעִיל?

Hah-ZOHT seem-LAH, oh meh-EEL?
Is this a dress or a coat?

לֹא, זֹאת לֹא שִׂמְלָה, אַף לֹא מְעִיל, זֹאת כֻּתֹּנֶת.

Lo, zoht lo seem-LAH, aff lo meh-EEL, zoht koo-TOH-net.
No, this is neither a dress nor a coat; this is a shirt.

שִׁשָּׁה	שִׁבְעָה	שְׁמוֹנָה	תִּשְׁעָה	עֲשָׂרָה
shee-SHAH	*sheev-AH*	*sh'moh-NAH*	*teesh-AH*	*ah-sah-RAH*
6	7	8	9	10

THINKING IN HEBREW

(Answers on page 278)

1. מַה זֶה?

    Mah zeh?

2. הֲזֹאת נַעַל אוֹ כְּפָפָה?

    Hah-ZOHT NAH-ahl oh kfah-FAH?

3. הֲזֹאת עֲנִיבָה, אוֹ מִטְפַּחַת?

    Hah-ZOHT ah-nee-VAH, oh meet-PAH-haht?

4. מַה זֶה?

    Mah zeh?

5. הֲזֹאת מִטְפַּחַת אוֹ כְּפָפָה?

    Hah-ZOHT meet-PAH-haht oh kfah-FAH?

6. הֲזֶה עִפָּרוֹן?

    Hah-ZEH ee-pah-ROHN?

7. מַה זֶה?

    Mah zeh?

8. הֲזֹאת שִׂמְלָה?

    Hah-ZOHT seem-LAH?

9. הֲזֶה מְעִיל אוֹ כּוֹבַע?

    Hah-ZEH meh-EEL, oh KOH-vah?

10. הֲזֹאת עֲנִיבָה?

    Hah-ZOHT ah-nee-VAH?

11. הֲזֶה כּוֹבַע?

    Hah-ZEH KOH-vah?

שִׁעוּר 3

הַצְּבָעִים

Hah-tsvah-EEM

The colors

שָׁחוֹר	לָבָן	אָדֹם	כָּחֹל
shah-HOHR	*lah*-VAHN	*ah*-DOHM	*kah*-HOHL
black	white	red	blue

יָרֹק	צָהֹב	חוּם	אָפוֹר
yah-ROHK	*tsah*-HOHV	*hoom*	*ah*-FOOR
green	yellow	brown	gray

הַכּוֹבַע שָׁחוֹר.

Hah-KOH-*vah shah*-HOHR.
The hat is black.

הַמְעִיל אָפוֹר.

Hah-meh-EEL *ah*-FOOR.
The coat is gray.

9

הַנַעַל שְׁחוֹרָה.

*Hah-*NAH*-ahl sh'hoh-*RAH.
The shoe is black.

הַכְּפָפָה אֲפוּרָה.

*Hah-kfah-*FAH *ah-foo-*RAH.
The glove is gray.

WATCH OUT: Adjectives agree in gender with the noun. Therefore, each adjective has two forms, as you have seen above. Watch the rest of this lesson for the masculine and feminine forms of each color.

NOTE ON THE ARTICLE: As we mentioned before, הָ or הַ (*hah*) means "the". This article is used to denote a definite person or thing.

הַמְעִיל אָפוּר.

*Hah-meh-*EEL *ah-*FOOR.
The coat is gray.

הַשִׂמְלָה יְרוּקָה.

*Hah-seem-*LAH *y'roo-*KAH.
The dress is green.

מַה צֶבַע הַנַעַל?

Mah TSEH-*vah hah-*NAH*-ahl?*
What color is the shoe?

הַנַעַל שְׁחוֹרָה.

*Hah-*NAH*-ahl sh'hoh-*RAH.
The shoe is black.

מַה צֶבַע הַצַוַארוֹן?

Mah TSEH-*vah hah-tsah-vah-*ROHN?
What color is the collar?

הַצַוַארוֹן לָבָן.

*Hah-tsah-vah-*ROHN *lah-*VAHN.
The collar is white.

הַסֵפֶר יָרוֹק וְצָהוֹב.

*Hah-*SEH*-fer yah-*ROHK *v'tsah-*HOHV.
The book is green and yellow.

הָעֲנִיבָה כְּחוּלָה וּלְבָנָה.

*Hah-ah-nee-*VAH *k'hoo-*LAH *oo-l'vah-*NAH.
The tie is blue and white.

HELPFUL HINT: The two words for "and" וְ (*veh*) and וּ (*oo*) are written together as prefixes to the second of the two words they are connecting. וְ (*veh*) is usually used, but וּ (*oo*) is used when the second

word starts with .פ ,מ ,ו or ב or when the word begins with the short
vowel , (eh).

Example: וּשְׁנַיִם (oo-sh'NAH-yim) — "and two".

מַה צֶבַע הָעִפָּרוֹן?	**הָעִפָּרוֹן שָׁחוֹר.**
Mah TSEH-*vah hah-ee-pah-*ROHN?	*Hah-ee-pah-*ROHN *shah-*HOHR.
What color is the pencil?	The pencil is black.
מַה צֶבַע הָעֵט?	**הָעֵט שָׁחוֹר.**
Mah TSEH-*vah hah-*EHT?	*Hah-*EHT *shah-*HOHR.
What color is the pen?	The pen is black.
מַה צֶבַע הַסֵפֶּר?	**הַסֵפֶר שָׁחוֹר.**
Mah TSEH-*vah hah-*SEH-*fer?*	*Hah-*SEH-*fer shah-*HOHR.
What color is the book?	The book is black.
מַה צֶבַע הָעֲנִיבָה?	**הָעֲנִיבָה שְׁחוֹרָה.**
Mah TSEH-*vah hah-ah-nee-*VAH?	*Hah-ah-nee-*VAH *sh'hoh-*RAH.
What color is the tie?	The tie is black.

BE CAREFUL with the pronunciation of שְׁחוֹרָה
(*sh'hoh-*RAH). Pronounce the first part of the word as
if it were one syllable, with just a slight hesitation
where we have placed the apostrophe.

מַה צֶבַע הַשּׁוּלְחָן?	**הַכִּסֵא?**	**הַקִיר?**
Mah TSEH-*vah hah-shool-*HAHN?	*Hah-kis-*SEH?	*Hah-*KEER?
What color is the table?	The chair?	The wall?

הַשִׂמְלָה?

*Hah-seem-*LAH?
The dress?

הָאָדוֹם הָעִפָּרוֹן?	**כֵּן, הָעִפָּרוֹן אָדוֹם.**
*Hah-ah-*DOHM *hah-ee-pah-*ROHN?	*Kehn, hah-ee-pah-*ROHN *ah-*DOHM.
Is the pencil red?	Yes, the pencil is red.
הַחוּם הָעֵט?	**לֹא, הָעֵט לֹא חוּם.**
*Hah-*HOOM *hah-*EHT?	*Lo, hah-*EHT *lo hoom.*
Is the pen brown?	No, the pen is not brown.

הַיָרֹק הַסֵּפֶר אוֹ כָּחֹל ?

*Hah-yah-*ROHK *hah-*SEH-*fer oh kah-*HOHL?
Is the book green or blue?

הַסֵּפֶר כָּחֹל.

*Hah-*SEH-*fer kah-*HOHL.
The book is blue.

הָעִפָּרוֹן כָּחֹל.

*Hah-ee-pah-*ROHN *kah-*HOHL.
The pencil is blue.

הָעֵט כָּחֹל.

*Hah-*EHT *kah-*HOHL.
The pen is blue.

זֶה הָעִפָּרוֹן הָאָדֹם.

*Zeh hah-ee-pah-*ROHN *hah-ah-*DOHM.
This is the red pencil.

זֶה הָעִפָּרוֹן הַיָרֹק.

*Zeh hah-ee-pah-*ROHN *hah-yah-*ROHK.
This is the green pencil.

זֶה הָעֵט הָאָדֹם.

*Zeh hah-*EHT *hah-ah-*DOHM
This is the red pen.

זֶה הָעֵט הַיָרֹק.

*Zeh hah-*EHT *hah-yah-*ROHK.
This is the green pen.

זֶה הַסֵּפֶר הָאָדֹם.

*Zeh hah-*SEH-*fer hah-ah-*DOHM.
This is the red book.

זֶה הַסֵּפֶר הַיָרֹק.

*Zeh hah-*SEH-*fer hah-yah-*ROHK.
This is the green book.

הָעִפָּרוֹן הַזֶה אָדֹם.

*Hah-ee-pah-*ROHN *hah-*ZEH *ah-*DOHM.
This pencil is red.

הָעִפָּרוֹן הַזֶה שָׁחֹר.

*Hah-ee-pah-*ROHN *hah-*ZEH *shah-*HOHR.
This pencil is black.

הָעֲנִיבָה הַזֹאת כְּחֻלָה.

*Hah-ah-nee-*VAH *hah-*ZOHT *k'hoo-*LAH.
This tie is blue.

הָעֲנִיבָה הַזֹאת יְרֻקָה.

*Hah-ah-nee-*VAH *hah-*ZOHT *y'roo-*KAH.
This tie is green.

הַנְיָר הַהוּא צָהוֹב.

*Hah-n'*YAHR *hah-*HOO *tsah-*HOV.
That paper is yellow.

הַנְיָר הַזֶה לָבָן.

*Hah-n'*YAHR *hah-*ZEH *lah-*VAHN.
This paper is white.

הָעִפָּרוֹן הַזֶּה אָדוֹם.   הַנְּיָר הַהוּא שָׁחוֹר.

*Hah-ee-pah-*ROHN *hah-*ZEH *ah-*DOHM.   *Hah-n'*YAHR *hah-*HOO *shah-*HOHR.

This pencil is red.   That paper is black.

הָעֲנִיבָה הַזֹּאת כְּחוּלָה.

*Hah-ah-nee-*VAH *hah-*ZOHT *k'hoo-*LAH.

This tie is blue.

הָעֲנִיבָה הַהִיא יְרוּקָה.

*Hah-ah-nee-*VAH *hah-*HEE *y'roo-*KAH.

That tie is green.

GRAMMATICAL NOTE: The demonstrative adjectives "this" and "that" are placed after the noun and agree in gender with it. The masculine forms are הַזֶּה (*hah-*ZEH) and הַהוּא (*hah-*HOO), and the feminine forms are הַזֹּאת (*hah-*ZOHT) and הַהִיא (*hah-*HEE).

הַשָּׁחוֹר הָעֵט?   כֵּן, הוּא שָׁחוֹר.

*Hah-shah-*HOHR *hah-*EHT?   *Kehn, hoo shah-*HOHR.

Is the pen black?   Yes, it is black.

לֹא, הוּא לֹא שָׁחוֹר, הוּא יָרוֹק.

*Lo, hoo lo shah-*HOHR, *hoo yah-*ROHK.

No, it is not black, it is green.

הֲלְבָנָה הַכּוּתוֹנֶת?   כֵּן, הִיא לְבָנָה.

*Hah-l'vah-*NAH *hah-koo-*TOH-*net?*   *Kehn, hee l'vah-*NAH.

Is the shirt white?   Yes, it is white.

לֹא, הִיא לֹא לְבָנָה, הִיא כְּחוּלָה.

*Lo, hee lo l'vah-*NAH, *hee k'hoo-*LAH.

No, it is not white, it is blue.

DON'T BE CONFUSED: "He and "she" are הוּא (*hoo*) and הִיא (*hee*) respectively. At first glance, this may befuddle you, but it will help you remember them: *hoo* sounds like "who" and means "he", while *hee* sounds like "he" and means "she".

REMEMBER: There is no neuter in Hebrew. Everything is "he" or "she", even tables, chairs, pencils, etc.

זָהוּ הַנְיָר הַלָּבָן.   זָהוּ הַנְיָר הַצָהוֹב.

zeh-*hoo* hah-n'yahr *hah-lah-vahn*. zeh-*hoo* hah-n'yahr *hah-tsah-*hohv.
This is the white paper.   This is the yellow paper.

הֲזֶה הָעִפָּרוֹן הָאָדוֹם?

Hah-zeh *hah-ee-pah-*rohn *hah-ah-*dohm?
Is this the red pencil?

כֵּן, זָהוּ הָעִפָּרוֹן הָאָדוֹם.

Kehn, zeh-*hoo* hah-ee-pah-rohn *hah-ah-*dohm.
Yes, this is the red pencil.

GRAMMATICAL NOTE: הַ (hah) is used with the adjective as well as the noun. In other words, in the above case you are really saying "Is this the pencil, the red one?"

אֵיזֶה עִפָּרוֹן זֶה?   זֶה עִפָּרוֹן אָדוֹם.

eh-*zeh* ee-pah-rohn zeh?   *Zeh* ee-pah-rohn ah-dohm.
Which pencil is this?   This is a red pencil.

אֵיזוֹ עֲנִיבָה זֹאת?   זֹאת עֲנִיבָה אֲדוּמָה.

eh-*zoh* ah-nee-vah zoht?   *Zoht* ah-nee-vah *ah-doo-*mah.
Which tie is this?   This is a red tie.

NOTE TO STUDENT: Even "which" must vary in gender according to the noun it modifies. The masculine form is אֵיזֶה (eh-zeh) and the feminine אֵיזוֹ (eh-zoh).

אַחַד־עָשָׂר   שְׁנַיִם־עָשָׂר   שְׁלוֹשָׁה־עָשָׂר

Ah-*hahd-ah-*sahr   Sh'nehm-ah-sahr   Sh'loh-shah-*ah-*sahr
11   12   13

אַרְבָּעָה־עָשָׂר   חֲמִשָׁה־עָשָׂר

Ahr-bah-*ah-ah-*sahr   Hah-mee-shah-*ah-*sahr
14   15

THINKING IN HEBREW

(Answers on page 279)

1. הַכָּחוֹל הָעֵט?

*Hah-kah-*HOHL *hah-*EHT?

2. מַה צֶּבַע הָעֵט?

Mah TSEH-*vah hah-*EHT?

3. הָאָדוֹם הָעֵט?

*Hah-ah-*DOHM *hah-*EHT?

4. הֲלָבָן הָעֵט אוֹ שָׁחוֹר?

*Hah-lah-*VAHN *hah-*EHT *oh shah-*HOHR?

5. מַה זֶה?   6. הָאָדוֹם הָעִפָּרוֹן?

Mah zeh?   *Hah-ah-*DOHM *hah-ee-pah-*ROHN?

7. הֲשָׁחוֹר הָעִפָּרוֹן?

*Hah-shah-*HOHR *hah-ee-pah-*ROHN?

8. מַה צֶבַע הָעִפָּרוֹן?

Mah TSEH-*vah hah-ee-pah-*ROHN?

9. מַה זֶה?   10. מַה צֶבַע הַמְנוֹרָה?

Mah zeh?   *Mah* TSEH-*vah hah-m'noh-*RAH?

11. הָאֲדוּמָה הִיא?   12. הָאֲפוּרָה הִיא?

*Hah-ah-doo-*MAH *hee?*   *Hah-ah-foo-*RAH *hee?*

13. הֲזֶה הַסֵּפֶר הָאָדוֹם?

*Hah-*ZEH *hah-*SEH-*fer hah-ah-*DOHM?

14. הֲזֶה הַסֵפֶר הַצָהוֹב?

*Hah-*ZEH *hah-*SEH-*fer hah-tsah-*HOHV?

15. מַה צֶבַע הַסֵּפֶר?

Mah TSEH-*vah hah-*SEH-*fer?*

שִׁעוּר 4

מִדוֹת

Mee-DOHT

The dimensions

הָעִפָּרוֹן הַשָּׁחוֹר אָרוֹךְ.

*Hah-ee-pah-*ROHN *hah-shah-*HOHR *ah-*ROKH.
The black pencil is long.

הָעִפָּרוֹן הָאָדֹם לֹא אָרוֹךְ.   הוּא קָצָר.

*Hah-ee-pah-*ROHN *hah-ah-*DOHM *lo ah-*ROKH.   *Hoo kah-*TSAHR.
The red pencil is not long.   It is short.

אֵיךְ הָעִפָּרוֹן הַשָּׁחוֹר ?   הוּא אָרוֹךְ.

*Ehkh hah-ee-pah-*ROHN *hah-shah-*HOHR?   *Hoo ah-*ROKH.
How is the black pencil?   It is long.

REMEMBER: Adjectives in Hebrew come *after* the noun. There are no exceptions, as in other languages. This is easy, so remember it! In questions this order is reversed.

16

אֵיךְ הָעִפָּרוֹן הָאָדוֹם?

*Ehkh hah-ee-pah-*ROHN *hah-ah-*DOHM?
How is the red pencil?

הוּא קָצָר.

*Hoo kah-*TSAHR.
It is short.

הַקוּפְסָה הַצְהוּבָה אֲרוּכָּה.

*Hah-koof-*SAH *hah-ts'hoo-*VAH *ah-roo-*KAH.
The yellow box is long.

הַקוּפְסָה הַשְׁחוֹרָה קְצָרָה.

*Hah-koof-*SAH *hah-sh'hoh-*RAH *k'tsah-*RAH.
The black box is short.

הַקְצָרָה הַשִּׂמְלָה הַצְהוּבָה?

*Hah-k'tsah-*RAH *hah-seem-*LAH *hah-ts'hoo-*VAH?
Is the yellow dress short?

NOTE: It is grammatically correct to say צְהוּבָּה (*ts'hoo-*BAH). However, colloquially, the form צְהוּבָה (*ts'hoo-*VAH) is more currently used.

הַקְצָרָה הַשִּׂמְלָה הַצְהוּבָה, אוֹ אֲרוּכָּה?

*Hah-k'tsah-*RAH *hah-seem-*LAH *hah-ts'hoo-*VAH, *oh ah-roo-*KAH?
Is the yellow dress short or long?

אֵיזֶה עִפָּרוֹן אָרוֹךְ, הַשָּׁחוֹר, אוֹ הָאָדוֹם?

EH-*zeh ee-pah-*ROHN *ah-*ROKH, *hah-shah-*HOHR, *oh hah-ah-*DOHM?
Which pencil is long, the black one or the red one?

הַשָּׁחוֹר אָרוֹךְ.

*Hah-shah-*HOHR *ah-*ROKH.
The black one is long.

הַסֵפֶר הָאָדוֹם קָצָר.

*Hah-*SEH-*fer hah-ah-*DOHM *kah-*TSAHR.
The red book is short.

הַסֵפֶר הַשָּׁחוֹר לֹא רָחָב;

*Hah-*SEH-*fer hah-shah-*HOHR *lo rah-*HAHV;
The black book is not wide;

הוּא צָר.

hoo tsahr.
it is narrow.

אֵיךְ הַסֵפֶר הַחוֹם?   הָרָחָב הוּא אוֹ צָר?

Ehkh hah-SEH-fer hah-HOOM?   *Hah-rah-HAHV hoo oh tsahr?*
How is the brown book?   Is it wide or narrow?

 NOTE: When we say in Hebrew? אֵיךְ הַסֵפֶר(*Ehkh hah-SEH-fer?*) ("How is the book?") we are not asking about its health, but for a description of its dimensions, quality, etc.

אֵיזֶהוּ הַסֵפֶר הַצָר?

EH-zeh-hoo hah-SEH-fer hah-TSAHR?
Which one is the narrow book?

הַחַלוֹן רָחָב.   הַדֶלֶת צָרָה.

Hah-hah-LOHN rah-HAHV.   *Hah-DEH-let tsah-RAH.*
The window is wide.   The door is narrow.

הַצָרָה הַקוּפְסָה הַצְהוּבָה אוֹ רְחָבָה?

Hah-tsah-RAH hah-koof-SAH hah-ts'hoo-VAH oh r'hah-VAH?
Is the yellow box narrow or wide?

הַצָר הַחַלוֹן?   אֵיךְ הַסֵפֶר הָאָדוֹם?

Hah-TSAHR hah-hah-LOHN?   *Ehkh hah-SEH-fer hah-ah-DOHM?*
Is the window narrow?   How is the red book?

אֵיךְ הַשִׂמְלָה הַצְהוּבָה?

Ehkh hah-seem-LAH hah-ts'hoo-VAH?
How is the yellow dress?

אֵיזֶה עִפָּרוֹן קָצָר וָצָר?

EH-zeh ee-pah-ROHN kah-TSAHR vah-TSAHR?
Which pencil is short and narrow?

הַסֵפֶר הַחוֹם אָרוֹךְ וְרָחָב; הוּא נָדוֹל.

Hah-SEH-fer hah-HOOM ah-ROKH v'rah-HAHV; hoo gah-DOHL.
The brown book is long and wide; it is large.

הַסֵּפֶר הָאָדוֹם קָצָר וָצָר; הוּא קָטָן.

Hah-SEH-fer hah-ah-DOHM kah-TSAHR vah-TSAHR; hoo kah-TAHN.
The red book is short and narrow; it is small.

הַגְּדוֹלָה הַשִּׂמְלָה הַצְּהוּבָה?

Hah-g'doh-LAH hah-seem-LAH hah-ts'hoo-VAH?
Is the yellow dress large?

הַקְטַנָּה הַקוּפְסָה הַשְּׁחוֹרָה?

Hah-k'tah-NAH hah-koof-SAH hah-sh'hoh-RAH?
Is the black box small?

הַגָּדוֹל הַחַלוֹן אוֹ קָטָן?

Hah-gah-DOHL hah-hah-LOHN oh kah-TAHN?
Is the window large or small?

הַגָּדוֹל הַשּׁוּלְחָן?

Hah-gah-DOHL hah-shool-HAHN?
Is the table large?

NOTE ABOUT GENDER: Even countries and cities have gender! Remember: all countries and cities are feminine. However, the word "village" is masculine.

תֵּל־אָבִיב גְּדוֹלָה.

Tel-Ah-VEEV g'doh-LAH.
Tel-Aviv is large.

חֲדָרָה קְטַנָּה.

Hah-DEH-rah k'tah-NAH.
Hederah is small.

הַקְטַנָּה יְרוּשָׁלַיִם?

Hah-k'tah-NAH Yeh-roo-shah-LAH-yim?
Is Jerusalem small?

לֹא, יְרוּשָׁלַיִם לֹא קְטַנָּה, הִיא גְּדוֹלָה.

Lo, Yeh-roo-shah-LAH-yim lo k'tah-NAH, hee g'doh-LAH.
No, Jerusalem is not small, it is large.

אֵיךְ חֵיפָה?   חֵיפָה לֹא קְטַנָה, הִיא גְדוֹלָה.

Ehkh HAY-*fah?*   HAY-*fah lo k'tah-*NAH, *hee gdoh-*LAH.

How is Haifa?   Haifa is not small, it is large.

הַגְדוֹלָה אֲמֶרִיקָה אוֹ קְטַנָה?

*Hah-g'doh-*LAH *Ah-*MEH-*ree-kah oh k'tah-*NAH?

Is America large or small?

שִׁשָׁה־עָשָׂר	שִׁבְעָה־עָשָׂר	שְׁמוֹנָה־עָשָׂר
Shee-SHAH-*ah-*SAHR	*Sheev-*AH-*ah-*SAHR	*Sh'mo-*NAH-*ah-*SAHR
16	17	18

תִּשְׁעָה־עָשָׂר	עֶשְׂרִים
*Tesh-*AH-*ah-*SAHR	*Ess-*REEM
19	20

THINKING IN HEBREW
(Answers on page 279)

1. ‏הָאָרוֹךְ הַסֵּפֶר הָאָדוֹם?
*Hah-ah-*ROKH *hah-*SEH-*fer hah-ah-*DOHM?

3. ‏הַגָּדוֹל הוּא? 2. ‏הָרָחָב הוּא?
*Hah-gah-*DOHL *hoo?* *Hah-rah-*HAHV *hoo?*

4. ‏הַקָּצָר הַסֵּפֶר הַיָּרוֹק?
*Hah-kah-*TSAHR *hah-*SEH-*fer*
*hah-yah-*ROHK?

6. ‏הַצַּר הוּא? 5. ‏הַקָּטָן הוּא?
*Hah-*TSAHR *hoo?* *Hah-kah-*TAHN *hoo?*

7. ‏אֵיךְ הַשִּׂמְלָה הָאֲרוּכָה?
*Ehkh hah-seem-*LAH *hah-ah-roo-*KAH?

8. ‏אֵיזוֹ שִׂמְלָה קְצָרָה?
EH-*zoh seem-*LAH *k'tsah-*RAH?

9. ‏אֵיךְ הַשִּׂמְלָה הַקְּצָרָה?
*Ehkh hah-seem-*LAH
*hah-k'tsah-*RAH?

10. ‏הַשְּׁחוֹרָה הִיא אוֹ כְּחוּלָה?
*Hah-sh'hoh-*RAH *hee*
*oh k'hoo-*LAH?

11. ‏הַכָּחוֹל הַחַלּוֹן
‏הָרָחָב, אוֹ אָדוֹם?
*Hah-kah-*HOHL
*hah-hah-*LOHN
*hah-rah-*HAHV,
*oh ah-*DOHM?

12. ‏אֵיזֶה חַלּוֹן קָצָר?
EH-*zeh hah-*LOHN
*kah-*TSAHR?

13. הֲקָטָן הַחַלּוֹן הַכָּחוֹל ?

*Hah-kah-*TAHN *hah-hah-*LOHN *hah-kah-*HOHL?

14. הֲרָחָב הַסֵּפֶר הַיָּרוֹק ?

*Hah-rah-*HAHV *hah-*SEH-*fer hah-yah-*ROHK?

15. אֵיזֶה סֵפֶר צָר ?

EH-*zeh* SEH-*fer tsahr?*

16. הַכָּחוֹל הַחַלּוֹן הַגָדוֹל, אוֹ שָׁחוֹר ?

*Hah-kah-*HOHL *hah-hah-*LOHN *hah-gah-*DOHL, *oh shah-*HOHR?

17. אֵיךְ הַסֵּפֶר הַיָּרוֹק, קָצָר אוֹ אָרוֹךְ ?

*Ehkh hah-*SEH-*fer hah-yah-*ROHK, *kah-*TSAHR *oh ah-*ROKH?

18. הֲקָצָר הַסֵּפֶר הָאָדוֹם ?

*Hah-kah-*TSAHR *hah-*SEH-*fer hah-ah-*DOHM?

שִׁעוּר 5

מִי הוּא?
Mee hoo?
Who is that?

אָדוֹן	נְבֶרֶת
Ah-DOHN	*G'VEH-ret*
a gentleman	a lady
הָאָדוֹן זָה?	הַגְבֶרֶת זֹאת?
Ha-ah-DOHN zeh?	*Hah-G'VEH-ret zoht?*
Is this a gentleman?	Is this a lady?
זָה הָאָדוֹן בֶּרְלִיץ.	זֹאת הַגְבֶרֶת בֶּרְלִיץ.
Zeh hah-ah-DOHN Berlitz.	*Zoht hah-G'VEH-ret Berlitz.*
This is Mr. Berlitz.	This is Mrs. Berlitz.

NOTE ON POLITENESS: There is no word for "Miss." נְבֶרֶת (*G'VEH-ret*) is used for both married and unmarried women. It is perhaps more polite this way, don't you think?

23

כֵּן, זֶהוּ אָדוֹן בָּרְלִיץ.

Kehn, ZEH-hoo ah-DOHN Berlitz.
Yes, this is Mr. Berlitz.

הַזֶה אָדוֹן בָּרְלִיץ?

Hah-ZEH ah-DOHN Berlitz?
Is this Mr. Berlitz?

לֹא, זֶה לֹא אָדוֹן בָּרְלִיץ.

Lo, zeh lo ah-DOHN Berlitz.
No, this is not Mr. Berlitz.

לֹא, זֹאת לֹא גְבֶרֶת בָּרְלִיץ.

Lo, zoht lo g'VEH-ret Berlitz.
No, this is not Mrs. Berlitz.

הַזֹאת גְבֶרֶת בָּרְלִיץ?

Hah-ZOHT g'VEH-ret Berlitz?
Is this Mrs. Berlitz?

אַתָּה תַּלְמִיד.

ah-TAH tahl-MEED.
you are a pupil.

אֲנִי מוֹרָה,

Ah-NEE moh-REH,
I am a teacher,

זֹאת גְבֶרֶת תָּבוֹר.

Zoht g'VEH-fer Tah-VOHR.
This is Mrs. Tavor.

 GENDER AGAIN: Even the word "you" must show whether the person you are addressing is masculine or feminine. אַתָּה (*ah-TAH*) is masculine and אַתְּ (*aht*) is feminine, both singular.

אָדוֹן בֶּן-גוּרִיוֹן יִשְׂרָאֵלִי.

Ah-DOHN Ben-Goor-YOHN Yis-reh-eh-LEE.
Mr. Ben-Gurion is Israeli.

אָדוֹן סְמִיט אֲמֶרִיקָאִי.

Ah-DOHN Smeet Ah-meh-ree-KAH-ee.
Mr. Smith is American.

אָדוֹן דוּפוֹן הוּא צָרְפָתִי.

Ah-DOHN Du-POHN hoo-Tsohr-fah-TEE.
Mr. Dupont is French.

אָדוֹן טוֹסְקָאנִינִי הוּא אִיטַלְקִי.

Ah-DOHN Toss-kah-NEE-nee hoo Ee-tahl-KEE.
Mr. Toscanini is Italian.

הַיִשְׂרָאֵלִי אַתָּה?

Hah-Yis-reh-eh-LEE ah-TAH?
Are you Israeli?

אָדוֹן אִידָן הוּא אַנְגְלִי.

Ah-DOHN EE-*den* hoo Ahn-GLEE.
Mr. Eden is English.

אָדוֹן גוֹמֵיז הוּא סְפָרַדִי.

Ah-DOHN Goh-MEZ hoo S'fah-rah-DEE.
Mr. Gomez is Spanish.

הַאַתְּ אֲמֶרִיקָאִית?

Hah-AHT Ah-meh-ree-kah-EET?
Are you American? (fem.)

הַאַתְּ יִשְׂרְאֵלִית?

Hah-AHT Yis-reh-eh-LEET?
Are you Israeli? (fem.)

 HELPFUL HINT: The ending ת (t) is another indication of the feminine adjectives. The other feminine ending was ־ָה (ah), which you encountered in the preceding lesson.

מִי אֲנִי?

Mee ah-NEE?
Who am I?

אַתָּה מוֹרֶה.

Ah-TAH moh-REH.
You are a teacher.

מִי אַתְּ?

Mee aht?
Who are you? (fem.)

אֲנִי תַּלְמִידָה.

Ah-NEE tahl-mee-DAH.
I am a pupil (fem.)

הַאֲנִי אָדוֹן אַינְשְׁטַין?

Hah-ah-NEE ah-DOHN Ine-shtane?
Am I Mr. Einstein?

לֹא, אַתָּה לֹא אָדוֹן אַינְשְׁטַין.

Lo, ah-TAH lo ah-DOHN Ine-shtane.
No, you are not Mr. Einstein.

הַאַתְּ גְּבֶרֶת מַימוֹן?

Hah-AHT G'VEH-ret MY-mon?
Are you Mrs. Mymon?

לֹא, אֲנִי לֹא גְבֶרֶת מַימוֹן.

Lo, ah-NEE lo G'VEH-ret MY-mon.
No, I am not Mrs. Mymon.

מִי הַגְּבֶרֶת הַזֹּאת?

Mee hah-G'VEH-ret hah-ZOHT?
Who is this lady?

זֹאת הַגְּבֶרֶת כַּרְמִי.

Zoht hah-G'VEH-ret KAHR-mee.
That is Mrs. Carme.

עֶשְׂרִים וְאֶחָד

Ess-REEM veh-eh-HAHD
21

עֶשְׂרִים וּשְׁנַיִם

Ess-REEM oo-sh'NAH-yim
22

עֶשְׂרִים וּשְׁלוֹשָׁה

Ess-REEM oo-sh'loh-SHAH
23

עֶשְׂרִים וְאַרְבָּעָה

Ess-REEM veh-ahr-bah-AH
24

עֶשְׂרִים וַחֲמִשָּׁה

Ess-REEM vah-hah-mee-SHAH
25

THINKING IN HEBREW
(Answers on page 280)

1. מִי אַתָּה?
*Mee ah-*TAH?

מִי אַתְּ?
Mee aht?

2. הַאַתָּה אֲמֶרִיקָאִי?
*Hah-ah-*TAH *Ah-meh-ree-*KAH*-ee?*

הַאַתְּ אֲמֶרִיקָאִית?
(*Hah-*AHT *Ah-meh-ree-kah-*EET?)

3. הַאַתָּה מוֹרֶה?
*Hah-ah-*TAH *moh-*REH?

4. הַאַתָּה יִשְׂרְאֵלִי?
*Hah-ah-*TAH *Yis-reh-eh-*LEE?

הַאַתְּ יִשְׂרְאֵלִית?
(*Hah-*AHT *Yis-reh-eh-*LEET?)

5. אֲנִי אָדוֹן נָבוֹן.
*Ah-*NEE *ah-*DOHN *Nah-*VOHN.

אֲנִי מוֹרָה.
*Ah-*NEE *moh-*REH.

מִי אֲנִי?
*Mee ah-*NEE?

6. הַמוֹרָה אֲנִי ?   7.   הַאֲנִי אֲמֶרִיקָאִי ?
Hah-moh-REH ah-NEE?   Hah-ah-NEE Ah-meh-ree-KAH-ee?

8. הַאֲנִי סְפָרַדִי ?   Hah-ah-NEE S'fah-rah-DEE?

9. הַאֲמֶרִיקָאִית הִיא חַנָה רוֹבִינָה, אוֹ יִשְׂרָאֵלִית ?
Hah-Ah-meh-ree-kah-EET hee
Hah-NAH Roh-VEE-nah, oh Yis-reh-eh-LEET?

10. הַצָרְפָתִי הַנָשִׂיא אִיזְנְהַאוֹר ?
Hah-Tsohr-fah-TEE hah-nah-SEE Eisenhower?

11. הַיִשְׂרָאֵלִי קְלַארְק נָבְּל ?   Hah-Yis-reh-eh-LEE Clark Gable?

12. הַאַנְגְלִי אַתָה ?   הַאַנְגְלִיָה אַתְ ?
Hah-Ahn-GLEE ah-TAH?   Hah-Ahn-glee-YAH aht?

13. מִי צָרְפָתִי, קָרִי גְרַנְט אוֹ מוֹרִיס שָׁבַלְיָה.
Mee Tsohr-fah-TEE, Cary Grant, oh Maurice Chevalier?

14. הַצָרְפָתִיָה הַגְבֶרֶת בֶּן־גוּרְיוֹן אוֹ אִיטַלְקִיָה ?
Hah-Tsohr-fah-tee-YAH hah-G'VEH-ret
Ben-Goor-YOHN, oh Ee-tahl-kee-YAH?

15. הַאֲמֶרִיקָאִי אִידָן ?   Hah-Ah-meh-ree-KAH-ee EE-den?

16. הַסְפַרְדִיָה מַרְלִין דִיטְרִיךְ ?
Hah-S'fahr-dee-YAH Marlene Dietrich?

17. הֲקָטָן הַכּוֹבַע הַזֶה אוֹ נָדוֹל ?
Hah-kah-TAHN hah-KOH-vah hah-ZEH oh gah-DOHL?

18. הֲרָחָב הַצַוָארוֹן הַזֶה אוֹ צָר ?
Hah-rah-HAHV hah-tsah-vah-ROHN hah-ZEH oh tsahr?

19. הַתַלְמִיד אַתָה אוֹ מוֹרָה ?
Hah-tahl-MEED ah-TAH oh moh-REH?

20. הַתַלְמִידָה אַתְ אוֹ מוֹרָה ?
Hah-tahl-mee-DAH aht oh moh-RAH?

שִׁעוּר 6

אֵיפֹה זֶה?

Eh-FOH zeh?

Where is it?

הַכּוֹבַע עַל הַכִּסֵּא.

Hah-KOH-vah ahl hah-kis-SEH.
The hat is on the chair.

הַסֵּפֶר עַל הַשֻּׁלְחָן.

Hah-SEH-fer ahl hah-shool-HAHN.
The book is on the table.

הוּא עַל הַכִּסֵּא.

Hoo ahl hah-kis-SEH.
It is on the chair.

אֵיפֹה הַכּוֹבַע?

Eh-FOH hah-KOH-vah?
Where is the hat?

הוּא עַל־יַד הַחַלּוֹן.

Hoo ahl-YAHD hah-hah-LOHN.
He is at the window.

אֵיפֹה אָדוֹן סְמִיט?

Eh-FOH ah-DOHN Smeet?
Where is Mr. Smith?

הוּא עַל הַנְּיָר.

Hoo ahl hah-n'YAHR?
It is on the paper.

אֵיפֹה הָעֵט?

Eh-FOH hah-EHT?
Where is the pen?

אֵיפֹה הַנְּיָר?

Eh-FOH hah-n'YAHR?
Where is the paper?

הוּא בְּתוֹךְ הַסֵּפֶר.

Hoo b'tokh hah-SEH-fer.
It is inside the book.

NOTE TO STUDENT:

בַּ (*bah*) means "in the" and בְּ (*b'*) means "in."

There is still another form בְּתוֹךְ (*b'tokh*) which has

the connotation of an article being contained within

another article.

Ex: **אֵיפֹה הַכֶּסֶף?** (*Eh-FOH hah-KEH-seff?*) "Where is the money?"

בַּבַּנְק. (*Bah-BAHNK.*) "In the bank."

אֵיפֹה הָעִפָּרוֹן? (*Eh-FOH hah-ee-pah-ROHN?*) "Where is the pencil?"

בְּתוֹךְ הַקּוּפְסָה. (*B'tokh hah-koof-SAH.*) "Inside the box."

אֵיפֹה הַמִּטְפַּחַת?

Eh-FOH hah meet-PAH-haht?
Where is the handkerchief?

הִיא בַּכִּיס.

Hee bah-KISS.
It is in the pocket.

אֵיפֹה הַקּוּפְסָה?

Eh-FOH hah-koof-SAH?
Where is the box?

הִיא מִתַּחַת לַשּׁוּלְחָן.

Hee mee-TAH-haht lah-shool-HAHN.
It is under the table.

הַחַלּוֹן לְפָנַי.

Hah-hah-LOHN l'fah-NIGH.
The window is in front of me.

הַדֶּלֶת מֵאֲחוֹרַי.

Hah-DEH-let meh-ah-hoh-RIGH.
The door is behind me.

הַשּׁוּלְחָן לְפָנֶיךָ.

Hah-shool-HAHN l'fah-NEH-hah.
The table is in front of you.

הַקִּיר מֵאֲחוֹרֶיךָ.

Hah-KEER meh-ah-hoh-REH-hah.
The wall is behind you.

WATCH THOSE ENDINGS: The endings ־י (*-igh*)

and ָיךָ (EH-*hah*) indicate "me" and "you" respec-

tively. But, if the "you" refers to a female, the end-

ing is ַיִךְ (AH-*yikh*). These suffixes are attached to

the prepositions with which they are used.

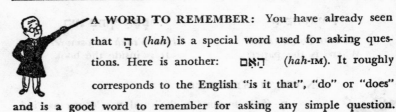

A WORD TO REMEMBER: You have already seen that הַ (hah) is a special word used for asking questions. Here is another: הַאִם (hah-IM). It roughly corresponds to the English "is it that", "do" or "does" and is a good word to remember for asking any simple question.

הַאִם הַשּׁוּלְחָן לְפָנֶיךָ?

Hah-IM hah-shool-HAHN l'fah-NEH-hah?
Is the table before you?

כֵּן, הַשּׁוּלְחָן לְפָנַי.

Kehn, hah-shool-HAHN l'fah-NIGH.
Yes, the table is before me.

הַאִם הַכִּסֵּא לְפָנַי?	לֹא, הַכִּסֵּא לֹא לְפָנֶיךָ.
Hah-IM hah kis-SEH l'fah-NIGH?	*Lo, hah-kis-SEH lo l'fah-NEH-hah.*
Is the chair before me?	No, the chair is not before you.
הַאִם אַתָּה לְפָנַי?	כֵּן, אֲנִי לְפָנֶיךָ.
Hah-IM ah-TAH l'fah-NIGH?	*Kehn, ah-NEE l'fah-NEH-hah.*
Are you before me?	Yes, I am before you.
מַה מֵאֲחוֹרַי?	הַחַלּוֹן מֵאֲחוֹרֶיךָ.
Mah meh-ah-hoh-RIGH?	*Hah-hah-LOHN meh-ah-hoh-REH-hah.*
What is behind me?	The window is behind you.
מַה מֵאֲחוֹרֶיךָ?	הַקִּיר מֵאֲחוֹרַי.
Mah meh-ah-hoh-REH-hah?	*Hah-KEER meh-ah-hoh-RIGH.*
What is behind you?	The wall is behind me.
אֵיפֹה הַסֵּפֶר?	הוּא לְפָנַי.
Eh-FOH hah-SEH-fer?	*Hoo l'fah-NIGH.*
Where is the book?	It is before me.
אֵיפֹה הַקֻּפְסָה?	הִיא מֵאֲחוֹרֶיךָ.
Eh-FOH hah-koof-SAH?	*Hee meh-ah-hoh-REH-hah.*
Where is the box?	It is behind you.

מִי אֲנִי?

*Mee ah-*NEE?
Who am I?

אַתָּה מוֹרֶה.

*Ah-*TAH *moh-*REH.
You are a teacher.

אֵיפֹה אֲנִי?

*Eh-*FOH *ah-*NEE?
Where am I?

אַתָּה מֵאֲחוֹרֵי הַשֻּׁלְחָן.

*Ah-*TAH *meh-ah-hoh-*REH *hah-shool-*HAHN.
You are behind the table.

הַסֵּפֶר הָאָדֹם פֹּה.

*Hah-*SEH-*fer hah-ah-*DOHM *poh.*
The red book is here.

הַסֵּפֶר הָאָפוֹר שָׁם.

*Hah-*SEH-*fer hah-ah-*FOOR *shahm.*
The gray book is there.

אֵיפֹה הַסֵּפֶר הָאָדֹם?

*Eh-*FOH *hah-*SEH-*fer hah-ah-*DOHM?
Where is the red book?

פֹּה.

Poh.
Here.

אֵיפֹה הַסֵּפֶר הָאָפוֹר?

*Eh-*FOH *hah-*SEH-*fer hah-ah-*FOOR?
Where is the gray book?

שָׁם.

Shahm.
There.

הָאָדוֹן בֶּרְלִיץ פֹּה?

*Heh-ah-*DOHN *Berlitz poh?*
Is Mr. Berlitz here?

לֹא, הוּא אֵינֶנּוּ פֹּה; הוּא בְּבֵית־הַסֵּפֶר בֶּרְלִיץ.

*Lo, hoo eh-*NEH-*noo poh; hoo b'veht-hah-*SEH-*fer Berlitz.*
No, he is not here; he is at the Berlitz School.

SAME WORD — THREE MEANINGS:

ה *(hah)* has three uses. It means "the"; it is
used to indicate a question; and it means "of." An
example of this last use is בֵּית־הַסֵּפֶר *(beht-hah-*SEH-*fer)* "house of the book," or "school."

עֶשְׂרִים וְשִׁשָּׁה

*Ess-*REEM *v'shee-*SHAH
26

עֶשְׂרִים וְשִׁבְעָה

*Ess-*REEM *v'sheev-*AH
27

עֶשְׂרִים וּשְׁמוֹנָה

*Ess-*REEM *oo-sh'moh-*NAH
28

עֶשְׂרִים וְתִשְׁעָה

*Ess-*REEM *v'teesh-*AH
29

שְׁלוֹשִׁים

*Sh'loh-*SHEEM
30

אֲנִי עַל־יַד הַדֶּלֶת.

*Ah-*NEE *ahl-*YAHD *hah-*DEH-*let.*
I am at the door.

אֵיפֹה אַתָּה?

*Eh-*FOH *ah-*TAH?
Where are you?

הַאִם הַכִּסֵּא לְפְנֵי הַגְּבֶרֶת נָבוֹן?

*Hah-*IM *hah-kis-*SEH *leef-*NEH *hah-g'*VEH-*ret Nah-*VOHN?
Is the chair in front of Mrs. Navon?

לֹא, הַכִּסֵּא לֹא לְפָנֶיהָ, הוּא מֵאֲחוֹרֶיהָ.

*Lo, hah-kis-*SEH *lo l'fah-*NEH-*hah, hoo meh-ah-hoh-*REH-*hah.*
No, the chair is not in front of her, it is behind her.

מִיהוּ מֵאֲחוֹרֵי הַמּוֹרָה?

MEE-*hoo meh-ah-hoh-*REH *hah-moh-*REH?
Who is behind the teacher?

אָדוֹן יַהְרְבְּלוּם הוּא מֵאֲחוֹרָיו.

*Ah-*DOHN YAHR-*bloom hoo meh-ah-hoh-*RAHV.
Mr. Jahrblum is behind him.

THOSE ENDINGS AGAIN: You have just noted (we hope!) the prepositional suffixes for "him" and "her." They are ־יו (*ahv*) and ־יהָ (EH-*hah*) respectively.

יְרוּשָׁלַיִם הִיא בְּיִשְׂרָאֵל.

*Yeh-roo-shah-*LAH-*yim hee b'Yis-rah-*EHL.
Jerusalem is in Israel.

נְיוּ־יוֹרְק הִיא בַּאֲמֶרִיקָה.

*New York hee bah-Ah-*MEH-*ree-kah.*
New York is in America.

פָּרִיז הִיא בְּצָרְפַת.

Pah-REEZ *hee b'Tsohr-*FAHT.
Paris is in France.

לוֹנְדוֹן הִיא בְּאַנְגְלְיָה.

LOHN-*don hee b'Ahn-glee-*YAH.
London is in England.

לֹא, הִיא בְּיִשְׂרָאֵל.

*Lo, hee b'Yis-rah-*EHL.
No, it is in Israel.

הַאִם יְרוּשָׁלַיִם בְּצָרְפַת?

*Hah-*IM *Yeh-roo-shah-*LAH-*yim b'Tsohr-*FAHT?
Is Jerusalem in France?

THINKING IN HEBREW
(Answers on page 281)

1.   ‏אֵיפֹה הַסֵּפֶר ?‏   2.   ‏הַאִם הוּא עַל הַשּׁוּלְחָן ?‏

*Eh-*FOH *hah-*SEH-*fer?*   *Hah-*IM *hoo ahl hah-shool-*HAHN?

3.   ‏הַאִם הוּא מִתַּחַת לַשּׁוּלְחָן ?‏   4. ‏אֵיפֹה הָעֵט ?‏

*Hah-*IM *hoo mee-*TAH-*haht lah-shool-*HAHN?   *Eh-*FOH *hah-*EHT?

5. ‏הַאִם הוּא עַל הַסֵּפֶר ?‏   6.   ‏אֵיפֹה הַחַלּוֹן ?‏

*Hah-*IM *hoo ahl hah-*SEH-*fer?*   *Eh-*FOH *hah-hah-*LOHN?

7.   ‏אֵיפֹה הַמּוֹרֶה ?‏   *Eh-*FOH *hah-moh-*REH?

8.   ‏הַאִם הַמּוֹרֶה מִתַּחַת לַשּׁוּלְחָן ?‏

*Hah-*IM *hah-moh-*REH *mee-*TAH-*haht lah-shool-*HAHN?

9. ‏הַאִם הוּא לִפְנֵי הַשּׁוּלְחָן ?‏   10.   ‏מַה מֵאֲחוֹרָיו ?‏

*Hah-*IM *hoo leef-*NEH *hah-shool-*HAHN?   *Mah meh-ah-hoh-*RAHV?

11.   ?הַאִם הַדֶּלֶת בַּקִיר

Hah-IM hah-DEH-let bah-KEER?

12.   ?הַאִם הַנְיָר בְּתוֹךְ הַסֵּפֶר   13.   ?אֵיפֹה הַקוּפְסָה

Hah-IM hah-n'YAHR b'tokh hah-SEH-fer?   Eh-FOH hah-koof-SAH?

14.   ?מַה בְּתוֹךְ הַקוּפְסָה   15.   ?הַאִם הַמַפְתֵּחַ בַּכִּיס

Mah b'tokh ha-koof-SAH?   Hah-IM hah-mahf-TEH-akh bah-KISS?

16.   ?הֲגָדוֹל הַסֵּפֶר הַזֶה אוֹ קָטָן

Hah-gah-DOHL hah-SEH-fer hah-ZEH oh kah-TAHN?

17.   ?הֲגָדוֹל הַכּוֹבַע שָׁעַל הַכִּסֵא, אוֹ קָטָן

Hah-gah-DOHL hah-KOH-vah sheh-AHL hah-kis-SEH, oh kah-TAHN?

18.   ?הַאִם תֵּל־אָבִיב בְּאַנְגְלִיָה

Hah-IM Tel-Ah-VEEV b'Ahn-glee-YAH?

19.   ?אֵיפֹה נְיוּ־יוֹרְק   20.   ?אֵיפֹה אַתָּה

Eh-FOH New York?   Eh-FOH ah-TAH?

מַה עוֹשֶׂה הַמּוֹרֶה?

*Mah oh-*SEH *hah-moh-*REH?

What does the teacher do?

הַמּוֹרֶה לוֹקֵחַ אֶת הַסֵּפֶר.

*Hah-moh-*REH *loh-*KAY-*akh ett hah-*SEH-*fer.*
The teacher takes the book.

הַמּוֹרֶה שָׂם אֶת הַסֵּפֶר עַל הַכִּסֵּא.

*Hah-moh-*REH *sahm ett hah-*SEH-*fer ahl hah-kis-*SEH.
The teacher puts the book on the chair.

הַמּוֹרֶה לוֹקֵחַ אֶת הַסַּרְגֵּל.

*Hah-moh-*REH *loh-*KAY-*akh ett hah-sahr-*GEHL.
The teacher takes the ruler.

35

הוּא שָׂם אֶת הַסַרְגֵל מִתַּחַת לַשֻׁלְחָן.

*Hoo sahm ett hah-sahr-*GEHL *mee-*TAH*-haht lah-shool-*HAHN.
He puts the ruler under the table.

הַמוֹרָה פּוֹתֵחַ אֶת הַסֵפֶר.

*Hah-moh-*REH *poh-*TAY*-akh ett hah-*SEH*-fer.*
The teacher opens the book.

הוּא סוֹגֵר אֶת הַסֵפֶר.

*Hoo soh-*GEHR *ett hah-*SEH*-fer.*
He closes the book.

HELPFUL HINT: You may be wondering what אֶת (*ett*) means. It has no meaning here other than to label the direct object of the verb, with the definite article ה (*hah*). Therefore when you refer to a particular object such as *the* table, *the* paper, *the* book, etc., you must use *ett* and *hah* as shown above, but when you refer to *a* table, *a* paper, or *any* book, neither is necessary. Example: "He takes *the* book". הוּא לוֹקֵחַ אֶת הַסֵפֶר. (*Hoo loh-*KAY*-akh ett hah-*SEH*-fer*). "He takes *a* book". הוּא לוֹקֵחַ סֵפֶר. (*Hoo loh-*KAY*-akh* SEH*-fer*).

הַמוֹרָה נוֹשֵׂא אֶת הַכִּסֵא אֶל הַחַלוֹן.

*Hah-moh-*REH *noh-*SEH *ett hah-kis-*SEH *ell hah-hah-*LOHN.
The teacher carries the chair to the window.

הַאִם הַמוֹרָה לוֹקֵחַ אֶת הָעִפָּרוֹן?

*Hah-*IM *hah-moh-*REH *loh-*KAY*-akh ett hah-ee-pah-*ROHN?
Does the teacher take the pencil?

הוּא לוֹקֵחַ אֶת הַסֵפֶר.

*Hoo loh-*KAY*-akh ett hah-*SEH*-fer.*
He takes the book.

הַאִם הוּא לוֹקֵחַ אֶת הַקוּפְסָה?

*Hah-*IM *hoo loh-*KAY*-akh ett hah-koof-*SAH?
Does he take the box?

לֹא, הוּא אֵינוֹ לוֹקֵחַ אֶת הַקּוּפְסָה.

Lo, hoo eh-NOH loh-KAY-akh ett hah-koof-SAH.
No, he does not take the box.

NOT A PRINTING ERROR: There exists a group of verbs which includes לוֹקֵחַ (*loh-KAY-akh*) and פּוֹתֵחַ (*poh-TAY-akh*) in which the last syllable is pronounced אַח (*akh*) although it is actually spelled חַ (*hah*). Before you protest too strongly about this, remember the difficulties students of English have with "through", "tough",' though", etc.

NOTE on the *negative* form of the verbs.

We have seen that לֹא (*lo*) is used to form the negative. However, the negative can also be formed through the use of the negative particle אֵין (*ehn*) followed by a contracted pronoun representing a repetition of the subject of the verb. Notice the following table of such negative forms:

In the *present* tense, the negative form of the verb is expressed by the following constructions, which roughly correspond in meaning to the English "don't" and "doesn't".

	MASC.		*FEM.*		
I	*eh-NEN-nee*	אֵינֶנִּי	(same as masc.)		
	eh-NEE	אֵינִי			
you	*ehn-HAH*	אֵינְךָ	you	*eh-NEHKH*	אֵינֵךְ
he	*eh-NOH*	אֵינוֹ	she	*eh-NAH*	אֵינָה
	eh-NEN-noo	אֵינֶנּוּ		*eh-NEN-ah*	אֵינֶנָּה
we	*eh-NEN-noo*		(same as masc.)		
you	*ehn-HEMM*	אֵינְכֶם	you	*ehn-HENN*	אֵינְכֶן
they	*eh-NAHM*	אֵינָם	they	*eh-NAHN*	אֵינָן

Examples:

אַתְּ אֵינֵךְ בָּאָה.

הוּא אֵינוּ הוֹלֵךְ.

Hoo eh-NOH hoh-LEHKH.
He doesn't go.

Aht eh-NEHKH bah-AH.
You don't come.

הַשָּׂם הַמּוֹרֶה אֶת הַקּוּפְסָה עַל הַשֻׁלְחָן ?

Hah-SAHM hah-moh-REH ett hah-koof-SAH ahl hah-shool-HAHN?
Does the teacher put the box on the table?

כֵּן, הוּא שָׂם אֶת הַקּוּפְסָה עַל הַשֻׁלְחָן.

Kehn, hoo sahm ett hah-koof-SAH ahl hah-shool-HAHN.
Yes, he puts the box on the table.

הַשָּׂם הוּא אֶת הַסַּרְגֵּל עַל הַכִּסֵּא ?

Hah-SAHM hoo ett hah-sahr-GEHL ahl hah-kis-SEH?
Does he put the ruler on the chair?

לֹא, הוּא אֵינוּ שָׂם אֶת הַסַּרְגֵּל עַל הַכִּסֵּא.

Lo, hoo eh-NOH sahm ett hah-sahr-GEHL ahl hah-kis-SEH.
No, he does not put the ruler on the chair.

אֵיפֹה שָׂם הַמּוֹרֶה אֶת הַסַּרְגֵּל ?

Eh-FOH sahm hah-moh-REH ett hah-sahr-GEHL?
Where does the teacher put the ruler?

הוּא שָׂם אֶת הַסַּרְגֵּל מִתַּחַת לַשֻׁלְחָן.

Hoo sahm ett hah-sahr-GEHL mee-TAH-haht lah-shool-HAHN.
He puts the ruler under the table.

הַפּוֹתֵחַ הַמּוֹרֶה אֶת הַסֵּפֶר ?

Hah-poh-TAY-akh hah-moh-REH ett hah-SEH-fer?
Does the teacher open the book?

כֵּן, הוּא פּוֹתֵחַ אֶת הַסֵּפֶר.

Kehn, hoo poh-TAY-akh ett hah-SEH-fer.
Yes, he opens the book.

הַפּוֹתֵחַ הַמּוֹרֶה אֶת הַדֶּלֶת?

Hah-poh-TAY-akh hah-moh-REH ett hah-DEH-let?
Does the teacher open the door?

כֵּן, הוּא פּוֹתֵחַ אֶת הַדֶּלֶת.

*Kehn, hoo poh-*TAY-*akh ett hah-*DEH-*let.*
Yes, he opens the door.

הַסּוֹגֵר הוּא אֶת הַדֶּלֶת?

*Hah-soh-*GEHR *hoo ett hah-*DEH-*let?*
Does he close the door?

לֹא, הוּא אֵינוֹ סוֹגֵר אֶת הַדֶּלֶת.

*Lo, hoo eh-*NOH *soh-*GEHR *ett hah-*DEH-*let.*
No, he does not close the door.

מַה עוֹשָׂה הַמּוֹרֶה?

*Mah oh-*SEH *hah-moh-*REH?
What does the teacher do?

NOTE TO STUDENT: עוֹשָׂה (*oh-*SEH) means "make"
or 'do". There is no distinction between "do" and
"make".

הוּא נוֹשֵׂא אֶת הַכִּסֵּא אֶל הַחַלּוֹן.

*Hoo noh-*SEH *et hah-kis-*SEH *ell hah-hah-*LOHN
He carries the chair to the window.

TAKE YOUR CHOICE:

You maye use *either* לְ (*leh*) or אֶל (*ell*) to mean
"to" or "into", indicating the *direction* of an action.
Examples: אֲנִי הוֹלֵךְ אֶל הַכִּתָּה (*Ah-*NEE *hoh-*LEHKH *ell*
*hah-kee-*TAH) — I go to the classroom.

אֲנִי הוֹלֵךְ לַכִּתָּה (*Ah-*NEE *hoh-*LEHKH *lah-kee-*TAH) I go to the classroom.

הַמּוֹרָה הוֹלֵךְ אֶל הַדֶּלֶת.

*Hah-moh-*REH *hoh-*LEHKH *ell hah-*DEH-*let.*
The teacher goes to the door.

הַהוֹלֵךְ הַמוֹרָה אֶל הַחַלוֹן?

*Hah-hoh-*LEHKH *hah-moh-*REH *ell hah-hah-*LOHN?
Does the teacher go to the window?

לֹא, הוּא אֵינוֹ הוֹלֵךְ אֶל הַחַלוֹן.

*Lo, hoo eh-*NOH *hoh-*LEHKH *ell hah-hah-*LOHN.
No, he does not go to the window.

לְאָן הוּא הוֹלֵךְ?   הוּא הוֹלֵךְ אֶל הַדָלֶת.

*Leh-*AHN *hoo hoh-*LEHKH?   *Hoo hoh-*LEHKH *ell hah-*DEH-*let.
Where does he go?   He goes to the door.

לְאָן הוֹלֵךְ הַתַּלְמִיד?   הוּא הוֹלֵךְ לְבֵית־הַסֵפֶר.

*Leh-*AHN *hoh-*LEHKH *hah-tahl-*MEED?*Hoo hoh-*LEHKH *l'veht-hah-*SEH-*fer.
Where does the student go?   He goes to the school.

הַהוֹלֵךְ אָדוֹן נָבוֹן לְבֵית־הַסֵפֶר?

*Hah-hoh-*LEHKH *ah-*DOHN *Nah-*VOHN *l'veht-hah-*SEH-*fer?
Does Mr. Navon go to school?

לֹא, הוּא אֵינֶנּוּ הוֹלֵךְ לְבֵית־הַסֵפֶר, הוּא הוֹלֵךְ לַתֵּיאַטְרוֹן.

*Lo, hoo eh-*NEN-*noo hoh-*LEHKH *l'veht-hah-*SEH-*fer, hoo hoh-*LEHKH
*lah-teh-aht-*ROHN.
No, he does not go to school; he goes to the theater.

לְאָן הוֹלֵךְ הָרַב עוּזִיאֵל?

*Leh-*AHN *hoh-*LEHKH *hah-*RAHV *Oo-zee-*ELL?
Where does Rabbi Uziel go?

הוּא הוֹלֵךְ לְבֵית הַכְּנֶסֶת.

*Hoo-hoh-*LEHKH *l'veht-hah-k'*NEH-*set.
He goes to the temple.

מִי בָּא אֶל הַחֶדֶר?

*Mee bah ell hah-*HEH-*der?
Who is coming into the room?

הַמוֹרָה בָּא אֶל הַחֶדֶר.

*Hah-moh-*REH *bah ell hah-*HEH-*der.
The teacher is coming into the room.

הַאִם אֲנִי בָּא אֵלֶיךָ?

Hah-IM ah-NEE bah eh-LEH-hah?
Do I come to you?

כֵּן, אַתָּה בָּא אֵלַי.

Kehn, ah-TAH bah eh-LIGH.
Yes, you come to me.

SOMETHING EASY: There is no difference in Hebrew verb construction between "I come" and "I am coming". The one form you have learned אֲנִי בָּא expresses both meanings. The same applies to all verbs.

קַח אֶת הַסֵּפֶר, אֲדוֹן נָבוֹן!

Kakh ett hah-SEH-fer, ah-DOHN Nah-VOHN!
Take the book, Mr. Navon!

מַה אַתָּה עוֹשֶׂה?

Mah ah-TAH oh-SEH?
What do you do?

אֲנִי לוֹקֵחַ אֶת הַסֵּפֶר.

Ah-NEE loh-KAY-akh ett hah-SEH-fer.
I take the book.

קְחִי אֶת הָעֵט, גְּבֶרֶת נָבוֹן!

K'hee ett hah-EHT, g'VEH-ret Nah-VOHN!
Take the pen, Mrs. Navon!

ATTENTION PLEASE: קַח *(kakh)* and קְחִי *(k'hee)* are the imperative forms of "to take". The former is for talking to a man, and the second form for giving orders to a woman. Learn these imperative forms individually until page 224 when the matter will be explained in some detail.

מַה אַתְּ עוֹשָׂה?

Mah aht oh-SAH?
What do you do?

אֲנִי לוֹקַחַת אֶת הָעֵט.

Ah-NEE loh-KAH-haht ett hah-EHT.
I take the pen.

VERBS CAN BE FEMININE: When Mrs. Navon speaks, she uses a different ending for the verb, because she is a woman. You can usually tell the feminine by the ending ת *(t)* and the changes in the vowels at the end of the verb. You will hear more about this later in this lesson.

אָדוֹן לַוִי, שִׂים אֶת הַסֵּפֶר עַל הַשּׁוּלְחָן!

Ah-DOHN Leh-VEE, seem ett hah-SEH-fer ahl hah-shool-HAHN!
Mr. Levy, put the book on the table!

מִי שָׂם אֶת הַסֵּפֶר עַל הַשּׁוּלְחָן?

Mee sahm ett hah-SEH-fer ahl hah-shool-HAHN?
Who puts the book on the table?

אָדוֹן לַוִי שָׂם אֶת הַסֵּפֶר עַל הַשּׁוּלְחָן.

Ah-DOHN Leh-VEE sahm ett hah-SEH-fer ahl hah-shool-HAHN.
Mr. Levy puts the book on the table.

הַאִם גְּבֶרֶת לַוִי שָׂמָה אֶת הָעִפָּרוֹן לְתוֹךְ הַקּוּפְסָה?

Hah-IM g'veh-ret Leh-VEE SAH-mah ett hah-ee-pah-ROHN l'tokh hah-koof-SAH?
Does Mrs. Levy put the pencil into the box?

לֹא, הִיא אֵינָה שָׂמָה אֶת הָעִפָּרוֹן לְתוֹךְ הַקּוּפְסָה.

Lo, hee eh-NAH SAH-mah ett hah-ee-pah-ROHN l'tokh hah-koof-SAH.
No, she does not put the pencil into the box.

אָדוֹן כַּסְפִּי, אֵיפֹה אַתָּה שָׂם אֶת הַכֶּסֶף?

Ah-DOHN KAHS-pee, eh-FOH ah-TAH sahm ett hah-KEH-sef?
Mr. Kaspy, where do you put the money?

אֲנִי שָׂם אֶת הַכֶּסֶף בַּכִּיס.

Ah-NEE sahm ett kah-KEH-sef bah-KISS.
I put the money into the pocket.

לִפְעָמִים אֲנִי שָׂם אֶת הַכֶּסֶף בַּבַּנְק.

Leef-ah-MEEM ah-NEE sahm ett hah-KEH-sef bah-BAHNK.
Sometimes I put the money into the bank.

הַהוֹלֶכֶת גְּבֶרֶת רוֹבִינָה לְתַל־אָבִיב?

Hah-hoh-LEH-het g'veh-ret Roh-VEE-nah l'Tel-Ah-VEEV?
Is Mrs. Rovina going to Tel-Aviv?

לֹא, הִיא אֵינָה הוֹלֶכֶת לְתַל־אָבִיב, הִיא הוֹלֶכֶת לִירוּשָׁלַיִם.

Lo, hee eh-NAH hoh-LEH-het l'Tel-Ah-VEEV, hee hoh-LEH-het lee-Yeh-roo-shah-LAH-yim.
No, she is not going to Tel-Aviv, she is going to Jerusalem.

IMPORTANT NOTE:
Observe the following comparative table for the English infinitives and corresponding Hebrew stems of the verbs contained in the preceding lesson.

ENGLISH	HEBREW STEM	ENGLISH	HEBREW STEM
"to close" —	סָגֹר (sah-GOHR)	"to take"—	לָקֹח (lah-KOH-akh)
"to open"—	פָּתֹחַ (pah-TOH-akh)	"to put"—	שִׂים (seem)
"to come"—	בֹּא (boh)	"to do"—	עָשֹׂה (ah-SOH)
"to go"—	הָלֹךְ (hah-LOKH)	"to carry"—	נָשֹׂא (nah-SOH)

Notice that these Hebrew verb stems (with the exception of those with one syllable) follow a uniform pattern in that they are based on the sequence of two fundamental vowel sounds, namely the *ah* and the *oh*, always occurring in that order and occasionally followed by a third syllable (*akh* or *ah*). The verbs with this sound pattern (*ah-oh*) in their stem belong to the first group of Hebrew verbs, which is the most important one, as it is the largest.

In constructing the individual forms of all verbs in the present tense, such as "I take", "he goes", "she opens", etc., always consider the *gender* and *number* of the person who is performing the verbal action. The *present* tense of most verbs contained in this lesson (first group) is based on the sequence of the vowel sounds *oh* and *eh*, instead of the *ah-oh* sounds peculiar to their stems.

Example: סוֹגֵר (soh-GEHR) — "I close, you close, he closes" (masculine). If the subject is feminine, the syllable (*et*) is added to the verb. Example: סוֹגֶרֶת (soh-GEH-ret) = "I close (feminine), you close, she closes". In the plural, the same verb (based on the vowels *oh-eh*, as in soh-GEHR) receives the addition of (*eem*) for the masculine and (*oht*) for the feminine, while the vowel (*eh*) in the middle syllable is shortened. We obtain in this way the following forms:

סוֹגְרִים (soh-g'REEM) — we, you, they (masculine) close.

סוֹגְרוֹת (soh-g'ROHT) — we, you, they (feminine) close.

But, you may say, what happens when the subject of the verb includes men *and* women? The answer is that the masculine prevails and the ים– (*eem*) ending is used.

Example: (אִישׁ אֶחָד וְעֶשְׂרִים נָשִׁים הוֹלְכִים)

*Eesh eh-*HAHD *veh-ess-*REEM *nah-*SHEEM *hoh-l'*HEEM.
"One man and twenty women go."

THINKING IN HEBREW
(Answers on page 282)

1.   מַה עוֹשֶׂה הַמוֹרֶה?

Mah oh-SEH hah-moh-REH?

2.   הֲלוֹקֵחַ הַמוֹרֶה אֶת הַסֵפֶר?

*Hah-loh-KAY-akh hah-moh-REH
ett hah-SEH-fer?*

3.   הֲשָׂם הַמוֹרֶה אֶת הַסֵפֶר
מִתַּחַת לַשׁוּלְחָן?

*Hah-SAHM hah-moh-REH ett hah-SEH-fer
mee-TAH-haht lah-shool-HAHN?*

4.   הֲלוֹקֵחַ הוּא אֶת הַקוּפְסָה?

Hah-loh-KAY-akh hoo ett hah-koof-SAH?

5.   הֲיוֹשֵׁב הַמוֹרֶה אוֹ עוֹמֵד?

Hah-yoh-SHEHV hah-moh-REH oh oh-MEHD?

6.   הֲסוֹגֵר הַמוֹרֶה אֶת הַחַלוֹן?

Hah-soh-GEHR hah-moh-REH ett hah-hah-LOHN?

7.   הֲפוֹתֵחַ הוּא אֶת הַדֶלֶת, אוֹ אֶת הַחַלוֹן?

*Hah-poh-TAY-akh hoo ett hah-DEH-let,
oh ett hah-hah-LOHN?*

8.   הֲפוֹתַחַת הַתַּלְמִידָה אֶת הַדֶלֶת?

*Hah-poh-TAH-haht hah-tahl-mee-DAH
ett hah-DEH-let?*

9.   הֲפוֹתַחַת גְבֶרֶת בֵּילָה אֶת הַדֶלֶת?

Hah-poh-TAH-haht G'VEH-ret BEH-leh ett hah-DEH-let?

10. הֲפוֹתֵחַ הַמוֹרֶה אֶת הַקוּפְסָה?

Hah-poh-TAY-akh hah-moh-REH ett hah-koof-SAH?

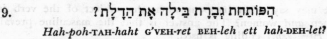

11. הַהוֹלֵךְ הַמּוֹרֶה
לְנִי־יוֹרְק?

*Hah-hoh-*LEHKH *hah-moh-*
REH *lee-New-*YORK?

12. הַהוֹלֵךְ הוּא לְפָּרִיז?

*Hah-hoh-*LEHKH *hoo*
*l'Pah-*REEZ?

13. הַאִם הַמּוֹרֶה בָּאֲוִירוֹן?

*Hah-*IM *hah-moh-*REH
*bah-ah-vee-*ROHN?

14. הַגְדוֹלָה נִי־יוֹרְק אוֹ קְטַנָה?

*Hah-g'doh-*LAH *New-*YORK *oh k'tah-*NAH?

15. הַאַתְּ בְּהוֹלִיבוּד?

*Hah-*AHT *b'*HOH-*lee-vood?*

16. הַהוֹלֶכֶת אַתְּ לְתֵל־אָבִיב אוֹ הַמּוֹרֶה?

*Hah-hoh-*LEH-*het aht l'Tel-Ah-*VEEV *oh hah-moh-*REH?

שָׁעוּר 8

מספרים

*Mees-pah-*REEM

Counting

---

masc.	*fem.*	*masc.*	*fem.*	*masc.*	*fem.*
אֶחָד	אַחַת	שְׁנַיִם	שְׁתַּיִם	שְׁלוֹשָׁה	שָׁלוֹשׁ
*eh-*HAHD	(*ah-*HAHT)	*sh'*NAH-*yim*	(*sh'*TAH-*yim*)	*sh'loh-*SHAH	(*shah-*LOSH)
1		2		3	

אַרְבָּעָה	אַרְבַּע	חֲמִשָּׁה	חָמֵשׁ	שִׁשָּׁה	שֵׁשׁ
*ahr-bah-*AH	(*ahr-*BAH)	*hah-mee-*SHAH	(*hah-*MEHSH)	*shee-*SHAH	(*shesh*)
4		5		6	

שִׁבְעָה	שֶׁבַע	שְׁמוֹנָה	שְׁמוֹנֶה	תִּשְׁעָה	תֵּשַׁע
*sheev-*AH	(*SHEH-vah*)	*sh'moh-*NAH	(*sh'moh-*NEH)	*teesh-*AH	(*TEH-shah*)
7		8		9	

46

עֶשָׂרָה   עֶשֶׂר   אַחַת־עֶשְׂרֵה   אַחַד־עָשָׂר

ah-sah-RAH (EH-ser)   ah-HAHD-ah-SAHR (ah-HAHT-ess-REH)

10   11

שְׁנֵים־עָשָׂר   שְׁתֵּים־עֶשְׂרֵה   שְׁלוֹשׁ־עֶשְׂרֵה   שְׁלוֹשָׁה־עָשָׂר

sh'NEHM-ah-SAHR (sh'TEHM-ess-REH)   sh'loh-SHAH-ah-SAHR (sh'LOSH-ess-REH)

12   13

אַרְבָּעָה־עָשָׂר   אַרְבַּע־עֶשְׂרֵה   חֲמִשָּׁה־עָשָׂר   הֲמֵשׁ־עֶשְׂרֵה

ahr-bah-AH-ah-SAHR (ahr-BAH-ess-REH)   hah-mee-SHAH-ah-SAHR (hah-MEHSH-ess-REH)

14   15

שִׁשָּׁה־עָשָׂר   שֵׁשׁ־עֶשְׂרֵה   שִׁבְעָה־עָשָׂר   שְׁבַע־עֶשְׂרֵה

shee-SHAH-ah-SAHR (shehsh-ess-REH)   sheev-AH-ah-SAHR (shvah-ess-REH)

16   17

שְׁמוֹנָה־עָשָׂר שְׁמוֹנֶה־עֶשְׂרֵה   תֵּשַׁע־עֶשְׂרֵה   תִּשְׁעָה־עָשָׂר

sh'moh-NAH-ah-SAHR (sh'moh-NEH-ess-REH)   teesh-AH-ah-SAHR (t'SHAH-ess-REH)

18   19

עֶשְׂרִים   עֶשְׂרִים וְאָחָד   עֶשְׂרִים וְאַחַת

ess-REEM   ess-REEM-veh-eh-HAHD (ess-REEM veh-ah-HAHT)

20   21

עֶשְׂרִים וּשְׁנַיִם   עֶשְׂרִים וּשְׁתַּיִם   עֶשְׂרִים וּשְׁלוֹשָׁה עֶשְׂרִים וְשָׁלוֹשׁ

ess-REEM oo-sh'NAH-yim (ess-REEM oo-sh'TAH-yim)   ess-REEM oo-sh'loh-SHAH (ess-REEM v'shah-LOSH)

22   23

עֶשְׂרִים וְאַרְבָּעָה עֶשְׂרִים וְאַרְבַּע   עֶשְׂרִים וַחֲמִשָּׁה עֶשְׂרִים וְחָמֵשׁ

ess-REEM veh-ahr-bah-AH (ess-REEM veh-ahr-BAH)   ess-REEM vah-hah-mee-SHAH (ess-REEM v'hah-MEHSH)

24   25

עֶשְׂרִים וְשִׁשָּׁה עֶשְׂרִים וָשֵׁשׁ

ess-REEM *v'shee*-SHAH
(*ess*-REEM *vah*-SHEHSH)
26

עֶשְׂרִים וְשִׁבְעָה עֶשְׂרִים וָשֶׁבַע

ess-REEM *v'sheev*-AH
(*ess*-REEM *vah*-SHEH-*vah*)
27

עֶשְׂרִים וּשְׁמוֹנָה עֶשְׂרִים וּשְׁמוֹנֶה

ess-REEM *oo-sh'moh*-NAH
(*ess*-REEM *oo'shmoh*-NEH)
28

עֶשְׂרִים וְתִשְׁעָה עֶשְׂרִים וָתֵשַׁע

ess-REEM *v'teesh*-AH
(*ess*-REEM *vah*-TEH-*shah*)
29

שְׁלוֹשִׁים

sh'loh-SHEEM
30

אַרְבָּעִים

ahr-bah-EEM
40

חֲמִשִּׁים

hah-mee-SHEEM
50

שִׁשִּׁים

shee-SHEEM
60

שִׁבְעִים

sheev-EEM
70

שְׁמוֹנִים

sh'moh-NEEM
80

תִּשְׁעִים

teesh-EEM
90

מֵאָה

meh-AH
100

חֲמֵשׁ מֵאוֹת

hah-MEHSH *meh*-OHT
500

אֶלֶף

EH-*leff*
1000

שְׁנֵי אֲלָפִים

sh'NEH ah-lah-FEEM
2000

מִילְיוֹן

meel-YOHN
1 000 000

שְׁלוֹשׁ מֵאוֹת שִׁשִּׁים וַחֲמִשָּׁה

sh'LOSH meh-OHT *shee*-SHEEM *vah-hah-mee*-SHAH
365

GENDER AGAIN: All numbers ending in 0, except the number 10, have only one form. The rest have two forms, for masculine and feminine. But, you may wonder, what if you say a number which includes men *and* women? In this mixed case, use the masculine gender.

Examples: חֲמִשָּׁה עָשָׂר אֲנָשִׁים

(*hah-mee*-SHAH-*ah*-SAHR *ah-nah*-SHEEM) fifteen men.

חֲמֵשׁ-עֶשְׂרֵה נָשִׁים (*hah*-MEHSH-*ess*-REH *nah*-SHEEM) fifteen women.

חֲמִשָּׁה עָשָׂר אֲנָשִׁים וְנָשִׁים (*hah-mee*-SHAH-*ah*-SAHR *ah-nah*-SHEEM *v'nah*-SHEEM) fifteen men and women.

סְפֹר.　　　　אֲנִי סוֹפֵר.　　　　אַתָּה סוֹפֵר.

S'fohr.　　　Ah-NEE soh-FEHR.　　Ah-TAH soh-FEHR.
Count!　　　I count.　　　　　　You count.

אַתָּה סוֹפֵר מֵאֶחָד עַד אַרְבָּעָה.

Ah-TAH soh-FEHR meh-eh-HAHD ahd ahr-bah-AH.
You count from one to four.

אֲנִי סוֹפֵר מֵעֲשָׂרָה עַד חֲמִשָּׁה-עָשָׂר.

Ah-NEE soh-FEHR meh-ah-sah-RAH ahd hah-mee-SHAH-ah-SAHR.
I count from ten to fifteen.

מַה אֲנִי עוֹשֶׂה?　　　　אַתָּה סוֹפֵר.

Mah ah-NEE oh-SEH?　　Ah-TAH soh-FEHR.
What do I do?　　　　　You count.

מַה אַתָּה עוֹשֶׂה?　　　　אֲנִי סוֹפֵר.

Mah ah-TAH oh-SEH?　　Ah-NEE soh-FEHR.
What do you do?　　　　I count.

סְפֹר מֵעֶשְׂרִים עַד שְׁלוֹשִׁים.

S'fohr meh-ess-REEM ahd sh'loh-SHEEM.
Count from twenty to thirty.

מֵאֵיזֶה מִסְפָּר אַתָּה סוֹפֵר?

Meh-EH-zeh mees-PAHR ah-TAH soh-FEHR?
From what number do you count?

עַד אֵיזֶה מִסְפָּר סוֹפֵר הָאָדוֹן?

Ahd EH-zeh mees-PAHR soh-FEHR hah-ah-DOHN?
Up to what number does the gentleman count?

אֵילוּ מִסְפָּרִים הֵם?

EH-loo mees-pah-REEM hehm?
What numbers are these?

שְׁלוֹשָׁה	שְׁלוֹשָׁה-עָשָׂר	שְׁלוֹשִׁים	חֲמִשִּׁים
sh'loh-SHAH	sh'loh-SHAH-ah-SAHR	sh'loh-SHEEM	hah-mee-SHEEM
three	thirteen	thirty	fifty

שְׁלוֹשָׁה סְפָרִים	שְׁנֵי סְפָרִים	סֵפֶר אֶחָד
sh'loh-SHAH s'fah-REEM	sh'NEH s'fah-REEM	SEH-fer eh-HAHD
three books	two books	one book

שְׁלוֹשָׁה כִּסְאוֹת	שְׁנֵי כִּסְאוֹת	כִּסֵא אֶחָד
sh'loh-SHAH kis-OHT	sh'NEH kis-OHT	Kis-SEH eh-HAHD
three chairs	two chairs	one chair

NOTE ON THE PLURAL: The plural of nouns is formed by adding the endings ‎יִ־ (eem) or וֹת (oht)

Examples: "Boy students" תַּלְמִידִים (tahl-mee-DEEM)

"girl students" תַּלְמִידוֹת (tahl-mee-DOHT)

יִ־ (eem) is usually used for the masculine and וֹת (oht) for the feminine, but there are exceptions.

NOTE ON 1—10: Numbers from 1 to 10, have an abbreviated form for both genders. This form is employed when the number is used with a noun preceded by the definite article הַ (hah). Here are the abbreviated forms of the numbers from 1 to 10.

	Masc.		*Fem.*	
1.	ah-HAHD	אֶחָד—	ah-HAHT	אַחַת—
2.	sh'NEH	שְׁנֵי—	sh'TEH	שְׁתֵּי—
3.	sh'LOH-shett	שְׁלוֹשֶׁת—	sh'LOSH	שָׁלוֹשׁ—
4.	ahr-BAH-aht	אַרְבַּעַת—	ahr-BAH	אַרְבַּע—
5.	hah-MEH-shett	חֲמֵשֶׁת—	hah-MEHSH	חָמֵשׁ—
6.	SHEH-shett	שֵׁשֶׁת—	shehsh	שֵׁשׁ—
7.	sheev-AHT	שִׁבְעַת—	sh'VAH	שֶׁבַע—
8.	sh'moh-NAHT	שְׁמוֹנַת—	sh-moh-NEH	שְׁמוֹנָה—
9.	teesh-AHT	תִּשְׁעַת—	t'SHAH	תֵּשַׁע—
10.	ah-SEH-ret	עֲשֶׂרֶת—	EH-ser	עֶשֶׂר—

Here is how the abbreviation is used.

חֲמֵשֶׁת הַסְפָרִים (hah-MEH-shet hah-s'fah-REEM) "the five books".

שְׁלוֹשׁ הַתְּמוּנוֹת (sh'losh hah-t'moo-NOHT) "the three pictures".

The same abbreviations are used for counting thousands and millions. Hold your hats! There is an exception to all this. The number 2 is used in the abbreviated form with a noun regardless of whether or not the article "the" precedes the noun.

Example: שְׁנֵי אֲנָשִׁים   (sh'NEH ah-nah-SHEEM) "two men"

שְׁתֵּי נָשִׁים   (sh'TEH nah-SHEEM) "two women".

שְׁנַיִם וְעוֹד שְׁנַיִם הֵם אַרְבָּעָה.

Sh'NAH-yim veh-OHD sh'NAH-yim hehm ahr-bah-AH.
Two and two are four.

כַּמָּה הֵם שְׁלוֹשָׁה וְעוֹד חֲמִשָּׁה?

KAH-mah hehm sh'loh-SHAH veh-OHD hah-mee-SHAH?
How much are three and five?

שְׁלוֹשָׁה וְעוֹד חֲמִשָּׁה הֵם שְׁמוֹנָה.

Sh'loh-SHAH veh-OHD hah-mee-SHAH hehm sh'moh-NAH.
Three and five are eight.

כַּמָּה הֵן חָמֵשׁ פְּעָמִים שָׁלוֹשׁ?

KAH-mah hehn hah-MEHSH peh-ah-MEEM shah-LOSH?
How much are five times three?

חָמֵשׁ פְּעָמִים שָׁלוֹשׁ הֵן חֲמֵשׁ-עֶשְׂרֵה.

Hah-MEHSH peh-ah-MEEM shah-LOSH hehn hah-MEHSH-ess-REH.
Five times three are fifteen.

הָעִתּוֹן הַזֶּה עוֹלֶה בַּחֲמִשָּׁה-עָשָׂר סֶנְט.

Hah-ee-TOHN hah-ZEH oh-LEH bah-hah-mee-SHAH-ah-SAHR sent.
This newspaper costs fifteen cents.

הַכּוֹבַע עוֹלֶה בַּעֲשָׂרָה דוֹלַר.

Hah-KOH-vah oh-LEH bah-ah-sah-RAH DOH-lahr.
The hat costs ten dollars.

הַסֵּפֶר הַזֶּה עוֹלֶה בְּשָׁלוֹשׁ לִירוֹת יִשְׂרְאֵלִיּוֹת.

Hah-SEH-fer hah-ZEH oh-LEH b'shah-LOSH LEE-roht Yis-reh-eh-lee-YOHT
This book costs three Israeli pounds.

כַּמָּה סְפָרִים יֵשׁ עַל הַשֻׁלְחָן?   שִׁשָׁה.

KAH-*mah s'fah*-REEM *yehsh ahl hah-shool*-HAHN?   Shee-SHAH.
How many books are there on the table?   Six.

כַּמָּה עֶפְרוֹנוֹת יֵשׁ שָׁם?   שְׁמוֹנָה.

KAH-*mah eff-roh*-NOHT *yehsh shahm?*   Sh'moh-NAH.
How many pencils are over there?   Eight.

כַּמָּה כִּסְאוֹת יֵשׁ בַּחֶדֶר הַזֶה?   עֲשָׂרָה.

KAH-*mah kis*-OHT *yehsh bah*-HEH-*dehr hah*-ZEH?   Ah-sah-RAH.
How many chairs are there in this room?   Ten.

כַּמָּה דְלָתוֹת?   כַּמָּה חַלוֹנוֹת?

KAH-*mah hah-loh*-NOHT?   KAH-*mah d'lah*-TOHT?
How many windows?   How many doors?

כַּמָּה מִילִין מִתֵּל־אָבִיב לִירוּשָׁלַיִם?

KAH-*mah mee*-LEEN *m'Tel-Ah*-VEEV *lee-Yeh-roo-shah*-LAH-*yim?*
How many miles is it from Tel-Aviv to Jerusalem?

בְּכַמָּה עוֹלֶה סֵפֶר זֶה?

B'HAH-*mah oh*-LEH SEH-*fer zeh?*
How much does this book cost?

זֶה עוֹלֶה בִּשְׁלוֹשָׁה דוֹלַרִים.

Zeh oh-LEH *besh-loh*-SHAH *doh*-LAH-*reem.*
It costs three dollars.

זֶה עוֹלֶה בְּשִׁשִׁים לִירוֹת.   בְּכַמָּה עוֹלֶה שָׁעוֹן זֶה?

B'HAH-*mah oh*-LEH *shah*-OHN *zeh?*   Zeh oh-LEH *b'shee*-SHEEM LEE-*roht.*
How much does this watch cost?   It costs sixty pounds.

A LAST WORD ON NUMBERS:

All numbers come before the noun except "one".

Example: "Five hundred books"   חֲמֵשׁ מֵאוֹת סְפָרִים

(hah-MEHSH *meh*-OHT *s'fah*-REEM)

"One book"   סֵפֶר אֶחָד   (SEH-*fer eh*-HAHD).

THINKING IN HEBREW
(Answers on page 283)

1. מַה אַתָּה עוֹשֶׂה? ‏ סְפֹר מֵאֶחָד עַד עֲשָׂרָה.

*Mah ah-*TAH *oh-*SEH?   *S'fohr meh-eh-*HAHD *ahd ah-sah-*RAH.

2. אֲנִי סוֹפֵר: אֶחָד שְׁנַיִם שְׁלוֹשָׁה וְכוּ'

*Ah-*NEE *soh-*FEHR: *eh-*HAHD *sh'NAH-yim sh'loh-*SHAH *v'hoo.*

3. מַה עוֹשֶׂה הַמּוֹרֶה?   מַה אֲנִי עוֹשֶׂה?

*Mah oh-*SEH *hah-moh-*REH?   *Mah ah-*NEE *oh-*SEH?

4. כַּמָּה כִּסְאוֹת יֵשׁ בַּחֶדֶר הַזֶּה?

*KAH-mah kis-*OHT *yehsh bah-*HEH-*der hah-*ZEH?

5. הֲיֵשׁ שָׁם שׁוּלְחָן?

*Hah-*YEHSH *shahm shool-*HAHN?

6. כַּמָה קוּפְסָאוֹת יֵשׁ עַל הַשּׁוּלְחָן?

KAH-*mah* koof-sah-OHT *yehsh ahl* hah-shool-HAHN?

7. כַּמָה הֵן שֵׁשׁ פְּעָמִים חָמֵשׁ?

KAH-*mah* hehn shesh peh-ah-MEEM *hah-*MEHSH?

8. הַאִם שְׁתֵּי פְּעָמִים שְׁתַּיִם הֵן חָמֵשׁ?

*Hah-*IM *sh'teh* peh-ah-MEEM *sh'*TAH-*yim* hehn *hah-*MEHSH?

9. כַּמָה הֵן שֶׁבַע פְּעָמִים שָׁלוֹשׁ?

KAH-*mah* hehn SHEH-*vah* peh-ah-MEEM shah-LOSH?

10. בְּכַמָה עוֹלָה הַנִיוּ־יוֹרְק טַיְמְס?

*B'*HAH-*mah* oh-LEH hah-NEW-YORK-TIMES?

11. בְּכַמָה עוֹלָה סֵפֶר זֶה?

*B'*HAH-*mah* oh-LEH SEH-*feh* zeh?

12. הַעוֹלָה הַסֵפֶר הַזֶה בַּעֲשָׂרָה דוֹלַר?

*Hah-*oh-LEH *hah-*SEH-*fer* hah-ZEH bah-ah-sah-RAH DOH-*lahr*?

13. הַעוֹלָה הַשָׁעוֹן הַזֶה בְּמֵאָה לִירוֹת?

*Hah-*oh-LEH *hah-*shah-OHN hah-ZEH *b'meh-*AH LEE-*roht*?

14. הַאִם שִׁשָׁה וּשְׁנַיִם הֵם שִׁבְעָה?

*Hah-*IM shee-SHAH oo-*sh'*NAH-*yim* hehm sheev-AH?

שִׁעוּר 9 ⑨

נוּף הָאָדָם

*Goof hah-ah-*DAHM

The human body

רֹאשׁ	שֵׂעָר	אַף	פֶּה
Rosh	*seh-*AHR	*ahf*	*peh*
head	hair	nose	mouth

כָּתֵף	עַיִן	אֹזֶן	רֶגֶל	יָד
*Kah-*TEHF	AH-*yin*	OH-*zehn*	REH-*gehl*	*yahd*
shoulder	eye	ear	foot	hand

בֶּרֶךְ	שָׂפָה	שֵׁן	לֶחִי
BEH-*rekh*	*sah-*FAH	*shehn*	LEH-*hee*
knee	lip	tooth	cheek

55

HELPFUL HINT:

The parts of the body which come in two's, such as eyes, ears, hands, etc., as well as the teeth (32!), are all feminine and have a special dual plural ending: ‑ַיִם (AH-*yim*). Fingers and arms, however, form their plural in the normal way. Observe the following plurals:

Examples:

רַגְלַיִם	יָדַיִם	אָזְנַיִם	עֵינַיִם	כְּתֵפַיִם
rahg-LAH-*yim*	yah-DAH-*yim*	ohz-NAH-*yim*	eh-NAH-*yim*	k'teh-FAH-*yim*
feet	hands	ears	eyes	shoulders

לְחָיַיִם	שִׁנַּיִם	שְׂפָתַיִם	בִּרְכַּיִם
l'hah-YAH-*yim*	shee-NAH-*yim*	s'fah-TAH-*yim*	beer-KAH-*yim*
cheeks	teeth	lips	knees

אֶצְבַּע	חָזֶה	שְׁכֶם	צַוָּאר	מֵצַח
ETZ-*bah*	hah-ZEH	SHEH-*hemm*	tsah-VAHR	MEH-*tzakh*
finger	chest	back	neck	forehead

זְרוֹעַ
z'ROH-*ah*
arm

הַיָּד הַיְּמָנִית.
*Hah-*YAHD *hah-y'mah-*NEET.
The right hand.

הַיָּד הַשְּׂמָאלִית.
*Hah-*YAHD *hah-s'moh-*LEET.
The left hand.

מַה צֶּבַע הַסְּפָרִים הָאֵלֶה?
Mah TSEH-*vah hah-s'fah-*REEM *hah-*EH-*leh?*
What color are these books?

הֵם אֲדוּמִים.
*Hehm ah-doo-*MEEM.
They are red.

הַאֲפוֹרוֹת הַקֻּפְסוֹת הָאֵלֶה?
*Hah-ah-foo-*ROHT *hah-koof-*SOHT *hah-*EH-*leh?*
Are these boxes gray?

לֹא, הֵן לֹא אֲפוֹרוֹת!
*Lo, hehn lo ah-foo-*ROHT.
No, they are not gray.

מִיהוּ הָאָדוֹן הַזֶה?

MEE-*hoo* hah-ah-DOHN hah-ZEH?
Who is this gentleman?

זֶה אָדוֹן נָבוֹן.

Zeh ah-DOHN *Nah*-VOHN.
It is Mr. Navon.

מִי הֵם הָאֲדוֹנִים הָאֵלֶה?

Mee hehm hah-ah-doh-NEEM hah-EH-*leh?*
Who are these gentlemen?

אֵלֶה הֵם אָדוֹן נָבוֹן וְאָדוֹן כַּסְפִּי.

EH-*leh* hehm ah-DOHN *Nah*-VOHN vah-ah-DOHN KAHS-*pee*.
They are Mr. Navon and Mr. Kaspy.

מִיהִי הַגְבֶרֶת הַזֹאת?

MEE-*hee* hah-G'VEH-*ret* hah-ZOHT?
Who is this lady?

זֹאת הַגְבֶרֶת כַּסְפִּי.

Zoht hah-G'VEH-*ret* KAHS-*pee*.
It is Mrs. Kaspy.

מִיהֵן הַגְבִירוֹת הָאֵלֶה?

MEE-*hehn* hah-g'vee-ROHT hah-EH-*leh?*
Who are these ladies?

אֵלֶה הֵן הַגְבֶרֶת נָבוֹן וְהַגְבֶרֶת כַּסְפִּי.

EH-*leh* hehn hah-G'VEH-*ret* *Nah*-VOHN veh-hah-G'VEH-*ret* KAHS-*pee*.
They are Mrs. Navon and Mrs. Kaspy.

הָאָמְרִיקָאִים אַתֶם?

*Hah-Ah-meh-ree-kah-*EEM *ah*-TEMM?
Are you Americans?

כֵּן, אֲנַחְנוּ אָמְרִיקָאִים.

Kehn, ah-NAKH-*noo* Ah-meh-ree-kah-EEM.
Yes, we are Americans.

הַיִשְׂרָאֵלִים אַתֶם?

*Hah-Yis-reh-eh-*LEEM *ah*-TEMM?
(Gentlemen) are you Israelis?

לֹא, אֲנַחְנוּ לֹא יִשְׂרָאֵלִים.

Lo, ah-NAKH-*oo* lo Yis-reh-eh-LEEM.
No, we are not Israelis.

הַאֲמֶרִיקָאִיּוֹת אַתֶּן?

*Hah-Ah-meh-ree-kah-ee-*YOHT *ah-*TENN?

Ladies, are you Americans?

לֹא, אֲנַחְנוּ לֹא אֲמֶרִיקָאִיּוֹת.

*Lo, ah-*NAKH*-noo lo ah-meh-ree-kah-ee-*YOHT.

Not, we are not Americans.

הַיִשְׂרְאֵלִיּוֹת אַתֶּן?

*Hah-Yis-reh-eh-lee-*YOHT *ah-*TENN?

Are you Israelis?

כֵּן, אֲנַחְנוּ יִשְׂרְאֵלִיּוֹת.

*Kehn, ah-*NAKH*-noo Yis-reh-eh-lee-*YOHT.

Yes, we are Israelis.

אֵלֶּה הַכְּפָפוֹת שֶׁלִי.	זֶה הַכּוֹבַע שֶׁלִי.
EH-*leh hah-k'fah-*FOHT *sheh-*LEE.	*Zeh hah-*KOH*-vah sheh-*LEE.
These are my gloves.	This is my hat.
אֵלֶּה הַנַּעֲלַיִם שֶׁלָּךְ.	זֹאת הָעֲנִיבָה שֶׁלָּךְ.
EH-*leh hah-nah-ah-*LAH*-yim shell-*HAH.	*Zoht hah-ah-nee-*VAH *shell-*HAH.
These are your shoes.	This is your tie.
הַכּוֹבַע הַזֶה.	אֵיזֶהוּ הַכּוֹבַע שֶׁלִי?
*Hah-*KOH*-vah hah-*ZEH.	EH-*zeh-hoo hah-*KOH*-vah sheh-*LEE?
This one.	Which is my hat?
הָעֲנִיבָה הַזֹאת.	אֵיזוֹהִי הָעֲנִיבָה שֶׁלָּךְ?
*Hah-ah-nee-*VAH *hah-*ZOHT.	EH-*zoh-hee hah-ah-nee-*VAH *shell-*HAH?
This one.	Which is your tie?
הָעֵט הַהוּא.	אֵיזֶהוּ עֵט הַתַּלְמִיד?
*Hah-*EHT *hah-*HOO.	EH-*zeh-hoo* EHT *hah-tahl-*MEED?
That one.	Which is the pupil's pen?

אֵילוּ הֵם הָעֵטִים שֶׁלְּךָ?

EH-loo hehm hah-eh-TEEM shell-HAH?
Which are your pens?

הָעֵטִים הָאֵלֶה.

Hah-eh-TEEM hah-EH-leh.
These pens.

שֶׁל מִי הַכּוֹבַע הַזֶה?

Shell mee hah-KOH-vah hah-ZEH?
Whose hat is this?

הוּא שֶׁל אָדוֹן כַּסְפִּי.

Hoo shell ah-DOHN KAHS-pee.
It is Mr. Kaspy's.

אֵילוּ הֵם סִפְרֵי הַתַּלְמִידִים?

EH-loo hehm seef-REH hah-tahl-mee-DEEM?
Which are the pupils' books?

הַסְפָרִים הָהֵם.

Hah-s'fah-REEM hah-HEHM.
Those are.

שֶׁל מִי הַכִּסְאוֹת הָאֵלֶה?

Shell mee hah-kis-OHT hah-EH-leh?
Whose chairs are these?

שֶׁל הַגְבִירוֹת נָבוֹן וְכַסְפִּי.

Shell hah-g'vee-ROHT Nah-VOHN v'KAHS-pee.
They are Mrs. Navon's and Mrs. Kaspy's.

PLURAL OF ADJECTIVES:

The adjectives form the plural like the nouns, that is with the endings ‫ים‬– (eem) for masculine plural and

וֹת (oht) for feminine plural.

Examples:

סֵפֶר גָדוֹל   (SEH-fer gah-DOHL) "big book"

סְפָרִים גְדוֹלִים   (s'fah-REEM g'doh-LEEM) "big books"

תְּמוּנָה גְדוֹלָה   (t'moo-NAH g'doh-LAH) "big picture"

תְּמוּנוֹת גְדוֹלוֹת   (t'moo-NOHT g'doh-LOHT) "big pictures"

However, (zeh) which is the masculine and (zoht) which is the feminine form of "this", have as their plural אֵלֶה (EH-leh), in both genders; while הַהוּא (hah-HOO) and הַהִיא (hah-HEE) meaning "that" become הָהֵם (hah-HEHM) and הָהֵן (hahn-HEHN) respectively in the plural, meaning "those".

THINKING IN HEBREW
(Answers on page 284)

1. מַה מִתַּחַת לִזְרוֹעַ הַמוֹרֶה?

Mah mee-TAH-haht lee-z'ROH-ah hah-moh-REH?

2. הַאִם זֶה עִתּוֹן מִתַּחַת לִזְרוֹעַ הַמוֹרֶה?

Hah-IM zeh ee-TOHN mee-TAH-haht lee-z'ROH-ah hah-moh-REH?

3. הַאִם זֶה עִפָּרוֹן בְּכִיס הַמוֹרֶה?

Hah-IM zeh ee-pah-ROHN b'hiss hah-moh-REH?

4. אֵיפֹה הָעִתּוֹן?

Eh-FOH hah-ee-TOHN?

5. הַאִם הַסַרְגֵל מִתַּחַת לְרַגְלוֹ הַיְמָנִית שֶל הַמוֹרֶה?

Hah-IM hah-sahr-GEHL mee-TAH-haht l'rahg-LOH hah-y'mah-NEET shell hah-moh-REH?

6. מַה בְּיָד הַיְמָנִית שֶׁל הַמּוֹרָה?

Mah bah-YAHD hah-y'mah-NEET shell hah-moh-REH?

7. הֲיֵשׁ אֵלּוּ עֶפְרוֹנוֹת בַּקֻּפְסָה?

Hah-YEHSH EH-loo eff-roh-NOHT bah-koof-SAH?

8. הֲיֵשׁ אֵלּוּ מַפְתְּחוֹת עַל הַשֻּׁלְחָן?

Hah-YEHSH EH-loo mahf-t'HOHT ahl hah-shool-HAHN?

9. אֵיפֹה הַסְּפָרִים?

Eh-FOH hah-s'fah-REEM?

10. הַאִם כֶּלֶב אֶחָד אוֹ שְׁנֵי כְּלָבִים מִתַּחַת לַשֻּׁלְחָן?

Hah-IM KEH-lev eh-HAHD oh sh'NEH k'lah-VEEM mee-TAH-haht lah-shool-HAHN?

11. הֲיֵשׁ אֵלּוּ תְּמוּנוֹת עַל הַקִּיר?

Hah-YEHSH EH-loo t'moo-NOHT ahl hah-KEER?

12. כַּמָּה סְפָרִים עַל הַשֻּׁלְחָן?

KAH-mah s'fah-REEM ahl hah-shool-HAHN?

13. הֲיֵשׁ אֵלּוּ כְּסָפִים בְּכִיס הַמּוֹרֶה?

Hah-YEHSH EH-loo k'sah-FEEM b'hiss hah-moh-REH?

14. הַאִם הַכּוֹבַע עַל הַכִּסֵּא הַקָּטָן?

Hah-IM hah-KOH-vah ahl hah-kis-SEH hah-kah-TAHN?

שִׁעוּר 10

אֲנִי כּוֹתֵב אֶת הָאָלֶף־בֵּית

Ah-NEE koh-TEHV ett hah-AH-lef-beht

I write the alphabet

הַמּוֹרֶה לוֹקֵחַ גִּיר.	הוּא כּוֹתֵב עַל הַלּוּחַ.
Hah-moh-REH loh-KAY-akh geer.	*Hoo koh-TEHV ahl hah-LOO-akh.*
The teacher takes chalk.	He writes on the blackboard.

הוּא כּוֹתֵב אֶת הָאָלֶף־בֵּית.

Hoo koh-TEHV ett hah-AH-lef-beht.

He writes the alphabet.

מַה עוֹשֶׂה הַמּוֹרֶה?	הוּא לוֹקֵחַ גִּיר וְכוֹתֵב.
Mah oh-SEH hah-moh-REH?	*Hoo loh-KAY-akh geer v'hoh-TEHV.*
What does the teacher do?	He takes chalk and writes.
עַל מַה הוּא כּוֹתֵב?	עַל הַלּוּחַ.
Ahl mah hoo koh-TEHV?	*Ahl hah-LOO-akh.*
On what does he write?	On the blackboard.

מַה הוּא כּוֹתֵב?

Mah hoo koh-TEHV?
What does he write?

אֶת הָאָלֶף־בֵּית.

Ett hah-AH-lef-beht.
The alphabet.

מִי כּוֹתֵב עַל הַלּוּחַ?

Mee koh-TEHV ahl hah-LOO-akh?
Who is writing on the blackboard?

הַמּוֹרֶה.

Hah-moh-REH.
The teacher.

אָדוֹן נָבוֹן, קַח עִפָּרוֹן וּנְיָר!

Ah-DOHN Nah-VOHN, kakh ee-pah-ROHN oo-n'YAHR!
Mr. Navon, take a pencil and paper!

כְּתֹב אֶת הָאָלֶף־בֵּית!

K'TOHV ett hah-AH-lef-beht!
Write the alphabet!

אַתָּה כּוֹתֵב אֶת הָאָלֶף־בֵּית עַל הַנְּיָר.

Ah-TAH koh-TEHV ett hah-AH-lef-beht ahl hah-n'YAHR.
You write the alphabet on the paper.

קַח גִּיר וּכְתֹב אֶת הָאָלֶף־בֵּית עַל הַלּוּחַ!

Kakh geer oo-h'TOHV ett hah-AH-lef-beht ahl hah-LOO-akh!
Take chalk and write the alphabet on the blackboard!

אֲנִי כּוֹתֵב.

Ah-NEE koh-TEHV.
I write.

אַתָּה כּוֹתֵב.

Ah-TAH koh-TEHV.
You write.

אֲנִי כּוֹתֵב אֶת הָאָלֶף־בֵּית.

Ah-NEE koh-TEHV ett hah-AH-lef-beht.
I write the alphabet.

הַכּוֹתֵב אַתָּה?

Hah-koh-TEHV ah-TAH?
Do you write?

מַה אַתָּה כּוֹתֵב?

Mah ah-TAH koh-TEHV?
What do you write?

אֲנִי כּוֹתֵב אוֹתִיּוֹת.

Ah-NEE koh-TEHV oh-tee-YOHT.
I write letters.

קַח סֵפֶר וּקְרָא!   אֲנִי קוֹרֵא.   אַתָּה קוֹרֵא.

Kakh SEH-*fer* oo-k'RAH!   *Ah*-NEE *koh*-REH.   *Ah*-TAH *koh*-REH.
Take a book and read!   I read.   You read.

מַה אַתָּה עוֹשֶׂה?   אֲנִי קוֹרֵא.

Mah ah-TAH *oh*-SEH?   *Ah*-NEE *koh*-REH.
What are you doing?   I am reading.

מַה אֲנִי עוֹשֶׂה?   אַתָּה קוֹרֵא עִתּוֹן.

Mah ah-NEE *oh*-SEH?   *Ah*-TAH *koh*-REH *ee*-TOHN.
What am I doing?   You are reading a newspaper.

אֲנִי קוֹרֵא אֶת הָאָלֶף־בֵּית.   א   ב   ג   וְכוּ'

Ah-NEE *koh*-REH *ett hah*-AH-*lef-beht*.   AH-*lef* Beht GHEE-*mel* v'HOO.
I read the alphabet.   A   B   G   etc.

אֲנִי כּוֹתֵב מִסְפָּרִים עַל הַלּוּחַ.

Ah-NEE *koh*-TEHV *mees-pah*-REEM *ahl hah*-LOO-*akh*.
I write numbers on the blackboard.

אֲנִי כּוֹתֵב אֶת הָאוֹתִיּוֹת אָלֶף, בֵּית.

Ah-NEE *koh*-TEHV *ett hah-oh-tee*-YOHT AH-*lef, beht*.
I write the letters A, B.

פֹּה אוֹת אַחַת.   פֹּה אוֹת אַחֶרֶת.   מַה זֹּאת?

Poh oht ah-HAHT.   *Poh oht ah*-HEH-*ret*.   *Mah zoht?*
Here is a letter.   Here is another letter.   What is this?

זֹאת אוֹת.   אֵיזוֹ אוֹת זֹאת?   הָאוֹת אָלֶף.

Zoht oht.   EH-*zoh oht zoht?*   *Hah*-OHT AH-*lef*.
This is a letter.   What letter is this?   The letter A.

פֹּה הָאוֹת גִּימֶל.   אֵילוּ אוֹתִיּוֹת הֵן?

Poh hah-OHT GHEE-*mel*.   EH-*loo oh-tee*-YOHT *hehn?*
Here is the letter G.   What letters are these?

אֵלֶּה הָאוֹתִיּוֹת הֵן אָלֶף, בֵּית.   אֲנִי כּוֹתֵב מִלִּים.

EH-*leh hah-oh-tee*-YOHT *hehn* AH-*lef, beht*. *Ah*-NEE *koh*-TEHV *mee*-LEEM.
They are the letters A, B.   I am writing words.

אֲנִי כּוֹתֵב אֶת הַמִּלָה „שׁוּלְחָן".

Ah-NEE koh-TEHV ett hah-mee-LAH "shool-HAHN".
I write the word "table".

קְרָא אֶת הַמִּלָה הַזֹאת, בְּבַקָשָׁה!

K'rah ett hah-mee-LAH hah-ZOHT, b'vah-kah-SHAH!
Read this word, please!

קִרְאִי בְּבַקָשָׁה מֵעַל הַלוּחַ, גְבֶרֶת נָבוֹן!

Keer-EE b'vah-kah-SHAH meh-AHL hah-LOO-akh, g'VEH-ret Nah-VOHN!
Please, read from the blackboard, Mrs. Navon!

מַה אַתְּ עוֹשָׂה?	אֲנִי קוֹרֵאת מֵעַל הַלוּחַ.
Mah aht oh-SAH?	*Ah-NEE koh-REHT meh-AHL hah-LOO-akh.*
What are you doing?	I read from the blackboard.
מַה הִיא עוֹשָׂה?	הִיא קוֹרֵאת מֵעַל הַלוּחַ.
Mah hee oh-SAH?	*Hee koh-REHT meh-AHL hah-LOO-akh.*
What does she do?	She reads from the blackboard.

פֹּה מִלָה אַחֶרֶת: „קִיר".

Poh mee-LAH ah-HEH-ret: "keer".
Here is another word: "wall".

כַּמָה אוֹתִיוֹת בַּמִּלָה אֲמֶרִיקָה?

KAH-mah oh-tee-YOHT bah-mee-LAH "America"?
How many letters are there in the word "America"?

בַּמִּלָה אֲמֶרִיקָה יֵשׁ שֵׁשׁ אוֹתִיוֹת

Bah-mee-LAH "America" yehsh shehsh oh-tee-YOHT.
In the word "America" there are six letters.

THINGS ARE NOT WHAT THEY SEEM:
Although it is clear to us that "America" has seven
letters, it has only six in Hebrew, inasmuch as the letters themselves become combined with vowels, according to the "dots" underneath. You will remember this
(we hope!) from the introduction on the alphabet.
However, starting with the next lesson we shall leave
the dots out!

‫פֹּה מְלָה עִבְרִית „אָדוֹן".‬   ‫„מִיסְטֶר" הִיא מִלָה אַנְגְלִית.‬

*Poh mee-*LAH *Eev-*REET *"Ah-*DOHN". *"Mister" hee mee-*LAH *Ahn-*GLEET.
Here is a Hebrew word, "Adon".   "Mister" is an English word.

‫„חַוַנ'ה" הִיא מִלָה עַרְבִית.‬   ‫הַאִם זֶה סֵפֶר רוּסִי?‬

*Khah-*WAH*-zhah hee mee-*LAH *Ahr-*VEET.   *Hah-*IM *zeh* SEH*-fer Roo-*SEE?
"Khawahzhah" is an Arabic word.   Is this a Russian book?

‫אֲנִי אוֹמֵר אֶת הָאָלֶף־בִּית הָעִבְרִי.‬

*Ah-*NEE *oh-*MEHR *ett hah-*AH*-lef-beht hah-Eev-*REE.
I say the Hebrew alphabet.

א	בּ	ג	ד	ה	ו
Ah-lef	*Beht*	GHEE-*mel*	DAH-*let*	*Heh*	*Vahv*
A	B	G	D	H	V

ז	ח	ט	י	כּ	ל
ZAH-*yin*	*Het*	*Tet*	*Yood*	*Kahf*	LAH-*med*
Z	KH	T	Y	K	L

מ	נ	ס	ע	פּ	צ
Memm	*Noon*	SAH-*mekh*	AH-*yin*	*Peh*	ZAH-*dee*
M	N	S	A	P	TS

ק	ר	שׁ	ת
Koof	*Rehsh*	*Sheen*	*Tahv*
K	R	SH	T

ONE LETTER IN ENGLISH; TWO IN HEBREW:
As you can see, there are two letters for "A", two for "K", two for "T", etc. In each case, the difference in pronunciation which formerly existed has disappeared.

WATCH OUT:
Five letters are written differently *when they come at the end of a word.* The following letters ‫כ' מ' נ' פ' צ‬ become ‫ך' ם' ן' ף' ץ'‬ in their end-of-a-word form.

A LAST WORD ON LETTERS:
Although the Hebrew alphabet officially has 22 letters, some of these modify themselves to make other letters. They are ‫בּ' כּ' פּ'‬ (p, k, b), which become, when the dot is left out, ‫ב' כ' פ'‬ (f, kh, and v, respectively).

מַה עוֹשֶׂה הַמוֹרָה?   הוּא אוֹמֵר אֶת הָאָלֶף־בֵּית.

*Mah oh-*SEH *hah-moh-*REH?   *Hoo oh-*MEHR *ett hah-*AH-*lef-beht.*
What does the teacher do?   He says the alphabet.

אֱמֹר בְּבַקָשָׁה אֶת הָאָלֶף־בֵּית, אֲדוֹנִי!

*Eh-*MOHR *b'vah-kah-*SHAH *ett hah-*AH-*lef-beht, ah-doh-*NEE!
Please, say the alphabet, sir!

אֲנִי כּוֹתֵב מִשְׁפָּט „הַכּוֹבַע עַל הַכִּסֵא".

*Ah-*NEE *koh-*TEHV *meesh-*PAHT *"hah-*KOH-*vah ahl hah-kis-*SEH".
I write a sentence—"The hat is on the chair".

כַּמָה מִלִים בַּמִשְׁפָּט הַזֶה?

KAH-*mah mee-*LEEM *bah-meesh-*PAHT *hah-*ZEH?
How many words are there in this sentence?

בַּמִשְׁפָּט הַזֶה שָׁלוֹשׁ מִלִים.

*Bah-meesh-*PAHT *hah-*ZEH *shah-*LOSH *mee-*LEEM.
In this sentence there are three words.

בְּאַנְגְלִיָה מְדַבְּרִים אַנְגְלִית, בְּיִשְׂרָאֵל–עִבְרִית.

*Beh-Ahn-glee-*YAH *m'dah-b'*REEM *Ahn-*GLEET, *b'Yis-rah-*EHL *Eev-*REET.
In England, they speak English; in Israel, Hebrew.

בְּתֵל־אָבִיב מְדַבְּרִים עִבְרִית.

*B'Tel-Ah-*VEEV *m'dah-b'*REEM *Eev-*REET.
In Tel-Aviv they speak Hebrew.

בְּפָרִיז מְדַבְּרִים צָרְפָתִית.

*B'Pah-*REEZ *m'dah-b'*REEM *Tsohr-fah-*TEET.
In Paris, they speak French.

בְּאֵיזוֹ שָׂפָה מְדַבְּרִים בְּלוֹנְדוֹן?

*Beh-EH-zo sah-*FAH *m'dah-b'*REEM *b'*LOHN-*dohn?
What language do they speak in London?

בְּלוֹנְדוֹן מְדַבְּרִים אַנְגְלִית.

*B'*LOHN-*dohn m'dah-b'*REEM *Ahn-*GLEET.
In London they speak English.

THE IMPERSONAL USE OF "THEY":

The form מְדַבְּרִים (*m'dah-b'*REEM) of the verb דַבֵּר (*dah-*BEHR), which means "to speak", is, in fact, the masculine plural of the present tense of that same verb, used *without* a subject. This form can best be rendered by the English translation "they speak".

הַמְדַבֵּר אַתָּה עִבְרִית?

*Hah-m'dah-*BEHR *ah-*TAH *Eev-*REET?
Do you speak Hebrew?

כֵּן, אֲנִי מְדַבֵּר מְעַט עִבְרִית.

*Kehn, ah-*NEE *m'dah-*BEHR *meh-*AHT *Eev-*REET.
Yes, I speak it a little.

GRAMMATICAL NOTE:

On page 43 we encountered the first group of verbs. דַבֵּר (*dah-*BEHR) is an example of the second group.

This group is recognizable by the alternation of the vowel sounds ַ (*ah*) and ֶ (*eh*), *both* in the stem and in the present tense. In the present tense an initial (*m'*) consonant is added to the verb. Observe the following conjugation:

דַבֵּר   *Dah-*BEHR = "to speak". (stem)

אֲנִי מְדַבֵּר   *Ah-*NEE *m'dah-*BEHR = "I speak".

הִיא מְדַבֶּרֶת   *Hee m'dah-*BEH-*rett* = "she speaks".

אָנוּ מְדַבְּרִים   *AH-noo m'dah-*B'REEM = "we (men) speak".

אָנוּ מְדַבְּרוֹת   *AH-noo m'dah-*B'ROHT = "we (women) speak".

THINKING IN HEBREW
(Answers on page 285)

1. ‏כְּתֹב אֶת הָאוֹת אָלֶף עַל הַנְיָר. מַה אַתָּה עוֹשֶׂה?‏

*K'tohv ett hah-*OHT *AH-lef ahl hah-n'*YAHR. *Mah ah-*TAH *oh-*SEH?

2. ‏אֲנִי כּוֹתֵב אֶת הַמִּלָּה „חוֹפֶשׁ". מַה אֲנִי כּוֹתֵב?‏

*Ah-*NEE *koh-*TEHV *ett hah-mee-*LAH "HOH-*fesh". Mah ah-*NEE *koh-*TEHV?

3. ‏אָדוֹן נַמְזוּ כּוֹתֵב אֶת הָאָלֶף־בֵּית עַל הַלּוּחַ.‏

‏מִי כּוֹתֵב אֶת הָאָלֶף־בֵּית עַל הַלּוּחַ?‏

*Ah-*DOHN GAHM-*zoo koh-*TEHV *ett hah-*AH-*lef-beht ahl hah-*LOO-*akh.*
*Mee koh-*TEHV *ett hah-*AH-*lef-beht ahl hah-*LOO-*akh?*

4. ‏קְרָא אֶת הַמִּשְׁפָּט „אֲנִי יִשְׂרְאֵלִי". מַה אַתָּה עוֹשֶׂה?‏

*K'rah ett hah-meesh-*PAHT "*ah-*NEE *Yis-reh-eh-*LEE". *Mah ah-*TAH *oh-*SEH?

5. ‏כַּמָּה אוֹתִיּוֹת בַּמִּשְׁפָּט הַזֶּה?‏

KAH-*mah oh-tee-*YOHT *bah-meesh-*PAHT *hah-*ZEH?

6. הַקוֹרֵא אַתָּה עִבְרִית?

*Hah-koh-*REH *ah-*TAH *Eev-*REET?

7. הַקוֹרֵא אָדוֹן בֶּרְלִיץ עִבְרִית?

*Hah-koh-*REH *ah-*DOHN *Berlitz Eev-*REET?

8. הַמְדַבֵּר הוּא עִבְרִית?

*Hah-m'dah-*BEHR *hoo Eev-*REET?

9. הַמְדַבֵּר אָדוֹן נָבוֹן אַנְגְלִית?

*Hh-m'dah-*BEHR *ah-*DOHN *Nah-*VOHN *Ahn-*GLEET?

10. מַה אַתָּה מְדַבֵּר, עִבְרִית אוֹ צָרְפָתִית?

*Mah ah-*TAH *m'dah-*BEHR, *Eev-*REET *oh Tsohr-fah-*TEET?

11. הַמְדַבֵּר אָדוֹן יַהרְבְּלוֹם צָרְפָתִית?

*Hak-m'dah-*BEHR *ah-*DOHN *JAHR-blum Tsohr-fah-*TEET?

12. הָעִבְרִית הִיא הַמִלָה „גֶ'נְטְלְמָן", אוֹ אַנְגְלִית?

*Hah-eev-*REET *hee hah-mee-*LAH *"Gentleman", oh Ahn-*GLEET?

13. אֲנִי אוֹמֵר, אָלֶף בֵּית גִימֶל דָלֶת וְכוּ'. הָאוֹמֵר אֲנִי אֶת הָאָלֶף־בֵּית?

*Ah-*NEE *oh-*MEHR: AH-*lef Beht* GHEE-*mel* DAH-*let v'hoo.*
*Hah-oh-*MEHR *ah-*NEE *ett hah-*AH-*lef-beht?*

14. הָאוֹמֵר אַתָּה אֶת הָאָלֶף־בֵּית הָרוּסִי?

*Hah-oh-*MEHR *ah-*TAH *ett hah-*AH-*lef-beht hah-*Roo-SEE?

15. אֵיזָה אָלֶף־בֵּית אוֹמֵר הַמוֹרֶה הָעִבְרִי?

EH-*zeh* AH-*lef-beht oh-*MEHR *hah-moh-*REH *hah-*Eev-REE?

16. בְּאֵיזוֹ שָׂפָה מְדַבְּרִים בִּירוּשָׁלַיִם?

*Beh-*EH-*zoh sah-*FAH *m'dah-b'*REEM *bee-Yeh-roo-shah-*LAH-*yim?*

17. הַמְדַבְּרִים סְפָרַדִית בְּעִיר מֶקְסִיקוֹ?

*Hah-m'dah-b'*REEM *S'fah-rah-*DEET *beh-*EER *Mexico?*

18. הַמְדַבְּרִים רוּסִית בְּמַדְרִיד?

*Hah-m'dah-b'*REEM *Roo-*SEET *b'*MAHD-*reed?*

שִׁעוּר 11

מאלף עד תיו
Meh-AH-lef ahd TAHV

From A to T

האלף-בית העברי מתחיל מאות אלף, וגומר באות תיו.
Hah-AH-lef-beht hah-Eev-REE maht-HEEL meh-OHT AH-lef v'goh-MEHR beh-OHT Tahv.
The Hebrew alphabet begins with the letter **A**
and ends with the letter **T**.

STILL ANOTHER VERB GROUP:

With התחל (*haht*-HEHL)—"to begin" we encounter a representative of the third group.

This group is recognizable by the alternation of the vowel sounds ַ (*ah*) and ֶ (*eh*) in the stem, which always begins with an ה (*h*). In the present tense the verbe begins with מַ (*mah*) and its conjugation is usually based on the alternation of the vowel sounds ַ (*ah*) and ִי (*ee*).

Observe the following examples:

הַתְחֵל (*Haht*-HEHL)="to begin". (stem)

אֲנִי מַתְחִיל (*Ah*-NEE *maht*-HEEL)="I begin".

הִיא מַתְחִילָה (*Hee maht-hee*-LAH)="she begins".

אָנוּ מַתְחִילִים (AH-*noo maht-hee*-LEEM)="we begin" (masc.)

אָנוּ מַתְחִילוֹת (AH-*noo maht-hee*-LOHT)="we begin" (fem.)

אלף היא האות הראשונה.
AH-*lef hee hah*-OHT *hah-ree-shoh*-NAH.
A is the first letter.

בית היא השניה.
Beht hee hah-sh'nee-YAH.
B is the second.

גימל היא השלישית,
GHEE-*mel hee hah-sh'lee*-SHEET,
G is the third,

דלת היא הרביעית,
DAH-*let hee hah-r'vee*-EET,
D is the fourth,

הא היא החמשית,
Heh hee hah-hah-mee-SHEET,
H is the fifth,

ואו היא הששית,
Vahv hee hah-shee-SHEET,
V is the sixth,

זין היא השביעית,
ZAH-*yin hee hah-sh'vee*-EET,
Z is the seventh,

חית היא השמינית,
Het hee hah-sh'mee-NEET,
Kh is the eighth,

טית היא התשיעית,
Tet hee hah-t'shee-EET,
T is the ninth,

יוד היא העשירית,
Yood hee hah-ah-see-REET,
Y is the tenth,

תיו היא האות האחרונה.
Tahv hee hah-OHT *hah-akh-roh*-NAH.
T is the last letter.

כַּמָה אוֹתִיוֹת בְּאָלֶף־בֵּית הָעִבְרִי ?
KAH-*mah* oh-tee-YOHT *beh*-AH-*lef-beht* hah-Eev-REE?
How many letters are there in the Hebrew alphabet?

בְּאָלֶף־בֵּית הָעִבְרִי יֵשׁ עֶשְׂרִים וּשְׁתַּיִם אוֹתִיוֹת.
Beh-AH-*lef-beht* hah-Eev-REE *yehsh* ess-REEM *oo-sh'*TAH-*yim* oh-tee-YOHT.
In the Hebrew alphabet there are twenty-two letters.

THE VANISHING DOTS:

The Hebrew alphabet forms its vowels by a system of "dots" under the consonants, as we have seen in the introduction. We have placed dots for your convenience under all the words you have so far encountered. But in current Hebrew writing, "dots" are seldom used.

Therefore, in order better to prepare for what you will encounter in Israel, we too shall drop the "dots" from this lesson on. There are, however, four letters which can be used as vowels. ה and א may have the vowel sound of *ah* or *eh*, ו that of *oo* or *oh*, and י that of *ee* or *eh*. But do not despair! We shall continue with the phonetic transliteration.

אֵיזוֹ אוֹת הִיא דָלֶת, הַשְּׁלִישִׁית אוֹ הָרְבִיעִית ?
EH-*zoh* oht *hee* DAH-*let*, hah-*sh'lee*-SHEET *oh* hah-*r'vee*-EET?
Which letter is D, the third or the fourth?

הִיא הָרְבִיעִית.
Hee hah-*r'vee*-EET.
It is the fourth.

בְּאֵיזוֹ אוֹת מַתְחִיל הָאָלֶף־בֵּית הָעִבְרִי ?
Beh-EH-*zoh* oht *maht*-HEEL hah-AH-*lef-beht* hah-Eev-REE?
With what letter does the Hebrew alphabet begin?

בְּאוֹת אָלֶף.
Beh-OHT AH-*lef*.
With the letter A.

בְּאֵיזוֹ אוֹת הָאָלֶף־בֵּית הָעִבְרִי גּוֹמֵר ?
Beh-EH-*zoh* oht hah-AH-*lef-beht* hah-Eev-REE *goh*-MEHR?
With what letter does the Hebrew alphabet end?

בְּאוֹת תָּיו.
Beh-OHT tahv.
With the letter T.

בְּאֵיזֶה עַמוּד גּוֹמֵר הַשִּׁעוּר הָרִאשׁוֹן בְּסֵפֶר זֶה ?
Beh-EH-*zeh* ah-MOOD *goh*-MEHR hah-*she*-OOR hah-*ree*-SHON b'SEH-*fer zeh*?
On what page does the first lesson in this book end?

השעור הראשון בספר זה גומר בעמוד 5.
Hah-shee-OOR hah-ree-SHON b'SEH-fer zeh goh-MEHR beh-ah-MOOD 5.
The first lesson in this book ends on page 5.

איזה עמוד זה ?
EH-*zeh ah-*MOOD *zeh?*
What page is this?

זה עמוד 74.
*Zeh ah-*MOOD 74.
This is page 74.

באיזה עמוד מתחיל השעור השלישי ?
*Beh-*EH-*zeh ah-*MOOD *maht-*HEEL *hah-shee-*OOR *hah-sh'lee-*SHEE?
On what page does the third lesson begin?

השעור השלישי מתחיל בעמוד 9.
*Hah-shee-*OOR *hah-sh'lee-*SHEE *maht-*HEEL *beh-ah-*MOOD 9.
The third lesson begins on page 9.

האות אלף היא לפני האות בית.
*Hah-*OHT AH-*lef hee leef-*NEH *hah-*OHT *Beht.*
The letter A is before the letter B.

האות גימל היא אחרי האות בית.
*Hah-*OHT GHEE-*mel hee akh-*RAY *hah-*OHT *Beht.*
The letter G is after the letter B.

האות הא היא בין האות דלת והאות ואו.
*Hah-*OHT *Heh hee behn hah-*OHT DAH-*let v'hah-*OHT VAH*ʋ.*
The letter H is between the letter D and the letter V.

איפה האות חית לפני האות זין, או אחריה ?
*Eh-*FOH *hah-*OHT *het leef-*NEH *hah-*OHT ZAH-*yin, oh akh-*REH-*hah*?
Where is the letter KH, before the letter Z or after?

איזו אות היא לפני האות תיו ?
EH-*zoh oht hee leef-*NEH *hah-*OHT *Tahv?*
Which letter is before the letter T?

איזו אות היא אחרי האות יוד ?
EH-*zoh oht hee akh-ray hah-*OHT *Yood?*
Which letter is after the letter Y?

איזו אות היא בין מים וסמך ?
EH-*zoh oht hee behn memm v'*SAH-*mekh?*
Which letter is between M and S?

שואל אני שאלה : „מיהו האדון הזה "?
*Shoh-*EHL *ah-*NEE *sheh-eh-*LAH: "MEE-*hoo hah-ah-*DOHN *hah-*ZEH"?
I ask a question: "Who is this gentleman?"

עני על השאלה, גברת
*Ah-*NEE *ahl hah-sheh-eh-*LAH, G'VEH-*ret.*
Answer the question, Madam.

זה אדון כרמי.
Zeh ah-DOHN KAHR-mee.
It is Mr. Carmy.

מה את עושה ?
Mah aht oh-SAH?
What are you doing?

אני עונה על שאלה.
Ah-NEE oh-NAH ahl sheh-eh-LAH.
I am answering a question.

WATCH OUT FOR THE IDIOM:

In Hebrew, we "answer on a question" not simply "answer a question." You will find many such unusual constructions, but, instead of rationalizing about them, simply accept them as they come.

שאל שאלה את אדון נבון ?
Sheh-AHL sheh-eh-LAH ett ah-DOHN nah-VOHN.
Ask Mr. Navon a question.

מי שואל את השאלה ?
Mee shoh-EHL ett hah-sheh-eh-LAH?
Who asks the question?

אני שואל את השאלה.
Ah-NEE shoh-EHL ett hah-sheh-eh-LAH.
I ask the question.

אדוני, ענה על שאלת הגברת !
Ah-doh-NEE, ah-NEH ahl sheh-eh-LAHT hah-G'VEH-ret!
Sir, answer the lady's question!

בסיום השאלה אנו מעמידים סמן שאלה (?).
B'see-YOOM hah-sheh-eh-LAH AH-noo mah-ah-mee-DEEM see-MAHN sheh-eh-LAH (?).
At the end of a question we put a question mark (?).

בסיום תשובה, או משפט אנו שמים נקודה (.).
B'see-YOOM t'shoo-VAH, oh meesh-PAHT AH-noo sah-MEEM n'koo-DAH (.).
At the end of an answer, or a sentence, we put a period (.).

פה הפסיק (,).
Poh hah-p'SEEK (,).
Here is the comma (,).

פה סמן הקריאה (!).
Poh see-MAHN hah-k'ree-AH (!).
Here is the exclamation mark (!).

פה המקף (-).
Poh hah-mah-KAHF (-).
Here is the hyphen (-).

פה המירכא (').
Poh hah-mehr-HAH (').
Here is the apostrophe (').

THINKING IN HEBREW
(Answers on page 286)

1. מי כותב על הלוח?
   Mee koh-TEHV ahl hah-LOO-akh?

2. הכותבת הגברת בילה?
   Hah-koh-TEH-vet hah-G'VEH-ret BEH-leh?

3. הקוראת התלמידה?
   Hah-koh-REHT hah-tahl-mee-DAH?

4. איזו מלה כותב המורה על הלוח?
   EH-zoh mee-LAH koh-TEHV hah-moh-REH ahl hah-LOO-akh?

5. הכותב המורה בעפרון או בגיר?
   Hah-koh-TEHV hah-moh-REH bah-ee-pah-ROHN oh bah-GEER?

6. הכותב המורה את האלף-בית?
   Hah-koh-TEHV hah-moh-REH ett hah-AH-lef-beht?

7. הקוראת הגברת כספי עתון עברי?
   Hah-koh-REHT hah-G'VEH-ret KAHS-pee ee-TOHN Eev-REE?

8. ‏המדבר המורה עברית?‏

Hah-m'dah-BEHR hah-moh-REH Eev-REET?

9. ‏איזה עתון היא קוראת?‏

EH-zeh ee-TOHN hee koh-REHT?

10. ‏הקורא אתה עברית?‏

Hah-koh-REH ah-TAH Eev-REET?

11. ‏המדבר אתה ספרדית?‏

Hah-m'dah-BEHR ah-TAH S'fah-rah-DEET?

12. ‏המדבר אדון ברליץ צרפתית?‏

Hah-m'dah-BEHR ah-DOHN Berlitz Tsohr-fah-TEET?

13. ‏המדבר אדון ספיר אנגלית?‏

Hah-m'dah-BEHR ah-DOHN Sah-PEER Ahn-GLEET?

14. ‏היושבת הגברת בילה או עומדת?‏

Hah-yoh-SHEV-vet hah-G'VEH-ret BEH-leh oh oh-MEH-det?

שִׁעוּר 12

מה יש לנו ?

Mah yehsh LAH-*noo?*

What have we?

קח עפרון.	לי (יש) עפרון.
*Kakh ee-pah-*ROHN.	*Lee (yehsh) ee-pah-*ROHN.
Take a pencil.	I have a pencil.

GRAMMATICAL NOTE:

There is no word in Hebrew for "to have." It is expressed by "is" with the *subject* in the dative case. Therefore, to say "I have a pencil," you must put the subject, which here is the pronoun "I", into the dative case, and literally say, "To me (is) pencil." You can use the following table to express "have" with the different pronouns:

"to me" — (meaning "I have")	לִי (*lee*)
"to you" — (meaning "you have")	לְךָ (*l'hah*)
"to him" — (meaning "he has")	לוֹ (*lo*)
"to us" — (meaning "we have")	לָנוּ (LAH-*noo*)
"to them" — (meaning "they have")	לָהֶם (*lah-*HEMM)

78

To sum it all up, "to be" is used instead of "to have", and, in order to make it even more confusing—or easier, according to your point of view—the word "is" may be dropped. Example:

לְךָ (יֵשׁ) שָׁעוֹן? (L'hah (yehsh) shah-OHN?) — "Have you a watch?"

כֵּן, לִי שָׁעוֹן. (Kehn, lee shah-OHN.) — "Yes, I have a watch."

We have put *yehsh* in parenthesis to show that it may or may not be used.

לֵךָ (יֵשׁ) עִפָּרוֹן.
L'hah (yehsh) ee-pah-ROHN.
You have a pencil.

לוֹ (יֵשׁ) שָׁעוֹן.
Lo (yehsh) shah-OHN.
He has a watch.

DON'T BE CONFUSED:

לוֹ (*lo*), meaning "to him," has exactly the same sound as לֹא (*lo*), meaning "no."

לָהּ (יֵשׁ) מִטְרִיָּה.
Lah (yehsh) meet-ree-YAH.
She has an umbrella.

לָנוּ מְכוֹנִית.
LAH-noo m'hoh-NEET.
We have an automobile.

לָהֶם בַּיִת.
Lah-HEMM BAH-yit.
They have a house.

לוֹ אֵין כּוֹבַע.
Lo ehn KOH-vah.
He has no hat.

WATCH OUT:

אֵין (*ehn*) is the negative for יֵשׁ (*yehsh*). It may NOT be omitted. Both are used only in the present tense.

Example:

לִי יֵשׁ עִפָּרוֹן.
Lee yehsh ee-pah-ROHN.
I have a pencil.

לִי אֵין עִפָּרוֹן.
Lee ehn ee-pah-ROHN.
I have no pencil.

לָהֶם שֵׂעָר קָצָר.
Lah-HEMM seh-AHR kah-TSAHR.
They have short hair.

לָהֶם שֵׂעָר אָרוֹךְ.
Lah-HEMM seh-AHR ah-ROKH.
They have long hair.

למורה אין שער.

Lah-moh-REH *ehn seh*-AHR.

The teacher has no hair.

כן, יש לי עט.   היש לך עט ?

Kehn, yehsh lee eht.   Hah-YEHSH *l'hah eht?*

Yes, I have a pen.   Have you a pen?

בידך פרח.   מה בידי ?

B'yahd-HAH PEH-*rakh.*   *Mah b'yah*-DEE?

You have a flower in your hand.   What have I in my hand?

בידינו ספרים.   מה בידינו ?

B'yah-DEH-*noo s'fah*-REEM.   *Mah b'yah*-DEH-*noo?*

We have books in our hands.   What have we in our hands?

GRAMMATICAL NOTE: Four important prepositions,
בְּ "in"   כְּ "like"   לְ "to"   מ "from"
are used as prefixes to nouns. When used with the definite article, they form contractions, in which (*heh*) is eliminated and the vowel ־ , ְ or ֵ becomes a part of the prefix. Examples:

בְּקוּפְסָה "in a box"   בַּקוּפְסָה "in the box"

לְאָדוֹן "to a gentleman"   לָאָדוֹן "to the gentleman"

The same prefixes frequently occur with verbs to indicate purpose, direction, etc. Example: לְדַבֵּר "to speak".

לה שער שחור.   איזה שער יש לרחל ?

Lah seh-AHR *shah*-HOHR.   EH-*zeh seh*-AHR *yehsh l'Rah*-HEHL?

She has black hair.   What (color) hair has Rachel?

לה שער חום.   איזה שער לשרה ?

Lah seh-AHR *hoom.*   EH-*zeh seh*-AHR *l'Sah*-RAH?

She has brown hair.   What color of hair has Sarah?

לה עינים כחולות.   אילו עינים לה ?

Lah eh-NAH-*yim k'hoo*-LOHT.   EH-*loo eh*-NAH-*yim lah?*

She has blue eyes.   What (color) eyes does she have?

לה עינים שחורות.   אילו עינים לרבקה ?

Lah eh-NAH-*yim sh'hoh*-ROHT.   EH-*loo eh*-NAH-*yim l'Reev*-KAH?

She has dark (black) eyes.   What (color) eyes has Rebecca?

כן, אתה חובש.   החובש אני כובע לראשי ?

Kehn, ah-TAH *hoh*-VEHSH.   Hah-hoh-VEHSH *ah*-NEE KOH-*vah l'roh*-SHEE?

Yes, you wear one.   Do I wear a hat on my head?

CLOTHING NOTE:

Although in English we say "I have a hat on my head," Hebrew insists that we say חובש (*hoh-*VEHSH) "put on," which not only means "put on," but also "wear". For dresses, coats, etc., we use לובש (*loh-*VEHSH) but not for shoes, in which case we use נועל (*noh-*EHL)—"to be shod." For wearing eye-glasses, however, we must use still another word — (*mahr-*KEEV) מרכיב

איזה כובע חובשת גברת מזרחי ?
EH-*zeh* KOH-*vah* hoh-VEH-*shet* G'VEH-*ret Meez-*RAH-*hee?*
What kind of hat has Mrs. Mizrahi?

היא חובשת כובע לבן.
Hee hoh-VEH-*shet* KOH-*vah* lah-VAHN.
She has a white hat on her head.

איזו שמלה לובשת גברת ספיר ?
EH-*zoh* seem-LAH loh-VEH-*shet* G'VEH-*ret Sah-*PEER?
What kind of dress has Mrs. Sapir?

היא לובשת שמלה כחולה.
Hee loh-VEH-*shet* seem-LAH k'hoo-LAH.
She has a blue dress.

אילו נעלים אתה נועל ?
EH-*loo* nah-ah-LAH-*yim* ah-TAH noh-EHL?
What kind of shoes have you?

אני נועל נעלים שחורות.
*Ah-*NEE noh-EHL nah-ah-LAH-*yim* sh'hoh-ROHT.
I have black shoes.

המרכיב המורה משקפים ?
*Hah-mahr-*KEEV hah-moh-REH meesh-kah-FAH-*yim?*
Has the teacher glasses?

כן, המורה מרכיב משקפים.
Kehn, hah-moh-REH mahr-KEEV meesh-kah-FAH-*yim.*
Yes, the teacher has glasses.

THINKING IN HEBREW
(Answers on page 286)

1. מה יש למורה על הראש ?
Mah yehsh lah-moh-REH ahl hah-ROHSH?

2. היש לרותי שערות שחורות ?
Hah-YEHSH l'ROO-tee seh-ah-ROHT sh'hoh-ROHT?

3. היש לך עפרון ?   Hah-YEHSH l'hah ee-pah-ROHN?

4. היש לתלמידים ספרים ?   Hah-YEHSH l'tahl-mee-DEEM s'fah-REEM?

5. כמה רגלים לשולחן ?   KAH-mah rahg-LAH-yim lah-shool-HAHN?

6. היש למורה שערות רבות ?
Hah-YEHSH lah-moh-REH seh-ah-ROHT rah-BOHT?

7. היש לרותי מטריה ?   Hah-YEHSH l'ROO-tee meet-ree-YAH?

8. כמה אותיות לאלף־בית העברי ?
KAH-mah oh-tee-YOHT leh-AH-lef-beht hah-Eev-REE?

9. למי עתון בידו ?   L'mee ee-TOHN b'yah-DOH?

10. כמה תלמידים לכתה ?   KAH-mah tahl-mee-DEEM lah-kee-TAH?

11. היש לרוקפלר הרבה כסף ?
Hah-YEHSH l'Rocke-feller hahr-BEH KEH-seff?

12. היש לבית־הספר ברליץ הרבה תלמידים ?
Hah-YEHSH l'veht-hah-SEH-fer Berlitz hahr-BEH tahl-mee-DEEM?

לְמִי סְפָרִים יוֹתֵר ?

*L'mee s'fah-*REEM *yoh-*TEHR?

Who has more books?

לְךָ חֲמִשָּׁה סְפָרִים.	לִי שְׁנֵי סְפָרִים.
*L'hah hah-mee-*SHAH *s'fah-*REEM.	*Lee sh'*NEH *s'fah-*REEM.
You have five books.	I have two books.

לָנוּ שְׁמוֹנָה סְפָרִים.	כַּמָּה סְפָרִים לָנוּ ?
LAH-*noo sh'moh-*NAH *s'fah-*REEM.	KAH-*mah s'fah-*REEM LAH-*noo?*
We have eight books.	How many books have we?

לְךָ סְפָרִים יוֹתֵר.	לְמִי סְפָרִים יוֹתֵר ?
*L'hah s'fah-*REEM *yoh-*TEHR.	*L'mee s'fah-*REEM *yoh-*TEHR?
You have more books.	Who has more books?

לִי סְפָרִים פָּחוּת.	לְמִי סְפָרִים פָּחוּת ?
*Lee s'fah-*REEM *pah-*HOOT.	*L'mee s'fah-*REEM *pah-*HOHT?
I have fewer books.	Who has fewer books?

83

לי פחות ממך.
Lee pah-HOHT meem-HAH.
I have fewer than you.

לך ספרים יותר ממני.
L'hah s'fah-REEM yoh-TEHR mee-MEN-nee.
You have more books than I.

לך שערות רבות.
L'hah seh-ah-ROHT rah-BOHT.
You have much hair.

לאדון ברליץ שערות מעטות.
Lah-ah-DOHN Berlitz seh-ah-ROHT meh-ah-TOHT.
Mr. Berlitz has little hair.

בספר הגדול חמש מאות עמודים.
Bah-SEH-fer hah-gah-DOHL hah-MEHSH meh-OHT ah-moo-DEEM.
In the large book there are 500 pages.

בספר הקטן שלוש מאות עמוד.
Bah-SEH-fer hah-kah-TAHN sh'LOSH meh-OHT ah-MOOD.
In the small book there are 300 pages.

NOTE ON THE PLURALS AFTER 10:

As you see, we use עמוד (ah-MOOD) and עמודים (ah-moo-DEEM) indiscriminately. This is because for numbers over *ten*, the noun following can be in either the singular or the plural form.

באיזה ספר יותר עמודים, ובאיזה ספר פחות ?
Beh-EH-zeh SEH-fer yoh-TEHR ah-moo-DEEM,
oo-veh-EH-zeh SEH-fer pah-HOHT?
In which book are there more pages, and in which fewer?

NOTE TO STUDENT:

יותר (yoh-TEHR) means *more*, and פחות (pah-HOHT) means *fewer*. Though these words should normally *follow* the noun they modify, they can also *precede* it to give more stress to the idea they convey, both in the question, and in the answer. So it is correct to say the above either way:

באיזה ספר יותר עמודים ?
1) Beh-EH-zeh SEH-fer yoh-TEHR ah-moo-DEEM?

באיזה ספר עמודים יותר ?
2) Beh-EH-zeh SEH-fer ah-moo-DEEM yoh-TEHR?

בספר הגדול יותר עמודים, בספר הקטן פחות.
Bah-SEH-fer hah-gah-DOHL yoh-TEHR ah-moo-DEEM, bah-SEH-fer
hah-kah-TAHN pah-HOHT.
In the large book there are more pages, and in the small one there are fewer.

בבנק הרבה כסף.
Bah-BAHNK *hahr*-BEH KEH-*seff.*
In the bank there is much money.

בכיסי מעט כסף.
B'his-SEE *meh*-AHT KEH-*seff.*
In my pocket there is little money.

היש תושבים רבים בעיר זו ?
Hah-YEHSH *toh-shah*-VEEM *rah*-BEEM *beh*-EER *zoh?*
Are there many inhabitants in this town?

כן
Kehn.
Yes.

היש כסאות רבים בחדר זה ?
Hah-YEHSH *kis*-OHT *rah*-BEEM *bah*-HEH-*der zeh?*
Are there many chairs in this room?

לא, רק שני כסאות.
*Lo, rahk sh'*NEH *kis*-OHT.
No, only two chairs.

לי קופסת גפרורים.
Lee koof-SAHT *gahf-roo*-REEM.
I have a box of matches.

כמה גפרורים בקופסה ?
KAH-*mah gahf-roo*-REEM *bah-koof*-SAH?
How many matches are there in the box?

בסך הכל יש בה שלושה גפרורים.
B'sakh hah-KOHL *yehsh bah sh'loh*-SHAH *gahf-roo*-REEM.
There are three matches in it in all.

היש לך כה הרבה כסף כמו שיש לי ?
Hah-YEHSH *l'hah koh hahr*-BEH KEH-*seff k'moh sheh*-YEHSH *lee?*
Have you as much money as I?

כן, לי יש אותו סכום הכסף כמו לך.
Kehn, lee yehsh oh-TOH *s'hoom hah*-KEH-*seff k'moh l'hah.*
Yes, I have the same amount of money as you.

למורה יותר ספרים מאשר לתלמיד.
Lah-moh-REH *yoh*-TEHR *s'fah*-REEM *meh-ah*-SHERR *lah-tahl*-MEED.
The teacher has more books than the student.

למי מכולנו יותר ספרים ?
L'mee mee-koo-LAH-*noo yoh*-TEHR *s'fah*-REEM?
Who has more books of all of us?

NOTE ON THE COMPARATIVE:

Normally, it is necessary to use *"meh-ah*-SHERR" to express comparison in the same way as we use "than" in English. However, it is also possible to use simply the preposition מ (*mee*) or מ (*meh*), which literally means "from" for the same purpose.

Example: לי פחות ממך (*Lee pah*-HOHT *meem*-HAH) — "I have less than you."

THINKING IN HEBREW
(Answers on page 286)

1. ‏כמה כסף יש לגברת בילה?‏
KAH-*mah* KEH-*seff yehsh lah*-G'VEH-*ret* BEH-*leh?*

2. ‏היש לה כה הרבה כסף כמו למורה?‏
Hah-YEHSH *lah koh hahr*-BEH KEH-*seff k'moh lah-moh*-REH?

3. ‏למי כסף יותר, לרותי או למורה?‏
L'mee KEH-*seff yoh*-TEHR, *l'*ROO-*tee oh lah-moh*-REH?

4. ‏היש למורה עפרונות על אוזנו?‏
Hah-YEHSH *lah-moh*-REH *eff-roh*-NOHT *ahl ohz*-NOH?

5. ‏היש לו עפרונות יותר מאשר לרותי?‏
Hah-YEHSH *lo eff-roh*-NOHT *yoh*-TEHR *meh-ah*-SHERR *l'*ROO-*tee?*

6. ‏היש לגברת בילה פחות ספרים מאשר למורה?‏
Hah-YEHSH *lah*-G'VEH-*ret* BEH-*leh pah*-HOHT *s'fah*-REEM *meh-ah*-SHERR *lah-moh*-REH?

7. ‏למי מכולם יותר כסף?‏
L'mee *mee-koo*-LAHM *yoh*-TEHR KEH-*seff?*

8. ‏למי מכולם פחות כסף?‏
L'mee *mee-koo*-LAHM *pah*-HOHT KEH-*seff?*

9.   ? היש לרותי הרבה כסף

Hah-YEHSH *l'*ROO-*tee hahr*-BEH KEH-*seff?*

10.   ? היש למורה מעט ספרים

Hah-YEHSH *lah-moh*-REH *meh*-AHT *s'fah*-REEM?

11.   ? הקורא אתה הרבה ספרים עברים

Hah-koh-REH *ah*-TAH *hahr*-BEH *s'fah*-REEM *eev-ree*-YEEM?

12.   ? מי כותב יותר תרגילים, המורה או התלמיד

Mee koh-TEHV *yoh*-TEHR *tahr-gee*-LEEM, *hah-moh*-REH *oh hah-tahl*-MEED?

13.   ? היש הרבה עמודים בספר זה

Hah-YEHSH *hahr*-BEH *ah-moo*-DEEM *b'*SEH-*fer zeh?*

14.   ? היש בניו-יורק טימס כה הרבה עמודים כמו בספר זה

Hah-YEHSH *bah*-New York TIMES *koh hahr*-BEH *ah-moo*-DEEM
*k'moh b'*SEH-*fer zeh?*

15.   ? כמה כסף בכיסי

KAH-*mah* KEH-*seff b'hee*-SEE?

16.   ? כמה כסף יש לך

KAH-*mah* KEH-*seff yehsh l'hah?*

שִׁעוּר 14

אני נותן לך ספר.

Ah-NEE *noh*-TEHN *l'hah* SEH-*fer.*

I give you a book.

מַה אַתָּה מְקַבֵּל מִמֶּנִּי?   אני נותן לך ספר.

Ah-NEE *noh*-TEHN *l'hah* SEH-*fer.*   *Mah ah*-TAH *m'kah*-BEHL *mee*-MEN-*nee?*

I give you a book.   What do you receive from me?

אַתָּה מְקַבֵּל סֵפֶר מִמֶּנִּי.

Ah-TAH *m'kah*-BEHL SEH-*fer mee*-MEN-*nee.*

You receive a book from me.

GRAMMATICAL NOTE: In Hebrew, personal pronouns are *declined*, that is, they change according to their use in the sentence.

The following table shows the change the pronouns undergo in the dative and the genitive cases. The dative implies the use of the indirect object with verbs of giving, telling, saying, etc., and corresponds to the English form "to me, to you, to him," etc. The genitive corresponds to the English form "of me, from me," etc.

Dative

Masc.		Fem.	
"to me"	לי *lee*	(same as masc.)	
"to you"	לך *l'hah*	"to you"	לך *lakh*
"to him"	לו *lo*	"to her"	לה *lah*
"to us"	לנו LAH-*noo*	(same as masc.)	
Plural: "to you"	לכם *lah*-HEMM	"to you"	לכן *lah*-HENN
"to them"	להם *lah*-HEMM	"to them"	להן *lah*-HENN

Genitive

Masc.		Fem.	
"from me"	ממני *mee*-MEN-*nee*	(same as masc.)	
"from you"	ממך *meem*-HAH	"from you"	ממך *mee*-MEHKH
"from him"	ממנו *mee*-MEN-*noo*	"from her"	ממנה *mee*-MEN-*nah*
"from us"	ממנו *mee*-MEN-*noo*	(same as masc.)	
Plural: "from you"	מכם *mee*-KEMM	"from you"	מכן *mee*-KENN
"from them"	מהם *meh*-HEMM	"from them"	מהן *meh*-HENN

Examples: המורה נותן להם שעור   (*Hah-moh-*REH *noh-*TEHN *lah*-HEMM *shee-*OOR) "The teacher gives them a lesson."
התלמידים מקבלים ספר ממנו (*Hah-tahl-mee-*DEEM *m'kah-b'*LEEM SEH-*fer mee-*MEN-*noo*) "The pupils receive a book from him."

אתה מקבל אותו ממני.
*Ah-*TAH *m'kah-*BEHL *oh-*TOH *mee-*MEN-*nee.*
You receive it from me.

הדודה בילה נותנת את הכפפות לרותי.
*Hah-doh-*DAH BEH-*leh noh-*TEH-*net* ett *hah-k'fah-*FOHT *l'*ROO-*tee.*
Aunt Behle gives the gloves to Ruthie.

היא נותנת לה את הכפפות.
*Hee noh-*TEH-*net lah* ett *hah-k'fah-*FOHT.
She gives her the gloves.

רותי מקבלת את הכפפות מהדודה בילה.
ROO-*tee m'kah-*BEH-*let* ett *hah-k'fah-*FOHT *meh-hah-doh-*DAH BEH-*leh.*
Ruthie receives the gloves from Aunt Behle.

היא מקבלת אותן ממנה.

Hee m'kah-BEH-let oh-TAHN mee-MEN-nah.

She receives them from her.

מי נותן לך את הספר?

Mee noh-TEHN l'hah ett hah-SEH-fer?

Who gives you the book?

אתה נותן לי את הספר.

Ah-TAH noh-TEHN lee ett hah-SEH-fer.

You give me the book.

ממי אתה מקבל את הספר?

Mee-MEE ah-TAH m'kah-BEHL ett hah-SEH-fer?

From whom do you receive the book?

אני מקבל אותו ממך.

Ah-NEE m'kah-BEHL oh-TOH meem-HAH.

I receive it from you.

למי אתה נותן את הספר?

L'mee ah-TAH noh-TEHN ett hah-SEH-fer?

To whom do you give the book?

אתה נותן לי את הספר.

Ah-TAH noh-TEHN lee ett hah-SEH-fer.

You give the book to me.

מי נותן לרותי את הכפפות?

Mee noh-TEHN l'ROO-tee ett hah-k'fah-FOHT?

Who gives Ruthie the gloves?

הדודה בילה נותנת לה את הכפפות.

Hah-doh-DAH BEH-leh noh-TEH-net lah ett hah-k'fah-FOHT.

Aunt Behle gives her the gloves.

למי היא נותנת את הכפפות?

L'mee hee noh-TEH-net ett hah-k'fah-FOHT?

To whom does she give the gloves?

היא נותנת אותן לרותי.

Hee noh-TEH-net oh-TAHN l'ROO-tee.

She gives them to Ruthie.

למי אתה נותן את המכתב?

L'mee ah-TAH noh-TEHN ett hah-meekh-TAHV?

To whom do you give the letter?

אני נותן אותו לאדון נבון.

*Ah-*NEE *noh-*TEHN *oh-*TOH *lah-ah-*DOHN NAh-VOHN.

I give it to Mr. Navon.

מה הוא מקבל ממך?

*Mah hoo m'kah-*BEHL *meem-*HAH?

What does he receive from you?

הוא מקבל מכתב ממני.

*Hoo m'kah-*BEHL *meekh-*TAHV *mee-*MEN-*nee.*

He receives a letter from me.

תן את הכובע ואת המטריה לגברת ספיר.

*Tehn ett hah-*KOH-*vah veh-*ETT *hah-meet-ree-*YAH *lah-*G'VEH-*ret Sah-*PEER.

Give the hat and the umbrella to Mrs. Sapir.

מה אתה נותן לה?

*Mah ah-*TAH *noh-*TEHN *lah?*

What do you give her?

אני נותן לה את הכובע ואת המטריה.

*Ah-*NEE *noh-*TEHN *lah ett hah-*KOH-*vah veh-*ETT *hah-meet-ree-*YAH.

I give her the hat and the umbrella.

למי אתה נותן את הכובע ואת המטריה?

*L'mee ah-*TAH *noh-*TEHN *ett hah-*KOH-*vah veh-*ETT *hah-meet-ree-*YAH?

To whom do you give the hat and the umbrella?

לה, לגברת ספיר.

*Lah, lah-*G'VEH-*ret Sah-*PEER.

To her, to Mrs. Sapir.

מה עושים המורים?	הם נותנים שעורים.
*Mah oh-*SEEM *hah-moh-*REEM?	*Hehm noh-*T'NEEM *shee-oo-*REEM.
What are the teachers doing?	They are giving lessons.

למי הם נותנים שעורים?

*L'mee hehm noh-*T'NEEM *shee-oo-*REEM?

To whom are they giving lessons?

הם נותנים שעורים לתלמידים.

*Hehm noh-*T'NEEM *she-oo-*REEM *lah-tahl-mee-*DEEM.

They are giving lessons to the pupils.

מה נותנים המורים לתלמידים?

*Mah noh-*T'NEEM *hah-moh-*REEM *lah-tahl-mee-*DEEM?

What do the teachers give to the pupils?

הם נותנים להם שעורים.

Hehm noh-T'NEEM lah-HEMM she-oo-REEM.

They give them lessons.

מה שמך ?

Mah sheem-HAH?

What is your name?

שמי אברהם.

Sh'mee Ahv-rah-HAHM.

My name is Abraham.

אמר לי את שמך הראשון והאמצעי.

Eh-MOHR lee ett sheem-HAH hah-ree-SHOHN veh-hah-ehm-tsah-EE.

Tell me your first and middle name.

שמי הראשון אברהם, שמי האמצעי יוסף.

Sh'mee hah-ree-SHOHN Ahv-rah-HAHM, sh'mee hah-ehm-tsah-EE Yoh-SEHF.

My first name is Abraham, my middle name is Joseph.

מה שם משפחתך ?

Mah shehm meesh-pakh-t'HAH?

What is your family name?

שם משפחתי ספיר.

Shehm meesh-pakh-TEE Sah-PEER.

My family name is Sapir.

אמר לי מה על השולחן?

Eh-MOHR lee mah ahl hah-shool-HAHN?

Tell me what is on the table?

על השולחן יש שעון, ספר ועתון.

Ahl hah-shool-HAHN yehsh sha-OHN, SEH-fer veh-ee-TOHN.

On the table are a clock, a book, and a newspaper.

מה אתה אומר ?

Mah ah-TAH oh-MEHR?

What do you say?

אני אומר לך מה על השולחן.

Ah-NEE oh-MEHR l'hah mah ahl hah-shool-HAHN.

I tell you what is on the table.

מה אומר אדון כספי ?

Mah oh-MEHR ah-DOHN KAHS-pee?

What does Mr. Kaspi say?

הוא אינו אומר כלום.

Hoo eh-NOH oh-MEHR k'loom.

He says nothing.

האומרת לנו הגברת כספי משהו ?

Hah-oh-MEH-ret LAH-noo hah-G'VEH-ret KAHS-pee mah-sheh-HOO?

Does Mrs. Kaspi say anything to us?

כן, היא אומרת משהו. היא מספרת לנו שהמורה הוא טוב מאד.

Kehn, hee oh-MEH-ret mah-sheh-HOO. Hee m'sah-PEH-ret LAH-noo sheh-hah-moh-REH hoo tohv meh-OHD.

Yes, she says something. She tells us that the teacher is very good.

TWO WORDS IN ENGLISH, ONE IN HEBREW:
"Something" and "anything" are both translated by
משהו (mah-sheh-HOO) and "none' and "nothing" are
both expressed by כלום (k'loom) or לא כלום
(lo k'loom).

אמר לי מי עומד על יד הדלת.
Eh-MOHR *lee mee oh*-MEHD *ahl yahd hah*-DEH-*let.*
Tell me who is standing near the door.

אדון ברליץ עומד שם   אמר לי מה הוא עושה ?
Ah-DOHN *Berlitz oh*-MEHD *shahm.*   *Eh*-MOHR-*lee mah hoo oh*-SEH?
Mr. Berlitz is standing there.   Tell me, what is he doing?

הוא מדבר עם התלמידים.
Hoo m'dah-BEHR *im hah-tahl-mee*-DEEM.
He is speaking with the students.

מה הוא אומר להם ?
Mah hoo oh-MEHR *lah*-HEMM?
What is he telling them?

הוא מדבר אתם על השעור.
Hoo m'dah-BEHR *ee*-TAHM *ahl hah-shee*-OOR.
He is speaking with them about the lesson.

מה אומרים אליו התלמידים אחרי השעור ?
*Mah oh-m'*REEM *eh*-LAHV *hah-tahl-mee*-DEEM *akh*-RAY *hah-shee-*OOR?
What do the students say to him after the lesson?

הם אומרים „תודה", ואחרי כן אומרים „שלום".
*Hehm oh-m'*REEM "*toh*-DAH", *veh-akh*-RAY *hehn oh-m'*REEM
"*shah*-LOHM".
They say "thank you," and then they say "good-bye."

מה הוא עונה להם ?
Mah hoo oh-NEH *lah*-HEMM?
What does he answer them?

הוא עונה „שלום" ו„להתראות".
Hoo ohn-NEH "*shah*-LOHM" *oo*-"*leh-heet-rah*-OHT."
He answers "good-bye" and "see you again."

THINKING IN HEBREW
(Answers on page 287)

1. הנותן המורה ספר לגברת בילה?

*Hah-noh-*TEHN *hah-moh-*REH SEH-*fer lah-*G'VEH-*ret* BEH-*leh?*

2. מה נותן המורה לרותי?

*Mah noh-*TEHN *hah-moh-*REH *l'*ROO-*tee?*

3. מה עושה הגברת בילה?

*Mah oh-*SAH *hah-*G'VEH-*ret* BEH-*leh?*

4. הנותנות בילה ורותי כובע למורה?

*Hah-noh-t'*NOHT BEH-*leh v'*ROO-*tee* KOH-*vah lah-moh-*REH?

5. מי מדבר לרותי?

*Mee m'dah-*BEHR *l'*ROO-*tee?*

6. מה אומר לה המורה?

*Mah oh-*MEHR *lah hah-moh-*REH?

7. האומרת הגברת בילה משהו לאביר?

*Hah-oh-*MEH-*ret hah-*G'VEH-*ret* BEH-*leh mah-sheh-*HOO *leh-ah-*BEER?

8. הנותנת היא לו משהו?

*Hah-noh-*TEH-*net hee lo mah-sheh-*HOO?

9. ‏מה אומר אביר ?‏

Mah oh-MEHR Ah-BEER?

10. ‏המדברים התלמידים אל המורה בשעת השעור ?‏

Hah-m'dah-b'REEM hah-tahl-mee-DEEM ell hah-moh-REH beesh-AHT
hah-shee-OOR?

11. ‏האומרים הם לו „שלום" לפני השעור ?‏

Hah-oh-m'REEM hehm lo "Shah-LOM" leef-NEH hah-shee-OOR?

12. ‏מה אומר להם המורה אחרי השעור ?‏

Mah oh-MEHR lah-HEMM hah-moh-REH akh-RAY hah-shee-OOR?

13. ‏אמר לי מה ביד השמאלית של הגברת בילה ?‏

Eh-MOHR lee mah b'yahd hah-s'moh-LEET shell hah-G'VEH-ret BEH-leh?

14. ‏מה אתה מספר לי ?‏

Mah ah-TAH m'sah-PEHR lee?

15. ‏מה אומר המורה לגברת בילה ?‏

Mah oh-MEHR hah-moh-REH lah-G'VEH-ret BEH-leh?

16. ‏מה היא אומרת לו ?‏

Mah hee oh-MEH-ret lo?

שָׁעוּר 15

הִכָּנֵס !
*Hee-kah-*NEHs!
Come in!

מִישֶׁהוּ דוֹפֵק בַּדֶּלֶת.
*Mee-sheh-*HOO *doh-*FEHK *bah-*DEH-*let.*
Somebody knocks at the door.

הַמּוֹרֶה אוֹמֵר: „הִכָּנֵס, בְּבַקָּשָׁה!"
*Hah-moh-*REH *oh-*MEHR: "*Hee-kah-*NEHs, *b'vah-kah-*SHAH!"
The teacher says: "Come in, please!"

זֶה אָדוֹן נָבוֹן מִתֵּל-אָבִיב.
*Zeh ah-*DOHN *Nah-*VOHN *mee-Tel-Ah-*VEEV.
It is Mr. Navon from Tel-Aviv.

הַמּוֹרֶה אוֹמֵר: „שֵׁב, בְּבַקָּשָׁה!"
*Hah-moh-*REH *oh-*MEHR: "*Shehv, b'vah-kah-*SHAH!"
The teacher says: "Please sit down!"

96

קח סגריה!

Kakh see-gah-ree-YAH!

Take a cigarette!

אדון נבון אומר : "תודה, יש לי אחדות משלי"

Ah-DOHN Nah-VOHN oh-MEHR: "Toh-DAH, yehsh lee ah-hah-DOHT mee-sheh-LEE."

Mr. Navon says: "Thank you, I have some of my own."

הם יושבים אל השולחן.

Hehm yoh-sh'VEEM ell hah-shool-HAHN.

They sit down at the table.

אדון נבון מספר לו דברים שונים על ישראל.

Ah-DOHN Nah-VOHN m'sah-PEHR lo d'vah-REEM shoh-NEEM ahl Yis-rah-EHL.

Mr. Navon tells him different things about Israel.

יש לו כמה תמונות מעיניות משם.

Yehsh lo KAH-mah t'moo-NOHT meh-ahn-y'NOHT mee-SHAHM.

He has some interesting pictures from there.

המדברים הם אנגלית?

Hah-m'dah-b'REEM hehm ahn-g'LEET?

Do they speak English?

לא, הם מדברים רק עברית.

Lo, hehm m'dah-b'REEM rahk eev-REET.

No, they speak only Hebrew.

המדבר מישהו בחדר צרפתית?

Hah-m'dah-BEHR mee-sheh-HOO bah-HEH-der tsohr-fah-TEET?

Does any one in the room speak French?

לא, אף אחד אינו מדבר צרפתית.

Lo, aff eh-HAHD eh-NOH m'dah-BEHR tsohr-fah-TEET.

No, no one speaks French.

אדון נבון נותן למורה ספרים אחדים וממתקים מישראל.

Ah-DOHN Nah-VOHN noh-TEHN lah-moh-REH s'fah-REEM ah-hah-DEEM oo-mahm-tah-KEEM mee-Yis-rah-EHL.

Mr.Navon gives the teacher some books and some candy from Israel.

המורה מקבל אותם ואומר "תודה רבה".

Hah-moh-REH m'kah-BEHL oh-TAHM veh-oh-MEHR "Toh-DAH rah-BAH".

The teacher accepts them and says, "Thank you very much."

IMPORTANT NOTE: "Some" or "a few" is אחדים (*ah-hah-*DEEM) (masculine) or אחדות (*ah-hah-*DOHT) (feminine). Since it is an adjective *only*, in Hebrew, it can be used *only with a noun.*

Examples:

ספרים אחדים (*s'fah-*REEM *ah-hah-*DEEM) "some books"

תמונות אחדות (*t'moo-*NOHT *ah-hah-*DOHT) "some pictures"

The word כמה (KAH-*mah*) is also currently used in both genders for "some." The same word means, as you noticed, "how much" or "how many" when used in a question.

Example: יש לו כמה תמונות מעיינות מישראל.
Yehsh lo KAH-*mah t'moo-*NOHT *meh-ahn-y'*NOHT *mee-Yis-rah-*EHL.
He has some interesting pictures from Israel.

Another word is also used for "some," "a few," or "a little". This word is קצת (*k'tsaht*).

Example:

היש לאדון ספיר קצת כסף?   יש לו קצת.
*Hah-*YEHSH *lah-ah-*DOHN *Sah-*PEER *k'tsaht* KEH-*seff?*   *Yehsh lo k'tsaht.*
Has Mr. Sapir a little money?   He has a little.

מישהו דופק בדלת.   בילה ורותי נכנסות.
*Mee-sheh-*HOO *doh-*FEHK *bah-*DEH-*let.*   BEH-*leh v'*ROO-*tee neekh-nah-*SOHT.
Someone knocks at the door.   Behle and Ruthie come in.

המורה ואדון נבון קמים.
*Hah-moh-*REH *vah-ah-*DOHN NAh-VOHN *kah-*MEEM.
The teacher and Mr. Navon get up.

רותי אומרת „היש לך ממתקים?"
ROO-*tee oh-*MEH-*ret* "*Hah-*YEHSH *l'hah mahm-tah-*KEEM?"
Ruthie says, "Have you any candy?"

אדון נבון נותן לה קצת.
*Ah-*DOHN *Nah-*VOHN *noh-*TEHN *lah k'tsaht.*
Mr. Navon gives her some.

אחרי הפקור אדון נבון הולך והיתר נשארים.
*Akh-*RAY *hah-bee-*KOOR *ah-*DOHN *Nah-*VOHN *hoh-*LEHKH
*veh-hah-*YEH-*ter neesh-ah-*REEM.
After the visit Mr. Navon goes, and the others remain.

THINKING IN HEBREW
(Answers on page 287)

1.   היש למורה סיגריה בידו?
*Hah-*YEHSH *lah-moh-*REH *see-gah-ree-*YAH *b'yah-*DOH?

2.   מה ביד השמאלית של הגברת בילה?
*Mah bah-*YAHD *hah-smoh-*LEET *shell hah-*G'VEH-*ret* BEH-*leh?*

3.   היש לרותי משהו בידה הימנית?
*Hah-*YEHSH *l'*ROO-*tee mah-sheh-*HOO *b'yah-*DAH *hah-y'mah-*NEET?

4.   מה בידה השמאלית?
*Mah b'yah-*DAH *hah-smoh-*LEET?

5.   העומד מישהו לידו השמאלית של המורה?
*Hah-oh-*MEHD *mee-sheh-*HOO *l'yah-*DOH *hah-smoh-*LEET
*shell hah-moh-*REH?

6.   איפה רותי?
*Eh-*FOH ROO-*tee?*

7.   היש ספר בידה הימנית של הגברת בילה?
*Hah-*YEHSH SEH-*fer b'yah-*DAH *hah-y'mah-*NEET
*shell hah-*G'VEH-*ret* BEH-*leh?*

8. ‏מי יושב על הכסא?‏
*Mee yoh-*SHEHV *ahl hah-kis-*SEH?

9. ‏היש משהו על השולחן?‏
*Hah-*YEHSH *mah-sheh-*HOO *ahl hah-shool-*HAHN?

10. ‏מה בידו הימנית של המורה?‏
*Mah b'yah-*DOH *hah-y'mah-*NEET *shell hah-moh-*REH?

11. ‏מי עומד לידו השמאלית?‏
*Mee oh-*MEHD *l'yah-*DOH *hah-smoh-*LEET?

12. ‏מה מתחת לכסא?‏
*Mah mee-*TAH-*haht lah-kis-*SEH?

13. ‏העומד מישהו לפני רותי?‏
*Hah-oh-*MEHD *mee-sheh-*HOO *leef-*NEH ROO-*tee?

14. ‏מי לידה השמאלית?‏
*Mee l'yah-*DAH *hah-smoh-*LEET?

15. ‏העומד מישהו מאחורי השולחן?‏
*Hah-oh-*MEHD *mee-sheh-*HOO *meh-ah-hoh-*REH *hah-shool-*HAHN?

16. ‏החובש המורה כובע לראשו?‏
*Hah-hoh-*VEHSH *hah-moh-*REH KOH-*vah l'roh-*SHOH?

17. ‏מה חובש המורה לראשו?‏
*Mah hoh-*VEHSH *hah-moh-*REH l'roh-*SHOH?

בְּמַה אַתָּה הוֹלֵךְ ?

Bah-MEH *ah*-TAH *hoh*-LEHKH?

With what do you walk?

אֲנִי הוֹלֵךְ בְּרַגְלַיִם.

Ah-NEE *hoh*-LEHKH *bah-rahg*-LAH-*yim*.

I walk with the feet.

אֲנַחְנוּ כּוֹתְבִים בְּעִפָּרוֹן.

Ah-NAKH-*noo koh*-T'VEEM *bah-ee-pah*-ROHN.

We write with the pencil.

אַתֶּם חוֹתְכִים אֶת הַלֶּחֶם בְּסַכִּין.

Ah-TEMM *hoh-t'*HEEM *ett hah-*LEH-*hemm bah-sah*-KEEN.

You cut the bread with the knife.

מַה אָנוּ עוֹשִׂים בְּעֵט ?	בְּעֵט אָנוּ כּוֹתְבִים.
Mah AH-*noo oh*-SEEM *bah*-EHT?	*Bah*-EHT AH-*noo koh*-T'VEEM.
What do we do with the pen?	We write with the pen.

101

NOTE TO STUDENT: אָנוּ (AH-*noo*)—"we" is an abbreviation of אֲנַחְנוּ (*Ah*-NAKH-*noo*). Both forms are in use.

מה אנו עושים במפתח, בסכין, בעט?
Mah AH-*noo* oh-SEEM *bah-mahf*-TEH-*akh, bah-sah*-KEEN, *bah*-EHT?
What do we do with the key, the knife, the pen?

מה אנו עושים בידים, ברגלים?
Mah AH-*noo* oh-SEEM *bah-yah*-DAH-*yim, bah-rahg*-LAH-*yim?*
What do we do with the hands, the legs?

במה אנו כותבים, לוקחים, חותכים?
Bah-MEH AH-*noo koh-t'*VEEM, *loh-k'*HEEM, *hoh-t'*HEEM?
With what do we write, take, cut?

במה אנו הולכים?
Bah-MEH AH-*noo hoh-l'*HEEM?
With what do we walk?

במה אנו פותחים את הדלת?
Bah-MEH AH-*noo poh-t'*HEEM *ett hah*-DEH-*let?*
With what do we open the door?

אנו רואים בעינים.
AH-*noo roh*-EEM *bah-eh*-NAH-*yim.*
We see with the eyes.

אנו שומעים באוזנים.
AH-*noo shoh-meh*-EEM *bah-ohz*-NAH-*yim.*
We hear with the ears.

אני עוצם את העינים, אינני רואה.
Ah-NEE *oh*-TSEHM *ett hah-eh*-NAH-*yim, eh*-NEN-*nee roh*-EH.
I close the eyes; I don't see.

אני פוקח אותן; אני רואה.
Ah-NEE *poh*-KAY-*akh oh*-TAHN; *ah*-NEE *roh*-EH.
I open them; I see.

אתה פה; אני רואה אותך.
Ah-TAH *poh; ah*-NEE *roh*-EH *oh-t'*HAH.
You are here; I see you.

היא שם; איני רואה אותה.
Hee shahm; eh-NEE *roh*-EH *oh*-TAH.
She is there; I do not see her.

GRAMMATICAL NOTE: In Hebrew, when a personal pronoun is the direct object of an action, it takes the *accusative* case. Note the following table, showing the accusative declension for masculine and feminine forms.

	Masculine			Feminine	
me	אוֹתִי	(*oh*-TEE)		(same as masculine)	
you	אוֹתְךָ	(*oh-t'*HAH)	you	אוֹתָךְ	(*oh*-TAKH)
him	אוֹתוֹ	(*oh*-TOH)	her	אוֹתָה	(*oh*-TAH)
us	אוֹתָנוּ	(*oh*-TAH-*noo*)		(same as masculine)	
you (plural)	אתכם	(*ett*-HEMM)	you (plural)	אתכן	(*ett*-HENN)
them	אוֹתם	(*oh*-TAHM)	them	אוֹתן	(*oh*-TAHN)

NOTE TO STUDENT: To "close" eyes is expressed by a special word עוֹצֵם (*oh*-TSEHM) and not by סוֹגֵר (*soh*-GEHR). To "open" eyes requires a special word פּוֹקֵחַ (*poh*-KAY-*akh*) and not פּוֹתֵחַ (*poh*-TAY-*akh*).

עצם עיניך.
Ah-TSOHM *eh*-NEH-*hah*.
Close your eyes.

הרואה אתה?
Hah-roh-EH *ah*-TAH?
Do you see?

פקח עיניך.
P'kakh eh-NEH-*hah*.
Open your eyes.

מה אתה רואה ברחוב?
Mah ah-TAH *roh*-EH *bah-r'*HOHV?
What do you see in the street?

את מי אתה רואה שם?
Ett mee ah-TAH *roh*-EH shahm?
Whom do you see there?

איני רואה שם איש.
Eh-NEE *roh*-EH shahm eesh.
I don't see anyone there.

WATCH THAT IDIOM: איני רואה איש (*eh*-NEE *roh*-EH eesh) is an idiomatic expression actually meaning "I don't see any man" but used in the sense of "I don't see anyone".

מה אתה רואה בפנה?
Mah ah-TAH *roh*-EH *bah-pee*-NAH?
What do you see in the corner?

איני רואה שם כלום.
Eh-NEE *roh*-EH shahm *k'loom*.
I do not see anything there.

את מי אתה שומע?
Ett mee ah-TAH shoh-MEH-ah?
Whom do you hear?

אני שומע אותך.
Ah-NEE shoh-MEH-ah oh-t'HAH.
I hear you.

אני דופק.
Ah-NEE doh-FEHK.
I knock.

השומע אתה מה אני עושה?
Hah-shoh-MEH-ah ah-TAH mah ah-NEE oh-SEH?
Do you hear what I am doing?

הרואה אתה מה אני עושה?
Hah-roh-EH ah-TAH mah ah-NEE oh-SEH?
Do you see what I am doing?

כן, אני רואה ושומע מה שאתה עושה.
Kehn, ah-NEE roh-EH v'shoh-MEH-ah mah sheh-ah-TAH oh-SEH.
Yes, I see and hear what you are doing.

אני מריח את השושנה.
Ah-NEE m'REE-akh ett hah-shoh-shah-NAH.
I smell the rose.

אנו מריחים באף.
AH-noo m'ree-HEEM bah-AFF.
We smell with the nose.

השושנה נותנת ריח טוב.
Hah-shoh-shah-NAH noh-TEH-net REH-akh tohv.
The rose smells good.

הרח את הגבינה.
Hah-RAKH ett hah-g'vee-NAH.
Smell the cheese.

היא מריחה רע.
Hee m'ree-HAH rah.
It smells bad.

במה אנו מריחים?
Bah-MEH AH-noo m'ree-HEEM?
With what do we smell?

איזה ריח נותנת הכלניה, רע או טוב?
EH-zeh REH-akh noh-TEH-net hah-kah-lah-nee-YAH, rah oh tohv?
How does the anemone (flower) smell, good or bad?

אנו אוכלים בפה.
AH-noo oh-h'LEEM bah-PEH.
We eat with the mouth.

אנו שותים בפה.
AH-noo shoh-TEEM bah-PEH.
We drink with the mouth.

NOTE: In Hebrew the word "with" can have two meanings: either an instrumental one, conveying the idea "by means of" in which case ב (bah) is used as a prefix to the noun, or a meaning simply indicative of joint presence ("together with") in which case we use עם (im).

Examples:

אני כותב ביד.

Ah-NEE *koh*-TEHV *bah*-YAHD.

I write with the hand.

אתה מדבר עם אדון ברליץ.

Ah-TAH *m'dah*-BEHR *im ah*-DOHN *Berlitz.*

You speak with Mr. Berlitz.

אנו אוכלים לחם, בשר, פירות, ירקות.

AH-*noo oh-h'*LEEM LEH-*hemm, bah*-SAHR, *peh*-ROHT, *y'rah*-KOHT.

We eat bread, meat, fruit, vegetables.

אנו שותים מים, קפה, תה ומשקאות אחרים.

AH-*noo shoh*-TEEM MAH-*yim, kah*-FEH, *tay, oo-mahsh-kah*-OHT

ah-heh-REEM.

We drink water, coffee, tea, and other beverages.

האוכל אתה לחם ?

Hah-oh-HEHL *ah*-TAH LEH-*hemm?*

Do you eat bread?

כן, אני אוכל לחם כל יום.

Kehn, ah-NEE *oh*-HEHL LEH-*hemm kohl yohm.*

Yes, I eat bread every day.

השותה אתה קפה ?	לא, אני שותה תה.
Hah-shoh-TEH *ah*-TAH *kah*-FEH?	*Lo, ah*-NEE *shoh*-TEH *tay.*
Do you drink coffee?	No, I drink tea.

השותה אתה תה עם חלב ?	לא, עם לימון.
Hah-shoh-TEH *ah*-TAH *tay im hah*-LAHV?	*Lo, im lee*-MOHN.
Do you drink tea with milk?	No, with lemon.

לכל מה שאנו אוכלים קוראים אוכל.

L'hohl mah sheh-AH-*noo oh-h'*LEEM *koh-reh*-EEM OH-*hell.*

What we eat is called food.

לכל מה שאנו שותים קוראים משקאות.

L'hohl mah sheh-AH-*noo shoh*-TEEM *koh-reh*-EEM *mahsh-kah*-OHT.

What we drink is called beverages.

אמר לי בבקשה מה אנו אוכלים?

Eh-MOHR *lee b'vah-kah*-SHAH *mah* AH-*noo oh-h'*LEEM?

Please tell me what we eat?

אמר לי שמות אחדים של משקאות.

Eh-MOHR *lee sheh*-MOHT *ah-hah*-DEEM *shell mahsh-kah*-OHT.

Tell me the names of some beverages.

ממה עושים יין ?   האם לימונדה משקה ?
Mee-MAH *oh*-SEEM YAH-*yin?*   *Hah*-IM *lee-moh*-NAH-*dah* mahsh-KEH?
What is wine made from?   Is lemonade a beverage?

יין עושים מענבים.
YAH-*yin oh*-SEEM *meh-ah-nah*-VEEM.
Wine is made from grapes.

ענבים	דובדבן	אגס	תפוח	פירות :
ah-nah-VEEM	*doov-d'*VAHN	*ah*-GAHS	tah-POO-*akh*	*Peh*-ROHT:
grapes	cherry	pear	apple	*Fruit:*

אפרסק	תפוח זהב
ah-fahr-SEHK	tah-POO-*akh zah*-HAHV
peach	orange

תות השדה	פטל	משמש
toot hah-sah-DEH	PEH-*tell*	*meesh*-MEHSH
strawberry	raspberry	apricot

ירקות :
Y'rah-KOHT:
Vegetables:

שעועית	גזר	תפוח אדמה
sheh-oo-EET	GEH-*zer*	tah-POO-*akh ah-dah*-MAH
beans	carrot	potato

פטריה	סלק	אפונה	כרוב
peet-ree-YAH	SEH-*lehk*	*ah-foo*-NAH	*kroov*
mushroom	beets	peas	cabbage

עגבניה	צנונית	חסה
ahg-vah-nee-YAH	*ts'noh*-NEET	HAH-*sah*
tomato	radish	lettuce

בשר-עגל	בשר-בקר	מיני בשר :
b'sahr EH-*gell*	*b'sahr* bah-KAHR	*mee*-NEH *bah*-SAHR:
veal	beef	*Meats:*

נקניק	קציצה	כבש	בשר צלוי
nahk-NEEK	*ktsee*-TSAH	KEH-*vess*	bah-SAHR *tsah*-LOOY
sausage	chopped meat	lamb	beef steak

תרנגול הודו	אוז	ברוז	בשר-עוף
*tahr-n'*GOHL HOH-*doo*	*ah*-VAHZ	*bah-rah*-VAHZ	*b'sahr-ohf*
turkey	goose	duck	chicken

THINKING IN HEBREW
(Answers on page 287)

1. ‏במה מריח המורה את הבצל?‏
*Bah-*MEH *m'*REE-*akh hah-moh-*REH *ett hah-bah-*TSAHL?

2. ‏היש לבצל ריח טוב?‏
*Hah-*YEHSH *lah-bah-*TSAHL REH-*akh tohv?*

3. ‏היש לשושנה ריח טוב?‏
*Hah-*YEHSH *lah-shoh-shah-*NAH REH-*akh tohv?*

4. ‏המריחה הגברת בילה שושנה או בצל?‏
*Hah-m'ree-*HAH *hah-*G'VEH-*ret* BEH-*leh shoh-shah-*NAH *oh bah-*TSAHL?

5. ‏הרואה אתה את הדברים שמאחוריך?‏
*Hah-roh-*EH *ah-*TAH *ett hah-d'vah-*REEM *sheh-meh-ah-hoh-*REH-*hah?*

6. ‏הרואים אנו את הדברים שלפנינו?‏
*Hah-roh-*EEM AH-*noo ett hah-d'vah-*REEM *sheh-l'fah-*NEH-*noo?*

7. ‏השומעים אנו מישהו דופק בדלת?‏
*Hah-shoh-meh-*EEM AH-*noo mee-sheh-*HOO *doh-*FEHK *bah-*DEH-*let?*

8.   ‏האוכלים אנו לחם?‏

*Hah-oh-h'*LEEM AH-*noo* LEH-*hemm?*

9.   ‏הרואים אנו את קלרק גיבל בקולנוע?‏

*Hah-roh-*EEM AH-*noo ett Clark Gable bah-kohl-*NOH-*ah?*

10.   ‏השמים אנו סוכר בקפה?‏

*Hah-sah-*MEEM AH-*noo soo-*KAHR *bah-kah-*FEH?

11.   ‏האוכלים אנשים רבים לחם לבן?‏

*Hah-oh-h'*LEEM *ah-nah-*SHEEM *rah-*BEEM LEH-*hemm lah-*VAHN?

22.   ‏השותים אמריקאים הרבה קוקה-קולה?‏

*Hah-shoh-*TEEM *ah-meh-ree-kah-*EEM *hahr-*BEH **Coca-Cola?**

13.   ‏השמים אנו חלב בתה?‏

*Hah-sah-*MEEM AH-*noo hah-*LAHV *bah-*TAY?

14.   ‏השמים אנו סוכר בבשר?‏

*Hah-sah-*MEEM AH-*noo soo-*KAHR *b'vah-*SAHR?

15.   ‏במה אנו חותכים בשר?‏

*Bah-*MEH AH-*noo hoh-t'*HEEM *bah-*SAHR?

16.   ‏האוכלים אנו אפונה בסכין?‏

*Hah-oh-h'*LEEM AH-*noo Ah-foo-*NAH *b'sah-*KEEN?

17.   ‏הכותבים אנו בעט או בעפרון?‏

*Hah-koh-t'*VEEM AH-*noo bah-*EHT *oh bah-ee-pah-*ROHN?

18.   ‏השותים אנו באף?‏

*Hah-shoh-*TEEM AH-*noo bah-*AFF?

19.   ‏במה אנו שותים?‏

*Bah-*MEH AH-*noo shoh-*TEEM?

בְּמָה אָנוּ אוֹכְלִים?

Bah-MEH AH-*noo oh-h'*LEEM?

With what do we eat?

צלחת	תחתית	קערה	ספין	מזלג	כף
*tsah-*LAH-*haht*	*takh-*TEET	*kah-ah-*RAH	*sah-*KEEN	*mahz-*LEHG	*kahf*
plate	saucer	dish or platter	knife	fork	spoon

מגש	מפה	בקבוק	מפית	ספל	כום
*mah-*GAHSH	*mah-*PAH	*bahk-*BOOK	*mah-*PEET	SEH-*fell*	*kohs*
tray	tablecloth	bottle	napkin	cup	glass

אנחנו אוכלים מרק בכף, ובשר במזלג.

*Ah-*NAKH-*noo oh-h'*LEEM *mah-*RAHK *bah-*KAHF, *oo-vah-*SAHR
*bah-mahz-*LEHG.

We eat soup with the spoon, and meat with the fork.

אנו שותים מים בכוס, וקפה בספפל.

AH-*noo* shoh-TEEM MAH-*yim* b'hohs, v'kah-FEH b'SEH-*fell*.

We drink water from a glass, and coffee from a cup.

במה אנו אוכלים מרק?	בכף.
Bah-MEH AH-*noo* oh-h'LEEM *mah*-RAHK?	Bah-KAHF.
With what do we eat soup?	With the spoon.

במה אנו שותים יין?	בכוס.
Bah-MEH AH-*noo* shoh-TEEM YAH-*yin*?	Bah-KOHS.
With what do we drink wine?	With the glass.

השותים אנו בירה מתוך הבקבוק?

Hah-shoh-TEEM AH-*noo* BEE-*rah* mee-TOKH hah-bahk-BOOK?

Do we drink beer from the bottle?

לא, אנו מוזגים את הבירה מן הבקבוק לתוך הכום.

Lo, AH-*noo* moh-z'GEEM ett hah-BEE-*rah* meen hah-bahk-BOOK
l'tokh hah-KOHS.

No, we pour the beer from the bottle into the glass.

במה שותים אנו קפה?	בספפל.
Bah-MEH shoh-TEEM AH-*noo* kah-FEH?	In the cup.
In what do we drink coffee?	Bah-SEH-*fell*.

NOTE TO STUDENT: The preposition בַ (bah) can

mean "with" and "in."

לסוכר טעם מתוק.	ללימון טעם חמוץ.
Lah-soo-KAHR TAH-*ahm* mah-TOHK.	L'lee-MOHN TAH-*ahm* hah-MOOTS.
Sugar has a sweet taste.	Lemon has a sour taste.

בלשון אנו טועמים אוכל ומשקה.

Bah-lah-SHOHN AH-*noo* toh-ah-MEEM OH-*hell* oo-mahsh-KEH.

With the tongue we taste food and drink.

לחם הוא אוכל, תה הוא משקה.

LEH-*hemm* hoo OH-*hell*, teh hoo mahsh-KEH.

Bread is food, tea is beverage.

אנו שמים סוכר לתוך קפה.

AH-*noo* sah-MEEM soo-KAHR l'tokh kah-FEH.

We put sugar into coffee.

לקפה עם סוכר טעם נעים.

L'kah-FEH im soo-KAHR TAH-ahm nah-EEM.
Coffee with sugar has a pleasant taste.

לקפה בלי סוכר טעם מר.

L'kah-FEH b'lee soo-KAHR TAH-ahm mahr.
Coffee without sugar has a bitter taste.

REMEMBER: עם (im) means "with" and בלי

(b'lee) means "without." The former must not be
confused with ב (bah) — "with," which really means
"by means of."

במה טועמים אנו את האוכל?

Bah-MEH toh-ah-MEEM AH-noo ett hah-OH-hell?
With what do we taste food?

בלשון.
Bah-lah-SHOHN.
With the tongue.

הטעים קפה בלי סוכר?

Hah-tah-EEM kah-FEH b'lee soo-KAHR?
Is coffee without sugar tasty?

לא, זה לא טעים.
Lo, zeh lo tah-EEM.
No, it is not tasty.

איזה טעם יש לסוכר?

EH-zeh TAH-ahm yehsh lah-soo-KAHR?
What taste has sugar?

מתוק.
Mah-TOHK.
Sweet.

איזה טעם יש ללימון?

EH-zeh TAH-ahm yehsh l'lee-MOHN?
What taste has lemon?

חמוץ.
Hah-MOOTs.
Sour.

השושנה מריחה יפה, יש לה ריח נעים.

Hah-shoh-shah-NAH m'ree-HAH yah-FEH, yehsh lah REH-akh nah-EEM.
The rose smells good; it has a pleasant smell.

גז מריח רע; ריחו בלתי נעים.

Gahz m'REE-akh rah; reh-HOH beel-TEE nah-EEM.
Gas smells bad; its odor is unpleasant.

הדובדבן טעים, יש לו טעם טוב.

Hah-DOOV-d'vahn tah-EEM, yehsh lo TAH-ahm tohv.
The cherry is tasty, it has a good taste.

הפרח מריח יפה.

Hah-PEH-rakh m'REE-akh yah-FEH.
The flower smells good.

טעם תות השדה נעים.

TAH-*ahm* toot *hah-sah*-DEH *nah*-EEM.

The taste of the strawberry is pleasant.

טעם הלימון לא נעים.

TAH-*ahm hah-lee*-MOHN lo *nah*-EEM.

The taste of lemon is unpleasant.

?היש לשושנה ריח נעים

Hah-YEHSH *lah-shoh-shah*-NAH REH-*akh nah*-EEM?

Has the rose a pleasant smell?

HOW TO EXPRESS ADMIRATION:

יפה (*yah*-FEH) and טוב (*tohv*) are practically syno-
nymous and mean "good" and|or "nice". מזל טוב
(*mah*-ZAHL *tohv*) — "good luck!"

?היש לגבינה ריח נעים

Hah-YEHSH *lah-g'vee*-NAH REH-*akh nah*-EEM?

Has cheese a pleasant smell?

שפת הים של תל-אביב יפה מאד.

S'*faht hah*-YAHM shell *Tel-Ah*-VEEV *yah*-FAH *meh*-OHD.

The beach of Tel-Aviv is very beautiful.

מה שנעים לנו לראות הוא יפה.

Mah sheh-nah-EEM LAH-*noo leer*-OHT hoo *yah*-FEH.

What we like to look at is beautiful.

הרי הגליל יפים מאד.

Hah-REH *hah-gah*-LEEL *yah*-FEEM *meh*-OHD.

The Galilee Mountains are very beautiful.

במוזיאון יש תמונות יפות.

Bah-moo-zeh-OHN yehsh *t'moo*-NOHT *yah*-FOHT.

In the museum there are beautiful pictures.

מה שאיננו מחבבים לראות הוא מכוער.

Mah sheh-eh-NEN-*noo m'hah-b'*VEEM *leer*-OHT hoo *m'hoh*-AHR.

What we don't like to look at is ugly.

העכביש מכוער.   הקוף מכוער.

Hah-ah-kah-VEESH *m'hoh*-AHR.   *Hah*-KOHF *m'hoh*-AHR.

The spider is ugly.   The monkey is ugly.

אנחנו אוהבים ריחות נעימים.
*Ah-*NAKH-*noo oh-hah-*VEEM *reh-*HOHT *neh-ee-*MEEM.
We like pleasant odors.

אנחנו אוהבים לאכל מאכלים החביבים עלינו.
*Ah-*NAKH-*noo oh-hah-*VEEM *leh-eh-*HOHL. *mah-ah-hah-*LEEM
*hah-hah-vee-*VEEM *ah-*LEH-*noo.
We like to eat dishes we are fond of.

TO LOVE OR TO LIKE:

אָהֹב   (*ah-*HOHV) means "to love" as well as "to
like." However, חַבֵּב (*hah-*BEHV) means simply "to
like," "to be fond of."

רינה אינה אוכלת בשר.   אני אוכל בשר.
REE-*nah eh-*NAH *oh-*HEH-*let bah-*SAHR.   *Ah-*NEE *oh-*HEHL bah-*SAHR.
Rina does not eat meat.   I eat meat.

היא אוכלת ירקות.
*Hee oh-*HEH-*let y'rah-*KOHT.
She eats vegetables.

אדון כרמי אינו אוכל ירקות.
*Ah-*DOHN KAHR-*mee eh-*NOH *oh-*HEHL y'rah-*KOHT.
Mr. Carmi doesn't eat vegetables.

אנו שמים מלח במרק.
AH-*noo sah-*MEEM MEH-*lakh bah-mah-*RAHK.
We put salt in the soup.

אין אנו שמים מלח בקפה.
*Ehn AH-*noo sah-*MEEM MEH-*lakh bah-kah-*FEH.
We do not put salt in coffee.

יוסף אינו אוכל פירות.   אתה אוכל פירות.
*Yoh-*SEHF eh-*NOH *oh-*HEHL peh-*ROHT.   *Ah-*TAH *oh-*HEHL peh-*ROHT.
Joseph does not eat fruit.   You eat fruit.

אנו הולכים למסעדה לאכל ארוחת צהרים.
*Ah-noo hoh-l'*HEEM l'mees-ah-*DAH leh-eh-*HOHL ah-roo-*HAHT
tsoh-hoh-*RAH-yim.
We go to a restaurant to eat lunch.

אנו יושבים אל השולחן.
AH-*noo yoh-sh'*VEEM ell hah-shool-*HAHN.
We seat ourselves at the table.

המלצר בא לקראתנו ומגיש לנו את התפריט.

*Hah-mell-*TSAHR *bah leek-rah-*TEH*-noo oo-mah-*GEESH LAH*-noo*
*ett hah-tahf-*REET.

The waiter comes to us and gives us the menu.

אנו מזמינים חמיצת סלק, קציצות בשר עם אפונה ותה.

AH*-noo mahz-mee-*NEEM *hah-mee-*TSAHT SEH*-lehk, k'tsee-*TSOHT
*bah-*SAHR *im ah-foo-*NAH, *v'tay.*

We order borsht, chopped beef with peas, and tea.

אחרי הארוחה מגיש לנו המלצר את החשבון.

Akh*-*RAY *hah-ah-roo-*HAH *mah-*GEESH LAH*-noo hah-mell-*TSAHR
*ett hah-hesh-*BOHN.

After lunch the waiter gives us the check.

אנו משלמים, נותנים דמי שתיה, ויוצאים.

AH*-noo m'shahl-*MEEM, *noh-t'*NEEM *d'meh shtee-*YAH, *v'yoh-tseh-*EEM.
We pay, give a tip, and leave.

AVOID CONFUSION:

מגיש (*mah-*GEESH) means "he brings" (or "serves") and

מגש (*mah-*GASH), "tray."

מגיש (*mah-*GEESH) also means "waiter". Therefore,

המגיש מגיש מגש (*hah-mah-*GEESH *mah-*GEESH *mah-*GASH) means "the
waiter brings a tray."

THINKING IN HEBREW
(Answers on page 288)

1. ‎בּמה אנו חותכים בּשׂר?
*Bah-*MEH AH*-noo hoh-t'*HEEM *bah-*SAHR?

2. ‎האוכלים אנו בּשׂר בּכּף?
*Hah-oh-h'*LEEM AH*-noo bah-*SAHR *bah-*KAHF?

3. ‎מה אנו אוכלים בּכּף?
Mah AH*-noo oh-h'*LEEM *bah-*KAHF?

4. ‎האוהב אתה את ריח השושׁנה?
*Hah-oh-*HEHV *ah-*TAH *ett* REH*-akh hah-shoh-shah-*NAH?

5. ‎האוהב אתה את ריח הגבינה?
*Hah-oh-*HEHV *ah-*TAH *ett* REH*-akh hah-g'vee-*NAH?

6. ‎המחבּב אתה קפה בּסוכּר?
*Hah-m'hah-*BEHV *ah-*TAH *kah-*FEH *b'soo-*KAHR?

7.   האוהב אתה מרק בלי מלח ?
Hah-oh-HEHV ah-TAH mah-RAHK b'lee MEH-lakh?

8.   האוהב אתה את ריח השום ?
Hah-oh-HEHV ah-TAH ett REH-akh hah-shoom?

9.   האוהב אתה את טעם תות השדה ?
Hah-oh-HEHV ah-TAH ett TAH-ahm toot hah-sah-DEH?

10. המחבב אתה גבינה ?
Hah-m'hah-BEHV ah-TAH g'vee-NAH?

11. האוהב אתה תה בלי סוכר ?
Hah-oh-HEHV ah-TAH tay b'lee soo-KAHR?

12. האוהב אתה בירה ?
Hah-oh-HEHV ah-TAH BEE-rah?

13. האוהבות נשים צעירות פרחים ?
Hah-oh-hah-VOHT nah-SHEEM tseh-ee-ROHT p'rah-HEEM?

14. האוהב אתה לדבר עברית ?
Hah-oh-HEHV ah-TAH l'dah-BEHR eev-REET?

15. היפה שפת הים של תל-אביב ?
Hah-yah-FAH s'faht hah-YAHM shell Tel-Ah-VEEV?

16. היפים הבגדים בחלונות הראוה של רחוב בן-יהודה ?
Hah-yah-FEEM hah-b'gah-DEEM bah-hah-loh-NOHT hah-rah-ah-VAH
shell r'hohv Behn-Yeh-hoo-DAH?

17. היפה הנשר או מכוער ?
Hah-yah-FEH hah-NEH-sherr oh m'hoh-AHR?

18. היפה השפה העברית ?
Hah-yah-FAH hah-sah-FAH hah-eev-REET?

19. האוהב אתה לשמע אותה?
Hah-oh-HEHV ah-TAH leesh-MOH-ah oh-TAH?

אֵינִי יָכוֹל לִרְאוֹת.

Eh-NEE *yah*-HOHL *leer*-OHT.

I cannot see.

אֲנִי סוֹגֵר אֶת הַדֶּלֶת.
Ah-NEE *soh*-GEHR *ett hah*-DEH-*let*.
I close the door.

הַדֶּלֶת סְגוּרָה.
Hah-DEH-*let s'goo*-RAH.
The door is closed.

אֵינִי יָכוֹל לָצֵאת.
Eh-NEE *yah*-HOHL *lah*-TSEHT.
I cannot go out.

אֲנִי פּוֹתֵחַ אֶת הַדֶּלֶת.
Ah-NEE *poh*-TAY-*akh ett hah*-DEH-*let*.
I open the door.

הַדֶּלֶת פְּתוּחָה.
Hah-DEH-*let p'too*-HAH.
The door is open.

אֲנִי יָכוֹל לָצֵאת.
Ah-NEE *yah*-HOHL *lah*-TSEHT.
I can go out.

יֵשׁ לִי עִפָּרוֹן.
Yehsh lee ee-pah-ROHN.
I have a pencil.

אֲנִי יָכוֹל לִכְתֹּב.
Ah-NEE *yah*-HOHL *leekh*-TOHV.
I can write.

לך אין עפרון.
*L'hah ehn ee-pah-*ROHN.
You haven't a pencil.

אינך יכול לכתב.
*Ehn-*HAH *yah-*HOHL *leekh-*TOHV.
You cannot write.

ליעקב סכין.
*L'Yah-ah-*KOHV *sah-*KEEN.
Jacob has a knife.

יכול הוא לחתך את הניר.
*Yah-*HOHL *hoo lakh-*TOKH *ett hah-n'*YAHR.
He can cut the paper.

אני נוגע בשולחן.
*Ah-*NEE *noh-*GEH-*ah bah-shool-*HAHN.
I touch the table.

אתה נוגע בכסא.
*Ah-*TAH *noh-*GEH-*ah bah-kis-*SEH.
You touch the chair.

GRAMMATICAL NOTE: יכל (*yah-*HOHL) means both "can" and "to be able." Of course, it varies for number and gender as does every other verb in Hebrew. The verb that immediately follows must be in the infinitive, preceded by a particle expressing purpose, which is לַ (*lah*), לִ (*lee*), or לְ (*leh*) according to the verb in question (which corresponds to the English "to"). Note the following examples of such infinitives of some of the verbs which you already know:

Stem		Infinitive
*lah-*KOH-*akh—*לקח	to take	*lah-*KAH-*haht—*לקחת
*seem—*שים	to put	*lah-*SEEM—*לשים
*hah-*LOKH—*הלך	to go	*lah-*LEH-*het—*ללכת
*boh—*בוא	to come	*lah-*VOH—*לבוא
*kah-*TOHV—*כתב	to write	*leekh-*TOHV—*לכתב
*kah-*ROH—*קרא	to read	*leek-*ROH—*לקרא
*dah-*BEHR—*דבר	to speak	*l'dah-*BEHR—*לדבר
*sah-*FOHR—*ספר	to count	*lees-*POHR—*לספר
*yah-*TSOH—*יצא	to go out	*lah-*TSEHT—*לצאת
*rah-*OH—*ראה	to see	*leer-*OHT—*לראות
*shah-*MOH-*ah—*שמע	to hear	*leesh-*MOH-*ah—*לשמע
*ah-*HOHL—*אכל	to eat	*leh-eh-*HOHL—*לאכל
*shah-*TOH—*שתה	to drink	*leesh-*TOHT—*לשתות
*nah-*TOHN—*נתן	to give	*lah-*TEHT—*לתת

גע בתקרה.
*Gah bah-teek-*RAH.
Touch the ceiling.

התקרה גבוהת.
*Hah-teek-*RAH *g'voh-*HAH.
The ceiling is high.

אינך יכל לנגוע בּתקרה.

Ehn-HAH *yah*-HOHL *leen*-GOH-*ah bah-teek-*RAH.

You cannot touch the ceiling.

המנורה נמוכה.	יכול אני לנגע בּה.
*Hah-m'noh-*RAH *n'moo-*HAH.	*Yah-*HOHL *ah-*NEE *leen-*GOH-*ah bah.*
The lamp is low.	I can touch it.
אני נוגע בּה.	אני עוצם את עיני.
*Ah-*NEE *noh-*GEH-*ah bah.*	*Ah-*NEE *oh-*TSEHM *ett eh-*NIGH.
I touch it.	I close my eyes.
איני רואה אותך.	איני יכול לראות.
*Eh-*NEE *roh-*EH *oh-t'*HAH.	*Eh-*NEE *yah-*HOHL *leer-*OHT.
I do not see you.	I cannot see.
אני פוקח את עיני.	אני יכול לראות.
*Ah-*NEE *poh-*KAY-*akh ett eh-*NIGH.	*Ah-*NEE *yah-*HOHL *leer-*OHT.
I open my eyes.	I can see.

אני רואה אותך.

*Ah-*NEE *roh-*EH *oh-t'*HAH.

I see you.

היכולים אנו לאכל מרק בּמזלג ?

*Hah-y'yoh-*LEEM AH-*noo leh-eh-*HOHL *mah-*RAHK *bah-mahz-*LEHG?

Can we eat soup with the fork?

אנו הולכים בּרגלים.	לא, איננו יכולים.
AH-*noo hoh-l'*HEEM *bah-rahg-*LAH-*yim.*	*Lo, eh-*NEN-*noo y'hoh-*LEEM.
We walk with the legs.	No, we cannot.

אנו רואים בּעינינו.

AH-*noo roh-*EEM *beh-eh-*NEH-*noo.*

We see with our eyes.

היכולים אנו לראות בּחושך ?

*Hah-y'yoh-*LEEM AH-*noo leer-*OHT *bah-*HOH-*shekh?*

Can we see in the dark?

לא, אין אנו יכולים, אבל החתול יכול.

Lo, ehn AH-*noo y'hoh-*LEEM, *ah-*VAHL *heh-hah-*TOOL *yah-*HOHL.

No, we cannot, but the cat can.

ATTENTION:

In the case of the cat חָתוּל (*hah-*TOOL) the article

becomes הֶ (*heh*) instead of הַ (*hah*) because the

חָ (*hah*) is written with a ָ (*kah-*MAHTS).

There are several other words in this category which you will encounter later.

אין לי סכין.

*Ehn lee sah-*KEEN.
I have no knife.

איני יכול לחתך את הלחם.

*Eh-*NEE *yah-*HOHL *lakh-*TOKH *ett hah-*LEH-*hemm.
I cannot cut the bread.

מדוע אינך יכול?

*Mah-*DOO-*ah ehn-*HAH *yah-*HOHL?
Why can't you?

משום שאין לי סכין.

*Mee-*SHOOM *sheh-*EHN *lee sah-*KEEN.
Because I have no knife.

הדלת סגורה.

*Hah-*DEH-*let s'goo-*RAH.
The door is closed.

דינה אינה יכולה לצאת.

*Dee-*NAH *eh-*NAH *y'hoh-*LAH *lah-*TSEHT.
Dina cannot go out.

מדוע אינה יכולה לצאת?

*Mah-*DOO-*ah *eh-*NAH *y'hoh-*LAH *lah-*TSEHT?
Why can't she go out?

משום שהדלת סגורה.

*Mee-*SHOOM *sheh-hah-*DEH-*let s'goo-*RAH.
Because the door is closed.

REMEMBER THE FEMININE: As "closed" is an adjective, it must vary for gender and number as do
other adjectives. סגורה (s'goo-RAH) is the feminine
form and סגור (sah-GOOR), the masculine.
Note as well that the feminine form of the verb "to
be able" is יכולה (y'hoh-LAH). It does not end in ת (ett)
as we can usually expect with the majority of Hebrew verbs.

התיק קטן והספר גדול.

*Hah-*TEEK *kah-*TAHN *veh-hah-*SEH-*fer gah-*DOHL.
The briefcase is small, and the book is large.

מדוע אין אנו יכולים לשים את הספר בתיק?

*Mah-*DOO-*ah ehn* AH-*noo yeh-hohl-*EEM *lah-*SEEM *ett hah-*
SEH-*fer bah-*TEEK?
Why can we not put the book into the briefcase?

משום שהתיק קטן והספר גדול.

*Mee-*SHOOM *sheh-hah-*TEEK *kah-*TAHN *veh-hah-*SEH-*fer gah-*DOHL.
Because the briefcase is small and the book is large.

האדון ברליץ מרכיב משקפים.

*Hah-ah-*DOHN *Berlitz mahr-*KEEV *meesh-kah-*FAH-*yim.
Mr. Berlitz has eye-glasses.

היכול אתה לקרא בלי משקפים?
*Hah-yah-*HOHL *ah-*TAH *leek-*ROH *b'lee meesh-kah-*FAH*-yim?*
Can you read without eye-glasses?

אני יכול.   איני יכול.   אני סופר את הספרים.
*Ah-*NEE *yah-*HOHL. *Eh-*NEE *yah-*HOHL. *Ah-*NEE *soh-*FEHR *ett hah-s'fah-*REEM.
I can.   I cannot.   I count the books.

כמובן, אני יכול.   היכול אתה לספר אותם?
*Hah-yah-*HOHL *ah-*TAH *lees-*POHR *oh-*TAHM? *K'moo-*VAHN, *ah-*NEE *yah-*HOHL.
Can you count them?   Certainly I can.

היכול אתה לספר את הכוכבים בשמים?
*Hah-yah-*HOHL *ah-*TAH *lees-*POHR *ett hah-koh-hah-*VEEM
*bah-shah-*MAH*-yim?*
Can you count the stars in the sky?

איני יכול.   אתה שובר גפרור.
*Eh-*NEE *yah-*HOHL.   *Ah-*TAH *shoh-*VEHR *gahf-*ROOR.
I cannot.   You break a match.

אבל אינך יכול לשבר מפתח.
*Ah-*VAHL *ehn-*HAH *yah-*HOHL *leesh-*BOHR *mahf-*TEH-akh.*
But you cannot break a key.

עצם עיניך.   אינך יכול לראות.
*Ah-*TSOHM *eh-*NEH*-hah.*   *Ehn-*HAH *yah-*HOHL *leer-*OHT.
Close your eyes.   You cannot see.

מדוע אינך יכול?   משום שעיני עצומות.
*Mah-*DOO*-ah ehn-*HAH *yah-*HOHL? *Mee-*SHOOM *sheh-eh-*NIGH *ah-tsoo-*MOHT.
Why can't you?   Because my eyes are closed.

איפה אדון ברליץ?   הוא איננו פה.
*Eh-*FOH *ah-*DOHN *Berlitz?*   *Hoo eh-*NEN*-noo poh.*
Where is Mr. Berlitz?   He is not here.

היכולים התלמידים לראותו?
*Hah-y'hoh-*LEEM *hah-tahl-mee-*DEEM *leer-oh-*TOH?
Can the students see him?

לא, אינם יכולים.   מדוע אינם יכולים לראותו?
*Lo, eh-*NAHM *y'hoh-*LEEM. *Mah-*DOO*-ah eh-*NAHM *y'hoh-*LEEM *leer-oh-*TOH?
No, they cannot.   Why can they not see him?

משום שאיננו פה.
*Mee-*SHOOM *sheh-eh-*NEN*-noo poh.*
Because he is not here.

THINKING IN HEBREW
(Answer on page 288)

1. הנוגעת רותי באפיר ?
    Hah-noh-GAH-aht ROO-*tee beh-Ah-*BEER?

2. היכולה היא לנגע בידו הימנית של המורה ?
    *Hah-y'hoh-*LAH *hee leen-*GOH-*ah b'yah-*DOH *hah-y'mah-*NEET
    *shell hah-moh-*REH?

3. היכול המורה לנגע בכובעה של רותי ?
    *Hah-yah-*HOHL *hah-moh-*REH *leen-*GOH-*ah b'hoh-vah-*AH *shell* ROO-*tee?*

4. הנוגע הוא בה ?
    *Hah-noh-*GEH-*ah hoo bah?*

5. הנמוכה המנורה ?
    *Hah-n'moo-*HAH *hah-m'noh-*RAH?

6. היכול המורה לנגע בה ?
    *Hah-yah-*HOHL *hah-moh-*REH *leen-*GOH-*ah bah?*

7. במה נוגע המורה ?
    *Bah-*MEH *noh-*GEH-*ah hah-moh-*REH?

8.   ? המרפיב המורה משקפים

*Hah-mahr-*KEEV *hah-moh-*REH *meesh-kah-*FAH-*yim?*

9.   ? היכול הוא לראות בלי משקפים

*Hah-yah-*HOHL *hoo leer-*OHT *b'lee meesh-kah-*FAH-*yim?*

10.   ? הדלת פתוחה; היכול הוא לצאת מהחדר

*Hah-*DEH-*let p'too-*HAH; *hah-yah-*HOHL *hoo lah-*TSEHT *meh-hah-*HEH-*der?*

11.   ? אין לי לא עפרון אף לא עט; היכול אני לכתב

*Ehn lee lo ee-pah-*ROHN *aff lo eht; hah-yah-*HOHL *ah-*NEE *leekh-*TOHV?

12.   ? היכולים אנו לראות מה מאחורינו

*Hah-y'hoh-*LEEM AH-*noo leer-*OHT *mah meh-ah-hoh-reh-*NOO?

13.   ? היכולים התלמידים לנגע בתקרה

*Hah-y'hoh-*LEEM *hah-tahl-mee-*DEEM *leen-*GOH-*ah bah-teek-*RAH?

14.   ? היכול אתה לשבר גפרור

*Hah-yah-*HOHL *ah-*TAH *leesh-*BOHR *gahf-*ROOR?

15.   ? היכול אתה לשבר מפתח של הדלת

*Hah-yah-*HOHL *ah-*TAH *leesh-*BOHR *mahf-*TEH-*akh shell hah-*DEH-*let?*

16.   ? היכול אתה לנגע בספרך

*Hah-yah-*HOHL *ah-*TAH *leen-*GOH-*ah b'seef-r'*HAH?

מה מוכרח אני לעשות כדי לצאת?

*Mah mookh-*RAKH *ah-*NEE *lah-ah-*SOHT *k'day
lah-*TSEHT?

What must I do to go out?

הדלת פתוחה

*Hah-*DEH-*let p'too-*HAH.

The door is open.

היכול אתה לצאת מן החדר?

*Hah-yah-*HOHL *ah-*TAH *lah-*TSEHT *meen hah-*HEH-*der?*

Can you go out of the room?

כן, אני יכול.

*Kehn, ah-*NEE *yah-*HOHL.

Yes, I can.

מדוע אינך יוצא?

*Mah-*DOO-*ah ehn-*HAH *yoh-*TSEH?

Why don't you go out?

משום שאינני רוצה.

*Mee-*SHOOM *sheh-eh-*NEN-*nee roh-*TSEH.

Because I do not want to.

124

REMEMBER THIS WORD:

כְּדֵי (*k'day*) — "in order to" or "to" expressing purpose, is also followed by the infinitive of the verb as was "to be able" which you noticed in the preceding lesson.

היכול אתה לקרע את ספרך ?
Hah-yah-HOHL ah-TAH leek-ROH-ah ett seef-r'HAH?
Can you tear your book?

כן, אני יכול.   מדוע אינך קורע את ספרך ?
Kehn, ah-NEE yah-HOHL.   Mah-DOO-ah ehn-HAH koh-REH-ah ett seef-r'HAH?
Yes, I can.   Why don't you tear your book?

משום שאינני רוצה.
Mee-SHOOM sheh-eh-NEN-nee roh-TSEH.
Because I do not want to.

אם אתה רוצה לצאת, אתה מוכרח לפתח את הדלת.
Im ah-TAH roh-TSEH lah-TSEHT, ah-TAH mookh-RAKH leef-TOH-akh ett hah-DEH-let.
If you want to go out, you must open the door.

USE OF INFINITIVE:

"To want to" or "to wish" and "must" also cause the verb immediately following to fall into the infinitive. Examples:

אני מוכרח ללכת לבית-הספר   (*Ah-NEE mokh-RAKH lah-LEH-het l'veht-hah-SEH-fer.*)   "I must go to school."

הוא רוצה לדבר עם אדון ברליץ.   (*Hoo roh-TSEH l'dah-BEHR im ah-DOHN Berlitz.*)   "He wishes to speak with Mr. Berlitz."

אני מוכרח לפקח את עיני, אם אני רוצה לראות.
Ah-NEE mookh-RAKH leef-KOH-akh ett eh-NIGH, im ah-NEE roh-TSEH leer-OHT.
I must open my eyes, if I want to see.

אם אנחנו רוצים לאכל מרק, אנו מוכרחים להשתמש בכף.

Im ah-NAKH-noo roh-TSEEM leh-eh-HOHL mah-RAHK, AH-noo
mookh-rah-HEEM leh-heesh-tah-MESH bah-KAHF.

If we wish to eat soup, we must use the spoon.

אם אתה רוצה לחתך בשר, אתה מוכרח להשתמש בסכין.

Im ah-TAH roh-TSEH lakh-TOKH bah-SAHR, ah-TAH mookh-RAKH
leh-heesh-tah-MESH bah-sah-KEEN.

If you wish to cut meat, you must use the knife.

יכול אני לשבר את שעוני, אבל איני רוצה בזאת.

Yah-HOHL ah-NEE leesh-BOHR ett sheh-oh-NEE,
ah-VAHL eh-NEE roh-TSEH bah-ZOHT.

I can break my watch, but I do not want to.

THE FOURTH GROUP OF VERBS:

You will be able to recognize this group by the prefix
הִתְ (*heet*), הִשְׁ (*heesh*),   הִסְ (*hees*) or הִצְ (*heets*),
in the infinitive. This verb group can best be compared
in meaning and construction to reflexive verbs such as "to dress oneself," "to wash oneself," etc. The verb we have just encountered
הִשְׁתַּמֵּשׁ (*heesh-tah-MESH*), has been translated as "to use", as it
literally means "to serve oneself with".

יכול אני לקרע את מטפחתי, אבל איני רוצה בזאת.

Yah-HOHL ah-NEE lek-ROH-ah ett meet-PAKH-tee, ah-VAHL eh-NEE
roh-TSEH bah-ZOHT.

I can tear my handkerchief, but I do not want to.

היכול אתה לדבר עברית?	כן, אני יכול.
Hah-yah-HOHL ah-TAH l'dah-BEHR eev-REET?	*Kehn, ah-NEE yah-HOHL.*
Can you speak Hebrew?	Yes, I can.
הרוצה אתה לדבר עברית?	כן, אני רוצה.
Hah-roh-TSEH ah-TAH l'dah-BEHR eev-REET?	*Kehn, ah-NEE roh-TSEH.*
Do you want to speak Hebrew?	Yes, I want to.

מה אתה רוצה לקרא, עתון או ספר?

Mah ah-TAH roh-TSEH leek-ROH, ee-TOHN oh SEH-fer?

What do you want to read, a newspaper or a book?

אני רוצה לקרא ספר עברי.

Ah-NEE roh-TSEH leek-roh SEH-fer eev-REE.

I want to read a Hebrew book.

מה אתה רוצה לשתות, תה או קפה ?

Mah ah-TAH roh-TSEH leesh-TOHT, tay oh kah-FEH?

What do you want to drink, tea or coffee?

קפה, בבקשה עם סוכר.

Kah-FEH, b'vah-kah-SHAH, im soo-KAHR.

Coffee, please, with sugar.

היכולים התלמידים לכתב עברית ?

Hah-y'hoh-LEEM hah-tahl-mee-DEEM leekh-TOHV eev-REET?

Can the pupils write Hebrew?

כן, הם יכולים, קצת.

Kehn, hehm y'hoh-LEEM, k'tsaht.

Yes, they can, a little.

הרוצים הם לקרא עברית היטב ?   כמובן!

Hah-roh-TSEEM hehm leek-ROH eev-REET heh-TEHV?   *K'moo-VAHN!*

Do they want to read Hebrew well?   Certainly!

אם הדלת סגורה, אין אנו יכולים לצאת.

Im hah-DEH-let s'goo-RAH, ehn AH-noo y'hoh-LEEM lah-TSEHT.

If the door is closed, we cannot go out.

אם אנו עוצמים את עינינו, אין אנו יכולים לראות.

Im AH-noo oh-ts'MEEM ett eh-NEH-noo, ehn AH-noo y'hoh-LEEM leer-OHT.

If we close our eyes, we cannot see.

אם אין לי לא עפרון אף לא עט, איני יכול לכתב על הניר.

Im ehn lee lo ee-pah-ROHN aff lo eht, eh-NEE yah-HOHL leekh-TOHV ahl hah-n'YAHR.

If I have neither pencil nor pen, I cannot write on the paper.

היכולים אנו לצאת אם הדלת סגורה ?

Hah-y'hoh-LEEM AH-noo lah-TSEHT im hah-DEH-let s'goo-RAH?

Can we go out if the door is closed?

לא, איננו יכולים.

Lo, eh-NEN-noo y'hoh-LEEM.

No, we cannot.

היכול אתה לחתּך לחם בלי סכּין ?
*Hah-yah-*HOHL *ah-*TAH *lakh-*TOKH LEH-*hemm b'lee sah-*KEEN?
Can you cut bread without a knife?

לא, איננו יכולים.
*Lo, eh-*NEN-*noo y'hoh-*LEEM.
No, we cannot.

מה צריכה בּילה לעשׂות אם היא רוצה ללכת לקולנוע ?
*Mah ts'ree-*HAH BEH-*leh lah-ah-*SOHT *im hee roh-*TSAH
*lah-*LEH-*het l'kohl-*NOH-*ah?*
What must Behle do if she wants to go to the cinema?

היא צריכה לקנות כּרטיס.
*Hee ts'ree-*HAH *leek-*NOHT *kahr-*TISS.
She must buy a ticket.

בּמה אתה משתּמש כּדי לאכול מרק ?
*Bah-*MEH *ah-*TAH *meesh-tah-*MEHSH *k'deh leh-eh-*HOHL *mah-*RAHK?
What do you use in order to eat soup?

בּמה אתה משתּמש כּדי לחתּך בּשׂר ?
*Bah-*MEH *ah-*TAH *meesh-tah-*MEHSH *k'deh lakh-*TOKH *bah-*SAHR?
What do you use to cut meat?

היכול אדון כּספּי לנסע לישׂראל בּלי דרכּון ?
*Hah-yah-*HOHL, *ah-*DOHN KAHS-*pee leen-*SOH-*ah l'Yis-rah-*EHL
*b'lee dahr-*KOHN?
Can Mr. Kaspi travel to Israel without a passport?

NOTE TO STUDENT:

דרכּון (*dar-*KOHN) is a classical example of the creation of a new word to meet modern requirements. This word is derived from   דרך (DEH-*rekh*) which means "road."

מה הוא מוכרח לעשׂות כּדי לנסע לישׂראל ?
*Mah hoo mookh-*RAHKH *lah-ah-*SOHT *k'deh leen-*SOH-*ah l'Yis-rah-*EHL?
What must he do in order to go to Israel?

הוא מוכרח לקבּל דרכּון ואשרה.
*Hoo mookh-rakh leh-kah-*BEHL *dahr-*KOHN *veh-ahsh-*RAH.
He must get a passport and a visa.

הוא זקוק גּם לכסף.
*Hoo zah-*KOOK *gahm l'*HEH-*seff*.
He needs money, too.

THINKING IN HEBREW
(Answers on page 288)

1. ‏הרוצה רותי לאכל את התפוח?‏
*Hah-roh-*TSAH *ROO-tee leh-eh-*HOHL *ett hah-tah-*POO-*akh?*

2. ‏היכולה היא לנגע בו?‏
*Hah-y'hoh-*LAH *hee leen-*GOH-*ah boh?*

3. ‏הנותן המורה את התפוח לרותי?‏
*Hah-noh-*TEHN *hah-moh-*REH *ett hah-tah-*POO-*akh l'*ROO-*tee?*

4. ‏מדוע הוא אינו נותן אותו לרותי?‏
*Mah-*DOO-*ah hoo eh-*NOH *noh-*TEHN *oh-*TOH *l'*ROO-*tee?*

5. ‏הרוצה הוא לתת אותו לרותי?‏
*Hah-roh-*TSEH *hoo lah-*TEHT *oh-*TOH *l'*ROO-*tee?*

6. ‏המוכרח אתה לפתח את הדלת כדי לצאת?‏
*Hah-mookh-*RAKH *ah-*TAH *leef-*TOH-*akh ett hah-*DEH-*let k'deh lah-*TSEHT?*

7. ‏אם אנו רוצים לראות, המוכרחים אנו לפקח את עינינו ؟
Im AH-noo *roh*-TSEEM *leer*-OHT, *hah-mookh-rah*-HEEM AH-noo
leef-KOH-akh *ett eh*-NEH-noo?

8. ‏הזקוק אתה לכסף כדי לנסע ؟
Hah-zah-KOOK *ah*-TAH *l'*HEH-*seff k'deh leen*-SOH-*ah?*

9. ‏במה יש לנו צורך כדי לכתב ؟
Bah-MEH *yehsh* LAH-noo TSOH-*rekh k'deh leekh*-TOHV?

10. ‏מה אתה מוכרח לעשות אם הדלת סגורה, ואתה רוצה לצאת ؟
Mah ah-TAH *mookh*-RAKH *lah-ah*-SOHT *im hah*-DEH-*let s'goo*-RAH,
veh-ah-TAH *roh*-TSEH *lah*-TSEHT?

11. ‏היכול אדון ברליץ לראות בלי משקפים ؟
Hah yah-HOHL *ah*-DOHN *Berlitz leer*-OHT *b'lee meesh-kah*-FAH-*yim?*

12. ‏למה אתה זקוק כדי לקרא ؟
L'mah ah-TAH *zah*-KOOK *k'deh leek*-ROH?

13. ‏מה אנו מוכרחים לעשות כדי ללכת לאופרה ؟
Mah AH-noo *mookh-rah*-HEEM *lah-ah*-SOHT *k'deh lah*-LEH-*het*
leh-OH-*peh-rah?*

14. ‏היכול אתה לאכל מרק בספין ؟
Hah-yah-HOHL *ah*-TAH *leh-eh*-HOHL *mah*-RAHK *bah-sah*-KEEN?

15. ‏במה אנו משתמשים כדי לאכל מרק ؟
Bah-MEH AH-noo *mee-sh'tahm*-SHEEM *k'deh leh-eh*-HOHL *mah*-RAK?

16. ‏האם זקוק אני לכסף כדי ללכת לקולנוע ؟
Hah-IM *zah*-KOOK *ah*-NEE *l'*HEH-*seff k'deh lah*-LEH-*het l'kohl*-NOH-*ah?*

17. ‏המגיש המלצר את האוכל לשולחן במסעדה ؟
Hah-mah-GEESH *hah-mell*-TSAHR *ett hah*-OH-*hell lah-shool*-HAHN
bah-mis-ah-DAH?

18. ‏איפה אני משאיר דמי שתיה למלצר ؟
Eh-FOH *ah*-NEE *mahsh*-EER *d'meh shtee*-YAH *lah-mell*-TSAHR?

19. ‏המוכרח אני לשלם בעד האוכל ؟
Hah-mookh-RAKH *ah*-NEE *l'shah*-LEHM *beh*-AHD *hah*-OH-*hell!*

מה השעה ?

Mah hah-shah-AH?

What time is it?

פה שעון-כים.
Poh sheh-OHN-kiss.
Here is a pocket watch.

שם, על הקיר, שעון-קיר.
Shahm, ahl hah-KEER, sheh-OHN-keer.
There, on the wall, is a wall clock.

אנו נושאים את שעון-הכים בכים,
AH-*noo noh-seh-***EEM** *ett sheh-***OHN-***hah-***KISS** *bah-***KISS***,*
We carry the pocket watch in the pocket,

ושעון-הקיר תלוי על הקיר.
oo-sheh--OHN-hah-KEER tah-LOOY ahl hah-KEER.
and the wall clock hangs on the wall.

שעון-כים עשוי מזהב, כסף, ניקל או מפלדה.
Sheh-OHN-kiss ah-SOOY mee-zah-HAHV, KEH-seff, NEE-kel oh mee-p'lah-DAH.
A pocket watch is made of gold, silver, nickel or steel.

131

למורה שעון-זהב, לתלמיד שעון-כסף.

*Lah-moh-*REH *sheh-*OHN-*zah-*HAHV, *lah-tahl-*MEED *sheh-*OHN-*keh-*seff.

The teacher has a gold watch, the pupil a silver one.

NOTE ON ADJECTIVES: To form adjectives denoting materials, you can use the noun itself, placing it after the thing described. "A gold watch" שעון–זהב (*sheh-*OHN-*zah-*HAHV).

Adjectives can also be formed from nouns by the addition of the suffix י (*ee*) to the noun in question and by changing the vowel in the first syllable of the noun. Examples: טבע (TEH-*vah*) "nature", טבעי (*teev-*EE) "natural"; יום (*yohm*) "day", יומי (*yoh-*MEE) "daily", (masc.), יומית (*yoh-*MEET) (fem.).

בשעון שנים או שלושה מחוגים.

*Bah-shah-*OHN *sh'*NAH-*yim oh sh'loh-*SHAH *m'hoh-*GEEM.

On the watch there are two or three hands (arrows).

המחוג הגדול מראה את הדקות.

*Hah-mah-*HOHG *hah-gah-*DOHL *mahr-*EH *ett hah-dah-*KOHT.

The big hand shows the minutes.

המחוג הקטן מראה את השעות, והשלישי את השניות.

*Hah-mah-*HOHG *hah-kah-*TAHN *mahr-*EH *ett hah-shah-*OHT, *veh-hah-sh'lee-*SHEE *ett hah-sh'nee-*YOHT.

The small hand shows the hours, and the third one the seconds.

מה השעה ?

*Mah hah-shah-*AH?

What time is it?

השעה שלוש.	השעה שתים.	השעה אחת.
*Hah-shah-*AH *shah-*LOHSH.	*Hah-shah-*AH *sh'*TAH-*yim.*	*Hah-shah-*AH *ah-*HAHT.
Three o'clock.	Two o'clock.	It is one o'clock.

A NOTE ON TIME: Since the word for "hour" שָׁעָה (*shah-*AH) is feminine, all numbers expressing time, such as "one o'clock," "two o'clock, etc.", must also be feminine.

השעה שתים-עשרה ורבע.	אחת וחצי.
*Hah-shah-*AH *sh'tehm-ess-*REH *vah-*REH-*vah.*	*Ah-*HAHT *vah-*HEH-*tsee.*
It is a quarter past twelve.	Half past one.

רבע לשלוש.

REH-*vah* l'*shah*-LOHSH.

A quarter to three.

עשר (דקות) אחרי שלוש.

Eh-*ser* (dah-KOHT) akh-RAY shah-LOHSH.

(It is): ten (minutes) past three.

עשרים וחמש (דקות) אחרי שבע.

Ess-REEM veh-hah-MEHSH (dah-KOHT) akh-RAY SHEH-vah.

Twenty-five (minutes) past seven.

(השעה): עשרים וחמש לתשע.

(*Hah*-shah-AH): ess-REEM veh-hah-MEHSH l'TEH-shah.

(It is): twenty-five to nine.

עשר פחות שבע.

EH-ser pah-HOHT SHEH-vah.

Seven to ten.

מתי יוצאת הרכבת ?

Mah-TIGH yoh-TSEHT hah-rah-KEH-vet?

What time does the train leave?

הרכבת יוצאת בשתים וחצי, ומגעת בשלוש ועשר.

Hah-rah-KEH-vet yoh-TSEHT beesh-TAH-yim vah-HEH-tsee,
oo-mah-GAH-aht b'shah-LOHSH vah-EH-ser.

The train leaves at 2:30, and arrives at 3:10.

בצהרים.

Bah-tsoh-hoh-RAH-yim.

At noon.

בשתים-עשרה בצהרים.

Beesh-TEHM-ess-REH bah-tsoh-hoh-RAH-yim.

At twelve o'clock noon.

בחצות.

Bah-hah-TSOHT.

At midnight.

(השעה) אחת אחרי חצות.

(*Hah*-shah-AH) ah-HAHT akh-RAY hah-TSOHT.

(It is) 1:00 a.m.

אחת אחרי הצהרים.

Ah-HAHT akh-RAY hah-tsoh-hoh-RAH-yim.

One p.m.

שתים לפנות בוקר.

Sh'TAH-yim leef-NOHT BOH-ker.

Two a.m.

שתים אחרי הצהרים.

Sh'TAH-yim akh-RAY hah-tsoh-hoh-RAH-yim.

Two p.m.

בשש בבוקר   בארבע לפנות בוקר.

B'shehsh bah-BOH-ker.   Beh-ahr-BAH leef-NOHT BOH-ker.

At six o'clock in the morning.   At four o'clock in the morning.

בחמש לפנות ערב.

Beh-hah-MEHSH leef-NOHT EH-rehv.

At five o'clock in the evening.

TIME APPROACHES: The word לפנות (leef-NOHT) means literally "at the approach of." It is commonly used to express morning or evening hours, as in "five o'clock at the approach of morning," or "six o'clock at the approach of evening." Poetic, isn't it?

מה השעה עכשיו?   השעה אחת בדיוק.

Mah hah-shah-AH akh-SHAHV?   Hah-shah-AH ah-HAHT b'dee-YOOK.

What time is it now?   It is exactly one o'clock.

השעה כבר אחרי שתים.

Hah-shah-AH k'vahr akh-RAY sh'TAH-yim.

It is already past two.

בשעה ששים דקות.

Bah-shah-AH shee-SHEEM dah-KOHT.

In the hour there are sixty minutes.

ששים דקות הן שעה.

Shee-SHEEM dah-KOHT hehn shah-AH.

Sixty minutes make one hour.

אתה בא לשעור בשעה שתים, ועוזב בשעה חמש.

Ah-TAH bah lah-shee-OOR b'shah-AH sh'TAH-yim,

veh-oh-ZEHV b'shah-AH hah-MEHSH.

You come to the lesson at two o'clock, and you leave at five o'clock.

כמה שעות אתה לומד?

KAH-mah shah-OHT ah-TAH loh-MEHD?

How many hours do you study?

אני לומד שלוש שעות.

Ah-NEE loh-MEHD shah-LOHSH shah-OHT.

I study three hours.

באיזו שעה אתה בא הנה?
Beh-EH-zoh shah-ah ah-TAH bah HEH-nah?
At what time do you come here?

באיזו שעה אתה עוזב?
Beh-EH-zoh shah-AH ah-TAH oh-ZEHV?
At what time do you leave?

באיזו שעה אתם אוכלים ארוחת-צהרים?
Beh-EH-zoh shah-AH ah-TEMM oh-h'LEEM ah-roo-HAHT-tsoh-hoh-RAH-yim?
At what time do you have lunch?

אנו אוכלים ארוחת צהרים בשעה אחת.
AH-noo oh-h'LEEM ah-roo-HAHT tsoh-hoh-RAH-yim b'shah-AH ah-HAHT.
We eat lunch at one o'clock.

באיזו שעה אתם אוכלים ארוחת ערב?
Beh-EH-zoh shah-AH ah-TEMM oh-h'LEEM ah-roo-HAHT EH-rev?
At what time do you eat supper?

אנו אוכלים ארוחת ערב בשעה שבע.
AH-noo oh-kh'LEEM ah-roo-HAHT EH-rev b'shah-AH SHEH-vah.
We eat supper at seven o'clock.

NOTE ON MEALS:

In Hebrew there are no special names for the different meals as in English. Instead, the words "morning" בוקר (BOH-*ker*), "noon" צהרים (*tsoh-hoh-RAH-yim*) or "evening" ערב (EH-*rev*) are simply added to the word ארוחה (*ah-roo-HAH*) which means "meal," and we obtain the three composite words ארוחת בוקר (*ah-roo-HAHT BOH-ker*), ארוחת צהרים (*ah-roo-HAHT tsoh-hoh-RAH-yim*) and ארוחת ערב (*ah-roo-HAHT EH-rev*) which mean, respectively, breakfast, lunch and supper.

בחדר השנה יש לי שעון מעורר שאינו הולך.
Bah-h'DAHR hah-sheh-NAH yehsh lee shah-OHN meh-oh-REHR sheh-eh-NOH hoh-LEHKH.
I have an alarm clock in my bedroom which doesn't run.

מוכרחים לכונן אותן.   השעון עומד.
Mookh-rah-HEEM l'hoh-NEHN oh-TOH.   *Hah-shah-OHN oh-MEHD.*
One must wind it.   The watch is stopped.

אני מכונן אותו.

Ah-NEE m'hoh-NEHN oh-TOH.

I wind the watch.

שעוני אינו ממהר ואינו מפגר.

Sheh-oh-NEE eh-NOH m'mah-HEHR veh-eh-NOH m'fah-GEHR.

My watch is not fast and not slow.

הוא מדייק.

Hoo m'dah-YEHK.

It is accurate.

שעונך ממהר בחמש דקות.

Sheh-ohn-HAH m'mah-HEHR beh-hah-MEHSH dah-KOHT.

Your watch is five minutes fast.

שעונו מפגר בשלוש דקות.

Sheh-oh-NOH m'fah-GEHR b'shah-LOHSH dah-KOHT.

His watch is three minutes slow.

תודה רבה. אמור לי, בבקשה, מה השעה?

Eh-MOHR lee, b'vah-kah-SHAH, mah hah-shah-AH? Toh-DAH rah-BAH.

Tell me, please, what time is it?   Thank you.

ההצגה בתיאטרון „הבימה" מתחילה בשמונה.

Hah-hah-tsah-GAH b'teh-aht-ROHN "Hah-bee-MAH" maht-hee-LAH beesh-moh-NEH.

The show at the "Habima" theater starts at eight o'clock.

היא גומרת בשעה אחת-עשרה.

Hee goh-MEH-ret b'shah-AH ah-HAHT-ess-REH.

It ends at eleven.

היא אורכת שלוש שעות.

Hee oh-REH-het shah-LOHSH shah-OHT.

It lasts three hours.

איך קוראים לשעון שעל ידך?

Ehkk koh-reh-EEM lah-shah-OHN sheh-AHL yahd-HAH?

What do you call the watch which you have on your hand?

קוראים לזה שעון-יד.

Koh-reh-EEM lah-ZEH sheh-OHN-yahd.

It is called a wrist-watch.

עוזי פקח יותר מגדעון.

OO-zee pee-KAY-akh yoh-TEHR mee-Gheed-OHN.

Uzi is cleverer than Gideon.

יגאל אמיץ יותר מיוסף.

Yig-AHL ah-MEETS yoh-TEHR mee-Yoh-SEHF.

Yigal is braver than Joseph.

צבי אינטליגנטי יותר מדוד.

Z'vee een-teh-lee-GHEN-tee yoh-TEHR nee-Dah-VEED.

Zvi is more intelligent than David.

TO EXPRESS COMPARISON we normally use the word יותר (yoh-TEHR) which means "more" and which follows the adjective. Example: טוב יותר (tohv yoh-TEHR) — better (more good).

שרה רוקדת טוב יותר מרות.

Sah-RAH roh-KEH-det tohv yoh-TEHR meh-Ruth.

Sarah dances better than Ruth.

הנשר אמיץ יותר מן התרנגולת.

Hah-NEH-sherr ah-MEETS yoh-TEHR meen hah-tahr-n'GOH-let.

The eagle is braver than the hen.

השושנה מריחה יפה.

Hah-shoh-shah-NAH m'ree-HAH yah-FEH.

The rose smells good.

היא מריחה טוב יותר מן הלילך.

Hee m'ree-HAH tohv yoh-TEHR meen hah-lee-LAKH.

It smells better than the lilac.

גבינה מריחה רע, וגז מריח רע.

G'vee-NAH m'REE-hah rah, v'gahz m'REE-akh rah.

Cheese smells bad, and gas smells bad.

מה מריח רע יותר?

Mah m'REE-akh rah yoh-TEHR?

Which smells worse?

המריח היסמין יפה כמו השושנה?

Hah-m'REH-akh hah-yahs-MEEN yah-FEH k'moh hah-shoh-shah-NAH?

Does the jasmine smell as good as the rose?

היסמין, השושנה והלילך כולם מריחים היטב במדה שוה.

*Hah-yahs-MEEN, hah-shoh-shah-NAH veh-hah-lee-LAKH koo-LAHM
m'ree-HEHM heh-TEHV b'mee-DAH shah-VAH.*

The jasmine, the rose, and the lilac all smell equally good.

מה טוב יותר : תה עם סוכר או בלי סוכר ?

Mah tohv yoh-TEHR: tay im soo-KAHR oh b'lee soo-KAHR?

Which is better: tea with sugar or without sugar?

תה עם סוכר טוב יותר.

Tay im soo-KAHR tohv yoh-TEHR.

Tea with sugar is better.

אתה מדבר אנגלית היטב, אבל אתה מדבר עברית טוב יותר.

*Ah-TAH m'dah-BEHR ahn-g'LEET heh-TEHV, ah-VAHL ah-TAH
m'dah-BEHR eev-REET tohv yoh-TEHR.*

You speak English well, but you speak Hebrew better.

המבטא העברי שלך טוב (יותר) משלי.

Hah-meev-TAH hah-eev-ree sheh-l'HAH tohv (yoh-TEHR) mee-sheh-LEE.

Your Hebrew pronunciation is better than mine.

המבטא העברי של אדון יהרבלום הוא הטוב ביותר.

*Hah-meev-TAH hah-eev-REE shell ah-DOHN Yahrblum hoo
hah-tohv b'yoh-TEHR.*

The pronunciation of Mr. Jahrblum is the best.

 NOTE ON THE SUPERLATIVE: The superlative is formed also with the use of יותר (*yoh-TEHR*) plus the use of הַ (*hah*) and בְּ (*b'*) arranged in the following manner: "the biggest" הגדול ביותר (*hah-gah-dohl b'yoh-TEHR*).

Examples: "Jerusalem is big." ירושלים גדולה. (*Yeh-roo-shah-LAH-yim g'doh-LAH.*)

"Tel-Aviv is bigger." תל-אביב גדולה יותר. (*Tel-Ah-VEEV g'doh-LAH yoh-TEHR.*)

"New York is the biggest." ניו-יורק היא הגדולה ביותר. (*New York hee hah-g'doh-LAH b'yoh-TEHR.*)

המדבר אתה צרפתית כמו עברית?
*Hah-m'dah-*BEHR *ah-*TAH *tsohr-fah-*TEET *k'moh eev-*REET?
Do you speak French as well as Hebrew?

אדון ברליץ מרכיב משקפים.
*Ah-*DOHN *Berlitz mahr-*KEEV *meesh-kah-*FAH-*yim.*
Mr. Berlitz has eye-glasses.

אתה אינך מרכיב משקפים.
*Ah-*TAH *ehn-*HAH *mahr-*KEEV *meesh-kah-*FAH-*yim.*
You have no eye-glasses.

הרואה אתה טוב יותר מאדון ברליץ?
*Hah-roh-*EH *ah-*TAH *tohv yoh-*TEHR *meh-ah-*DOHN *Berlitz?*
Do you see better than Mr. Berlitz?

כן, אני רואה טוב יותר.
*Kehn, ah-*NEE *roh-*EH *tohv yoh-*TEHR.
Yes, I see better.

התלמיד יוסף חרוץ כמו התלמיד אורי.
*Hah-tahl-*MEED *Yoh-*SEHF *hah-*ROOTS *k'moh hah-tahl-*MEED OO-*ree.*
The pupil Joseph is as diligent as the pupil Uri.

לונדון עיר גדולה כמו ניו-יורק.
LOHN-*dohn eer g'doh-*LAH *k'moh New York.*
London is as large as New York.

המלון העברי עולה באותו מחיר כמו המלון האנגלי.
*Hah-mee-*LOHN *hah-eev-*REE *oh-*LEH *beh-oh-*TOH *m'heer k'moh hah-mee-*
LOHN *hah-ahn-*GLEE.
The Hebrew dictionary costs as much as the English
dictionary.

THINKING IN HEBREW
(Answers on page 289)

1. ?היש שעונים בחדר הזה

Hah-YEHSH sheh-oh-NEEM bah-HEH-der hah-zeh?

2. ?איפה השעונים

Eh-FOH hah-sheh-oh-NEEM?

3. ?היש לך שעון-יד או שעון-כים

Hah-YEHSH l'hah sheh-OHN-yahd oh sheh-OHN-kiss?

4. ?איפה אתה שם את שעון-הכים

Eh-FOH ah-TAH sahm ett sheh-OHN hah-KISS?

5. ?מאיזו מתכת הוא שעונך

Meh-EH-zoh mah-TEH-het hoo sheh-ohn-HAH?

6. היש לשעונך מחוג לשניות ?
Hah-YEHSH leesh-ohn-HAH mah-HOHG leesh-nee-YOHT?

7. כמה שעות יש ביום ?
KAH-mah shah-OHT yehsh bah-YOHM?

8. כמה שניות בדקה ?
KAH-mah sh'nee-YOHT b'dah-KAH?

9. הממהר שעונך ?
Hah-m'mah-HEHR sheh-ohn-HAH?

10. ממה עשוי השולחן ?
Mee-MAH ah-SOOY hah-shool-HAHN?

11. האם הכסא אף הוא מעץ ?
Hah-IM hah-kis-SEH aff hoo meh-EHTS?

12. הגדול השולחן מהכסא ?
Hah-gah-DOHL hah-shool-HAHN meh-hah-kiss-SEH?

13. הארוכה התמונה מהקיר ?
Hah-ah-roo-KAH hah-t'moo-NAH meh-hah-KEER?

14. הגדול החלון כמו הדלת ?
Hah-gah-DOHL hah-hah-LOHN k'moh hah-DEH-let?

15. הארוך המעיל מהחזיה ?
Hah-ah-ROKH hah-meh-EEL meh-heh-hah-zee-YAH?

16. הטוב האפרסק יותר מהתפוח ?
Hah-TOHV hah-ah-far-SEHK yoh-TEHR meh-hah-tah-POO-akh?

17. המבטא אתה עברית היטב ?
Hah-m'vah-TEH ah-TAH eev-REET heh-TEHV?

18. הרואה אתה היטב ?
Hah-roh-EH ah-TAH heh-TEHV?

19. הרואה אדון ברליץ היטב בלי משקפים ?
Hah-roh-EH ah-DOHN Berlitz heh-TEHV b'lee meesh-kah-FAH-yim.

20. הרואה הוא טוב יותר במשקפים ?
Hah-roh-EH hoo tohv yoh-TEHR b'meesh-kah-FAH-yim?

בְּאֵיזוֹ עוֹנָה אָנוּ?

Beh-EH-zoh oh-NAH AH-noo?

In what season are we?

הִנֵּה לוּחַ.
Hee-NEH LOO-akh.
Here is a calendar.

A USEFUL WORD: הִנֵּה (*hee-NEH*) means "here is," "there is," "here are" or "there are" when pointing to an object or objects.

הוּא מֵכִיל שְׁלֹשׁ מֵאוֹת שִׁשִּׁים וַחֲמִשָּׁה יוֹם.
Hoo meh-HEEL sh'lohsh meh-OHT shee-SHEEM vah-hah-mee-SHAH yohm.
It contains three hundred and sixty-five days.

142

השנה מחולקת לשנים-עשר חודש, וחמשים ושנים שבועות.

Hah-shah-NAH m'hoo-LEH-ket leesh-NEHM-ah-SAHR HOH-desh,
vah-hah-mee-SHEEM oo-sh'NAH-yim shah-voo-OHT.

The year is divided into twelve months and fifty-two weeks.

השבוע מורכב משבעה ימים הנקראים:

Hah-shah-VOO-ah mohr-KAHV mee-sheev-AH yah-MEEM hah-neek-rah-EEM:
A week is composed of seven days, which are called:

יום ראשון, יום שני, יום שלישי, יום רביעי,

Yohm ree-SHOHN, yohm sheh-NEE, yohm sh'lee-SHEE, yohm r'vee-EE,
Sunday, Monday, Tuesday, Wednesday,

יום חמשי, יום ששי, שבת.

yohm hah-mee-SHEE, yohm shee-SHEE, shah-BAHT.
Thursday, Friday, Saturday.

HOW TO FORM THE PASSIVE: If you look immediately above this note, you will note two examples of the "passive" form of the verb in English, and its corresponding use in Hebrew. They are: "is divided" and "is composed." An easy way to remember the passive is to keep in mind that the active voice concerns an action performed by the subject whereas the passive voice indicates that the action is undergone by the subject—in other words, the considerable difference that exists between "I shoot" (active) and "I am shot" (passive).

Note how the passive is constructed for the different groups that you already know, in the present tense:

FIRST GROUP

	Active			Passive	
(*soh*-GEHR)	סוגר	"close" "closes"	(*nees*-GAHR)	נסגר	"is closed"
(*koh*-TEHV)	כותב	"write" "writes"	(*neekh*-TAHV)	נכתב	"is written"

In the first group the prefix   נ   (*nee*) must be used and the vowel

"oh" of the first syllable disappears, the vowel of the second syllable becoming "ah." Examples:

"I write a letter." אני כותב מכתב. (*Ah*-NEE *koh*-TEHV *meekh*-TAHV.)

"A letter is written by me.". המכתב נכתב על ידי. (*Hah-meekh*-TAHV *neekh*-TAHV ahl yah-DEE.)

SECOND GROUP

	Active			Passive	
(*m'dah*-BEHR)	מדבר	"speak" "speaks"	(*m'doo*-BAHR)	מדובר	"is spoken of"
(*m'shah*-BEHR)	משבר	"break" "breaks"	(*m'shoo*-BAHR)	משובר	"is broken"

As you can see, in this group the vowel in the first syllable becomes "oo" and the vowel in the second syllable becomes "ah." Examples:

"I tell a story." אני מספר ספור.   (Ah-NEE m'sah-PEHR see-POOR.)

"The story is told." הספור מסופר.   (Hah-see-POOR m'soo-PAHR.)

THIRD GROUP

Active	Passive
(makh-TEEV) מכתיב	(mokh-TAHV) מוכתב
"dictate" "dictates"	"is dictated to"

The vowel in the first syllable changes to "o" or "oo" and that of the last syllable to "ah." Examples:

"I dictate a letter." אני מכתיב מכתב.   (Ah-NEE makh-TEEV meekh-TAHV.)

"The letter is dictated." המכתב מוכתב.   (Hah-meekh-TAHV mokh-TAHV.)

אנו עובדים חמשה או ששה ימים בשבוע.
AH-ROO oh-v'DEEM hah-mee-SHAH oh shee-SHAH yah-MEEM bah-shah-VOO-ah.
We work five or six days a week.

ביום השביעי, שבת, אין אנו עובדים; זה יום מנוחה.
Bah-yohm hah-sh'vee-EE, shah-BAHT, ehn AH-noo oh-v'DEEM; zeh yohm m'noo-HAH.
On the seventh day, Saturday, we do not work; it is a day of rest.

הנה שמות החודשים:
Hee-NEH sh'moht hah-hoh-dah-SHEEM:
Here are the names of the months:

ינואר, פברואר, מרס, אפריל, מאי, יוני, יולי,
JAH-noo-ahr, FEB-roo-ahr, Mahrs, Ahp-RILL, Migh, YOO-nee, YOO-lee,
January, February, March, April, May, June, July,

אוגוסט, ספטמבר, אוקטובר, נובמבר, דצמבר.
Oh-GOOST, Sep-TEM-ber, Ok-TOH-ber, Noh-VEM-ber, Deh-TSEM-ber.
August, September, October, November, December.

AN OLD HEBREW CUSTOM: The months you have just learned are those of the international calendar which are used in Israel for business and administrative purposes. The traditional Hebrew calendar has a different set of months, based on the phases of the moon, and in their names we can perceive the echoes of a distant past. They are: ניסן (Nee-SAHN), אייר (Ee-YAHR), סיון (See-VAHN), תמוז (Tah-MOOZ), אב (Ahv), אלול (El-LOOL), תשרי (Teesh-REH), חשון (Hesh-VAHN), כסלו (Kees-LEHV), טבת (Teh-VEHT), שבט (Sh'vaht) and אדר (Ah-DAHR). All of these names have come down from Babylonian times.

The year composed of these months consists of only 354 days, and for this reason a whole month is added nearly every three years, and is called אדר שני (ah-DAHR sheh-NEE) "Ah-DAHR the second" (!). The Hebrew holidays, including the Day of Independence, are observed according to this calendar.

השנה מחולקת לארבע עונות, הנקראות:

Hah-shah-NAH m'hoo-LEH-ket leh-ahr-BAH oh-NOHT, hah-neek-rah-OHT:
The year is divided into four seasons, called:

אביב, קיץ, סתיו, חורף.
Ah-VEEV, KAH-yits, s'tahv, HOH-reff.
Spring, summer, autumn, winter.

בארץ חמה כמו ישראל יש רק שתי עונות:
Beh-EH-rets hah-MAH k'moh Yis-rah-EHL yehsh rahk sh'teh oh-NOHT:
In a warm land like Israel there are only two seasons:

ימי החמה (קיץ), וימי הגשמים.
y'meh hah-hah-MAH (KAH-yits), vee-y'meh hah-g'shah-MEEM.
a sunny season (summer) and a rainy season.

בקיץ אנו הולכים לכפר או לשפת-הים, שבהם קריר יותר מאשר בעיר.
Bah-KAH-yits AH-noo hoh-l'HEEM leekh-FAHR oh lees-FAHT-hah-YAHM, sheh-bah-HEMM kah-REER yoh-TEHR meh-ah-SHERR bah-EER.
In summer we go to the country or to the seashore, where it is cooler than in the city.

על שפת הים אנו יכולים לשחות בים, או לשכב על החול.
Ahl s'faht hah-YAHM AH-noo y'hoh-LEEM lees-HOHT bah-YAHM, oh leesh-KAHV ahl hah-HOHL.
At the seashore we can swim in the sea, or lie on the sand.

בחורף אין אנו הולכים לכפר; אנו נשארים בעיר.
Bah-HOH-reff ehn AH-noo hoh-l'HEEM leekh-FAHR; AH-noo neesh-ah-REEM bah-EER.
In winter we do not go to the country; we remain in the city.

באביב רואים הרבה פרחים יפים.
Bah-ah-VEEV roh-EEM hahr-BEH p'rah-HEEM yah-FEEM.
In spring one sees many beautiful flowers.

בסתיו מחליפים העלים את צבעם ונושרים מן העצים.

Bahs-TAHV makh-lee-FEEM heh-ah-LEEM ett tseev-AHM v'noh-sh'REEM meen hah-eh-TSEEM.

In autumn the leaves change their color and fall from the trees.

בישראל האביב הוא העונה היפה ביותר.

B'Yis-rah-EHL hah-ah-VEEV hoo hah-oh-NAH hah-yah-FAH b'yoh-TEHR.

In Israel spring is the most beautiful season.

איזה יום בחודש היום?

EH-*zeh yohm bah-*HOH-*desh hah-*YOHM?

What day of the month is it today?

היום החמשה עשר בחודש.

*Hah-*YOHM *hah-hah-mee-*SHAH *ah-*SAHR *bah-*HOH-*desh.*

Today is the fifteenth.

איזה יום בשבוע היום?

EH-*zeh yohm bah-shah-*VOO-*ah hah-*YOHM?

What day of the week is today?

היום יום חמשי.

*Hah-*YOHM *yohm hah-mee-*SHEE.

Today is Thursday.

SOMETHING EASY:

Remember that the days in Hebrew have no names; only ordinal numbers with the exception of Saturday which is שבת (*Shah-*BAHT), meaning "rest."

החודש האחרון היה דצמבר.

*Hah-*HOH-*desh hah-*AH-*hah-*ROHN *hah-*YAH *Deh-*TSEM-*ber.*

Last month was December.

עתה חודש ינואר.

*Ah-*TAH HOH-*desh* YAH-*noo-ahr.*

Now it is January.

החודש הבא יהיה פברואר.

*Hah-*HOH-*desh hah-*BAH *yee-*YEH *Feb-roo-ahr.*

Next month will be February.

SAME SOUND — ANOTHER MEANING:

אתה (*ah-*TAH) means "you" and עתה (*ah-*TAH) means "now." Before protesting bitterly about this, re-member the English "to," "too" and "two."

אתמול היה יום שני.   היום יום שלישי.

Ett-MOHL *hah*-YAH *yohm sheh*-NEE.   *Hah*-YOHM *yohm sh'lee*-SHEE.

Yesterday was Monday.   Today is Tuesday.

מחר יהיה יום רביעי.

Mah-HAHR *yee*-YEH *yohm r'vee*-EE.

Tomorrow will be Wednesday.

אתמול היה הארבעה עשר; מחר יהיה יום הששה עשר.

Ett-MOHL *hah*-YAH *hah-ahr-bah*-AH *ah*-SAHR; *mah*-HAHR *yee*-YEH
yohm hah-shee-SHAH *ah*-SAHR.

Yesterday was the fourteenth; tomorrow will be the sixteenth.

ATTENTION, PLEASE: You have just encountered
two tenses, the past and the future. Simply learn these
two words as they stand היה (*hah*-YAH)—"was", and
יהיה (*yee*-YEH) — "will be." The past and future
tenses will be fully explained in later lessons.

אם אתה רוצה לדעת את התאריך, אתה מביט בלוח.

Im ah-TAH *roh*-TSEH *lah*-DAH-*aht ett hah-tah-ah*-REEKH, *ah*-TAH
mah-BEET *bah*-LOO-*akh.*

If you wish to know the date, you look at the calendar.

באיזה תאריך חל יום העצמאות בישראל ?

Beh-EH-*zeh tah-ah*-REEKH *hahl yohm hah-ahts-mah*-OOT *b'Yis-rah*-EHL?

On what date does Independence Day fall in Israel?

הוא חל בחמשי באייר.

Hoo hahl bah-hah-mee-SHEE *beh-ee*-YAHR.

It falls on the fifth of Eeyar.

היום הזה הוא חג לאומי בישראל.

Hah-YOHM *hah-zeh hoo hahg leh-oo*-MEE *b'Yis-rah-ehl.*

This day is a national holiday of Israel.

באיזה תאריך חל יום העצמאות בארצות-הברית ?

Beh-EH-*zeh tah-ah*-REEKH *hahl yohm hah-ahts-mah*-OOT
beh-Ahr-TSOHT-*Hah-b'*REET?

On what date does Independence Day fall in the United States?

הוא חל ברביעי ביולי.

Hoo hahl bah-r'vee-EE *b'YOO-lee.*

It falls on the Fourth of July.

THINKING IN HEBREW
(Answers on page 289)

1. ‏כמה ימים בשנה?‏
   KAH-*mah yah*-MEEM *bah-shah*-NAH?

2. ‏מכמה ימים מורכב השבוע?‏
   Mee-KAH-*mah yah*-MEEM *mohr*-KAHV *hah-shah-*VOO-*ah?*

3. ‏מתי מתחילה השנה?‏
   Mah-TIGH *maht-hee*-LAH *hah-shah*-NAH?

4. ‏מתי היא נגמרת?‏
   Mah-TIGH *hee neeg*-MEH-*ret?*

5. ‏מה שם החודש הראשון, השלישי והחמשי בשנה?‏
   Mah shehm *hah*-HOH-*desh hah-ree*-SHOHN, *hah-sh'lee*-SHEE
   veh-hah-hah-mee-SHEE *bah-shah*-NAH?

6. ‏מה שמות חודשי השנה?‏
   Mah sh'moht *hohd*-SHEH *hah-shah*-NAH?

7. ‏מה שם היום האחרון בשבוע?‏
   Mah shehm *hah*-YOHM *hah-ah-hah*-ROHN *bah-shah-*VOO-*ah?*

8.   איזה יום בשבוע הוא היום?
EH-zeh yohm bah-shah-VOO-ah hoo hah-YOHM?

9.   ההיה אתמול יום ראשון?   :
Heh-hah-YAH ett-MOHL yohm ree-SHOHN?

10.   באיזה יום אין אתה הולך לבית-הספר?
Beh-EH-zeh yohm ehn ah-TAH hoh-LEHKH l'veht-hah-SEH-fer?

11.   היהיה יום ששי יום החמשה עשר בחודש?
Hah-yee-YEH yohm shee-SHEE yohm hah-hah-mee-SHAH ah-SAHR
bah-HOH-desh?

12.   איזה יום בחודש הוא היום?
EH-zeh yohm bah-HOH-desh hoo hah-YOHM?

13.   איזה יום בחודש יהיה יום שני הבא?
EH-zeh yohm bah-HOH-dehsh yee-YEH yohm sheh-NEE hah-BAH?

14.   איזה יום בחודש היה יום שני שעבר?
EH-zeh yohm bah-HOH-dehsh hah-YAH yohm sheh-NEE sheh-ah-VAHR?

15.   היהיה מחר היום האחרון בחודש?
Hah yee-YEH mah-HAHR hah-YOHM hah-ah-hah-ROHN bah-HOH-desh?

16.   כמה ימים בשבוע אנו עובדים?
KAH-mah yah-MEEM bah-shah-VOO-ah AH-noo oh-v'DEEM?

17.   העובד אתה בשבת?
Hah-oh-VEHD ah-TAH b'shah-BAHT?

18.   איזה חג חל בחמשי באייר?
EH-zeh hahg hahl bah-hah-mee-SHEE beh-ee-YAHR?

שָׁעוּר 22

יום ולילה

*Yohm vah-*LIGH-*lah*

Day and Night

עשרים וארבע השעות מחולקות לשני חלקים:

ESS-REEM *veh-ahr*-BAH *hah-shah*-OHT *m'hoo-lah*-KOHT *leesh*-NEH
hah-lah-KEEM:

The twenty-four hours are divided into two parts:

לשעות היום ולשעות הלילה

leesh-OHT *hah*-YOHM *v'leesh*-OHT *hah*-LIGH-*lah.*

the hours of the day and the hours of the night.

NOTE ON SPELLING:

The prefix וְ (*veh*) means "and." Before a stressed

syllable, however, it changes to וָ (*vah*), as above

יום ולילה (*yohm vah*-LIGH-*lah*) — "day and night."

150

A USEFUL IDIOM:

The Hebrew language has two special words indicating a 24-hour period. They are יממה (y'mah-MAH) and מעת-לעת (meh-EHT-leh-EHT).

במשך היום יש אור, ואנו יכולים לראות,

B'MEH-shekh hah-YOHM yehsh ohr, veh-AH-noo y'hoh-LEEM leer-OHT,
During the day it is light and we can see,

אבל במשך הלילה חושך, ואנחנו מוכרחים להדליק את האור,
אם אנו רוצים לראות.

ah-VAHL b'MEH-shekh hah-LIGH-lah HOH-shekh, veh-ah-NAKH-noo mookh-rah-HEEM leh-hahd-LEEK ett hah-OHR, im AH-noo roh-TSEEM leer-OHT.
but during the night it is dark, and we must turn on the light
if we want to see.

בחדר הזה אין די אור; הדלק את החשמל, בבקשה!

Bah-HEH-der hah-ZEH ehn digh ohr; hahd-LEHK ett hah-hahsh-MAHL,
b'vah-kah-SHAH!

In this room it isn't light enough; turn on the light, please!

עכשו מאיר המאור החשמלי את החדר.

Akh-SHAHV meh-EER hah-mah-OHR hah-hahsh-mahl-LEE ett hah-HEH-der.
Now the electric light lights up the room.

אל תגע במנורה דולקת, משום, שאף-על-פי

Ahl tee-GAH beem-noh-RAH doh-LEH-ket, mee-SHOOM, sheh-aff-ahl-PEE
Don't touch a burning lamp, because, though

שאין לה להבה, אתה יכול להכוות בה.

sheh-EHN lah leh-hah-VAH, ah-TAH yah-HOHL leh-hee-kah-VOHT bah.
it has no flame, you can get burned by it.

NOTE FOR PARENTS:

When you wish to say "don't touch" to your children, say אל תגע (ahl tee-GAH). The word אל (ahl) or בל (bahl) is used for the negative imperative as לא (lo) and אין (ehn) is used for the ordinary negative. DO NOT CONFUSE this אל (ahl) meaning "don't!" with the other על (ahl) meaning "on."

אנו מדליקים את הסיגריה בגפרור.

AH-noo mahd-lee-KEEM ett hah-see-gah-ree-YAH b'gahf-ROOR.
We light the cigarette with a match.

אין אנו זקוקים לגפרורים כדי להדליק את החשמל.

Ehn AH-*noo* z'koo-KEEM *l'gahf-roo-*REEM *k'deh leh-hahd-*LEEK
*ett hah-hahsh-*MAHL.

We do not need matches to turn on the electric light.

אם ילד קטן מדליק גפרור, אנו אומרים לו:

Im YEH-*led kah-*TAHN *mahd-*LEEK *gahf-*ROOR, AH-*noo oh-m'*REEM *lo*:

If a small child lights a match, we say to him:

הזהר! בל תכוה.

*Hee-zah-*HEHR! *bahl tee-kah-*VEH.

Be careful! don't burn yourself.

היש עכשו אור מספיק בחדר ?

*Hah-*YEHSH *akh-*SHAHV *ohr mahs-*PEEK *bah-*HEH-*der?*

Is there enough light in the room now?

כן אדוני, יש אור מספיק בחדר.

*Kehn, ah-doh-*NEE, *yehsh ohr mahs-*PEEK *bah-*HEH-*der.*

Yes, sir, there is enough light in the room.

היכול אתה לראות אותנו היטב ?

*Hah-yah-*HOHL *ah-*TAH *leer-*OHT *oh-*TAH-*noo heh-*TEHV?

Can you see us well?

אני יכול לראותך היטב.

*Ah-*NEE *yah-*HOHL *leer-oh-t'*HAH *heh-*TEHV.

I can see you well.

בדרך כלל אין אנו משתמשים באור החשמל במשך היום.

B'DEH-*rekh k'lahl ehn* AH-*noo meesh-tahm-*SHEEM *beh-*OHR
*hah-hahsh-*MAHL *b'*MEH-*shekh hah-*YOHM.

Generally we do not use electric light during the day.

A WORD FROM THE PAST:
As the concept of "electricity" did not exist in ancient times, the word חשמל (*hahsh-*MAHL) has been adopted to express it. The word comes from the first chapter of Ezekiel and refers to the radiating halo the prophet saw around the vision of the Almighty that appeared to him. (Ezekiel 1:4) Rather a good word to express electricity, don't you think?

כבה את החשמל, בבקשה.

*Kah-*BEH *ett hah-hahsh-*MAHL, *b'vah-kah-*SHAH.

Turn off the light, please.

מה אתה עושה?

Mah ah-TAH oh-SEH?

What do you do?

אני מכבה את החשמל.

Ah-NEE m'hah-BEH ett hah-hahsh-MAHL.

I turn off the light.

הדולק עתה החשמל, או לא?

Hah-doh-LEHK ah-TAH hah-hahsh-MAHL oh lo?

Is the light on or off now?

החשמל כבה.

Hah-hahsh-MAHL kah-VAH.

The light is off.

מתי אתה מדליק את החשמל?

Mah-TIGH ah-TAH mahd-LEEK ett hah-hahsh-MAHL?

When do you turn on the light?

אני מדליק את החשמל בחושך.

Ah-NEE mahd-LEEK ett hah-hahsh-MAHL bah-HOH-shekh.

I turn on the electric light when it is dark.

אור היום בא מן השמש אשר בשמים.

Ohr hah-YOHM bah meen hah-SHEH-mesh ah-SHERR bah-shah-MAH-yim.

The light of the day comes from the sun which is in the sky.

הבט החוצה דרך החלון.

Hah-BEHT hah-HOO-tsah DEH-rekh hah-hah-LOHN.

Look out of the window.

WATCH OUT FOR THE IDIOM:

The literal translation of the above is "Look toward the outside of the window." The word for "outside" is חוץ (*hoots*) and הָ (*lah*) is added to this as a suffix to indicate the direction.

Observe the following examples showing how this suffix is used:

אני נוסע תל-אביבה.   (*Ah-NEE noh-SEH-ah Tel-Ah-VEE-vah.*)

אני נוסע לתל-אביב   (*Ah-NEE noh-SEH-ah leh-Tel-Ah-VEEV.*)

Both mean: "I am going to Tel-Aviv."

הרואה אתה את השמים הכחולים?

Hah-roh-EH ah-TAH ett hah-shah-MAH-yim hah-k'hoo-LEEM?

Do you see the blue sky?

בלילה השמש אינה נראית; אין אנו יכולים לראותה,

Bah-LIGH-lah hah-SHEH-mesh eh-NAH neer-EHT; ehn AH-noo y'hoh-LEEM leer-oh-TAH,

At night the sun is not visible; we cannot see it,

אבל יכולים אנו לראות את הירח והכוכבים.

ah-VAHL *y'hoh*-LEEM AH-*noo* leer-OHT *ett hah-yah*-REH-*akh*
veh-hah-koh-hah-VEEM.

but we can see the moon and the stars.

הכוכבים רבים מספר; אי-אפשר לספר אותם.

Hah-KOH-*hah*-VEEM *rah*-BEEM *mees*-FOHR; *ee-eff*-SHAHR
lees-POHR *oh*-TAHM.

The stars are innumerable; it is impossible to count them.

A USEFUL PREFIX:

Note: אפשר   (*eff*-SHAHR) "possible"

אי-אפשר   (*ee-eff*-SHAHR) "impossible"

ברצון   (*b'rah*-TSOHN) "willingly"

באי-רצון   (*beh*-EE-*rah*-TSOHN) "unwillingly"

החלק הראשון של היום נקרא בוקר.

Hah-HEH-*lek hah-ree*-SHON *shell hah*-YOHM *neek*-RAH BOH-*ker*.

The first part of the day is called morning.

הוא נגמר בשתים-עשרה בצהרים.

Hoo neeg-MAHR *beesh*-TEHM-*ess*-REH *bah-tsoh-hoh*-RAH-*yim*.

It ends at twelve o'clock noon.

החלק האחרון של היום נקרא ערב.

Hah-HEH-*lek hah-ah-hah*-ROHN *shell hah*-YOHM *neek*-RAH EH-*rev*.

The last part of the day is called evening.

הוא מתחיל בשש אחרי הצהרים.

Hoo maht-HEEL *b'shehsh akh*-RAY *hah-tsoh-hoh*-RAH-*yim*.

It begins at six p.m.

הזמן בין שתים-עשרה בצהרים ושש בערב נקרא אחרי הצהרים.

*Hah-z'*MAHN *behn sh'tehm-ess*-REH *bah-tsoh-hoh*-RAH-*yim v'shehsh*
bah-EH-*rev neek*-RAH *akh*-RAY *hah-tsoh-hoh*-RAH-*yim*.

The time between twelve noon and six p.m. is called **afternoon.**

השמש זורחת בבוקר, ושוקעת בערב.

Hah-SHEH-*mesh zoh*-RAH-*haht bah*-BOH-*ker*, *v'shoh*-KAH-*aht bah*-EH-*rev*.

In the morning the sun rises, and it sets in the evening.

ארבע רוחות יש בעולם: צפון, דרום, מזרח ומערב.

Ahr-BAH *roo*-HOHT *yehsh bah-oh*-LAHM: *tsah*-FOHN, *dah*-ROHM,
meez-RAKH *oo-mah-ah*-RAHV.

There are four cardinal points: north, south, east, and west.

השמש זורחת במזרח ושוקעת במערב.

Hah-SHEH-mesh zoh-RAH-haht bah-meez-RAKH v'shoh-KAH-aht bah-mah-ah-RAHV.

The sun rises in the east and sets in the west.

בקיץ השמש מקדימה לזרח, בחמש

Bah-KAH-yits hah-SHEH-mesh mahk-dee-MAH leez-ROH-akh, beh-hah-MEHSH

In the summer the sun rises early, at five

או בשש, והימים ארוכים;

oh b'shehsh, veh-hah-yah-MEEM ah-roo-KEEM;

or six, and the days are long;

בחורף השמש מאחרת לזרח, והימים קצרים.

bah-HOH-reff hah-SHEH-mesh meh-ah-HEH-ret leez-ROH-akh, veh-hah-yah-MEEM k'tsah-REEM.

in the winter the sun rises late, and the days are short.

ולכן הלילות בחורף ארוכים מאשר בקיץ.

V'lah-HEHN hah-leh-LOHT bah-HOH-reff ah-roo-KEEM meh-ah-SHERR bah-KAH-yits.

The nights are therefore longer in winter than in summer.

בלילה, כאשר אנו רוצים לישון, אנחנו שוכבים במטה,

Bah-LIGH-lah, kah-ah-SHERR AH-noo roh-TSEEM lee-SHOHN, ah-NAKH-noo shoh-h'VEEM bah-mee-TAH,

At night, when we are sleepy, we go to bed,

מכבים את האור וישנים.

m'hah-BEEM ett hah-OHR vee-y'sheh-NEEM.

turn off the light, and sleep.

אנו קמים בבוקר, מתרחצים, מתגלחים, סורקים את שערותינו,

AH-noo kah-MEEM bah-BOH-ker, meet-rah-hah-TSEEM, meet-gahl-HEEM, soh-r'KEEM ett seh-ah-roh-TEH-noo,

In the morning, we get up, we wash ourselves, we shave, we comb our hair,

מתלבשים ואוכלים ארוחת-בוקר.

meet-lah-b'SHEEM veh-oh-h'LEEM ah-roo-HAHT-BOH-ker.

we dress, and have breakfast.

אחרי-כן אנו מוכנים ללכת לעבודה.

Akh-RAY-hehn AH-noo moo-hah-NEEM lah-LEH-het lah-ah-voh-DAH.

After that we are ready to go work.

THINKING IN HEBREW

(Answers on page 290)

1.   איך מחולקות עשרים וארבע שעות-היום?
*Ehkh m'hoo-lah-*KOHT *ess-*REEM *veh-ahr-*BAH *sheh-*OHT-*hah-*YOHM?

2.   מתי אור?
*Mah-*TIGH *ohr?*

3.   החושך עכשו?
*Hah-*HOH-*shekh akh-*SHAHV?

4.   מאין בא אור היום?
*Meh-*AH-*yin bah ohr hah-*YOHM?

5.   איפה השמש?
*Eh-*FOH *hah-*SHEH-*mesh?*

6.   מה מאיר את החדר בלילה?
*Mah meh-*EER *ett hah-*HEH-*der bah-*LIGH-*lah?*

7.   מה אנו מדליקים בלילה כדי לראות?
*Mah-*AH-*noo mahd-lee-*KEEM *bah-*LIGH-*lah k'deh leer-*OHT?

8.   מה אנו רואים בשמים בלילה?
Mah AH-*noo roh-*EEM *bah-shah-*MAH-*yim bah-*LIGH-*lah?*

9.   ?מאיזו רוח זורחת השמש
Meh-EH-zoh ROO-akh zoh-RAH-haht hah-SHEH-mesh?

10.   ? באיזו שעה זורחת השמש בחודש מרס
Beh-EH-zoh shah-AH zoh-RAH-haht hah-SHEH-mesh b'HOH-desh Mahrs?

11.   ?באיזו עונה ארוכים הימים
Beh-EH-zoh oh-NAH ah-roo-KEEM hah-yah-MʰEM?

12.   ? הארוכים הימים בקיץ מן הלילות
Hah-ah-roo-KEEM hah-yah-MEEM bah-KAH-yits meen hah-leh-LOHT?

13.   ? באיזו עונה ארוכים הלילות
Beh-EH-zoh oh-NAH ah-roo-KEEM hah-leh-LOHT?

14.   ? מתי מדליקים אנו את האור
Mah-TIGH mahd-lee-KEEM AH-noo ett hah-OHR?

15.   ? מתי אתה הולך לישון בדרך כלל
Mah-TIGH ah-TAH hoh-LEHKH lee-SHOHN b'DEH-rekh k'lahl?

16.   ?באיזו שעה אתה קם
Beh-EH-zoh shah-AH ah-TAH kahm?

17.   ? מתי אתה אוכל ארוחת בוקר
Mah-TIGH ah-TAH oh-HEHL ah-roo-HAHT BOH-ker?

18.   ? באיזו שעה אתה מתחיל לעבד
Beh-EH-zoh shah-AH ah-TAH maht-HEEL lah-ah-VOHD?

19.   ? מתי אתה גומר את עבודתך
Mah-TIGH ah-TAH goh-MEHR ett ah-voh-daht-HAH?

20.   ? האוהב אתה לעבד
Hah-oh-HEHV ah-TAH lah-ah-VOHD?

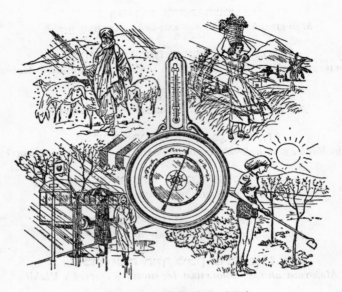

אֵיךְ מֶזֶג הָאַוִיר הַיּוֹם?

Ehkh MEH-*zeg hah-ah*-VEER *hah*-YOHM?

How is the weather today?

מַה צֶּבַע הַשָּׁמַיִם?
Mah TSEH-*vah hah-shah*-MAH-*yim?*
What color is the sky?

הַשָּׁמַיִם אֲפוֹרִים.
Hah-shah-MAH-*yim ah-foo*-REEM.
The sky is gray.

בַּמֶּה מְכֻסִּים הַשָּׁמַיִם?
Bah-MEH *m'hoo*-SEEM *hah-shah*-MAH-*yim?*
With what is the sky covered?

בַּעֲנָנִים.
Bah-ah-nah-NEEM.
With clouds.

מַה צֶּבַע הָעֲנָנִים?
Mah TSEH-*vah hah-ah-nah*-NEEM?
What color are the clouds?

הֵם אֲפוֹרִים.
Hehm ah-foo-REEM.
They are gray.

עַתָּה יוֹרֵד גֶּשֶׁם.
Ah-TAH *yoh*-REHD GEH-*shemm.*
Now, it is raining.

בַּחוֹרֶף יוֹרֵד שֶׁלֶג.
Bah-HOH-*reff yoh*-REHD SHEH-*leg.*
In winter snow falls.

158

השלג לבן.

*Hah-*SHEH-*leg lah-*VAHN.

The snow is white.

כאשר השמים בהירים, והשמש זורחת, מזג האויר יפה.

*Kah-ah-*SHERR *hah-shah-*MAH-*yim beh-hee-*REEM, *veh-hah-*SHEH-*mesh
zoh-*RAH-*haht,* MEH-*zeg hah-ah-*VEER *yah-*FEH.

When the sky is clear, and the sun is shining, the weather is good.

A USEFUL ABBREVIATION:

The word כאשר (*kah-ah-*SHERR) which means "when"
is usually abbreviated to . . . כש (*k'sheh*...) when used
in conjunction with a verb. The same abbreviation is
in use in conjunction with a noun.   Example:
כשאדם רעב, הוא רוצה לאכל. (*k'sheh-ah-*DAHM *rah-*EHV, *hoo roh-*TSEH
*leh-eh-*HOHL.)—"When a man is hungry, he wishes to eat."

כשיורדים גשמים ושלג, מזג האויר רע.

*K'sheh-yoh-r'*DEEM *g'shah-*MEEM *vah-*SHEH-*leg,* MEH-*zeg hah-ah-*VEER *rah.

When it rains and snows, the weather is bad.

METEOROLOGICAL NOTE:

There are no special verbs in Hebrew like "to rain"
or "to snow." So we have to say, literally describing
such natural phenomena: "The rain (or snow) falls."
Example: בחורף יורד שלג, ולפעמים גשם (*Bah-*HOH-*reff
yoh-*REHD SHEH-*leg v'leef-ah-*MEEM GEH-*shemm*) — "In
winter it snows and sometimes it rains."

כשיורד גשם אנו פותחים את מטריותינו.

*K'sheh-yoh-*REHD GEH-*shemm* AH-*noo poh-t'*HEEM *ett
meet-ree-yoh-*TEH-*noo.

When it rains we open our umbrellas.

מה צבע השמים כשיורדים גשמים ?

Mah TSEH-*vah hah-shah-*MAH-*yim k'sheh-yoh-r'*DEEM *g'shah-*MEEM?

What color is the sky when it rains?

השמים אפורים.

*Hah-shah-*MAH-*yim ah-foo-*REEM.

The sky is gray.

היורדים תמיד גשמים בדצמבר ?

*Hah-yoh-r'*DEEM *tah-*MEED *g'shah-*MEEM *b'Deh-*TSEM-*ber?

Does it always rain in December?

כֵּן, בְּדֶצֶמְבֶּר יוֹרְדִים תְּכוּפוֹת גְּשָׁמִים.
*Kehn, b'Deh-*TSEM*-ber yoh-r'*DEEM *t'hoo-*FOHT *g'shah-*MEEM.
Yes, in December it often rains.

הֲיוֹרֵד שֶׁלֶג בַּקַּיִץ?
*Hah-yoh-*REHD SHEH-*leg bah-*KAH*-yits?*
Does it snow in summer?

לֹא, בַּקַּיִץ אַף פַּעַם אֵין שֶׁלֶג.
*Lo, bah-*KAH*-yits aff* PAH*-ahm ehn* SHEH*-leg.*
No, in summer it never snows.

הֲיוֹרֵד שֶׁלֶג בַּחוֹרֶף?
*Hah-yoh-*REHD SHEH*-leg bah-*HOH*-reff?*
Does it snow in winter?

כֵּן, בַּחוֹרֶף יוֹרֵד שֶׁלֶג תְּכוּפוֹת.
*Kehn, bah-*HOH*-reff yoh-*REHD SHEH*-leg t'hoo-*FOHT.
Yes, it snows often in winter.

כַּאֲשֶׁר יוֹרֵד שֶׁלֶג בַּמֶּה מְכֻסִּים הָרְחוֹבוֹת וְהַבָּתִּים?
*Kah-ah-*SHERR *yoh-*REHD SHEH*-leg bah-*MEH *m'hoo-*SEEM
*hah-r'hoh-*VOHT *veh-hah-bah-*TEEM?
With what are the houses and streets covered when it snows?

כְּשֶׁיּוֹרֵד שֶׁלֶג הֵם מְכֻסִּים בְּשֶׁלֶג.
*K'sheh-yoh-*REHD SHEH*-leg hehm m'hoo-*SEEM *ba-*SHEH*-leg.*
When it snows they are covered with snow.

אֵיזֶה מֶזֶג אֲוִיר יֵשׁ לָנוּ בִּינוּאָר?
EH*-zeh* MEH*-zeg ah-*VEER *yehsh* LAH*-noo b'*YAH*-noo-ahr?*
What sort of weather have we in January?

הוֹי! רוּחַ חֲזָקָה נוֹשֶׁבֶת.
Hoy! ROO*-akh hah-zah-*KAH *noh-*SHEH*-vet.*
Oh! A strong wind blows.

NOTE TO STUDENT:
What is meant here is "It is very windy," but, as there
is no word for "windy" in Hebrew, we have made a
literal translation.

כְּשֶׁיּוֹצְאִים בַּגֶּשֶׁם בְּלִי מִטְרִיָּה, אוֹ בְּלִי מְעִיל־גֶּשֶׁם, נִרְטָבִים.
*K'sheh-yoh-tseh-*EEM *bah-*GEH*-shemm b'lee meet-ree-*YAH. *oh b'lee*
*meh-*EEL-GEH*-shemm, neer-tah-*VEEM.
When one goes out in the rain without an umbrella or without a
raincoat, one gets wet.

אז עלינו לפשט את בגדינו הרטובים, וללבש בגדים יבשים.

*Ahz ah-*LEH*-noo leef-*SHOHT *ett b'gah-*DEH*-noo hah-r'too-*BEEM,
*v'leel-*BOHSH *b'gah-*DEEM *y'veh-*SHEEM.

Then we must take off our wet clothes, and put on dry clothes.

THIS IS ON ME:

As you have seen, the notion of "must" is usually expressed by the combination of the word מוכרח (*mookh-*RAKH) with the subject person. However, there is yet another very current and very short form, conveying the same notion and meaning, literally, "It is on me to..." and in fact "It is my (your, his, etc.) duty, or task, to..." Both forms are indiscriminately used to say "I (you, he, she, etc.) must." Observe the following table showing the second form:

	Masculine		*Feminine*	
on me	עלי	(*ah-*LIGH)	same as masculine	
on you	עליך	(*ah-*LEH*-hah*)	(*ah-lah-*yikh*)	עליך
on him, on her	עליו	(*ah-*LAHV)	(*ah-*LEH*-hah*)	עליה
on us	עלינו	(*ah-*LEH*-noo*)	same as masculine	
on you (plur.)	עליכם	(*ah-leh-*HEMM)	(*ah-leh-*HENN)	עליכן
on them	עליהם	(*ah-leh-*HEMM)	(*ah-leh-*HENN)	עליהן

Example of use:

"I must go": 1) אני מוכרח ללכת. (*Ah-*NEE *mookh-*RAKH *lah-*LEH*-het*)

2) עלי ללכת. (*Ah-*LIGH *lah-*LEH*-het*)

אם אין אנו פושטים את בגדינו הרטובים, אנו יכולים להצטנן.

Im ehn AH*-noo poh-sh'*TEEM *ett b'gah-*DEH*-noo hah-r'too-*BEEM,
AH*-noo y'hoh-*LEEM *leh-heets-tah-*NEHN.

If we don't take off our wet clothes, we can catch a cold.

היפה מזג האויר היום?

*Hah-yah-*FEH MEH*-zeg hah-ah-*VEER *hah-*YOHM?

Is it good weather today?

כן, היום מזג האויר יפה.

*Kehn, hah-*YOHM MEH*-zeg hah-ah-*VEER *yah-*FEH.

Yes, it is good weather today.

היוצא אתה החוצה במזג אויר רע?

*Hah-yoh-*TSEH *ah-*TAH *hah-*HOO*-htsah b'*MEH*-zeg ah-*VEER *rah?*

Do you go out when it is bad weather?

לא, אינני יוצא החוצה, ללא הכרח, במזג אויר רע.

*Lo, eh-*NEN-*nee yoh-*TSEH *hah-*HOO-*tsah, l'lo hekh-*RAKH,
*b'*MEH-*zeg ah-*VEER *rah.*

No, I do not go out in bad weather without necessity.

בקיץ אנו לובשים בגדים קלים.

*Bah-*KAH-*yits* AH-*noo loh-v'*SHEEM *b'gah-*DEEM *kah-*LEEM.

In summer we put on light clothes.

ATTENTION:

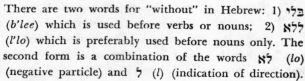

There are two words for "without" in Hebrew: 1) בּלי
(*b'lee*) which is used before verbs or nouns; 2) ללא
(*l'lo*) which is preferably used before nouns only. The
second form is a combination of the words לא (*lo*)
(negative particle) and ל (*l*) (indication of direction).

The combination ללא (*l'lo*) literally means "to no", but actually
expresses the notion of "without".

Example: ללא הכרח (*l'lo hekh-*RAKH) "without (to no) necessity."

בחורף אנו לובשים בגדים חמים.

*Bah-*HOH-*reff* AH-*noo loh-v'*SHEEM *b'gah-*DEEM *hah-*MEEM.

In winter we put on warm clothes.

בקיץ אנו פותחים את החלונות והדלתות.

*Bah-*KAH-*yits* AH-*noo poh-t'*HEEM *ett hah-hah-loh-*NOHT
*veh-hah-d'lah-*TOHT.

In summer we open the windows and doors.

בחורף אנו יושבים על-יד האש.

*Bah-*HOH-*reff* AH-*noo yoh-sh'*VEEM *ahl-yahd hah-*EHSH.

In winter we sit by the fire.

בקיץ חם.	בחורף קר.
*Bah-*KAH-*yits hahm.*	*Bah-*HOH-*reff kahr.*
In summer it is warm.	In winter it is cold.

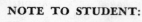

NOTE TO STUDENT:

There is no difference in Hebrew between "hot" and
"warm." Both notions are expressed by the same word
חם (*hahm*).

בישראל לא קר ביותר בחורף.

*B'Yis-rah-*EHL *lo kahr b'yoh-*TEHR *bah-*HOH-*reff.*

In Israel it is not very cold in winter.

בסביבת ים-המלח חם גם בחורף.
Bees-vee-VAHT yahm-hah-MEH-lakh hahm gahm bah-HOH-reff.
Around the Dead Sea it is warm also in winter.

גם בקרבת ים כנרת חם בחורף.
Gahm b'keer-VAHT yahm Kee-NEH-ret hahm bah-HOH-reff.
Near the Sea of Kineret it is also warm in winter.

שני הימים האלה נמצאים מתחת לפני הים.
*Sh'neh hah-yah-MEEM hah-EH-leh neem-tsah-EEM mee-TAH-haht
leef-NAY hah-YAHM.*
These two seas are below sea level.

הרוחות הקרות מן הים אינן מגיעות שמה.
*Hah-roo-HOHT hah-kah-ROHT meen ha-YAHM eh-NAHN
mah-gee-OHT SHAH-mah.*
The cold winds from the sea do not reach there.

בסביבת ים התיכון שורר אקלים ים-תיכוני.
Bees-vee-VAHT yahm hah-tee-HOHN soh-REHR ahk-LEEM yahm-tee-hoh-NEE.
In the vicinity of the Mediterranean Sea a mild climate prevails.

GEOGRAPHICAL NOTE:
To describe their climate, inhabitants of Israel usually
employ the adjective ים-תיכוני (*yahm-tee-hoh-NEE*)
meaning "Mediterranean" climate, which is very mild
and peculiar to that area from time immemorial.

החם באוגוסט?   כן, באוגוסט חם מאד.
Hah-HAHM beh-Oh-GOOST?   *Kehn, beh-Oh-GOOST hahm meh-OHD.*
Is it warm in August?   Yes, in August it is very warm.

החם במרכז אפריקה?
Hah-HAHM b'mer-KAHZ AHF-ree-kah?
Is it warm in the center of Africa?

כן, שם תמיד חם מאד.
Kehn, shahm tah-MEED hahm meh-OHD.
Yes, it is always very hot there.

הקר בקוטב הצפוני?
Hah-KAHR bah-KOH-tevv hah-ts'foh-NEE?
Is it cold at the North Pole?

כֵּן, שָׁם קַר מְאֹד.
Kehn, shahm kahr meh-OHD.
Yes, it is very cold there.

שָׁם אַף פַּעַם לֹא חַם.
Shahm aff PAH-ahm lo hahm.
It is never warm there.

כַּאֲשֶׁר אָנוּ לוֹבְשִׁים בְּגָדִים חַמִּים, חַם לָנוּ.
Kah-ah-SHERR AH-noo loh-v'SHEEM b'gah-DEEM hah-MEEM, hahm LAH-noo.
When we wear warm clothes, we are warm.

כְּשֶׁאָנוּ יוֹצְאִים הַחוּצָה בַּחוֹרֶף בְּלִי מְעִיל, קַר לָנוּ.
Ksheh-AH-noo yoh-tseh-EEM hah-HOO-tsah bah-HOH-reff b'lee meh-EEL, kahr LAH-noo.
When we go out without a coat in winter, we are cold.

הַקַר לָנוּ בַּחוֹרֶף כְּשֶׁהַחַלּוֹן פָּתוּחַ?
Hah-KAHR LAH-noo bah-HOH-reff k'sheh-hah-hah-LOHN pah-TOO-akh?
Are we cold when the window is open in winter?

בַּבַּיִת חַם.
Bah-BAH-yit hahm.
In the house it is warm.

בַּחוּץ קַר.
Bah-HOOTS kahr.
Outside it is cold.

גַּע בַּמְּקָרֵר; הֲקַר הוּא אוֹ חַם?
Gah bah-m'kah-REHR; hah-kahr hoo oh hahm?
Touch the refrigerator; is it cold or hot?

הוּא קַר.
Hoo kahr.
It is cold.

הֲחַם לְךָ עַכְשָׁו אוֹ קַר?
Hah-HAHM l'hah akh-SHAHV oh kahr?
Are you hot or cold now?

לֹא קַר לִי, אַף לֹא חַם; נוֹחַ לִי.
Lo kahr lee, aff lo hahm; NOH-akh lee.
I am neither cold nor hot; I am comfortable.

בְּנִיוּ יוֹרְק קַר בַּחוֹרֶף וְחַם בַּקַּיִץ.
Bee-New York kahr b'HOH-reff v'hahm b'KAH-yits.
In New York it is cold in winter and it is warm in summer.

בִּירוּשָׁלַיִם, לִפְעָמִים קַר בַּחוֹרֶף, וְלִפְעָמִים חַם.
Bee-Yeh-roo-shah-LAH-yim leef-ah-MEEM kahr bah-HOH-reff, v'leef-ah-MEEM hahm.
In Jerusalem it is sometimes cold in winter, and it is sometimes warm.

בַּגָּלִיל, לִפְעָמִים יוֹרֵד שֶׁלֶג בַּחוֹרֶף. אֲבָל אַף פַּעַם לֹא בַּקַּיִץ.
Bah-gah-LEEL leef-ah-MEEM yoh-REHD SHEH-leg bah-HOH-reff, ah-VAHL aff PAH-ahm lo bah-KAH-yits.
In Galilee it sometimes snows in winter, but never in summer.

היורד לפעמים שלג גם במרם באמריקה?

*Hah-yoh-*REHD *leef-ah-*MEEM SHEH-*leg gahm b'Mahrs beh-Ah-*MEH-*ree-kah?*

Does it sometimes snow in March in America?

כן, לפעמים יורד שלג במרם.

*Kehn, leef-ah-*MEEM *yoh-*REHD SHEH-*leg b'Mahrs.*

Yes, it sometimes snows in March.

היורד לפעמים שלג באוגוסט?

*Hah-yoh-*REHD *leef-ah-*MEEM SHEH-*leg beh-Oh-*GOOST?

Does it sometimes snow in August?

לא, באוגוסט אף פעם אין שלג.

*Lo, beh-Oh-*GOOST *aff* PAH-*ahm ehn* SHEH-*leg.*

No, in August it never snows.

בלונדון יורדים גשמים תכופות.

*B'*LOHN-*dohn yoh-r'*DEEM *g'shah-*MEEM *t'hoo-*FOHT.

In London it often rains.

בנגב הגשמים נדירים.

*Bah-*NEH-*gevv hah-g'shah-*MEEM *n'dee-*REEM.

In the Negev it rarely rains.

THE DRY LAND:

נֶגֶב Negev, where important irrigational develop-
ments are now taking place, was formerly practically
a desert. In fact the literal meaning of Negev is "dry."
Other interesting and useful derivations of this word are נֶגֶב
(*nah-*GEHV) — "to dry" and מגבת (*mah-*GEH-*vet*) — "towel."

מזג האויר בחורף שם נפלא.

MEH-*zeg hah-ah-*VEER *bah-*HOH-*reff shahm neef-*LAH.

It is wonderful weather there in winter.

בישראל יורדים גשמים רק בחורף.

*B'Yis-rah-*EHL *yoh-r'*DEEM *g'shah-*MEEM *rahk bah-*HOH-*reff.*

In Israel it rains only in the winter.

בקיץ משקים את השדות השקאה מלאכותית.

*Bah-*KAH-*yits mash-*KEEM *ett hah-sah-*DOHT *hahsh-kah-*AH *m'lah-hoo-*TEET.

In summer, the fields are watered by irrigation.

THINKING IN HEBREW
(Answers on page 290)

1.   מה מראה השמים במזג אויר רע?
Mah mahr-EH hah-shah-MAH-yim b'MEH-zeg ah-VEER rah?

2.   במה מכוסים השמים?
Bah-MEH m'hoo-SEEM hah-shah-MAH-yim?

3.   היורדים גשמים עתה?
Hah-yoh-r'DEEM g'shah-MEEM ah-TAH?

4.   האוהב אתה לטיל ברחובות בגשם?
Hah-oh-HEHV ah-TAH l'tah-YEHL bahr-hoh-VOHT bah-GEH-shemm?

5.   מה אתה לוקח אתך בגשם?
Mah ah-TAH loh-KAY-akh eet-HAH bah-GEH-shemm?

6. מה מזג האויר היום?   *Mah MEH-zeg hah-ah-VEER hah-YOHM?*

7.   היוצא אתה לרחוב במזג אויר רע?
Hah-yoh-TSEH ah-TAH lahr-HOHV b'MEH-zeg ah-VEER rah?

8.   הקר בקוטב הצפוני?
Hah-KAHR b'KOH-tevv hah-t'sfoh-NEE?

9.   באיזה חודש יורד שלג?
Beh-EH-zeh HOH-desh yoh-REHD SHEH-leg?

10.   ? היורד תמיד שלג בפברואר

*Hah-yoh-*REHD *tah-*MEED SHEH-*leg b'*FEB-*roo-ahr?*

11.   ? היורד תמיד שלג באפריל

*Hah-yoh-*REHD *tah-*MEED SHEH-*leg beh-Ahp-*REEL?

12. ? מאין באים הגשמים   *Meh-*AH-*yin bah-*EEM *hah-g'shah-*MEEM?

13.   ? הנעים ללכת בחוץ בגשם

*Hah-nah-*EEM *lah-*LEH-*het bah-*HOOTS *bah-*GEH-*shemm?*

14.   ? באילו חדשים אנו לובשים בגדים חמים

*Beh-*EH-*loo hoh-dah-*SHEEM AH-*noo loh-v'*SHEEM *b'gah-*DEEM *hah-*MEEM?

15.   ? מהו מזג האויר בישראל בדרך כלל

MAH-*hoo* MEH-*zeg hah-ah-*VEER *b'Yis-rah-*EHL *b'*DEH-*rekh k'lahl?*

16.   ? איפה אתה יושב כדי להתחמם

*Eh-*FOH *ah-*TAH *yoh-*SHEHV *k'deh leh-heet-hah-*MEHM?

17 ? מתי זורחת השמש   *Mah-*TIGH *zoh-*RAH-*haht hah-*SHEH-*mesh?*

שִׁעוּר 24

קצת היסטוריה
K'tsaht hees-TOHR-yah
A little history

יוסף: בּוֹקֶר טוֹב יְהוּדָה.
Yoh-SEHF: *BOH-ker tohv, Yeh-hoo*-DAH.
Joseph: Good morning, Yehuda.

מַה שְׁלוֹמְךָ ?
Mah sh'lohm-HAH?
How are you?

יהודה: טוֹב מְאֹד, תּוֹדָה.
Yeh-hoo-DAH: *Tohv meh*-OHD, *toh*-DAH.
Yehuda: Very well, thank you.

וְאַתָּה ?
Veh-ah-TAH?
And you?

יוסף: עָיֵף אֲנִי. הַלַּיְלָה הָלַכְתִּי מְאוּחָר לִישׁוֹן.
Ah-YEHF *ah*-NEE. *Hah*-LIGH-*lah hah*-LAKH-*tee meh-oo*-HAHR *lee*-SHOHN.
Joseph: I am tired. I went to bed late last night.

PAST TENSE OF HEBREW VERBS:

THE FIRST GROUP:
In Hebrew there is only one past tense, which is formed by the addition of the following suffixes to the consonant stem of the verb:

SINGULAR

Masculine			Feminine		
(I)	תִּי	(tee)	(I)	Same as masculine	
(you)	תָּ	(tah)	(you)	תְּ	(t)
(he)	—	(....)	(she)	הָ	(ah)

PLURAL

Masculine			Feminine		
(we)	נוּ	(noo)	(we)	Same as masculine	
(you)	תֶּם	(temm)	(you)	תֶּן	(tenn)
(they)	וּ	(oo)	(they)	Same as masculine	

As a rule, in verbs of the first group the invariable part of the verb is, at the same time, patterned on the sequence of vowel sounds ־ ֳ (ah-AH) with stress on the second syllable, regardless of what vowels are found in the present tense or the stem. Example:

	Masculine			Feminine	
I wrote	כתבתי	(kah-TAHV-tee)		Same as masculine	
You wrote	כתבת	(kah-TAHV-tah)			
He wrote	כתב	(kah-TAHV)	She wrote	כתבה	(kah-t'VAH)
We wrote	כתבנו	(kah-TAHV-noo)		Same as masculine	
You wrote (plur.)					
	כתבתם	(k'tahv-TEMM)		כתבתן	(k'tahv-TENN)
They wrote	כתבו	(kah-t'VOO)		Same as masculine	

MORE ABOUT THE PAST:

There are, however, several groups of verbs, in which other sequences of vowel sounds occur in the past tense. So, for example, verbs ending in ה (h) form the past tense with the vowels ־ . (ah-ee), and we say שתיתי (shah-TEE-tee) — "I drank" (from שתה (shah-TOH) — "to drink"). We shall analyze such verbs as they occur in the following lessons.

The one-syllable verbs add the same suffixes to their basic syllable in the past tense. Moreover, the vowel of that single syllable becomes — (ah) in the past tense.

Example: רוץ (roots) "to run". רצתי (RAHTS-tee) "I ran".

REMEMBER that the interrogative form of a Hebrew verb remains the same in the past, and in any other tense, as we saw it in the present tense, and is always formed with the prefixes הַ (hah) or הֲ (heh).

יהודה : אַף אֲנִי הָלַכְתִּי מְאוּחָר לִישׁוֹן. הָיִיתִי
*Aff ah-*NEE *hah-*LAHKH*-tee meh-oo-*HAHR *lee-*SHOHN. *Hah-*YEE*-tee*
Yehuda: I also went to bed late. I was

אֶמֶשׁ בְּהַרְצָאָה. הֲהֲכִינוֹת אֶת שִׁעוּרְךָ?
*eh-*MEHSH *beh-hahr-tsah-*AH. *Hah-hah-hee-*NOH*-tah* ett *shee-oor-*HAH?
at a lecture last night. Did you prepare your lesson?

PAST TENSE OF THE VERB "TO BE":

You have seen that the verb "to be" is not used in the
present tense, but only implied. However, it is used
in the past tense, in the future, and sometimes as an
auxiliary verb in the conditional. You will observe
these forms as they occur in the following lessons.
In the preceding sentence, you find the past tense form "I was".
The complete conjugation of "to be" in the past tense is shown
in the following table:

	Masculine			*Feminine*	
I was	הָיִיתִי	*hah-*YEE*-tee*		Same as masculine	
You were	הָיִיתָ	*hah-*YEE*-tah*			
He was	הָיָה	*hah-*YAH			
				She was	הָיְתָה *hah-y'*TAH
We were	הָיִינוּ	*hah-*YEE*-noo*		Same as masculine	
You were (plur.)					
	הֱיִיתֶם	*heh-yee-*TEMM		הֱיִיתֶן *heh-yee-*TENN
They were	הָיוּ	*hah-*YOO		Same as masculine	

יוֹסֵף : לֹא הָיָה לִי פְּנַאי לִלְמֹד. בִּקַּרְתִּי בְּבֵיתוֹ שֶׁל דָּוִד, וּמִשָּׁם
הָלַכְנוּ בְּיַחַד לַתֵּיאַטְרוֹן.
*Lo hah-*YAH *lee p'nigh leel-*MOHD. *Bee-*KAHR*-tee b'veh-*TOH *shell*
*Dah-*VEED, *oo-mee-*SHAHM *hah-*LAKH*-noo b'*YAH*-hahd l'teh-aht-*ROHN.
Joseph: I did not have leisure to study. I went to David's house,
and from there we went to a theater together.

HOW TO SAY "I HAD":

As you have already seen, there is no word really meaning "to have", so we must say "to me is" יֵשׁ לִי (YEHSH*-
lee*). Even in this case we are not saying "to me is"
but simply "to me". "To be" has no present tense in
Hebrew. There does exist a past tense, however, of
the verb "to be". Therefore, to express the idea of "I had", etc., we
say "to me was" — הָיָה לִי (*hah-*YAH *lee*) or "to me were" הָיוּ לִי
(*hah-*YOO *lee*).

Therefore we say, "There was to me a book", meaning "I had a book": היה לי ספר (hah-YAH lee SEH-fer). "I had books" will be, accordingly, היו לי ספרים (hah-YOO lee s'fah-REEM). Of course, the verb will change in this case, too, according to gender. So, we shall have to say: היתה לי תמונה (high-TAH lee t'moo-NAH): "I had a picture", and היו לי תמונות (hah-YOO lee t'moo-NOHT): "I had pictures".

In the sentence לא היה לי פנאי (Lo hah-YAH lee p'nigh) observe the negative use of the same construction, which automatically becomes negative if preceded by the word לא (lo).

A USEFUL CONTRACTION:

Observe the contraction משם (mee-SHAHM), which means "from there". Two words, מן (meen) "from" and שם (shahm) "there" are contracted into a single word in Hebrew.

יהודה: הראית הצגה טובה?
Hah-rah-EE-tah hah-tsah-GAH toh-VAH?
Yehuda: Did you see a good show?

יוסף: ראינו הצגה חדשה עם חנה רובינה בתפקיד ראשי.
Rah-EE-noo hah-tsah-GAH hah-dah-SHAH im Hah-NAH Roh-VEE-nah b'tahf-KEED roh-SHEE.
Joseph: We saw a new show with Hanna Rovina in the main role.

בלינו יפה. רובינה שחקה נפלא.
Bee-LEE-noo yah-FEH. Roh-VEE-nah see-hah-KAH neef-LAH.
We had a good time. Rovina performed wonderfully.

PAST TENSE OF THE SECOND GROUP OF VERBS:

To indicate the passing of time, the Hebrew language currently uses the verb בלה (bah-LEH), which means "to spend time." In the preceding sentence, you encounter the past tense of that verb, which is one of the second group described on page 68. Observe the following table, showing the conjugation, in the past tense, of a typical verb of that group, such as דבר (dah-BEHR) "to speak".

	Masculine		Feminine	
(I)	דברתי	(dee-BAHR-tee)	Same as masculine	
(you)	דברת	(dee-BAHR-tah)	דברת	(dee-BAHRT)
(he)	דבר	(dee-BEHR)	דברה	(dee-b'RAH)
(we)	דברנו	(dee-BAHR-noo)	Same as masculine	
(you) plur.	דברתם	(dee-bahr-TEMM)	דברתן	(dee-bahr-TENN)
(they)	דברו	(dee-b'ROO)	Same as masculine	

The reason the verb בלה (bah-LEH), which appears in the past tense
in the foregoing sentence, does not exactly follow the above pattern
is that it has a ה (h) at the end of its stem. You have already seen
that a verb in this category acquires the vowel sound יִ (ee) in its
last basic syllable in the past tense. You saw this happen in the case
of the first group verb שתיתי (shah-TEE-tee).

יהודה: מה עשיתם אחרי כן?

*Mah ah-see-*TEMM *akh-*RAY *hehn?*

Yehuda: What did you do afterwards?

יוסף: אחרי ההצגה הלכנו למסבה לבית יהודית.

*Akh-*RAY *hah-hah-tsah-*GAH *hah-*LAKH-*noo leem-see-*BAH
*l'veht Yeh-hoo-*DEET.

Joseph: After the show we went to a party at Judith's house.

יהודה: מי עוד ממכרי היה שם?

*Mee ohd mee-mah-kah-*RIGH *hah-*YAH *shahm?*

Yehuda: Who else of my acquaintances was there?

יוסף: נילי, רבקה, עוזי וגדעון, ועוד ידידים רבים,

NEE-*lee, reev-*KAH, OO-*zee v'Gee-deh-*OHN, *veh-*OHD *y'dee-*DEEM *rah-*BEEM,

Joseph: Nili, Rebecca, Uzi and Gideon, and many other friends,

כולם מבית-הספר.

*koo-*LAHM *mee-*BEHT-*hah-*SEH-*fer.

all of them from the school.

בראשונה הקשבנו לתכנית של שאלות ותשובות ברדיו.

*Bah-ree-shoh-*NAH *heek-*SHAHV-*noo l'tohkh-*NEET *shell sheh-eh-*LOHT
*oo-t'shoo-*VOHT *bah-*RAHD-*yoh.

First we listened to a question-and-answer program on the radio.

אחרי כן שמענו תקליטים חדשים.

*Akh-*RAY *hehn shah-*MAH-*noo tahk-lee-*TEEM *hah-dah-*SHEEM.

Then we listened to some new records.

רקדנו עד חצות. אחרי כן הכינה יהודית ארוחת-ערב,
שאכלנו אותה בתיאבון רב.

*Rah-*KAHD-*noo ahd hah-*TSOHT. *Akh-*RAY *hehn heh-*HEE-*nah Yeh-hoo-*DEET
*ah-roo-*HAHT-*EH-*rev, sheh-ah-*HAHL-*noo oh-*TAH b'teh-ah-*VOHN *rahv.

We danced until midnight. Then Judith prepared supper, which
we ate with a great appetite.

יהודה: אני מתאר לעצמי...

*Ah-*NEE *m'tah-*EHR *leh-ahts-*MEE...

Yehuda: I can imagine...

הנה המורה! בוקר טוב, אדוני!

*Hee-*NEH *hah-moh-*REH! BOH-*ker tohv, ah-doh-*NEE!

Here is the teacher! Good morning, sir!

(בכתה.)

(*Bah-kee-*TAH.)

(In the class.)

בוקר טוב לכם רבותי!

BOH-*ker tohv lah-*HEMM *rah-boh-*TIGH!

Good morning, gentlemen!

המורה: היום יש לנו סקירה על כמה תאריכים היסטוריים.

*Hah-moh-*REH: *Hah-*YOHM *yehsh* LAH-*noo s'kee-*RAH *ahl* KAH-*mah tah-ah-ree-*HEEM *hees-*TOH-*ree-yim.

The Professor: Today we have a review of some historical dates.

יהודה, מתי התחילה רשמית תנועת „חבת-ציון"?

*Yeh-hoo-*DAH, *mah-*TIGH *heet-*HEE-*lah reesh-*MEET *t'noo-*AHT "*Hee-*BAHT-*Tsee-*YOHN?"

Yehuda, when did the "Hebat-Zion" movement officially begin?

PAST TENSE OF THE THIRD GROUP OF VERBS: These verbs have, as you know, ה (*h*) at the beginning of their stems. This *h*, substituted for by מ (*m'*) in the present tense, reappears in the past tense, and the basic syllables normally follow, in the past tense, the sequence of vowel sounds ◌ַ◌ִ (AH-*ee*) for all persons, except the third person singular, masculine and feminine, which is formed on the pattern of vowel sounds ◌ִי (*ee-*EE). The characteristic suffixes of the past tense are the same for all groups of verbs. Observe the following table showing the conjugation of a typical verb of this group הקשב (*hahk-*SHEHV), which means "to listen", in the past tense:

SINGULAR

Masculine		Feminine	
I listened	הקשבתי (*heek-*SHAHV-*tee*)	Same as masculine	
You listened	הקשבת (*heek-*SHAHV-*tah*)	הקשבת (*heek-*SHAHVT)	
He listened	הקשיב (*heek-*SHEEV)	she listened	הקשיבה (*heek-*SHEE-*vah*)

PLURAL

Masculine		*Feminine*
We listened (הקשבנו	*heek-*SHAHV*-noo*)	Same as masculine
You listened הקשבתם	(*heek-shahv-*TEMM)	(*heek-shahv-*TENN) הקשבתן
They listened הקשיבו	(*heek-*SHEE*-voo*)	Same as masculine

יהודה: ד"ר הרצל פתח את הקונגרס הראשון בבזל בשנת 1897.
*Dr. Herzl pah-*TAKH *ett hah-kohn-*GRESS *hah-ree-*SHOHN
*b'Basel beesh-*NAHT 1897.
Yehuda: Dr. Herzl opened the first Zionist Congress in Basel in 1897.

המורה: לא שאלתי אותך כלל על-אודות ד"ר הרצל.
*Hah-moh-*REH: *Lo shah-*AHL*-tee oht-*HAH *k'lahl ahl oh-*DOHT *Dr. Herzl.*
The Professor: I didn't ask you anything about Dr. Herzl.

TWO WORDS, SAME MEANING:

In the above sentence, observe the words על-אודות
(*ahl oh-*DOHT) which mean "about". We can use this
combination or merely the word על (*ahl*) to say
"about" in Hebrew.

ענה על שאלתי.   יהודה: (שקט)
*Ah-*NEH *ahl sheh-eh-lah-*TEE.   (SHEH*-kett*)
Answer my question.   Yehuda: (Silence)

המורה: יוסף, ואתה יודע?
*Yoh-*SEHF, *veh-ah-*TAH *yoh-*DEH*-ah?*
Professor: Joseph, do you know?

יוסף: תנועת „חבת-ציון" התחילה רשמית
*T'noo-*AHT *"Hee-*BAHT*-Tsee-*YOHN*" heet-*HEE*-lah reesh-*MEET
Joseph: The "Hebat-Zion" movement officially began

עם ועידת קטוביץ בשנת 1885, שתים-עשרה
*im veh-ee-*DAHT KAH*-toh-veets beesh-*NAHT 1885, *sh'tehm-ess-*REH
with the Katovitz Convention in 1885, twelve

שנה לפני הקונגרם הציוני הראשון (1897).
*shah-*NAH *leef-*NEH *hah-kohn-*GRESS *hah-tsee-yoh-*NEE *hah-ree-*SHOHN (1897).
years before the first Zionist Congress (1897).

המורה: נכון. עכשו יהודה, ספר לי משהו על ד"ר הרצל.
*Nah-*HOHN. *Akh-*SHAHV *Yeh-hoo-*DAH, *sah-*PEHR *lee*
*mah-sheh-*HOO *ahl Dr. Herzl.*
Professor: Right. Now, Yehuda, tell me something about Dr. Herzl.

יהודה: ד"ר הרצל היה המנהיג הציוני הגדול.
Dr. Herzl hah-YAH hah-mahn-HEEG hah-tsee-yoh-NEE hah-gah-DOHL.
Yehuda: Dr. Herzl was the great Zionist leader.

הוא הביא לראשונה את השאלה
Hoo heh-VEE lah-ree-shoh-NAH ett hah-sheh-eh-LAH
He first brought the Zionist problem

הציונית לפני העולם כולו כשאלה עולמית.
hah-tsee-yoh-NEET leef-NEH hah-oh-LAHM koo-LOH keesh-eh-LAH
oh-lah-MEET.
before the world forum as a world problem.

הוא נולד באונגריה.
Hoo noh-LAHD beh-Oon-GAHR-yah.
He was born in Hungary.

המורה: האינך יודע מתי נולד ומתי מת?
Hah-ehn-HAH yoh-DEH-ah mah-TIGH noh-LAHD oo-mah-TIGH meht?
Professor: Don't you know when he was born and when he died?

PAST TENSE OF THE PASSIVE VERB GROUPS:
Observe the past tense of the passive verb "to be born"
in the foregoing sentence. Normally, the past tense of
all passive verbs is formed by the addition of the same
standard suffixes, that characterize the past tense in
general, to the present tense form of the passive verb.
So, נסגר (*nees-GAHR*): "is closed" becomes נסגרתי
(*nees-GAHR-tee*): "was closed", etc.

REMEMBER that the second group verbs, which have a prefix (*m'*)
in the present tense (passive), lose it in the past tense. Example:
מדובר (*m'doo-BAHR*) "spoken of" becomes דוברתי (*doo-BAHR-tee*)
"was spoken of"; etc.

The third group verbs (passive) receive not only the regular suffixes,
but also the prefix ה (*h*) instead of the initial מ (*m*), which they
had in the present tense. So, מוכתב (*mokh-TAHV*) "dictated to", becomes הוכתבתי (*hokh-TAHV-tee*) "was dictated to", etc., in the past
tense.

יהודה: לא אדוני, איני יודע בדיוק את השנה.
Lo ah-doh-NEE, eh-NEE yoh-DEH-ah b'dee-YOOK ett hah-shah-NAH.
Yehuda: No, sir, I do not exactly know the year.

המורה: יוסף, ואתה יודע?

Yoh-SEHF, veh-ah-TAH yoh-DEH-ah?

Professor: Joseph, do you know?

יוסף: ד"ר הרצל נולד באונגריה בשנת 1860.

Dr. Herzl noh-LAHD beh-Oon-GAHR-yah beesh-NAHT 1860.

Joseph: Dr. Herzl was born in Hungary in the year 1860.

הוא מת בוינה בשנת 1904 ממחלת לב.

Hoo meht b'VEE-nah beesh-NAHT 1904 mee-makh-LAHT lehv.

He died in Vienna in the year 1904 of a heart disease.

המורה: טוב, רואה אני שאחדים למדו את השעור אמש.

Tohv, roh-EH ah-NEE sheh-ah-hah-DEEM lah-m'DOO
ett hah-she-OOR EH-mesh.

Professor: Well, I see some (students) studied the lesson last night.

יהודה: איך ידעת לענות על השאלות?

Ehkh yah-DAH-tah lah-ah-NOHT ahl hah-sheh-eh-LOHT?

Yehuda: How did you know (to answer) the questions?

יוסף: הלא אמרתי לך שהקשבנו בבית יהודית שעה
קלה לתכנית של שאלות ותשובות ברדיו.

Hah-LOH ah-MAHR-tee l'hah sheh-heek-SHAHV-noo b'veht
Yeh-hoo-DEET shah-AH kah-LAH l'tokh-NEET shell sheh-eh-LOHT
oo-t'shoo-VOHT bah-RAHD-yoh.

Joseph: Well, I told you that at Judith's house we listened to a
radio question-and-answer program for a while.

A USEFUL IDIOM:

In the above sentence, observe the idiom שעה קלה
(*shah-AH kah-LAH*) literally meaning "an easy hour"
but actually used to convey the meaning of the expression "for a short while".

יהודה: עכשו ברור לי. מעתה אלך גם אני לשמע לתוכנית
זו, כדי ללמד משהו ממנה.

Ahk-SHAHV bah-ROOR lee. Meh-ah-TAH eh-LEHKH gahm ah-NEE leesh-
MOH-ah l'tokh-NEET zoh, k'deh leel-MOHD mah-sheh-HOO mee-MEN-nah.

Yehuda: Now it is clear to me. From now on I am also going to listen
to this program, in order to learn something from it.

THINKING IN HEBREW
(Answers on page 291)

1. מתי התחילה תנועת „חבת־ציון" רשמית ?

Mah-TIGH heet-HEE-lah t'noo-AHT "Hee-BAHT-Tsee-YOHN" reesh-MEET?

2. מי זה היה ד"ר הרצל ?   3. ועידת קטוביץ מהי ?

Mee zeh hah-YAH Dr. Herzl?   Veh-ee-DAHT KAH-toh-veets MAH-hee?

4. ההכין יהודה את שעורו בהיסטוריה ?

Hah-heh-HEEN Yeh-hoo-DAH ett shee-oo-ROH beh-hees-TOHR-yah?

5. לאן הלך יוסף אחרי ההצגה ?

Leh-AHN hah-LAKH Yoh-SEHF akh-RAY hah-hah-tsah-GAH?

6. את מי פגש במסבה ?

Ett mee pah-GAHSH bah-m'see-BAH?

7.   איזו שאלה שאל המורה את יהודה ?
EH-zoh sheh-eh-LAH shah-AHL hah-moh-REH ett Yeh-hoo-DAH?

8.   הידע יהודה את התשובה הנכונה ?
Hah-yah-DAH Yeh-hoo-DAH ett hah-t'shoo-VAH hah-n'hoh-NAH?

9.   באיזו שעה אתה קם בבוקר ?
Beh-EH-zoh shah-AH ah-TAH kahm bah-BOH-ker?

10.   באיזו שעה התעוררת אתמול ?
Beh-EH-zoh shah-AH heet-oh-RAHR-tah ett-MOHL?

11.   מתי קמת ?   Mah-TIGH KAHM-tah?

12.   מה עשית לפני ארוחת הבוקר ?
Meh ah-SEE-tah leef-NEH ah-roo-HAHT hah-BOH-ker?

13.   איזו חליפה לבשת ?   EH-zoh hah-lee-FAH lah-VAHSH-tah?

14.   ההתרחצת במים קרים ?
Hah-heet-rah-HAHTS-tah b'MAH-yim kah-REEM?

15.   המהרת להתלבש ?
Hah-mee-HAHR-tah leh-heet-lah-BEHSH?

16.   האכלת מוקדם ארוחת-בוקר ?
Heh-ah-HAHL-tah mook-DAHM ah-roo-HAHT-BOH-ker?

17.   השמת חלב לתוך הקפה ?
Hah-SAHM-tah hah-LAHV l'tohkh hah-kah-FEH?

18.   הקבלת אילו מכתבים בשבוע האחרון ?
Hah-kee-BAHL-tah EH-loo meekh-tah-VEEM bah-shah-VOO-ah
hah-ah-hah-ROHN?

19.   הענית עליהם ?   Heh-ah-NEE-tah ah-leh-HEMM?

20.   הטילת אתמול ?   Hah-tee-YAHL-tah ett-MOHL?

21.   לאן הלכת ?   Leh-AHN hah-LAKH-tah?

22.   השמעת הרבה קונצרטים בחורף האחרון ?
Hah-shah-MAH-tah hahr-BEH kohn-TSERR-teem bah-HOH-reff
hah-ah-hah-ROHN?

23.   הצחקת הרבה בהצגת ?
Hah-tsah-HAHK-tah hahr-BEH bah-hah-tsah-GAH?

מה נעשה מחר?

*Mah nah-ah-*SEH *mah-*HAHR?

What shall we do tomorrow?

משה: בּוֹקר טוב, יצחק. יודע אתה שמחר יהיה חג.
*Moh-*SHEH: BOH-*ker tohv, Yits-*HAHK. *Yoh-*DEH-*ah ah-*TAH,
*sheh-mah-*HAHR *yee-*YEH *hahg.*
Moshe: Good morning, Isaac. You know that tomorrow
will be a holiday.

לא נלך לבית-הספר. מה נעשה בחופש?
*Lo neh-*LEHKH *l'veht-hah-*SEH-*fer. Mah nah-ah-*SEH *bah-*HOH-*fesh?*
We shall not go to school. What shall we do in our free time?

HOW TO FORM THE FUTURE OF VERBS:

The future is formed with the aid of prefixes (that
are either merged with or placed before the first syllable of the verb) and, for some persons, with the addition of standard suffixes. In these prefixes we usually
find the same consonant as in the personal pronoun
they are connected with, as in the following table:

179

SINGULAR

	Masculine			Feminine	
	Prefix		*Suffix*	*Prefix*	*Suffix*
I	(*ah*-NEE)	א *eh* (or *ah*)	——	same as masculine	
He	(*hoo*)	ת *tee*	——	ת *tee*	ִי *ee*
You	(*ah*-TAH)	י *yee*	—— She	ת *tee*	

PLURAL

	Masculine			Feminine	
We	(AH-*noo*)	נ *nee*	——	same as masculine	
You	(*ah*-TEMM)	ת *tee*	ו *oo*	ת *tee*	נה *nah*
They	(*hehm*)	י *yee*	ו *oo*	ת *tee*	נה *nah*

As you see, the construction is identical for the 2nd person singular masculine and the 3rd person singular feminine. The same applies to the 2nd and 3rd persons feminine plural.

Examples: *First group:* Verb כתב (kah-TOHV): "to write".

	Masculine		Feminine	
I	אכתב	(ekh-TOHV)	same as masculine	
You	תכתב	(teekh-TOHV)	תכתבי	(teekh-t'VEE)
He	יכתב	(yeekh-TOHV)	She: תכתב	(teekh-TOHV)
We	נכתב	(neekh-TOHV)	same as masculine	
You (plur.)	תכתבו	(teekh-t'VOO)	תכתבנה	(teekh-TOHV-nah)
They	יכתבו	(yeekh-t'VOO)	תכתבנה	(teekh-TOHV-nah)

You have noticed that, in this case, the prefixes are merged with (and not added to) the first syllable of the verb.

Second group: Verb דבר (dah-BEHR): "to speak". This group uses the same prefixes, but with a shortened vowel. The first person singular requires the prefix ־ (ah). Suffixes remain unchanged.

	Masculine		Feminine	
I	אדבר	(ah-dah-BEHR)	same as masculine	
You	תדבר	(t'dah-BEHR)	תדברי	(t'dah-b'REE)
He	ידבר	(y'dah-BEHR)	She: תדבר	(t'dah-BEHR)
We	נדבר	(n'dah-BEHR)	same as masculine	
You (plur.)	תדברו	(t'dah-b'ROO)	תדברנה	(t'dah-BEHR-nah)
They	ידברו	(y'dah-b'ROO)	תדברנה	(t'dah-BEHR-nah)

Third group: Verb הקשב (*hahk-*SHEHV): "to listen". The same prefixes and suffixes as in the 2nd group are here applied not to the stem, but to the present tense form of the verb, stripped of its initial מ (*m'*).

	Masculine		Feminine	
I	אקשיב (*ahk-*SHEEV)		same as masculine	
You	תקשיב (*tahk-*SHEEV)		תקשיבי (*tahk-*SHEEV-*vee*)	
He	יקשיב (*yahk-*SHEEV)	She:	תקשיב (*tahk-*SHEEV)	
We	נקשיב (*nahk-*SHEEV)		same as masculine	
You (plur.)	תקשיבו (*tahk-*SHEE-*voo*)		תקשבנה (*tahk-*SHEHV-*nah*)	
They	יקשיבו (*yahk-*SHEEV-*oo*)		תקשבנה (*tahk-*SHEHV-*nah*)	

יצחק : ננוח קצת. אקום מאוחר יותר,
Yits-HAHK: *Nah-*NOO-*akh k'tsaht. Ah-*KOOM *meh-oo-*HAHR *yoh-*TEHR,
Isaac: We shall rest a little. I shall get up later,

ואפגש אתך בשעה עשר, אם תרצה בכך.
*veh-eh-pah-*GEHSH *eet-*HAH *b'shah-ah* EH-*ser, im teer-*TSEH *b'hahkh.*
and shall meet you at ten o'clock, if you so wish.

FUTURE OF PASSIVE VERBS:

In the foregoing sentence, observe the future tense אפגש (*eh-pah-*GEHSH) of the verb הפגש (*hee-pah-*GEHSH) "to meet with", which is in the passive voice in Hebrew. The future of passive verbs takes the same prefixes and suffixes as the active verbs of the same group.

משה : אהיה מוכן בזמן זה.
*Eh-*YEH *moo-*HAHN *beez-*MAHN *zeh.*
Moshe: I shall be ready at that time.

מקוה אני שמזג האויר יהיה כמו היום.
*M'kah-*VEH *ah-*NEE *sheh-*MEH-*zeg hah-ah-*VEER *yee-*YEH *k'moh hah-*YOHM.
I hope the weather will be as it is today.

יצחק: שמעתי שמחר יהיה יום יפה.
*Shah-*MAH-*tee sheh-mah-*HAHR *yee-*YEH *yohm yah-*FEH.
Isaac: I heard that tomorrow will be a fine day.

הנלך לשפת הים?
*Hah-neh-*LEHKH *lees-*FAHT-*hah-*YAHM?
Shall we go to the beach?

משה: כֵּן, זֶה רַעְיוֹן טוֹב, וְדֶרֶךְ אַגַּב נִקְרָא גַם לִיהוּדִית וּמִרְיָם.

*Kehn, zeh rah-YOHN tohv, v'DEH-rekh ah-GAHV neek-RAH
gahm lee-Yeh-hoo-DEET oo-Meer-YAHM.*

Moshe: Yes, that is a good idea, and, by the way, we shall also
call for Judith and Miriam.

A USEFUL IDIOM:

Remember the expression דֶּרֶךְ אַגַּב (DEH-*rekh* ah-
GAHV) which is widely used with the meaning of "in-
cidentally", "by the way", etc.

בָּטוּחַ אֲנִי שֶׁהֵן תִּהְיֶינָה שְׂמֵחוֹת לָלֶכֶת עִמָּנוּ.

*Bah-TOO-akh ah-NEE sheh-HEHN teeh-YEH-nah s'meh-HOHT
lah-LEH-het ee-MAH-noo.*

I am sure they will be delighted to come with us.

יצחק: יָפֶה. אָנוּ נַגִּיעַ אֵפוֹא לִשְׂפַת-הַיָּם בִּשְׁתֵּים-עֶשְׂרֵה בְּעֵרֶךְ.

*Yah-FEH. AH-noo nah-GEE-ah eh-FOH lees-FAHT-hah-YAHM
beesh-TEHM-ess-REH beh-EH-rekh.*

Isaac: Fine. We shall thus arrive at the beach by twelve o'clock.

ATTENTION:

Do not confuse אֵפוֹא (eh-FOH) "so", "thus", with
אֵיפֹה (eh-FOH) "where". Observe the difference in
the Hebrew spelling.

זֶה יִתֵּן לָנוּ זְמַן לִשְׂחִיָּה לִפְנֵי אֲרוּחַת-צָהֳרַיִם.

*Zeh yee-TEHN LAH-noo z'mahn lees-hee-YAH leef-NEH
ah-roo-HAHT-tsoh-hoh-RAH-yim.*

That will give us time for a swim before lunch.

משה: הֲנִסְעַד אֲרוּחַת-הַצָּהֳרַיִם בְּמִסְעָדָה,

Hah-nees-AHD ah-roo-HAHT-hah-tsoh-hoh-RAH-yim b'mis-ah-DAH,

Moshe: Shall we eat lunch at the restaurant,

אוֹ נִקַּח אִתָּנוּ אֹכֶל ?

oh nee-KAHKH ee-TAH-noo OH-hell?

or shall we take food with us?

יצחק: חַס וְחָלִילָה! הַנְּעָרוֹת כְּמוּבָן תִּרְצֶינָה לִסְעֹד בְּמִסְעָדָה.

*Hahs v'hah-LEE-lah! Hah-neh-ah-ROHT k'moo-VAHN teer-TSEH-nah
lees-OHD b'mis-ah-DAH.*

Isaac: God forbid! The girls will certainly like to lunch in a restaurant.

A USEFUL IDIOM:

The expression חם וחלילה (*hahs v'hah*-LEE-lah) means "may it not happen" and is used in contingencies where one might say, in English, "God forbid".

התודיע על כך למרים, או שעלי לטלפן ליהודית?
Hah-toh-DEE-*ah ahl kahkh l'Meer*-YAHM, *oh sheh-ah*-LIGH
l'tahl-FEHN *lee-Yeh-hoo*-DEET?
Will you notify Miriam, or shall I call Judith?

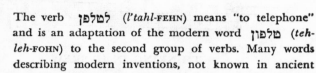

A NEW WORD:

The verb לטלפן (*l'tahl*-FEHN) means "to telephone" and is an adaptation of the modern word טלפון (*teh-leh*-FOHN) to the second group of verbs. Many words describing modern inventions, not known in ancient times, have been introduced into modern Hebrew with a slight change in pronunciation. Other modern words, where circumstances so permitted, have been formed from ancient roots. The creation of new words is decided upon by a special committee, located in Jerusalem, called the ועד-הלשון   "VAH-*ahd-hah-lah*-SHOHN".

משה: אני אטלפן אליהן בערב, כשהן תהיינה ודאי בבית.
Ah-NEE *ah-tahl*-FEHN *ah-lay*-HENN *bah-EH-rev, k'sheh*-HEHN *teeh*-YEH-*nah
vah-DIGH *bah*-BAH-*yit.*
Moshe: I will call them in the evening when they will surely
be at home.

יצחק: מתי תחזרנה הביתה מעבודתן?
Mah-TIGH *tahkh*-ZOHR-*nah hah*-BIGH-*tah meh-ah-voh-dah*-TAHN?
Isaac: When will they return home from their work?

משה: הן תהיינה בבית בשעה שבע.
Hehn teeh-YEH-*nah bah*-BAH-*yit b'shah*-AH SHEH-*vah.*
Moshe: They will be home at seven o'clock.

אני אבוא לקחת אותך בעשר בבוקר.
Ah-NEE *ah*-VOH *lah*-KAH-*haht oh-t'*HAH *beh*-EH-*ser bah*-BOH-*ker.*
I shall come to fetch you at ten o'clock in the morning.

יצחק: אני אחכה לך. שלום.
Ah-NEE *ah-hah*-KEH *l'hah.* Shah-LOHM.
Isaac: I'll be waiting for you. Goodbye.

THINKING IN HEBREW
(Answers on page 291)

1. ‎לאן ילך המורה הערב ?

*Leh-*AHN *yeh-*LEHKH *hah-moh-*REH *hah-*EH-*rev?*

2. ‎התהיה הגברת בילה בבית הלילה ?

*Hah-teeh-*YEH *hah-*G'VEH-*ret* BEH-*leh bah-*BAH-*yit hah-*LIGH-*lah?*

3. ‎מי יבוא לגברת בילה לארוחת-הצהרים ?

*Mee yah-*VOH *lah-*G'VEH-*ret* BEH-*leh lah-ah-roo-*HAHT-*hah-tsoh-
hoh-*RAH-*yim?*

4. ‎היקום המורה מאוחר מחר ?

*Hah-yah-*KOOM *hah-moh-*REH *meh-oo-*HAHR *mah-*HAHR?*

5. ‎מדוע לא ילך לבית-הספר ?

*Mah-*DOO-*ah lo yeh-*LEHKH *l'veht-hah-*SEH-*fer?*

6. ‎כמה ימים תעבד בשבוע הבא ?

KAH-*mah yah-*MEEM *tah-ah-*VOHD *b'shah-*VOO-*ah hah-*BAH?

7. ‎מה נעשה בשבת ?   *Mah nah-ah-*SEH *b'shah-*BAHT?

8. ‎לאן ילכו משה ויצחק מחר ?

*Leh-*AHN *yeh-l'*HOO *Moh-*SHEH *veh-Yits-*HAHK *mah-*HAHR?

9. ‎היזמינו את יהודית ומרים ?

*Hah-Yahz-*MEE-*noo ett Yeh-hoo-*DEET *oo-Meer-*YAHM?

10. ‏באיזו שעה יפגשו?‏ Beh-EH-zoh shah-AH yee-pah-g'SHOO?

11. ‏איפה יאכלו ארוחת-הצוהרים?‏
Eh-FOH yoh-h'LOO ah-roo-HAHT-hah-tsoh-hoh-RAH-yim?

12. ‏מי יטלפן לנערות?‏ Mee y'tahl-FEHN lah-neh-ah-ROHT?

13. ‏היקחו אתם אוכל?‏ Hah-yeek-HOO ee-TAHM OH-hell?

14. ‏התסע בקרוב לישראל?‏ Hah-tee-SAH b'kah-ROHV l'Yis-rah-EHL?

15. ‏איך תסע?‏ Ehkh tee-SAH?

16. ‏הנאכל יחד ארוחת-צוהרים בשבוע הבא?‏
Hah-noh-HAHL YAH-hahd ah-roo-HAHT-tsoh-hoh-RAH-yim
bah-shah-VOO-ah hah-BAH?

17. ‏באיזה יום, אתה רוצה, שאטלפן אליך?‏
Beh-EH-zeh yohm, ah-tah roh-TSEH, sheh-ah-tahl-FEHN eh-LEH-hah?

18. ‏האזמין את דוד ללכת אתנו?‏
Hah-ahz-MEEN ett Dah-VEED lah-LEH-het ee-TAH-noo?

19. ‏איפה נפגש?‏ Eh-FOH nee-pah-GEHSH?

שִׁעוּר 26

הַחַיּוֹת

*Hah-hah-*YOHT

Animals

הַסּוּס, הַפָּרָה, וְהַכֶּלֶב הֵם חַיּוֹת־בַּיִת.
*Hah-*SOOS, *hah-pah-*RAH *veh-hah-*KEH-*lev hehm hah-*YOHT-BAH-*yit.*
The horse, the cow, and the dog are domestic animals.

הִנֵּה אַרְיֵה, נָמֵר, פִּיל, זְאֵב.
*Hee-*NEH, *ahr-*YEH, *nah-*MEHR, *peel, zeh-*EHV.
Here are a lion, a tiger, an elephant, a wolf.

הֵם חַיּוֹת־שָׂדֶה.
*Hehm hah-*YOHT-*sah-*DEH.
They are wild animals.

186

AN ECHO FROM THE PAST:
The words חיות־שדה (*hah-*YOHT*-sah-*DEH) which we translate as "wild animals" actually mean "beasts of the field", as referred to in the Scriptures.

חיות־הבית עובדות בשביל האדם.
*Hah-*YOHT*-hah-*BAH*-yit oh-v'*DOHT *beesh-*VEEL *hah-ah-*DAHM.
The domestic animals work for man.

הכלב שומר את הבית.
*Hah-*KEH*-lev shoh-*MEHR *ett hah-*BAH*-yit.*
The dog watches the house.

החתול צד עכברים.
*Heh-hah-*TOOL *tsahd akh-bah-*REEM
The cat hunts mice.

הסוס מושך את העגלה.
*Hah-*SOOS *moh-*SHEHKH *ett hah-ah-gah-*LAH.
The horse pulls the wagon.

הפרה נותנת לנו חלב.
*Hah-pah-*RAH *noh-*TEH*-net* LAH*-noo hah-*LAHV.
The cow gives us milk.

אף הגמל חית־בית הוא, ונושא משאות.
*Aff hah-gah-*MAHL *hah-*YAHT*-*BAH*-yit hoo, v'noh-*SEH *mah-sah-*OHT.
The camel is also a domestic animal, and it carries loads.

הוא נקרא גם בשם ספינת־המדבר, ואנחנו יכולים לראות כיום גמלים רבים בנגב.
*Hoo neek-*RAH *gahm b'shehm "sfee-*NAHT*-hah-meed-*BAHR", *veh-ah-*NAHKH*-noo y'hoh-*LEEM *leer-*OHT *kah-*YOHM *g'mah-*LEEM *rah-*BEEM *bah-*NEH*-gev.*
It is also called the "ship-of-the-desert", and we can see many camels today in the Negev.

אבל חיות־השדה חיות ביער והן מסוכנות.
*Ah-*VAHL *hah-*YOHT*-hah-sah-*DEH *hah-*YOHT *bah-*YAH*-ahr veh-*HEHN *m'soo-kah-*NOHT.
But the wild animals live in the forest and are dangerous.

לסוס ארבע רגלים, ולנמר ארבע כפים.

Lah-soos ahr-BAH rahg-LAH-yim, v'lah-nah-MEHR ahr-BAH kah-PAH-yim.
The horse has four legs, and the tiger has four paws.

שניהם רצים, מהלכים ומקפצים.

Sh'neh-HEMM rah-TSEEM, meh-hah-l'HEEM oo-m'kah-p'TSEEM.
They both run, walk, and jump.

ATTENTION:

In Hebrew, there are several forms of the word "both" which are diversified according to the personal pronouns modified. So we say:

שנינו (sh'NEH-noo) "both of us".

שניכם (shneh-HEMM) "both of you" (masculine).

שתיכן (shteh-HENN) "both of you" (feminine).

שניהם (shneh-HEMM) "both of them" (masculine).

שתיהן (shteh-HENN) "both of them" (feminine).

הנשר, הנץ, היונה והתרנגול הם עופות.

Hah-NEH-sher, hah-NEHTS, hah-yoh-NAH, veh-hah-tahr-n'GOHL
hehm oh-FOHT.
The eagle, the hawk, the dove, and the rooster are birds.

לעופות שתי רגלים להלך בהן, ושתי כנפים לעוף בהן.

Lah-oh-FOHT sh'teh rahg-LAH-yim leh-hah-LEHKH bah-HENN, oo-sh'TEH
k'nah-FAH-yim lah-OOF bah-HENN.
Birds have two legs with which to walk, and two wings with which to fly.

החיות מהלכות ומקפצות על הארץ.

Hah-hah-YOHT meh-hah-l'HOHT oo-m'kah-p'TSOHT ahl hah-AH-rets.
Animals walk and jump on the ground.

העופות עפים באויר.

Hah-oh-FOHT ah-FEEM bah-ah-VEER.
Birds fly in the air.

ראשנו מכוסה שער.

Roh-SHEH-noo m'hoo-SEH seh-AHR.
Our head is covered with hair.

גוף החיות מכוסה פרוה.

Goof hah-hah-YOHT m'hoo-SEH pahr-VAH.
The body of the animals is covered with fur.

עור העופות מכוסה נוצות.

*Ohr hah-oh-*FOHT *m'hoo-*SEH *noh-*TSOHT.

The skin of the birds is covered with feathers.

דגים חיים במים.

*Dah-*GEEM *hah-*YIM *bah-*MAH*-yim.*

Fish live in the water.

אין להם לא רגלים אף לא כנפים.

*Ehn lah-*HEMM *lo rahg-*LAH*-yim aff lo k'nah-*FAH*-yim.*

They have neither legs nor wings.

יש להם סנפירים ונעים בשחיה.

*Yehsh lah-*HEMM *s'nah-pee-*REEM *v'nah-*EEM *bees-hee-*YAH.

They have fins and move by swimming.

עורם מכוסה קשקשים.

*Oh-*RAHM *m'hoo-*SEH *kahs-kah-*SEEM.

Their skin is covered with scales.

הכריש הוא הדג המסוכן ביותר.

*Hah-kah-*REESH *hoo hah-*DAHG *hah-m'soo-*KAHN *b'yoh-*TEHR.

The shark is the most dangerous fish.

את הכריש אפשר לפעמים לראות בחוף.

*Ett hah-kah-*REESH *eff-*SHAHR *leef-ah-*MEEM *leer-*OHT *bah-*HOFF.

A shark is sometimes seen off the coast.

כשאתה רואה כריש במקום שמתרחצים

*K'she-ah-*TAH *roh-*EH *kah-*REESH *bah-mah-*KOHM *sheh-meet-rah-hah-*TSEEM

If you see a shark in a place where there are people bathing,

אנשים, עליך להזהירים, ולצעק: „הזהרו מפני הכריש"!

*ah-nah-*SHEEM, *ah-*LEH*-hah leh-hahz-hee-*RAHM, *v'leets-*OHK:

"*hee-zah-hah-*ROO *meep-*NEH *hah-kah-*REESH!"

you must warn them, and cry: "Look out for the shark!"

IMPORTANT NOTE:

Here are some exclamations you must learn by heart because you won't have time to consult your dictionary if you need to use them!

הצילו !	(hah-TSEE-loo!)	Help!
עצר !	(ah-TSOHR!)	Stop!
גנב עצר !	(gah-NAHV ah-TSOHR!)	Stop thief!
הזהר !	(hee-zah-HEHR!)	Watch out!
משטרה !	(meesh-tah-RAH!)	Police!
רוץ !	(roots!)	Run!
לחיים !	(leh-hah-YIM!)	To your health!
אני אוהב אותך !	(ah-NEE oh-HEHV oh-TAKH!)	I love you!

GRAMMATICAL NOTE:

Take a deep breath; here is another verb group. This can be labeled the fourth group and includes reflexive verbs, such as "to wash oneself", "to dress oneself", etc. The verbs of this group have a three-syllable stem, patterned on the sequence of vowel sounds - - .
(ee-ah-eh), mingled with varying consonants. Observe the following table of conjugation of the verb התרחץ (heet-rah-HEHTs) "to wash oneself" or "to bathe", in the present, the past and the future tense.

PRESENT TENSE
SINGULAR

Masculine		Feminine	
I, you, he	מתרחץ	I, you, she	מתרחצת
	(meet-rah-HEHTs)		(meet-rah-HEH-tset)

PLURAL

We, you, they	מתרחצים	We, you, they	מתרחצות
	(meet-rah-hah-TSEEM)		(meet-rah-hah-TSOHT)

PAST TENSE

I	התרחצתי	same as masculine
	(heet-rah-HAHTs-tee)	
You	התרחצת	התרחצת
	(heet-rah-HAHTs-tah)	(heet-rah-HAHTST)
He	התרחץ	התרחצה
	(heet-rah-HEHTs)	(heet-rah-hah-TSAH)
We	התרחצנו	same as masculine
	(heet-rah-HAHTs-noo)	
You	התרחצתם	התרחצתן
	(heet-rah-hahts-TEMM)	(heet-rah-hahts-TENN)
They	התרחצו	same as masculine
	(heet-rah-hah-TSOO)	

FUTURE TENSE

	Masculine	Feminine
I	אתרחץ (*el-rah-*HEHTS)	same as masculine
You	תתרחץ (*teet-rah-*HEHTS)	תתרחצי (*teet-rah-hah-*TSEE)
He	יתרחץ (*yeet-rah-*HEHTS)	תתרחץ (*teet-rah-*HEHTS)
We	נתרחץ (*neet-rah-*HEHTS)	same as masculine
You	תתרחצו (*teet-rah-hah-*TSOO)	תתרחצנה (*teet-rah-*HEHTS-*nah*)
They	יתרחצו (*yeet-rah-hah-*TSOO)	תתרחצנה (*teet-rah-*HEHTS-*nah*)

הנחש שיך לזוחלים, ואין לו רגלים.

*Hah-nah-*HAHSH *shah-*YAHKH *l'zoh-hah-*LEEM, *veh-*EHN *lo rahg-*LAH-*yim.*

The snake belongs to the reptiles and has no legs.

הוא זוחל על הארץ.

*Hoo zoh-*HEHL *ahl hah-*AH-*rets.*

It crawls on the ground.

הצפרדע היא אמפיבית. היא יכולה לחיות בּמים וביבּשה.

*Hah-ts'fahr-*DEH-*ah hee ahm-*FEE-*beet. Hee y'hoh-*LAH *leekh-*YOHT *b'*MAH-*yim oo-v'yah-bah-*SHAH.

The frog is an amphibian. It can live in water and on the ground.

בּין הרמשים ישנם פרפרים, זבובים ויתושים.

*Behn hah-r'mah-*SEEM *yesh-*NAHM *pahr-pah-*REEM, *z'voo-*VEEM.
*v'yah-too-*SHEEM.

Among the insects, there are butterflies, flies, and mosquitoes.

הדבורה המיצרת דבש, ותולעת-המשי,

*Hah-d'voh-*RAH *hah-m'yah-*TSEH-*ret d'vahsh, v'toh-*LAH-*aht-hah-*MEH-*shee,*

The bee, which produces honey, and the silk-worm,

המיצרת משי, הן תועלתיות.

*hah-m'yah-*TSEH-*ret* MEH-*shee, hehn toh-ahl-tee-*YOHT.

which produces silk, are useful.

הזבוב והיתוש אינם תועלתיים ובלתי נעימים.

*Hahz-*VOOV *veh-hah-yah-*TOOSH *eh-*NAHM *toh-ahl-tee-*YEEM
*oo-veel-*TEE *neh-ee-*MEEM.

The fly and the mosquito are useless and unpleasant.

הם אינם מיצרים מאומה.

*Hehm ehn-*AHM *m'yah-ts'*REEM *meh-oo-*MAH.

They don't produce anything.

אדרבא, הם מזיקים.

*Ahd-rah-*BAH, *hehm mah-zee-*KEEM.

On the contrary, they are harmful.

ישנם אנשים האוהבים לצוד חיות או עופות.

*Yehsh-*NAHM *ah-nah-*SHEEM *hah-oh-hah-*VEEM *lah-*TSOOD
*hah-*YOHT *oh oh-*FOHT.

Some people like to hunt animals or birds.

לפני שנים רבות השמידו הצידים את האריה בישראל,

*Leef-*NEH *shah-*NEEM *rah-*BOHT *heesh-*MEE-*doo hah-tsah-yah-*DEEM
*ett hah-ahr-*YEH *b'Yis-rah-*EHL,

Many years ago hunters exterminated the lion in Israel,

כך, שפיום אין האריה מצוי בישראל.

*kakh, sheh-kah-*YOHM *ehn hah-ahr-*YEH *mah-*TSOOY *b'Yis-rah-*EHL.

so, that today the lion is not found in Israel.

לאדם וכמעט לכל החיות יש חמשה חושים,

*Lah-ah-*DAHM *v'heem-*AHT *l'hohl hah-hah-*YOHT *yehsh
*hah-mee-*SHAH *hoo-*SHEEM,

Man and almost all animals have five senses,

בהם יכולים לראות, לשמוע, להריח, לטעם, ולמשש.

*bah-*HEMM *y'hoh-*LEEM *leer-*OHT, *leesh-*MOH-*ah, leh-hah-*REE-*akh,
*leet-*OHM *oo-l'mah-*SHEHSH.

with which they can see, hear, smell, taste, and feel.

אנו רואים בעינינו.

AH-*noo roh-*EEM *beh-eh-*NEH-*noo.

We see with our eyes.

אנו שומעים באזנינו.   אנו מריחים באף.

AH-*noo shoh-meh-*EEM *beh-ohz-*NEH-*noo.   AH-*noo m'ree-*HEEM *bah-*aff.

We hear with our ears.   We smell with the nose.

בלשון ובחיך אנו טועמים אוכל ומשקה.

*Bah-lah-*SHOHN *oo-vah-*HEHKH AH-*noo toh-ah-*MEEM
OH-*hell oo-mahsh-*KEH.

With the tongue and the palate we taste food and drink.

בְּחוּשׁ הָרְאִיָּה אָנוּ רוֹאִים אֶת הַצֶּבַע הַצּוּרָה, הַמִּדּוֹת,

B'hoosh hah-reh-ee-YAH AH-noo roh-EEM ett hah-TSEH-vah,
hah-tsoo-RAH, hah-mee-DOHT,

With the sense of sight we see the color, the form, the dimensions,

וְהַמַּצָּב שֶׁל הַדָּבָר.

veh-hah-mah-TSAHV shell hah-dah-VAHR.

and the position of the object.

עַל יְדֵי הַשְּׁמִיעָה אָנוּ קוֹלְטִים קוֹלוֹת וְרַעַשׁ.

Ahl y'deh hahsh-mee-AH AH-noo koh-l'TEEM koh-LOHT vah-RAH-ahsh.

Through hearing we perceive sounds and noise.

עַל יְדֵי הַמִּשּׁוּשׁ אָנוּ מַרְגִּישִׁים אֶת קוֹר הַקֶּרַח,

Ahl y'deh hah-mee-SHOOSH AH-noo mahr-gee-SHEEM
ett kohr hah-KEH-rakh,

Through touch we feel the coldness of the ice,

אֶת חוֹם הָרַדְיָאטוֹר, וּכְאֵב, כַּאֲשֶׁר אָנוּ נִפְגָּעִים.

ett hohm hah-rahd-YAH-tohr, oo-h'EHV, kah-ah-SHERR AH-noo neef-gah-EEM.

the heat of the radiator, and pain, when we hurt ourselves.

יֶתֶר עַל כֵּן, עַל יְדֵי הַמִּשּׁוּשׁ אָנוּ מַרְגִּישִׁים אִם

YEH-ter ahl kehn, ahl y'deh hah-mee-SHOOSH AH-noo mahr-gee-SHEEM im

Moreover, through touch we perceive whether

הַדָּבָר רַךְ אוֹ קָשֶׁה.

hah-dah-VAHR rahkh oh kah-SHEH.

an object is soft or hard.

אָנוּ נוֹשְׁמִים אֲוִיר.	אָנוּ נוֹשְׁמִים בְּרֵיאוֹת.
AH-noo noh-sh'MEEM ah-VEER.	*AH-noo noh-sh'MEEM bah-reh-OHT.*
We breathe air.	We breathe with the lungs.
הָרֵיאוֹת בֶּחָזֶה.	אָנוּ אוֹכְלִים בַּפֶּה.
Hah-reh-OHT beh-hah-ZEH.	*AH-noo oh-h'LEEM bah-PEH.*
The lungs are in the chest.	We eat with the mouth.

הָאוֹכֶל יוֹרֵד אֶל הַקֵּיבָה, הַמְעַכֶּלֶת אוֹתוֹ.

Hah-OH-hell yoh-REHD ell hah-keh-VAH, hah-meh-ah-KEH-let oh-TOH.

Food goes down into the stomach, which digests it.

כַּאֲשֶׁר אֲנִי פּוֹצֵע אֶת עַצְמִי, נוֹזֵל אָדוֹם זוֹרֵם מִן הַפֶּצַע; זֶה דָם.

Kah-ah-SHERR ah-NEE poh-TSEH-ah ett ahts-MEE, noh-ZEHL ah-DOHM
zoh-REHM meen hah-PEH-tsah; zeh dahm.

If I cut myself, a red liquid flows out of the wound; it is blood.

AN INTERESTING FACT:

Note the similarity between the words דם "blood",

אָדֹם "red", and אָדָם "man".

הדם זורם בכל הגוף.

Hah-DAHM *zoh*-REHM *b'hohl hah*-GOOF.

Blood flows through the whole body.

הלב הוא הוא הגורם למחזור הדם.

Hah-LEHV *hoo hoo hah-goh*-REHM *l'mahkh*-ZOHR *hah*-DAHM.

It is the heart that causes circulation of the blood.

הלב בחזה.

Hah-LEHV *beh-hah*-ZEH.

The heart is in the chest.

אם האדם מעכל היטב, נושם היטב,

Im hah-ah-DAHM *meh-ah*-KEHL *heh*-TEHV, *noh*-SHEHM *heh*-TEHV,

If one digests well, if one breathes well,

ומחזור הדם בסדר הוא בריא.

oo-mahkh-ZOHR *hah*-DAHM *b'*SEH-*der*, *hoo bah*-REE.

and if the circulation of the blood is good, one is in good health.

אם האדם מעכל רע, אם כלי הנשימה שלו, או מחזור הדם

Im hah-ah-DAHM *meh-ah*-KEHL *rah*, *im k'leh hah-n'shee*-MAH *sheh*-LOH

oh mahkh-ZOHR *hah*-DAHM

If a person digests badly, if his breathing organs or blood circulation

לא נורמליים האדם הזה חולה.

lo nohr-MAH-*lee-yeem*, *hah-ah*-DAHM *hah*-ZEH *hoh*-LEH.

are not normal, that person is ill.

אז יש לקרא לרופא.

Ahz yehsh leek-ROH *lah-roh*-FEH.

Then one needs to call a doctor.

THINKING IN HEBREW
(Answers on page 291)

1. מה על החיות לעשות כדי לחיות?
Mah ahl hah-hah-YOHT lah-ah-SOHT k'deh leekh-YOHT?

2. למה אנו זקוקים כדי לחיות?
L'mah AH-noo z'koo-KEEM k'deh leekh-YOHT?

3. מה הם חמשת החושים?
Mah HEHM hah-MEH-shet hah-hoo-SHEEM?

4. מה שמות חיות-הבית העיקריות?
Mah sh'moht hah-YOHT-hah-BAH-yit hah-ee-kah-ree-YOHT?

5. במה אנו נושמים?
Bah-MEH AH-noo noh-sh'MEEM?

6. איפה חיים הדגים?
Eh-FOH hah-YIM hah-dah-GEEM?

7. כיצד מתנועע הנחש?
Keh-TSAHD meet-noh-EH-ah hah-nah-HAHSH?

8.   מדוע מביאה הדבורה תועלת?
*Mah-*DOO-*ah m'vee-*AH *hah-d'voh-*RAH *toh-*EH-*let?*

9.   קרא בשם חיות־השדה העיקריות?
*K'rah b'shehm hah-*YOHT-*hah-sah-*DEH *hah-ee-kah-ree-*YOHT?

10.   כמה כפים לכלב?
KAH-*mah kah-*PAH-*yim lah-*KEH-*lev?*

11.   כמה רגלים לעוף?
KAH-*mah rahg-*LAH-*yim lah-*OHF?

12.   מה עושות החיות ברגליהן?
*Mah oh-*SOHT *hah-hah-*YOHT *b'rahg-lay-*HENN?

13.   איפה עפים העופות?
*Eh-*FOH *ah-*FEEM *hah-oh-*FOHT?

14.   השוחים הדגים באוקינוס?
*Hah-soh-*HEEM *hah-dah-*GHEEM *bah-ohk-*YAH-*noos?*

15.   האפשר לנו לחיות בלי לאכל ולנשם?
*Hah-eff-*SHAHR LAH-*noo leekh-*YOHT *b'lee leh-eh-*HOHL *v'leen-*SHOHM?

16.   מה צבע הדם?
*Mah-*TSEH-*vah hah-*DAHM?

17.   מה גורם למחזור הדם?
*Mah goh-*REHM *l'makh-*ZOHR *hah-*DAHM?

18.   איפה מקום־הלב?
*Eh-*FOH *m'kohm-hah-*LEHV?

19.   הטוב מצב בריאותך?
*Hah-*TOHV *mah-*TSAHV *b'ree-oo-t'*HAH?

20.   אם תאכל הרבה, התעפל את האוכל בנקל?
*Im toh-*HAHL *hahr-*BEH, *hah-teh-ah-*KEHL ett *hah-*OH-*hell b'nah-*KEHL?

הָאָדָם וְתַחְשׁוּשׁוֹתָיו

*Hah-ah-*DAHM *oo-t'hoo-shoh-*TAHV

Man and his emotions

הָאָדָם דּוֹמֶה לַחַיּוֹת; מֻכְרָח הוּא לֶאֱכֹל, לִשְׁתּוֹת וְלִנְשׁוֹם.

*Hah-ah-*DAHM *doh-*MEH *lah-hah-*YOHT; *mooh-*RAHKH *hoo leh-eh-*HOHL,
*leesh-*TOHT *v'leen-*SHOHM.

Man resembles the animals; he must eat, drink and breathe.

אֲבָל שׁוֹנֶה הָאָדָם מִן הַחַיּוֹת,

*Ah-*VAHL *shoh-*NEH *hah-ah-*DAHM *meen hah-hah-*YOHT,

But man is different from the animals,

מִשּׁוּם שֶׁהוּא מְדַבֵּר וְחוֹשֵׁב.

*mee-*SHOOM *sheh-*HOO *m'dah-*BEHR *v'hoh-*SHEHV.

because he speaks and thinks.

אָנוּ חוֹשְׁבִים בַּמֹּחַ שֶׁבָּרֹאשׁ.

AH-*noo hoh-sh'*VEEM *bah-*MOH-*akh sheh-bah-*ROHSH.

We think with the brain, which is in the head.

197

המוח הוא אבר המחשבה.

*Hah-*MOH-*akh hoo* EH-*ver hah-mahkh-shah-*VAH.
The brain is the organ of thought.

? באילו דברים דומים אנו לחיות

*Beh-*EH-*loo d'vah-*REEM *doh-*MEEM AH-*noo l'hah-*YOHT?
In what ways are we similar to animals?

כמוהן אנו מוכרחים לאכל, לשתות ולנשום.

*K'moh-*HENN AH-*noo mookh-rah-*HEEM *leh-eh-*HOHL,
*leesh-*TOHT *v'leen-*SHOHM.
Like them we must eat, drink and breathe.

? מה מבדיל עקרונית את האדם מן החיות

*Mah mahv-*DEEL *ehk-roh-*NEET *ett hah-ah-*DAHM *meen hah-hah-*YOHT?
What principally distinguishes man from the animals?

דבור ומחשבה.

*Dee-*BOOR *oo-mahkh-shah-*VAH.
Speech and thought.

אנו חושבים על דברים נוכחים ונעדרים.

AH-*noo hoh-sh'*VEEM *ahl d'vah-*REEM *noh-h'*HEEM *v'neh-eh-dah-*REEM.
We think of things present and absent.

במוחנו מתהוות תמונות, הנקראות רעיונות.

*B'moh-*HEH-*noo meet-hah-*VOHT *t'moo-*NOHT, *hah-neek-rah-*OHT
*rah-ah-yoh-*NOHT.
In our brain images are formed, called ideas.

אנו מדברים כדי למסר לאחרים את רעיונותינו.

AH-*noo m'dah-b'*REEM *k'deh leem-*SOHR *lah-ah-heh-*REEM *ett
*rah-ah-yoh-noh-*TEH-*noo.
We speak to convey our ideas to others.

עכשו הנך חושב על שעורך.

*Akh-*SHAHV *heen-*HAH *hoh-*SHEHV *ahl shee-oor-*HAH.
Now you are thinking of your lesson.

A USEFUL IDIOM:

You will remember that the verb "to be" is not used in the present tense, but only implied. There is, however, another idiomatic construction, meaning literally "here I am", "here you are", etc., which is widely used as a substitute for that missing verb. It is, usually, a combination of the personal pronouns and the word הנה (*hee*-NAY) which means "here". Observe the following table showing the different forms of this construction, which is applied mainly to persons, and not to things.

	Masculine		*Feminine*	
I am:	הנני	(*hee-neh*-NEE)	same as masculine	
You are:	הנך	(*heen*-HAH)	הנך	(*hee*-NEHKH)
He is:	הנו	(*hee*-NOH)	She is: הנה	(*hee*-NAH)
We are:	הננו	(*hee-neh*-NOO)	same as masculine	
You are:	הנכם	(*heen*-HEMM)	הנכן	(*heen*-HENN)
They are:	הנם	(*hee*-NAHM)	הנן	(*hee*-NAHN)

The negative form of this construction has the prefix אינ (*ehn*) instead of הנ (*heen*). So we say, for example: אינך (*ehn*-HAH) "You are not", etc.

מה אתה עושה עכשו?
Mah *ah*-TAH *oh*-SEH *akh*-SHAHV?
What are you doing now?

אתה לומד עברית.
Ah-TAH *loh*-MEHD *eev*-REET.
You are learning Hebrew.

המורה מלמד.
Hah-moh-REH *m'lah*-MEHD.
The teacher teaches.

התלמיד לומד.
Hah-tahl-MEED *loh*-MEHD.
The pupil learns.

הלמדת עברית בשנה האחרונה?
Hah-lah-MAHD-*tah eev*-REET *bah-shah*-NAH *hah-ah-hah-roh*-NAH?
Did you learn Hebrew last year?

TAKE YOUR CHOICE:

You will frequently hear the word שעברה (*sheh-ahv*-RAH) also to mean "last" year, month, week, etc. It means the same as אחרונה (*ah-hah-roh*-NAH).

לצערי לא. נסיתי ללמוד, אבל לא היה לי ספר למוד טוב כזה.
L'tsah-ah-REE *lo*. *Nee*-SEE-*tee leel*-MOHD, *ah*-VAHL *lo hah*-YAH *lee* SEH-*fer lee*-MOOD *tohv kah*-ZEH.
To my regret, no. I tried to, but I hadn't a good book like this one.

כשלומדים משהו היטב, יודעים אותו.
*K'sheh-loh-m'*DEEM *mah-sheh*-HOO *heh*-TEHV, *yoh-deh*-EEM *oh*-TOH.
When one learns something well, he knows it.

יודע אתה לספר, יודע אתה לכתב,
Yoh-DEH-*ah ah*-TAH *lees*-POHR, *yoh*-DEH-*ah ah*-TAH *leekh*-TOHV,
You know how to count, you know how to write,

משום שלמדת זאת.

*mee-*SHOOM *sheh-lah-*MAHD*-tah zoht.*

because you have learned it.

יודע אתה שיש לי שעון, משום שראית אותו.

*Yoh-*DEH*-ah ah-*TAH *sheh-*YEHSH *lee shah-*OHN, *mee-*SHOOM
*sheh-rah-*EE*-tah oh-*TOH.

You know that I have a watch, because you have seen it.

למדת הרבה מלים עבריות,

*Lah-*MAHD*-tah hahr-*BEH *mee-*LEEM *eev-ree-*YOHT,

You have learned many Hebrew words,

אבל שכחת קצת מהן.

*ah-*VAHL *shah-*HAHKH*-tah k'tsaht meh-*HENN.

but you have forgotten some of them.

ההרגשות וההתחושות באדם מפותחות יותר מאשר בחיות.

*Hah-hahr-gah-*SHOHT *veh-haht'hoo-*SHOHT *bah-ah-*DAHM
*m'foo-tah-*HOHT *yoh-*TEHR *meh-ah-*SHERR *bah-hah-*YOHT.

In man, the sensations and the emotions are more developed
than in the animals.

החיות אוהבות את ולדותיהן,

*Hah-hah-*YOHT *oh-hah-*VOHT *ett v'lah-doh-teh-*HENN,

The animals love their young ones,

אבל אהבת האם לבנה חזקה יותר.

*ah-*VAHL *ah-hah-*VAHT *hah-*EHM *leev-*NAH *hah-zah-*KAH *yoh-*TEHR.

but the love of a mother for her child is much stronger.

אנו אוהבים לראות סרט יפה.

AH*-noo oh-hah-*VEEM *leer-*OHT SEH*-ret yah-*FEH.

We like to see a nice film.

אנו מחבבים יופי; ולהפך, איננו אוהבים כעור.

AH*-noo m'hah-b'*VEEM YOH*-fee;* oo*-l'*HEH*-fekh, eh-*NEN*-noo
oh-hah-*VEEM *kee-*OOR.

We like beauty and, on the contrary, we do not like ugliness.

אנו מרגישים בחילה, כשאנו נוגעים בדברים מלוכלכים.

AH*-noo mahr-gee-*SHEEM *b'hee-*LAH, *k'sheh-*AH*-noo noh-geh-*EEM
*beed-vah-*REEM *m'lookh-lah-*HEEM.

We feel repugnance when we touch dirty things.

אתה אוהב לראות ולשמע דברים נעימים.

*Ah-*TAH *oh-*HEHV *leer-*OHT *v'leesh-*MOH*-ah d'vah-*REEM *neh-ee-*MEEM.

You like to see and hear pleasant things.

פחד הוא תחושה.

PAH-*hahd hoo t'hoo*-SHAH.

Fear is an emotion.

חיות קטנות מפחדות מפני הגדולות.

Hah-YOHT *k'tah*-NOHT *m'fah-hah*-DOHT *meep*-NEH *hah-g'doh*-LOHT.

Small animals fear large ones.

ילדים מפחדים מפני החושך.

Y'lah-DEEM *m'fah-hah*-DEEM *meep*-NEH *hah*-HOH-*shekh*.

Children fear darkness.

המפחדות ילדות מצפרדעים, נחשים ועכברים?

Hah-m'fah-hah-DOHT *y'lah*-DOHT *mee-ts'fahr-deh*-EEM, *n'hah*-SHEEM *veh-akh-bah*-REEM?

Are girls afraid of frogs, snakes and mice?

כן, הן מפחדות מהם.

Kehn, hehn m'fah-hah-DOHT *meh*-HEMM.

Yes, they are afraid of them.

אדם שאינו מפחד הוא אמיץ.

Ah-DAHM *sheh-eh*-NOH *m'fah*-HEHD *hoo ah*-MEETS.

A person who has no fear is brave.

חילינו היו אמיצים בזמן המלחמה.

Hah-yah-LEH-*noo hah*-YOO *ah-mee*-TSEEM *beez*-MAHN *hah-meel-hah*-MAH.

Our soldiers were brave during the war.

כששומע אתה מוסיקה טובה, או רואה הצגה יפה

K'sheh-shoh-MEH-*ah ah*-TAH MOO-*see-kah toh*-VAH, *oh roh*-EH *hah-tsah*-GAH *yah*-FAH,

When you hear good music or see a beautiful show,

זה משביע את רצונך.

zeh mahs-BEE-*ah ett r'tsohn*-HAH.

it pleases you.

A USEFUL IDIOM:

The idiom משביע את רצונך (*mahs*-BEE-*ah ett r'tsohn*-HAH) is widely employed and literally means "it satisfies your desire", implying that you are pleased with something.

כשמורך אומר לך שתרגילך עשוי יפה,

K'sheh-moh-r'HAH oh-MEHR l'hah sheh-tahr-geel-HAH ah-SOOY yah-FEH,

When your teacher tells you that your exercise is well done,

אתה מרוצה.

ah-TAH m'roo-TSEH.

you are pleased.

אנו מופרעים כשרעש מונע בעדנו לישון.

AH-noo *moof-rah-EEM k'sheh-RAH-ahsh moh-NEH-ah bah-ah-DEH-noo lee-SHOHN.*

We are disturbed when noise prevents us from sleeping.

אין אנו מרוצים כשעלינו לחכות זמן רב

Ehn AH-noo *m'roo-TSEEM k'sheh-ah-LEH-noo l'hah-KOHT z'mahn rahv*

We are displeased when we have to wait a long time

למקום-ישיבה בקול-נוע.

leem-KOHM-y'shee-VAH b'kohl-NOH-ah.

for a seat at the movies.

CINEMATOGRAPHIC NOTE:

The construction קול-נוע (*kohl*-NOH-*ah*) literally means "moving voice", and is used for talking pictures. The silent movies were called ראי-נוע (*reh-eh*-NOH-*ah*): "moving mirror".

כשמרגיזים ילדים קטנים, הם בוכים.

K'sheh-mahr-gee-ZEEM yeh-lah-DEEM k'tah-NEEM, hehm boh-HEEM.

When one annoys small children, they cry.

אבל אנשים מבוגרים מראים את אי-רצונם בדרכים אחרות.

*Ah-*VAHL *ah-nah-*SHEEM *m'voo-gah-*REEM *mahr-*EEM *ett ee-r'tsoh-*NAHM *beed-rah-*HEEM *ah-heh-*ROHT.

But adults show their dissatisfaction in other ways.

בכל אופן מוטב לצחק מאשר לכעם או להתעצב.

B'hohl OH-*fen moo-*TAHV *leets-*HOHK *meh-ah-*SHERR *leekh-*OHS *oh leh-heet-ah-*TSEHV.

In any case it is better to laugh than to get angry or to be sad.

TWO USEFUL IDIOMS:

Remember the expression בכל אופן (*b'hohl-*OH-*fen*) meaning "in any case", "at any rate".

We have used מוטב (*moo-*TAHV) in the above sentence instead of טוב יותר (*tohv yoh-*TEHR), so you may become familiar with it. Either can be used.

THINKING IN HEBREW
(Answers on page 292)

1. מדוע שמח המורה?

Mah-DOO-ah sah-MEH-akh hah-moh-REH?

2. האם רותי מאושרת?

Hah-im ROO-tee meh-oo-SHEH-ret?

3. מדוע היא בּוכה?

Mah-DOO-ah hee boh-HAH?

4. העצובה הגברת בילה?

Hah-ah-tsoo-VAH hah-G'VEH-ret BEH-leh?

5. העולה האדם על החיות בּכל הדברים?

Hah-oh-LEH hah-ah-DAHM ahl hah-hah-YOHT b'hohl hah-d'vah-REEM?

6. היכולים לדבּר בּאופן נכון בּלי לחשוב?

Hah-y'hoh-LEEM l'dah-BEHR b'OH-fen nah-HOHN b'lee lah-hah-SHOHV?

7.   מה אתה לומד עכשו?
Mah ah-TAH loh-MEHD akh-SHAHV?

8.   הלמדת לרקד?
Hah-lah-MAHD-tah leer-KOHD?

9.   היודע אתה מה שם הנשיא של ישראל?
Hah-yoh-DEH-ah ah-TAH mah shehm hah-nah-SEE shell Yis-rah-EHL?

10.   היודע אני כמה כוכבים יש בשמים?
Hah-yoh-DEH-ah ah-NEE KAH-mah koh-hah-VEEM yehsh bah-shah-MAH-yim?

11.   היודעים אנו מה יהיה מזג האויר בשבוע הבא?
Hah-yoh-deh-EEM AH-noo mah yee-YEH MEH-zeg hah-ah-VEER
bah-shah-VOO-ah hah-BAH?

12.   היודע המורה את המרחק בין תל-אביב לירושלים?
Hah-yoh-DEH-ah hah-moh-REH ett hah-merr-HAHK behn Tel-Ah-VEEV
lee-Yeh-roo-shah-LAH-yim?

13.   הלמדת אנגלית?
Hah-lah-MAHD-tah ahn-GLEET?

14.   התזכר אותה עדיין?
Hah-teez-KOHR oh-TAH ah-DAH-yin?

15.   השכחת אותה?
Hah-shah-HAKH-tah oh-TAH?

16.   היש לך זכרון טוב?
Hah-YEHSH l'hah zee-kah-ROHN tohv?

17. המרוצה אתה כשהנך יודע שמזג האויר יהיה טוב?
Hah-m'roo-TSEH ah-TAH k'sheh-heen-HAH yoh-DEH-ah sheh-MEH-zeg
hah-ah-VEER yee-YEH tohv?

18.   המרוצה אתה כשהנך עוזב את העיר בקיץ?
Hah-m'roo-TSEH ah-TAH k'she-heen-HAH oh-ZEHV ett hah-EER bah-KAH-yits?

19.   המפחד אתה ללכת בחושך?
Hah-m'fah-HEHD ah-TAH lah-LEH-het bah-HOH-shekh?

שִׁעוּר 28

כשאנו נוסעים

K'sheh-AH-noo noh-seh-EEM

When we travel

ישראל היא ארץ.
Yees-rah-EHL hee EH-rets.
Israel is a country.

הנה כמה מהארצות הקרובות לישראל:
Hee-NEH KAH-mah meh-hah-ah-rah-TSOHT hah-k'roh-VOHT l'Yees-rah-EHL:
Here are some of the countries near Israel:

סוריה, לבנון, טורקיה, מצרים, עבר הירדן וקפריסין,
שהיא אי בים התיכון.

soor-*yah*, L'vah-NOHN, TOOR-*kee-yah*, Meets-RAH-*yim*, EH-*ver-hah-Yahr-*
DEHN v'Kahf-ree-SEEN, sheh-HEE ee bah-YAHM hah-tee-HOHN.

Syria, Lebanon, Turkey, Egypt, Trans-Jordan and Cyprus,
which is an island in the Mediterranean Sea.

הנה שמותיהן של כמה מארצות אירופה:

Hee-NEH sh'moh-tay-HENN shel KAH-*mah* meh-ahr-TSOHT Eh-ROH-*pah*:

Here are the names of some of the countries in Europe:

אנגליה, צרפת, איטליה, יון, גרמניה, ספרד ורוסיה.

Ahn-glee-YAH, Tsohr-FAHT, Ee-TAHL-*yah*, Yah-VAHN, Gerr-MAHN-*yah*,
Sfah-RAHD v'ROOS-*yah*.

England, France, Italy, Greece, Germany, Spain and Russia.

ארצות-הברית וקנדה הן בצפון אמריקה,

Ahr-TSOHT-hah-b'REET v'KAH-*nah-dah* hehn beets-FOHN Ah-MEH-*ree-kah*,

The United States and Canada are in North America,

והארצות הגדולות בדרום אמריקה הן ארגנטינה וברזיליה.

veh-hah-ah-rah-TSOHT hah-g'doh-LOHT beed-ROHM Ah-MEH-*ree-kah*
hehn Ahr-gen-TEE-*nah* oo-Brah-ZEEL-*yah*.

and the largest countries in South America are Argentina and Brazil.

סין, יפן, והודו הן באסיה.

Seen, YAH-*pahn*, veh-HOH-*doo* hehn beh-AHS-*yah*.

China, Japan and India are in Asia.

מה הן הערים הגדולות ביותר בעולם?

Mah hehn heh-ah-REEM hah-g'doh-LOHT b'yoh-TEHR bah-oh-LAHM?

What are the biggest cities in the world?

הערים הגדולות ביותר בעולם הן:

Heh-ah-REEM hah-g'doh-LOHT b'yoh-TEHR bah-oh-LAHM hehn:

The largest cities of the world are:

לונדון	ניו יורק	פריז	ברלין	מוסקבה	שנגחי
Lohn-DOHN	N'yoo-YOHRK	Pah-REEZ	Ber-LEEN	Mohs-k'VAH	Shahn-GHIGH
London	New York	Paris	Berlin	Moscow	Shanghai

כשעוברים מעיר לעיר, או מארץ לארץ, נוסעים.

K'sheh-oh-v'REEM meh-EER leh-EER, oh meh-EH-*rets* leh-EH-*rets*,
noh-seh-EEM.

When one goes from one city to another, or from one country to
another, one is traveling.

אנו נוסעים באוירון, באניה, במכונית או ברכבת.

AH-noo noh-seh-**EEM** bah-ah-vee-**ROHN**, bah-oh-nee-**YAH**, bah-m'hoh-**NEET**,
oh bah-rah-**KEH**-vet.

We travel by plane, by ship, by automobile, or by train.

אם המקום, אליו אנו נוסעים, הוא רחוק,

Im hah-mah-**KOHM**, eh-**LAHV** **AH**-noo noh-seh-**EEM**, hoo rah-**HOHK**,

If the place to which we are going is distant,

אנו נוסעים באוירון.

AH-noo noh-seh-**EEM** bah-ah-vee-**ROHN**.

we travel by plane.

אם זה קרוב אנו יכולים לנסע במכונית (באוטו), או ברכבת.

Im zeh kah-**ROHV**, **AH**-noo y'hoh-**LEEM** leen-**SOH**-ah bah-m'hoh-**NEET**
(bah-**OH**-toh), oh bah-rah-**KEH**-vet.

If it is nearby we can travel by automobile, or by train.

NOTE TO STUDENT:

The word מכונית (m'hoh-**NEET**) derived from מכונה
(m'hoh-**NAH**) "machine" and the adopted word אוטו
(**OH**-toh) can both be used to describe a motorcar.

לפני צאתנו לטיול, עלינו לארוז את חבילותינו, או את מזודותינו.

Leef-**NEH** tseh-**TEH**-noo l'tee-**YOOL**, ah-**LEH**-noo leh-eh-**ROHZ** ett
hah-vee-loh-**TAY**-noo, oh ett mez-v'doh-**TAY**-noo.

Before leaving on a trip, we must pack our bags, or our suitcases.

AN INTERESTING COMBINATION:

Idiomatic combinations of verb and pronoun are possible in the case of certain Hebrew verbs, like the one
in the foregoing sentence, where you find צאתנו (tseh-
TEH-noo) meaning literally "our leaving". Of course,
"my leaving" would be, accordingly, צאתי (tseh-**TEE**).
Such combinations are considered one of the beauties of the language.

אנו שמים במזודה כל מה שנצטרך להם בדרך:

AH-noo sah-**MEEM** bah-meez-vah-**DAH** kohl mah sheh-neets-tah-**REHKH**
lah-**HEMM** bah-**DEH**-rekh:

We put in the suitcase everything that we shall need on the way:

חליפות,   גרבים,   כותנות,   לבנים,
hah-lee-FOHT, *gahr*-BAH-*yim*, *koo-tah*-NOHT, *l'vah*-NEEM,
suits,   socks,   shirts,   underwear,

חפצי טואלט,   ודברים רבים אחרים.
heff-TSEH *too-ah*-LETT, *oo-d'vah*-REEM *rah*-BEEM *ah-heh*-REEM.
toilet articles,   and many other things.

NOTE TO STUDENT:

Observe the use of the word ש (*sheh*) "that" in the preceding sentence. This is an abbreviation of the relative pronoun אשר (*ah*-SHERR) "that" or "which".

אחרי כן אנו קוראים לטקסי, ואומרים לנהג:
Akh-RAY *hehn* AH-*noo koh-ree*-EEM *l'*TAHK-*see*, *veh-oh-m'*REEM
lah-neh-HAHG:
Then we call a taxi, and say to the chauffeur:

„לשדה-התעופה, בבקשה. סע מהר!"
"Lees-DEH-*hah-teh-oo*-FAH, *b'vah-kah*-SHAH. *Sah mah*-HEHR!"
"To the airport, please. Drive quickly!"

AN IMPORTANT IMPERATIVE:

You are probably wondering what is the verb of which the imperative is סע (*sah*). סע (*sah*) is the imperative of the verb נסע (*nah*-SOH-*ah*) meaning "to "travel", "to ride in a vehicle", etc. This is a masculine singular imperative. Its feminine counterpart would be סעי (*seh*-EE).

בתחנה נגשים אנו לקופאי לקנות כרטים.
Bah-tah-hah-NAH *nee-gah*-SHEEM AH-*noo lah-koo-pah*-EE
leek-NOHT *kahr*-TEES.
At the station, we go to the cashier to buy a ticket.

אנו אומרים לקופאי : „שני כרטיסים מחלקה ראשונה,
AH-*noo oh-m'*REEM *l'koo-pah*-EE: *"Sh'neh kahr-tee*-SEEM *makh-lah*-KAH
ree-shoh-NAH,
We say to the cashier: "Two first-class tickets,

ירושלים הלך וחזר, בבקשה."

*Yeh-roo-shah-*LAH-*yim, hah–*LOHKH *v'hah-*ZOHR *b'vah-kah-*SHAH".
round trips to Jerusalem, please".

A ROUND TRIP TICKET:

The expression used in Hebrew for "round trip" is
הלך וחזר (*hah-*LOHKH *v'hah-*ZOHR). As you see, this
idiom consists of two verb stems and literally means
"to go and to come back".

הסבל נושא את המזודות לתוך הקרון.

*Hah-sah-*BAHL *noh-*SEH *ett hah-meez-vah-*DOHT *l'tohkh hah-kah-*ROHN.
The porter carries your suitcases into the car.

ATTENTION:

The word   קרון (*kah-*ROHN) means exclusively a "rail-
road car" and not just any car.

אתה שואל אותו : כמה מגיע לך?

*Ah-*TAH *shoh-*EHL *oh-*TOH: KAH-*mah mah-*GHEE-*ah l'hah?*
You ask him: What do I owe you?

NOTE FOR SHOPPING:

To say "what do I owe you?" we use the current expression ? כמה מגיע לך (KAH-*mah mah-*GHEE-*ah l'hah?*)
which literally means "how much is coming to you?"

הנה כמה בטויים שתצטרך להם במשך הטיול :

*Hee-*NEH KAH-*mah bee-too-*YIM *sheh-teets-tah-*REHKH *lah-*HEMM
*b'*MEH-*shekh hah-tee-*YOOL:
Here are some expressions that you will need during the trip:

NOTE TO STUDENT:

The word   טיול (*tee-*YOOL) is very flexible and can
mean "stroll", "excursion", "trip", or "voyage".

האם תפוס המקום הזה?

*Hah-tah-*FOOS *hah-mah-*KOHM *hah-*ZEH?

Is this seat occupied?

כמה זמן מתעכבת הרכבת בלוד?

KAH-*mah z'mahn meet-ah-*KEH-*vet hah-rah-*KEH-*vet b'Lod?*

How long does the train stop at Lod?

מתי נגיע לירושלים?

*Mah-*TIGH *nah-*GEE-*ah lee-Yeh-roo-shah-*LAH-*yim?*

When shall we arrive in Jerusalem?

כמה שעות אורכת הנסיעה לחיפה?

KAH-*mah shah-*OHT *oh-*REH-*het hah-n'see-*AH *l'*HIGH-*fah?*

How many hours does the trip to Haifa take?

כשאתה מגיע למחוז חפצך הנך מתענין במלון טוב,

*K'sheh-ah-*TAH *mah-*GHEE-*ah leem-*HOHZ *hef-ts'*HAH *heen-*HAH

*meet-ahn-*YEHN *b'mah-*LOHN *tohv,*

When you arrive at your destination, you inquire about a good hotel,

ונוסע שמה במונית.

*v'noh-*SEH-*ah* SHAH-*mah b'moh-*NEET.

and go there by cab.

שואלים את פקיד-המלון:

*Shoh-ah-*LEEM *ett p'keed-hah-mah-*LOHN:

One asks the hotel clerk:

היש לך חדר עם אמבטיה?

*Hah-*YEHSH *l'hah* HEH-*der im ahm-*BAHT-*yah?*

Have you a room with bath?

אשהה כאן שבוע. מה מחירו?

*Esh-*HEH KAH-*ahn shah-voo-*AH. *Mah m'hee-*ROH?

I shall stay here a week. What is its price?

אם אתה אובד דרך בעיר, עליך לשאול שוטר:

*Im ah-*YAH *oh-*VEHD DEH-*rekh bah-*EER, *ah-*LEH-*hah leesh-*OHL *shoh-*TEHR:

If you lose your way in a city, you must ask a policeman:

סליחה אדוני, התוכל להראות לי את הדרך למלון „נורדאו פלאז'ה"?

*S'lee-*HAH *ah-doh-*NEE, *hah-too-*HAHL *leh-hahr-*OHT *lee ett hah-*DEH-*rekh*

*l'mah-*LOHN "NOHR-*dow* PLAH-*zhah"?*

Pardon me, sir, can you tell me the way to the "Nordau Plaza" Hotel?

FINANCIAL NOTE:

The verb אובד (*oh*-VEHD) means "to lose" in a general sense, for example, to lose an object, one's way, etc. For monetary loss resulting from business, another verb must be used. This verb is הפסד (*hahf*-SEHD). Example: אני מפסיד כסף (*ah*-NEE *mahf*-SEED KEH-*seff*) "I lose money".

אם אינך מבין את תשובתו, עליך לומר לו:

Im ehn-HAH *meh*-VEEN *ett t'shoo-vah*-TOH, *ah*-LEH-*hah leh*-MOHR *lo:*

If you do not understand his answer, you must say to him:

בבקשה, דבר לאט, אדוני, אינני מבין עברית יפה.

B'vah-kah-SHAH, *dah*-BEHR *leh*-AHT, *ah-doh*-NEE, *eh*-NEN-*nee meh*-VEEN *Eev*-REET *yah*-FEH.

Please speak slowly, sir, I do not understand Hebrew well.

NOTE ON ADVERBS:

In some cases, the Hebrew adverb is identical to the corresponding adjective. Example: יפה (*yah*-FEH) "nice", "nicely". In other cases, the adverb has a different formation.

בעיר גדולה ישנן חנויות גדולות.

Beh-EER *g'doh*-LAH *yehsh*-NAHN *hah-noo*-YOHT *g'doh*-LOHT.

In a large city there are big stores.

בחנות לספרים מוכרים ספרים.

Beh-hah-NOOT *lees-fah*-REEM *moh-h'*REEM *s'fah*-REEM.

In a bookstore, they sell books.

בחנות מכולת מוכרים צורכי אוכל.

Beh-hah-NOOT *mah*-KOH-*let moh-h'*REEM *tsohr*-KEH OH-*hell.*

In a grocery, they sell foodstuffs.

בחנות ירקות מוכרים ירקות.

Beh-hah-NOOT *y'rah*-KOHT *moh-h'*REEM *y'rah*-KOHT.

In a vegetable shop, they sell vegetables.

בשר תשיג באטליז, רפואות — בבית-מרקחת,

Bah-SAHR *tah*-SEEG *beh-eet*-LEEZ, *r'foo*-OHT *b'veht-meer*-KAH-*haht,*

You obtain meat in a butcher shop, medicines in a pharmacy,

פרחים — בחנות פרחים.
prah-HEEM *beh-hah*-NOOT *p'rah*-HEEM.
flowers in a florist's.

בחנויות כל־בו תמצא קצת מכל דבר.
Bah-hah-noo-YOHT *kohl*-BOH *teem*-TSAH *k'tsaht mee*-KOHL *dah*-VAHR.
In department stores, you find a little of everything.

כשהנך נכנס לחנות כל־בו לקנות כובע,
K'sheh-heen-HAH *neekh*-NAHS *leh-hah*-NOOT *kohl*-BOH *leek*-NOHT KOH-*vah*,
When you enter a department store to buy a hat,

אתה אומר בכניסתך: שלום, גברת,
ah-TAH *oh*-MEHR *beekh-nee-saht*-HAH: *Shah*-LOHM, *g'veh*-*ret*,
you say on entering: Good morning, miss,

איפה מחלקת הכובעים?
eh-FOH *makh*-LEH-*ket hah-koh-vah*-EEM?
where is the hat department?

היא מראה לך, ואחרי כן אתה אומר למוכר:
Hee mahr-AH *l'hah*, *veh-akh*-RAY *hehn ah*-TAH *oh*-MEHR *lah-moh*-HEHR:
She shows it to you, and then you say to the salesman:

הראה לי כובע אפור, בבקשה, מספר 7.
Hahr-EH *lee* KOH-*vah ah*-FOOR, *b'vah-kah*-SHAH, *mees*-PAHR 7.
Show me a gray hat, please, size 7.

אם המחיר יקר, הנך שואל: היש לך כובע זול יותר?
*Im hah-m'*HEER *yah*-KAHR, *heen*-HAH *shoh*-EHL:
Hah-YEHSH *l'hah* KOH-*vah zohl yoh*-TEHR?
If the price is high, you ask: Have you a cheaper hat?

אם החפץ מתאים לך, אתה אומר:
Im hah-HEH-*fets maht*-EEM *l'hah*, *ah*-TAH *oh*-MEHR:
If the article suits you, you say:

טוב, אקח את זה. התואיל לעטף אותו? לוקח אני זה אתי.
Tohv, *ek*-KAHKH *ett zeh*. *Hah-toh*-EEL *lah-ah*-TOHF *oh*-TOH?
Loh-KAY-*akh ah*-NEE *zeh ee*-TEE.
Good, I'll take it. Will you please wrap it up?
I shall take it with me.

THINKING IN HEBREW
(Answers on page 292)

1. ציין שמות כמה ארצות הקרובות לישראל?

*Tsah-*YEHN *sh'moht* KAH-*mah ah-rah-*TSOHT *hah-k'roh-*VOHT *l'Yis-rah-*EHL?

2. כיצד אנו נוסעים מישראל לארצות-הברית?

*Keh-*TSAHD AH-*noo noh-seh-*EEM *mee-Yis-rah-*EHL *leh-Ahr-*TSOHT-*Hah-b'*REET?

3. במה אנו נוסעים מתל-אביב לירושלים?

*Bah-*MEH AH-*noo noh-seh-*EEM *mee-Tel-Ah-*VEEV *lee-Yeh-roo-shah-*LAH-*yim?

4. מה אתה עושה לפני צאתך לטיול?

*Mah ah-*TAH *oh-*SEH *leef-*NEH *tseh-t'*HAH *leh-tee-*YOOL?

5. ההולך אתה לשדה-התעופה ברגל?

*Hah-hoh-*LEHKH *ah-*TAH *lees-*DEH *hah-teh-oo-*FAH *bah-*REH-*gϵl?

6. מה אתה אומר לנהג?

*Mah ah-*TAH *oh-*MEHR *lah-neh-*HAHG?

7. איפה קונים כרטיסי נסיעה ברכבת?

*Eh-*FOH *koh-*NEEM *kahr-tee-*SEH *n'see-*AH *bah-rah-*KEH-*vet?

8. מי נושא את המזודות לתוך הקרון?

Mee noh-SEH ett hah-meez-vah-DOHT l'tohkh hah-kah-ROHN?

9. כמה זמן לוקחת הנסיעה במכונית מתל-אביב לירושלים?

KAH-mah z'mahn loh-KAH-haht hah-n'see-AH beem-hoh-NEET
mee-Tel-Ah-VEEV lee-Yeh-roo-shah-LAH-yim?

10. מה אתה עושה אם אתה תועה בעיר?

Mah ah-TAH oh-SEH im ah-TAH toh-EH bah-EER?

11. מנה כמה חנויות שהנך מוצא בעיר, ומה מוכרים בהן.

M'neh KAH-mah hah-noo-YOHT she-heen-HAH moh-TSEH bah-EER,
oo-MAH mokh-REEM bah-HENN?

12. איזה שם תקרא לחנות שמוכרים בה מכל דבר?

EH-zeh shehm teek-RAH leh-hah-NOOT sheh-mokh-REEM bah
mee-KOHL dah-VAHR?

13. מי מוכר סחורה בחנות?

Mee moh-HEHR s'hoh-RAH beh-hah-NOOT?

14. מה אתה עושה אם אתה רוצה לקנות כובע?

Mah ah-TAH oh-SEH im ah-TAH roh-TSEH leek-NOHT KOH-vah?

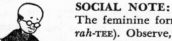

*Hah-p'gee-*SHAH

The meeting

(בשדה התעופה אליניקו — אתונה)
(*Bees-*DEH *hah-teh-oo-*FAH *Eh-lee-nee-*KOH—*Ah-*TOO-*nah*)
(Airport Elliniko—Athens)

אדון לוי : הוי ! איזו הפתעה !
*Ah-*DOHN *Leh-*VEE: *Hoy! EH-zoh hahf-tah-*AH!
Mr. Levy: Oh, what a surprise!

מה אתה עושה פה דן יקירי?
*Mah ah-*TAH *oh-*SEH *poh Dahn yah-kee-*REE?
What are you doing here, my dear Dan?

SOCIAL NOTE:
The feminine form of "my dear" is יקירתי (*yah-kee-rah-*TEE). Observe, here, that the letter ת (*T*) is introduced, instead of ה (*H*), for euphony. This euphonic rule is applied to all similar constructions.

215

אדון נבון: זוהי באמת פגישה בלתי צפויה!

*Ah-*DOHN *Nah-*VOHN: ZOH-*hee beh-eh-*METT *p'gee-*SHAH
*beel-*TEE *ts'foo-*YAH!

Mr. Navon: It is indeed an unexpected meeting!

בדעתי לטוס באוירון ההולך לישראל.

*B'dah-*TEE *lah-*TOOS *bah-ah-vee-*ROHN *hah-hoh-*LEHKH *l'Yis-rah-*EHL.

It is my intention to fly by plane leaving for Israel.

NOTE TO STUDENT:

The expression בדעתי (*b'dah-*TEE) literally means
"it is my intention to". "You intend to" will be, accordingly, בדעתך (*b'daht-*HAH), etc.

אדון לוי: מצוין! אף אני טס באותו אוירון.

*Ah-*DOHN *Leh-*VEE: *M'tsoo-*YAHN! *Aff ah-*NEE *tahs beh-oh-*TOH
*ah-vee-*ROHN.

Mr. Levy: Excellent! I am flying on that plane too.

כן, מפליא לפגש אותך פה!

*Kehn, mahf-*LEE *leef-*GOHSH *oh-t'*HAH *poh!

Well, it's amazing meeting you here!

ואני חשבתי שאתה עדין באמריקה.

*Vah-ah-*NEE *hah-*SHAHV-*tee *sheh-ah-*TAH *ah-*DAH-*yin *beh-Ah-*MEH-*ree-kah.

And I thought you were still in America.

מה מעשיך ביון?

*Mah mah-ah-*SEH-*hah *b'Yah-*VAHN?

What are you doing in Greece?

AN IDIOMATIC EXPRESSION:

The word מעשיך (*mah-ah-*SEH-*hah*) literally means
"your deeds". Above sentence illustrates a current way
of asking "what are you doing?"

אדון נבון: זה עתה סימתי בקור מסחרי קצר באתונה,

*Ah-*DOHN *Nah-*vohn: *Zeh ah-*TAH *see-*YAHM-*tee *bee-*KOOR *mees-hah-*REE
*kah-*TSAHR *beh-Ah-*TOO-nah,

Mr. Navon: I have just finished a short business visit to Athens,

והוזר הביתה לתל-אביב.   ואתה?
*veh-hoh-*ZEHR *hah-*BIGH*-tah l'Tel-Ah-*VEEV.   *Veh-ah-*TAH?
and am returning home to Tel-Aviv.   And you?

אדון לוי : אני בדרכי מניו-יורק לישראל;
*Ah-*DOHN *Leh-*VEE: *Ah-*NEE *b'dahr-*KEE *mee-New-York l'Yis-rah-*EHL;
Mr. Levy: I am on my way from New York to Israel;

יש לי עסקים בארצך.
*yehsh lee ah-sah-*KEEM *beh-ahr-ts'*HAH.
I have some business in your country.

תכופות שאפתי לנסע שמה,
*T'hoo-*FOHT *shah-*AHF*-tee leen-*SOH*-ah* SHAH*-mah,*
I have so often wished to go there,

אבל לא היתה לי אף פעם הזדמנות לכך.
*ah-*VAHL *lo hah-y'*TAH *lee aff* PAH*-ahm heez-dahm-*NOOT *l'hakh.*
but have never before had the opportunity.

אדון נבון : ובכן, הבה נעלה לאוירון.
*Ah-*DOHN *Nah-*VOHN: *Oo-v'*HEHN, *hah-*VAH *nah-ah-*LEH *lah-ah-vee-*ROHN.
Mr. Navon: Well, let us get into the plane.

הוא ימריא בעוד עשר דקות. אולי
*Hoo yahm-*REE *beh-*OHD EH*-ser dah-*KOHT. *Oo-*LIGH
It will take off in another ten minutes. Perhaps

נשיג מקומות ישיבה זה ליד זה.
*nah-*SEEG *m'koh-*MOHT *y'shee-*VAH *zeh l'yahd zeh.*
we will get seats near each other.

אדבר עם המארחת.
*Ah-dah-*BEHR *im hah-meh-ah-*RAH*-haht.*
I'll speak to the hostess.

(באוירון)
*(Bah-ah-vee-*ROHN)
(On the plane)

אדון לוי : כן, תמיד שמעתי אומרים ששום ים אינו כחול
כים התיכון.
*Ah-*DOHN *Leh-*VEE: *Kehn, tah-*MEED *shah-*MAH*-tee oh-m'*REEM *sheh-*SHOOM
*yahm eh-*NOH *kah-*HOHL *k'yahm hah-tee-*HOHN.
Mr. Levy: Well, I have always heard that no other sea is as blue
as the Mediterranean.

עתה נוכחתי בעצמי שכן הוא.

Ah-TAH *noh*-HAKH-*tee beh-ahts*-MEE *sheh*-KEHN *hoo*.

But now I have realized myself that it is so.

אדון נבון: לא כן? הבט! הרואה אתה את הקו הצהוב באופק?

Ah-DOHN *Nah*-VOHN: *Lo hehn? Hah*-BEHT! *Hah-roh*-EH *ah*-TAH
ett *hah*-KAHV *hah-tsah*-HOHV *bah-OH-fek*?

Mr. Navon: Isn't it so? Look! Do you see that yellow streak
on the horizon?

אדון לוי: כמעט שאיני רואה אותו.

Ah-DOHN *Leh*-VEE: *Keem*-AHT *sheh-eh*-NEE *roh*-EH *oh*-TOH.

Mr. Levy: I can barely see it.

אדון נבון: זהו קו החוף של ישראל. עד מהרה נהיה בתל-אביב.

Ah-DOHN *Nah*-VOHN: ZEH-*hoo kahv hah*-HOHF *shell Yis-rah*-EHL.
Ahd meh-heh-RAH *nee*-YEH *b'Tel-Ah*-VEEV.

Mr. Navon: That is the coastline of Israel. Soon we shall
be in Tel-Aviv.

אדון לוי: מדוע החוף צהוב? האם זה עדין מדבר?

Ah-DOHN *Leh*-VEE: *Mah*-DOO-*ah hah*-HOHF *tsah*-HOHV? *Hah*-IM *zeh*
ah-DAH-*yin meed*-BAHR?

Mr. Levy: Why is the shore yellow? Is it still desert?

אדון נבון: זה היה פעם מדבר, אבל לא כיום.

Ah-DOHN *Nah*-VOHN: *Zeh hah*-YAH PAH-*ahm meed*-BAHR,
ah-VAHL *lo kah*-YOHM.

Mr. Navon: It was desert once, but not today.

עכשו הכל מכוסה ירק.

Akh-SHAHV *hah*-KOHL *m'hoo*-SEH YEH-*rek*.

It is getting green all over now.

ההשקאה ופתוח החקלאות האינטנסיבי עשו נפלאות.

Hah-hahsh-kah-AH *oo-fee*-TOO-*akh hah-hahk-lah*-OOT *hah-een-tenn*-SEE-
vee ah-SOO *neef-lah*-OHT.

Irrigation and intensive development of agriculture have done wonders.

וערינו גדלו במהירות שאין דוגמתה בעולם.

Veh-ah-REH-*noo gah-d'LOO beem-hee*-ROOT *sheh*-EHN *doog-mah*-TAH
bah-oh-LAHM.

And our cities grew with a speed unparalleled in the world.

אדון לוי : אכן, זוהי באמת „הארץ המובטחה".

Ah-DOHN *Leh*-VEE: *Ah*-HEHN, ZOH-*hee beh-eh*-METT "hah-AH-rets
hah-moov-tah-HAH".

Mr. Levy: Really, it is indeed the "land of promise".

אדון נבון! ראה, העיר שלפני עינינו היא תל-אביב גאותנו :
המודרנית, המזהירה והמקסימה.

Ah-DOHN *Nah*-VOHN: *Reh*-EH, hah-EER *sheh-leef*-NEH *eh*-NEH-*noo hee*
Tel-*Ah*-VEEV, *gah-ah-vah-*TEH-*noo:* hah-moh-DER-neet, hah-mahz-hee-RAH
veh-hah-mahk-see-MAH.

Mr. Navon: See, the city you see before us is our pride: modern,
shining, fascinating Tel-Aviv.

ראה כיצד היא משתרעת בבניניה הלבנים,

Reh-EH *keh*-TSAHD *hee mees-tah*-RAH-*aht b'veen-yah*-NEH-hah
hah-l'vah-NEEM,

Look how it spreads out with its white buildings,

ונלחמת במדבר ההולך ונעלם מסביבה במדה שהיא גדלה.

v'neel-HEH-*met bah-meed*-BAHR *hah-hoh*-LEHKH *v'neh-eh*-LAHM
mees-vee-VAH *b'mee*-DAH *sheh*-HEE *g'deh*-LAH.

and fights the desert, which disappears around it as it grows.

אדון לוי : היא באמת עיר נפלאת. איזה מחזה!

Ah-DOHN *Leh*-VEE: *Hee beh-eh*-METT *eer neef-lah*-AH, EH-*zeh makh*-ZEH!

Mr. Levy: It is indeed a wonderful city. What a sight!

אבל איפה שדה-התעופה?

Ah-VAHL *eh*-FOH *s'deh-hah-teh-oo*-FAH?

But where is the airport?

אדון נבון : אנו עוברים על פני העיר,

Ah-DOHN *Nah*-VOHN: AH-*noo oh-v'*REEM *ahl p'neh* hah-EER,

Mr. Navon: We pass over the city,

ומגיעים תחלה לשדה-התעופה בלוד,

oo-mah-gee-EEM *t'hee*-LAH *less*-DEH-hah-teh-oo-FAH *b'Lod,*

and arrive first at the Lod airport,

הנמצא מאחוריה.

hah-neem-TSAH *meh-ah-hoh*-REH-hah.

which is right behind it.

זהו שדה־תעופה, מודרני, משוכלל כפי שתראה.
ZEH-hoo s'deh-teh-oo-FAH, moh-DER-nee, m'shookh-LAHL,
k'fee sheh-teer-EH.
It is a modern, well-equipped airfield, as you will see.

הנה הוא שם, התראה אותו?
Hee-NEH hoo shahm, hah-teer-EH oh-TOH?
There it is, do you see it?

אדון לוי: כן, באמת. נרגש אני עד מאד לחשוב
Ah-DOHN Leh-VEE: Kehn, beh-eh-METT. Neer-GAHSH ah-NEE
ahd meh-OHD lah-hah-SHOHV
Mr. Levy: Yes, indeed. I am very excited to think

שבעוד רגע אדרך על אדמת ארץ־ישראל העתיקה,
sheh-beh-OHD REH-gah edd-ROKH ahl ahd-MAHT EH-rets-Yis-rah-EHL
hah-ah-tee-KAH,
that in another moment I'll be treading the ancient ground of Israel,

מקום אבותינו חיו ועשו היסטוריה
mah-kohm ah-voh-TEH-noo hah-YOO veh-ah-SOO hees-TOHR-yah
the spot where our ancestors lived and made history

לפני אלפי שנים.
leef-NEH ahl-FEH shah-NEEM.
thousands of years ago.

אדון נבון: מבין אני יפה לרוחך,
Ah-DOHN Nah-VOHN: Meh-VEEN ah-NEE yah-FEH l'roo-hah-HAH,
Mr. Navon: I understand your feelings well,

ובטוח אני, כי תמצא את מדינת ישראל המודרנית
oo-vah-TOO-akh ah-NEE, kee teem-TSAH ett m'dee-NAHT Yis-rah-EHL
hah-moh-DER-neet
and I am sure you will find the modern State of Israel

ראויה לעברה המזהיר.
reh-oo-YAH lah-ah-vah-RAH hah-mahz-HEER.
worthy of its glorious past.

THINKING IN HEBREW
(Answers on page 293)

1. ‏לאן נוסעים האדונים לוי ונבון?‏

   Leh-AHN *noh-seh*-EEM *hah-ah-doh*-NEEM *Leh*-VEE *v'Nah*-VOHN?

2. ‏הנוסעים הם ברכבת או באניה?‏

   Hah-noh-seh-EEM *hehm bah-rah*-KEH-*vet oh bah-oh-nee*-YAH?

3. ‏במה אתה מעדיף לנסע?‏

   Bah-MEH *ah*-TAH *mah-ah*-DEEF *leen*-SOH-*ah?*

4. ‏מדוע?‏

   Mah-DOO-*ah?*

5. ‏איפה נפגשו הידידים לבסוף?‏

   Eh-FOH *neef-g'*SHOO *hah-y'dee*-DEEM *leev*-SOHF?

6. ‏מדוע שמחו הידידים על שנפגשו שוב?‏

   Mah-DOO-*ah sah-m'*HOO *hah-y'dee*-DEEM *ahl she-neef-g'*SHOO *shoov?*

7. ‏תאר את מה שרואים כשמתקרבים לחוף ישראל?‏

   Γah-EHR *ett mah she-roh*-EEM *k'sheh-meet-kahr*-VEEM *l'hohf Yis-rah*-EHL?

8. איך היה הנוף בישראל לפנים ?
Ehkh hah-YAH hah-NOHF b'Yis-rah-EHL l'fah-NEEM?

9. ואיך הנוף כיום ?
Veh-EHKH hah-NOHF kah-YOHM?

10. מהי הסבה לשנוי זה ?
MAH-hee hah-see-BAH l'shee-NOOY zeh?

11. מה דעתו של אדון לוי על תל־אביב ?
Mah dah-TOH shell ah-DOHN Leh-VEE ahl Tel-Ah-VEEV?

12. הקרוב שדה־התעופה לעיר תל־אביב ?
Hah-kah-ROHV s'deh-hah teh-oo-FAH leh-EER Tel-Ah-VEEV?

13. מדוע כה נרגש אדון לוי ?
Mah-DOO-ah koh neer-GAHSH ah-DOHN Leh-VEE?

14. מה עונה לו ידידו אדון נבון ?
Mah-oh-NEH lo y'dee-DOH ah-DOHN Nah-VOHN?

15. ההיית נוסע ברצון לישראל ?
Heh-hah-YEE-tah noh-SEH-ah b'rah-TSOHN l'Yis-rah-EHL?

16. מהן הערים הראשיות בישראל ?
MAH-hehn heh-ah-REEM hah-roh-shee-YOHT b'Yis-rah-EHL?

שִׁעוּר 30

הִגַּעְנוּ.

Hee-GAH-noo.

We have arrived.

הַמְאָרַחַת: בְּרוּכִים הַבָּאִים לְיִשְׂרָאֵל,

Hah-meh-ah-RAH-haht: B'roo-HEEM hah-bah-EEM l'Yis-rah-EHL,

Hostess: Welcome to Israel,

גְּבִירוֹתַי וְרַבּוֹתַי! הִנֵּה שְׂדֵה־הַתְּעוּפָה לוֹד.

g'vee-roh-TIGH veh-rah-boh-TIGH! Hee-NEH s'deh-hah-teh-oo-FAH Lod.

ladies and gentlemen! This is Lod Airport.

AN ECHO FROM THE PAST:

The ancient formula בָּרוּךְ הַבָּא (*bah-ROOKH hah-BAH*) or, in its plural form, בְּרוּכִים הַבָּאִים (*b'roo-HEEM hah-bah-EEM*) has been in use since times immemorial to welcome newcomers. It literally means "Blessed the coming".

223

הנוסעים יפנו, בבקשה, תחילה למשרד העליה, ואחרי כן למכם.
*Hah-noh-seh-EEM yeef-NOO, b'vah-kah-SHAH, t'hee-LAH l'mees-RAHD
hah-ah-lee-YAH, veh-akh-RAY hehn l'MEH-hess.*
Passengers will please go first to the immigration office, and then
to Customs.

אנו מקוים שהנסיעה היתת נעימה.
AH-*noo m'kah*-VEEM *sheh-hah-n'see*-AH *hah-y'*TAH *neh-ee*-MAH.
We hope the trip was pleasant.

(במשרד העליה)
(B'*mees*-RAHD *hah-ah-lee*-YAH)
(At the immigration office)

פקיד־משרד העליה : השם והאזרחות, אדוני ?
P'*keed-mees*-RAHD *hah-ah-lee*-YAH: *Hah*-SHEHM *veh-hah-ez-rah*-HOOT,
ah-doh-NEE?
Immigration inspector: Name and nationality, sir?

נבון : שמי דן נבון אזרח ישראלי.
Nah-VOHN: *Sh'mee Dahn Nah*-VOHN *ez*-RAKH *Yis-reh-eh*-LEE.
Navon: My name is Dan Navon, an Israeli citizen.

הנה הדרכון שלי.
Hee-NEH *hah-dahr*-KOHN *sheh*-LEE.
Here is my passport.

הפקיד : תודה רבה. סור לבדיקת החפצים.
Hah-pah-KEED: *Toh*-DAH *rah*-BAH. *Soor leev-dee*-KAHT *ha-hah-fah*-TSEEM.
Inspector: Thank you. Go now to the baggage inspection.

NOTE ON THE IMPERATIVE:
In the masculine singular, the imperative forms are
usually similar to the stem. Examples:

סגר	(s'*gohr*)	"Close!"
דבר	(*dah*-BEHR)	"Speak!"
הכתב	(*hakh*-TEHV)	"Dictate!"
התלבש	(*heet-lah*-BEHSH)	"Dress (yourself)!"

In the feminine singular and plural and the masculine plural, the
imperative usually resembles the future, stripped of its characteristic
prefixes: Examples:

סגרי	(*see*-GREE)	"Close!" fem. sing.
דברו	(*dah-b'*ROO)	"Speak!" masc. plur.
הכתבנה	(*hakh*-TEHV-nah)	"Dictate!" fem. plur.
התלבשו	(*heet-lah-b'*SHOO)	"Dress! (yourselves)" masc. plur.

ואתה, אדוני ?

*Veh-ah-*TAH, *ah-doh-*NEE?

And you, sir?

לוי : יצחק לוי, אזרח אמריקאי.

*Leh-*VEE: *Yits-*HAHK *Leh-*VEE, *ez-*RAKH *ah-meh-ree-*KAH-*ee*.

Levy: Isaac Levy, an American citizen.

הנה הדרכון שלי עם האשרה לישראל.

*Hee-*NEH *hah-dahr-*KOHN *sheh-*LEE *im hah-ahsh-*RAH *l'Yis-rah-*EHL.

Here is my passport with the visa for Israel.

הפקיד : הכל בסדר, אדוני. אתה מדבר עברית מצוין.

*Hah-pah-*KEED: *Hah-*KOHL *b'*SEH-*der, ah-doh-*NEE. *Ah-*TAH *m'dah-*BEHR
*eev-*REET *m'tsoo-*YAHN.

Inspector: That is all right, sir. You speak Hebrew excellently.

הלמדת את השפה בארצות הברית?

*Hah-lah-*MAHD-*tah ett hah-sah-*FAH *beh-Ahr-*TSOHT *Hah-b'*REET?

Did you learn the language in the United States?

לוי : תודה. למדתי קצת מהורי בעודני ילד,

*Leh-*VEE: *Toh-*DAH. *Lah-*MAHD-*tee k'tsaht meh-hoh-*RIGH
*beh-oh-*DEH-*nee* YEH-*led*,

Levy: Thanks. I learned some from my parents while I was
still a child,

ולפני בואי הנה לקחתי קורס מזורז

*v'leef-*NEH *boh-*EE *HEH-*nah lah-*KAKH-*tee koors m'zoh-*RAHZ

and before coming here I took a rapid course

בבית-הספר ברליץ בניו יורק.

*b'veht-hah-*SEH-*fer Berlitz bee-New York.

at the Berlitz School in New York.

הפקיד : אכן, אתה באמת למדת היטב את השפה.

*Hah-pah-*KEED: *Ah-*HEHN, *ah-*TAH *beh-eh-*METT *lah-*MAHD-*tah heh-*TEHV
ett *hah-sah-*FAH.

Inspector: Well, you certainly learned the language well.

האם זה הבקור הראשון שלך בישראל ?

*Hah-*IM *zeh hah-bee-*KOOR *hah-ree-*SHOHN *sheh-l'*HAH *b'Yis-rah-*EHL?

Is this your first visit to Israel?

לוי : כן, אני אהיה פה כמה שבועות.

*Leh-*VEE: *Kehn. *Ah-*NEE *eh-*YEH *poh* *KAH-*mah shah-voo-*OHT.

Levy: Yes. I shall be here for several weeks.

הפקיד: מקוה אני כי תיהנה מבקורך.

*Hah-pah-*KEED: *M'kah-*VEH *ah-*NEE *kee teh-hah-*NEH *mee-bee-koor-*HAH.

Inspector: I hope you will enjoy your visit.

סור, בבקשה, לבקור מזוודותיך.

*Soor b'vah-kah-*SHAH *l'vee-*KOOR *meez-v'doh-*TEH-*hah.*

Please go on to the baggage inspection.

(במכם)   נבון (אל לוי): הוי הנך פה!

*(Bah-*MEH-*hess)*   *Nah-*VOHN (*ell Leh-*VEE): Hoy, *heen-*HAH *poh!*

(At Customs)   Navon (to Levy): Oh, here you are!

הנה חבילותינו על השולחן.

*Hee-*NEH *hah-vee-loh-*TEH-*noo ahl hah-shool-*HAHN.

Our bags are over here on the counter (table).

לוי: האם הבדיקה חמורה מאד? מה אסור?

*Leh-*VEE: *Hah-*IM *hah-b'dee-*KAH *hah-moo-*RAH *meh-*OHD? *Mah ah-*SOOR?

Levy: Is the inspection very strict? What is forbidden?

נבון: בתור אמריקאי הבא הנה בפעם הראשונה לא יחמירו אתך.

*Nah-*VOHN: *B'tohr Ah-meh-ree-*KAH-*ee hah-*BAH HEH-*nah bah-*PAH-*ahm
*hah-ree-shoh-*NAH *lo yakh-*MEE-*roo it-*HAH.

Navon: As an American coming here for the first time, they will not
be strict with you.

לכן הצהר על כל דבר בלי פחד.

*Lah-*HEHN *hahts-*HEHR *ahl kohl dah-*VAHR *b'lee* PAH-*hahd.*

Therefore declare everything without fear.

לוי: ומה ביחם אליך?

*Leh-*VEE: *Oo-*MAH *b'yah-*hahs *eh-*LEH-*hah?*

Levy: And what about you?

NOTE TO STUDENT:

Observe the use of the expression ביחם (*b'yah-hahs*)
in the sentence. It literally means "in relation to" but
can best be conversationally rendered by the English
"about".

נבון: כישראלי עלי לשלם מכם על הקניות שעשיתי בחוץ לארץ.

*Nah-*VOHN: *K'Yis-reh-eh-*LEE, *ah-*LIGH *l'shah-*LEHM MEH-*hess ahl
*hah-knee-*YOHT *sheh-ah-*SEE-*tee b'hoots lah-*AH-*rets.*

Navon: As an Israeli I must pay duty on the purchases
I have made abroad.

TWO WORDS — SAME MEANING:

The word "as" can be indiscriminately rendered, in Hebrew, by either בְּתוֹר (*b'tohr*) or כְּמוֹ (*k'moh*), or simply (*k'*). Observe the following examples: בְּתוֹר אמריקאי (*b'tohr Ah-mee-ree-KAH-ee*)—"As an American" כְּיִשְׂרְאֵלִי (*k'Yis-reh-eh-LEE*)—"As an Israeli".

פקיד-המכס : (מתקרב) פתח את מזוודותיך, בבקשה.
P'keed-hah-MEH-hess: (meet-kah-REHV) Ptakh ett meez-v'doh-TEH-hah, b'vah-kah-SHAH.
Customs Inspector: (he comes nearer) Open your suitcases, please.

היש לך משהו להצהיר ?
Hah-YEHSH l'hah mah-sheh-HOO leh-hats-HEER?
Have you anything to declare?

לוי : יש אתי אך ורק שתי מזוודות אלה. זה כל מה שיש לי.
Leh-VEE: Yehsh it-TEE akh v'RAHK sh'teh meez-vah-DOHT EH-leh. Zeh kohl mah sheh-YEHSH lee.
Levy: I have only these two suitcases with me. That's all I have.

A USEFUL IDIOM:

The word אַך (*akh*) means "only". So does the word רק (RAHK). For more emphasis, ("nothing but", "just only") both words are used one after the other, as in the preceding sentence.

פקיד-המכס : היש לך מטבע חוץ ?
P'keed-hah-MEH-hess: Hah-YEHSH l'hah maht-BEH-ah hoots?
Customs Inspector: Have you any foreign currency?

לוי : יש לי כמאה וחמשים דולר מלבד מכתבי-אשראי.
Leh-VEE: Yehsh lee k'meh-AH vah-hah-mee-SHEEM DOH-lahr meel-VAHD meekh-t'VEH-ahsh-RIGH.
Levy: I have about one hundred and fifty dollars, besides letters of credit.

פקיד-המכס : החלף אותם בבקשה ללירות ישראליות ליד האשנב שם.
P'keed-hah-MEH-hess: Hakh-LEHF oh-TAHM b'vah-kah-SHAH l'LEE-roht Yis-reh-eh-lee-YOHT l'yahd hah-esh-NAHV shahm.
Customs Inspector: Please change them into Israeli pounds at that window over there.

לוי: תודה רבה. היכול אני עתה ללכת?
To-DAH *rah*-BAH. *Hah-yah*-HOHL, *ah*-NEE *ah*-TAH *lah*-LEH-*het?*
Levy: Thank you, very much. May I go now?

פקיד־המכס: טוב מאד. (לנבון) ואתה, אדוני?
P'keed-hah-MEH-*hess:* *Tohv meh*-OHD. (*L'Nah*-VOHN) *Veh-ah*-TAH,
ah-doh-NEE?
Customs Inspector: Very well. (To Navon) And you, sir?

נבון: הנה ההצהרה שלי. חכה לי ליד הדלת,
Hee-NEH *hah-hahts-hah*-RAH *sheh*-LEE. *Hah*-KEH *lee l'yahd hah*-DEH-*let,*
Navon: Here is my declaration. Wait for me at the door,

יצחק, אהיה שם במהרה.
Yeets-HAHK, *eh*-YEH *shahm beem-heh*-RAH.
Isaac, I shall be there soon.

(ביציאה)
(*Bee-y'tsee*-AH)
(At the exit)

לוי: ההיה לך לשלם הרבה מכס?
Heh-hah-YAH *l'hah l'shah*-LEHM *hahr*-BEH MEH-*hess?*
Levy: Did you have to pay much duty?

נבון: כן, קניתי מצלמה חדשה באיטליה.
Kehn, kah-NEE-*tee mahts-leh*-MAH *hah-dah*-SHAH *beh-Ee-*TAHL-*yah.*
Navon: Yes, I did. I bought a new camera in Italy.

הנה מונית. הה, מונית!
Hee-NEH *moh*-NEET. Heh, *moh*-NEET!
There is a taxi. Hey, taxi!

הנהג: כן אדוני! לאן?
Hah-neh-HAHG: *Kehn, ah-doh*-NEE! *Leh*-AHN?
Cab driver: Yes, sir! Where to?

נבון: למלון „נורדאו־פלאז׳ה", להוריד את ידידי,
L'mah-LOHN "NOHR-*dow*-PLAH-*zhah", leh-hoh*-REED *ett y'dee*-DEE,
Navon: To the "Nordau Plaza" Hotel to drop my friend,

ואחר־כך לביתי ברחוב אלנבי 91.
veh-ah-HAHR-*kakh l'veh*-TEE *beer*-HOHV Allenby 91.
and then to my house at 91 Allenby Street.

THINKING IN HEBREW
(Answers on page 293)

1. באילו מלים קבלה המארחת את הנוסעים בבואם?

*Beh-*EH-*loo mee-*LEEM *keeb-*LAH *hah-meh-ah-*RAH-*haht ett
hah-noh-seh-*EEM *b'voh-*AHM?

2. מה עשו הנוסעים לאחר שעזבו את האוירון?

*Meh ah-*SOO *hah-noh-seh-*EEM *leh-ah-*HAHR *she-ah-z'*VOO
*ett hah-ah-vee-*ROHN?

3. אילו שאלות שואלים כרגיל במשרד-העליה?

EH-*loo she-eh-*LOHT *shoh-ah-*LEEM *kah-rah-*GEEL
*b'mees-*RAHD-*hah-ah-lee-*YAH?

4. האם שניהם נבון ולוי אזרחים ישראליים הם?

*Hah-*IM *sh'neh-*HEMM *Nah-*VOHN *v'Leh-*VEE *ez-rah-*HEEM
*Yis-reh-eh-lee-*YEEM *hehm?

5. מה אמר הפקיד ל„עברית" של אדון לוי?

*Mah ah-*MAHR *hah-pah-*KEED "*lah-eev-*REET" *shell ah-*DOHN *Leh-*VEE?

6. איפה למד אדון לוי לדבר עברית?

*Eh-*FOH *lah-*MAHD *ah-*DOHN *Leh-*VEE *l'dah-*BEHR *eev-*REET?

7. המדבר אתה עברית היטב כמו אדון לוי?

*Hah-m'dah-*BEHR *ah-*TAH *eev-*REET *heh-*TEHV *k'moh ah-*DOHN *Leh-*VEE?

8.   ההיית פעם בישראל ?

Heh-hah-YEE-tah PAH-*ahm b'Yis-rah-*EHL?

9.   מה כרגיל אומר פקיד-המכס אל הנוסעים ?

*Mah kah-rah-*GEEL *oh-*MEHR *p'keed-hah-*MEH-*hess ell hah-noh-seh-*EEM?

10.   על מה יש להצהיר במכס ?

*Ahl mah yehsh leh-hahts-*HEER *bah-*MEH-*hess?

11.   מי משני הידידים גמר תחילה עם בדיקת חפציו, ומדוע ?

*Mee mee-sh'*NEH *hah-y'dee-*DEEM *gah-*MAHR *t'hee-*LAH *im b'dee-*KAHT *hah-fah-*TSAHV, *oo-mah-*DOO-*ah?

12.   מדוע שלם אדון נבון הרבה מכם ?

*Mah-*DOO-*ah shee-*LEHM *ah-*DOHN *Nah-*VOHN *hahr-*BEH MEH-*hess?

13.   מה עשה אדון לוי עם הדולרים שלו ?

*Meh ah-*SAH *ah-*DOHN *Leh-*VEE *im hah-do-*LAH-*reem sheh-*LOH?

14.   איפה נפגשו שוב הידידים לאחר הבדיקה ?

*Eh-*FOH *neef-g'*SHOO *shoov hah-y'dee-*DEEM *leh-ah-*HAHR *hah-b'dee-*KAH?

15.   הנסעו לתל-אביב במכונית ?

*Hah-nah-seh-*OO *l'Tel-Ah-*VEEV *bah-m'moh-*NEET?

16.   לאן הם הפנו את הנהג תחילה, ומדוע ?

*Leh-*AHN *hehm heef-*NOO *ett hah-neh-*HAHG *t'hee-*LAH, *oo-mah-*DOO-*ah?

לִיד הַמָּלוֹן
*L'yahd hah-mah-*LOHN
At the Hotel

נָבוֹן: הִנֵּה אֲנַחְנוּ לְיַד הַמָּלוֹן.
*Nah-*VOHN: *Hee-*NEH *ah-*NAKH*-noo l'yahd hah-mah-*LOHN.
Navon: Here we are at the hotel.

וְעַכְשָׁו לִפְנֵי לֶכְתְּךָ עָלֶיךָ לְהַבְטִיחַ לִי לָבוֹא
לְבֵיתִי לַאֲרוּחַת עֶרֶב.
*Veh-akh-*SHAV *leef-*NEH *lekh-t'*HAH *ah-*LEH*-hah leh-hahv-*TEE*-akh lee
lah-*VOH *l'veh-*TEE *lah-ah-roo-*HAHT EH*-rev.*
Now, before you go, you must promise me to come to my house
for dinner.

לֵוִי: אֶהְיֶה מְאוּשָׁר.
*Leh-*VEE: *Eh-*YEH *meh-oo-*SHAHR.
Levy: I'll be delighted.

נבון: הנה כתובתי, ואני אחכה לך בשעה שמונה.

*Nah-*VOHN: *Hee-*NEH *k'toov-*TEE, *vah-ah-*NEE *ah-hah-*KEH *l'hah
*b'shah-*AH *sh'moh-*NEH.

Navon: Here is my address, and I'll wait for you at eight o'c¹

תהיה לנו מסיבת חנוכה הערב,

*Tee-*YEH LAH-*noo m'see-*BAHT Hah-*noo-*KAH hah-*EH-rev,

We are having a Chanuka party tonight,

ושם תפגש הרבה מידידינו.

*v'shahm teef-*GOHSH hahr-*BEH *mee-y'dee-*DAY-noo.

and you will meet many of our friends there.

לוי: אל תדאג. אהיה שם, ותודה רבה לך בעד הזמנתך האדיבה.

*Leh-*VEE: *Ahl teed-*AHG. *Eh-*YEH shahm, *v'toh-*DAH *rah-*BAH *l'hah
*beh-*AHD *hahz-mah-naht-*HAH hah-ah-dee-*VAH.

Levy: Don't worry. I'll be there. And thank you very much
for your kind invitation.

(לוי נכנם למלון)

(*Leh-*VEE *neekh-*NAHS *lah-mah-*LOHN)

(Levy enters the hotel)

פקיד-המלון: במה אוכל לשרת אותך?

*P'keed-hah-mah-*LOHN: *Bah-*MEH *oo-*HAHL *l'shah-*REHT *oh-t'*HAH?

Hotel clerk: How can I serve you?

לוי: היש לך חדר בשבילי?

*Leh-*VEE: *Hah-*YEHSH *l'hah HEH-*der *beesh-vee-*LEE?

Levy: Have you a room for me?

שלחתי הנה מברק מרומא. שמי יצחק לוי.

*Sha'-*LAKH-*tee HEH-*nah *meev-*RAHK *meh-*ROH-mah. *Sh'mee Yits-*HAHK
*Leh-*VEE.

I sent a telegram from Rome. My name is Isaac Levy.

AS QUICK AS LIGHTNING:

The word מברק (*meev-*RAHK) meaning "telegram"
is another instance of the adaptation of old words to
modern meanings. It is formed from ברק (*bah-*RAHK)
meaning "lightning".

פקיד-המלון: כן, כן! אדון לוי מאמריקה?

*P'keed-hah-mah-*LOHN: *Kehn, kehn! *Ah-*DOHN *Leh-*VEE
*meh-*Ah-*MEH-ree-kah?

Hotel clerk: Oh, yes! Mr. Levy from America?

A DOUBLE AFFIRMATIVE:

To stress an affirmation, similar to the English "Oh, yes" or "Yes, indeed", all you have to do in Hebrew is to repeat the word כּן (*kehn*) twice, as in the preceding sentence.

יש לך חדר מספר 207.
Yehsh l'hah HEH-*der mees*-PAHR 207.
You have room number 207.

התּוֹאיל לחתום כּאן ?
Hah-toh-EEL *lakh*-TOHM KAH-*ahn?*
Would you be good enough to sign here?

לוי : טוב מאד. אשאר פה כּמה שבועות.
Leh-VEE: *Tohv meh*-OHD. *Eh-shah*-EHR *poh* KAH-*mah shah-voo*-OHT.
Levy: Very well. I shall stay here for several weeks.

מהו התּשלום השבועי בּעד חדרי ?
MAH-*hoo hah-tahsh*-LOOM *hahsh-voo*-EE *beh*-AHD *hedd*-REE?
What is the weekly payment for my room?

הפּקיד : זה יעלה לך בּעשרים לירות לשבוע, אדוני,
Hah-pah-KEED: *Zeh yah-ah*-LEH *l'hah beh-ess*-REEM LEE-*roht l'shah*-VOO-*ah, ah-doh*-NEE,
Clerk: It will cost you twenty pounds a week, sir,

הכּוללות גם ארוחת בּוקר.
*hah-koh-l'*LOHT *gahm ah-roo*-HAHT BOH-*kerr*.
including also breakfast.

הנה המפתּח לחדרך.
Hee-NEH *hah-mahf*-TEH-*akh leh-hed-r'*HAH.
Here is the key to your room.

לוי : תּודה רבּה.
Leh-VEE: *Toh*-DAH *rah*-BAH.
Levy: Thank you very much.

הפּקיד : ילד, קח את המזודות האלה לחדר 207.
Hah-pah-KEED: YEH-*led, kakh ett hah-meez-vah*-DOHT *hah*-EH-*leh l'*HEH-*der* 207.
Clerk: Boy, take these suitcases to Room 207.

לוי : שים לב! אל תשכח את החבילה הקטנה ההיא.

Leh-VEE: Seem lehv! Ahl teesh-KAKH ett hah-hah-vee-LAH
hah-k'tah-NAH hah-HEE.

Levy: Take care! Don't forget that little bag over there.

PUT YOUR HEART INTO IT!

The expression **שים לב** (*seem lehv*) literally means "put your heart", and is used for such exclamations as "take care", "pay attention!", etc. Another expression having a similar meaning ("take care!") is **השגח,** (*hahsh-GAKH*), as you will see later.

בתוכה ישנם כל הנירות שלי,

B'toh-HAH yehsh-NAHM kohl hah-n'yah-ROHT sheh-LEE,
It has all my papers in it,

ואיני רוצה לאבדה.

veh-eh-NEE roh-TSEH leh-ah-b'DAH.
and I don't want to lose it.

לוי הולך לחדרו, מתרחץ, מוציא את בגדיו,

Leh-VEE hoh-LEHKH l'hed-ROH, meet-rah-HEHTS, moh-TSEE ett b'gah-DAHV,
Levy goes to his room, washes, unpacks his suits,

מחליף לבושו, ויוצא לרחוב.

makh-LEEF l'voo-SHOH, v'yoh-TSEH lah-r'HOHV.
changes his clothes, and goes out into the street.

הוא מתפלא למראה החנויות היפות,

Hoo meet-pah-LEH l'mahr-EH hah-hah-noo-YOHT hah-yah-FOHT,
He admires the appearance of the beautiful shops,

AN IDIOMATIC EXPRESSION:

The expression **הוא מתפלא למראה...** (*hoo meet-pah-LEH l'mahr-EH*) rendered above by "he admires" literally means: "he is perplexed at the sight of..."

ונכנס לחנות פרחים.

v'neekh-NAHS leh-hah-NOOT p'rah-HEEM.
and enters a flower shop.

(בחנות לפרחים)

(*Beh-hah-*NOOT *leef-rah-*HEEM)

(In the flower shop)

הזבנית: שלום, אדוני! במה אוכל לשרתך?

*Hah-zah-bah-*NEET: *Shah-*LOHM, *ah-doh-*NEE! *Bah-*MEH *oo-*HAHL
*l'shah-ret-*HAH?

Salesgirl: Good day, sir. How can I serve you?

לוי: הביטי. הולך אני הערב למסיבה,

*Leh-*VEE: *Hah-*BEE-*tee.* *Hoh-*LEHKH *ah-*NEE *hah-*EH-*rev leem-see-*BAH,

Levy: Look. I am going to a party tonight,

ואני מבקש ממך לשלוח זר פרחים יפה לפי הכתובת הזאת

*vah-ah-*NEE *m'vah-*KEHSH *mee-*MEHKH *leesh-*LOH-*akh zehr prah-*HEEM
*yah-*FEH *l'fee hah-k'*TOH-*vet hah-*ZOHT

and I want you to send a nice bouquet of flowers to this address

(מראה לה פרטים עם כתובת אדון נבון).

(*mahr-*EH *lah kahr-*TEES *im k'*TOH-*vet ah-*DOHN *Nah-*VOHN).

(shows her a card with Mr. Navon's address).

הזבנית: התרצה את הסל הזה המקושט בגלדיולות,

*Hah-zah-bah-*NEET: *Hah-teer-*TSEH *ett hah-*SAHL *hah-*ZEH *hah-m'koo-*
SHAHT *bee-glahd-*YOH-*loht,

Salesgirl: Would you like this basket decorated with gladiolas,

או הנך מעדיף את השושנים האדומות האלה?

*oh heen-*HAH *mah-ah-*DEEF *ett hah-shoh-shah-*NEEM *hah-ah-doo-*MOHT
*hah-*EH-*leh?

or do you prefer these red roses?

לוי: אין זאת פגישה רומנטית. הואיל והזכרת שושנים,

*Leh-*VEE: *Ehn zoht p'gee-*SHAH *roh-*MAHN-*teet.* *Hoh-*EEL
*v'heez-*KAHRT *shoh-shah-*NEEM,

Levy: This is not such a romantic appointment. Since you
mentioned roses,

המשתמשים אתם עדיין בבטוי:

*hah-meesh-tahm-*SHEEM *ah-*TEMM *ah-*DAH-*yin bah-bee-*TOOY:

do you still use the expression:

„שושנת חברון" כדי לתאר בחורה נחמדה?

*"shoh-shah-*NAT *Hev-*ROHN" *k'deh l'tah-*EHR *bah-hoo-*RAH *nekh-mah-*DAH?

"rose of Hebron" to describe a lovely girl?

רבים בודאי יקראו לך תכופות כן.

Rah-BEEM *b'vah*-DIGH *yeek-reh*-OO *lakh t'hoo*-FOHT *kehn.*

People surely often call you so.

הזבנית: (צוחקת) איני זוכרת אם שמעתי זאת,

Hah-zah-bah-NEET: (*tsoh*-HEH-*ket*) *Eh*-NEE *zoh*-HEH-*ret im*
shah-MAH-*tee zoht,*

Salesgirl: (laughing) I don't remember having heard it,

אדוני. יתכן שמשתתמשים בבטוי זה.

ah-doh-NEE. *Yee-tah*-HEHN *sheh-meesh-tahm*-SHEEM *b'vee*-TOOY *zeh.*

sir. They may use it, though.

לוי: כן, בחוג משפחתי אומרים כך, וכמובן הבטוי

Leh-VEE: *Kehn, b'hoog meesh-pakh*-TEE *oh-m'*REEM *kakh, oo-h'moo*-VAHN
hah-bee-TOOY

Levy: Yes, my folks did, and it certainly

מתאים לך. בכמה עולה הסל הזה?

maht-EEM *lakh. B'*HAH-*mah oh*-LEH *hah*-SAHL *hah*-ZEH?

fits you. How much is this basket?

הזבנית: שלוש לירות, אדוני, כולל מם.

Hah-zah-bah-NEET: *Shah*-LOHSH LEE-*roht, ah-doh*-NEE, *koh*-LEHL *mahs.*

Salesgirl: Three pounds, sir, including tax.

לוי: הנה שלוש לירות, בבקשה לדאג לכך, כי הפרחים

Leh-VEE: *Hee*-NEH *shah*-LOHSH LEE-*roht, b'vah-kah*-SHAH *leed*-OHG *l'hakh,*
kee hah-p'rah-HEEM

Levy: There are three pounds. Please, see that the flowers

יגיעו לפני שמונה הערב.

yah-GEE-*oo leef*-NEH *sh'moh*-NEH *hah*-EH-*rev.*

are delivered before 8 o'clock this evening.

הזבנית: כמובן אדוני. תודה רבה. שלום.

Hah-zah-bah-NEET: *K'moo*-VAHN, *ah-doh*-NEE. *Toh*-DAH *rah*-BAH.
Shah-LOHM.

Salesgirl: Certainly, sir. Thank you. Goodbye.

THINKING IN HEBREW
(Answers on page 294)

1.   ‏מה אמר אדון נבון לאדון לוי ליד המלון ?‏

*Mah ah-*MAHR *ah-*DOHN *Nah-*VOHN *lah-ah-*DOHN *Leh-*VEE
*l'yahd hah-mah-*LOHN?

2.   ‏מתי יבוא אדון לוי לביתו של אדון נבון ?‏

*Mah-*TIGH *yah-*VOH *ah-*DOHN *Leh-*VEE *l'veh-*TOH *shell ah-*DOHN *Nah-*VOHN?

3.   ‏היערך אדון נבון מסיבה בביתו ?‏

*Hah-yah-ah-*ROHKH *ah-*DOHN *Nah-*VOHN *m'see-*BAH *b'veh-*TOH?

4.   ‏התערך בביתך מסיבת-חנוכה השנה ?‏

*Hah-tah-ah-*ROHKH *b'veh-t'*HAH *m'see-*BAHT-*Hah-noo-*KAH *hah-shah-*NAH?

5.   ‏כמה זמן ישהה אדון לוי בתל-אביב ?‏

KAH-*mah z'mahn yeesh-*HEH *ah-*DOHN *Leh-*VEE *b'Tel-Ah-*VEEV?

6. מי יביא את מזודותיו לחדרו?

*Mee yah-*VEE *ett meez-v'doh-*TAHV *l'hed-*ROH?

7. מה יעשה אדון לוי כשיכנס לחדרו?

*Mah yah-ah-*SEH *ah-*DOHN *Leh-*VEE *k'sheh-yee-kah-*NEHS *l'hed-*ROH?

8. איפה יאכל אדון לוי את ארוחת־הבוקר מחר?

*Eh-*FOH *yoh-*HAHL *ah-*DOHN *Leh-*VEE *ett ah-roo-*HAHT-*hah-*BOH-*ker*
*mah-*HAHR?

9. התלך מחר לעבודה?

*Hah-teh-*LEHKH *mah-*HAHR *lah-ah-voh-*DAH?

10. איפה קנה אדון לוי פרחים?

*Eh-*FOH *kah-*NAH *ah-*DOHN *Leh-*VEE *p'rah-*HEEM?

11. אמר לי בבקשה, את הצבעים?

*Eh-*MOHR *lee b'vah-kah-*SHAH, *ett hah-ts'vah-*EEM?

12. היביא אדון לוי בעצמו את הפרחים לביתו של אדון נבון?

*Hah-yah-*VEE *ah-*DOHN *Leh-*VEE *beh-ahts-*MOH *ett hah-p'rah-*HEEM
*l'veh-*TOH *shell ah-*DOHN *Na-*VOHN?

13. בכמה עלו הפרחים שקנה אדון לוי?

*B'HAH-mah ah-*LOO *hah-p'rah-*HEEM *sheh-kah-*NAH *ah-*DOHN *Leh-*VEE?

14. מתי יתקבלו הפרחים בבית נבון?

*Mah-*TIGH *yeet-kah-b'*LOO *hah-p'rah-*HEEM *b'veht Nah-*VOHN?

15. מדוע צריכים הפרחים להגיע לשם לפני שמונה?

*Mah-*DOO-*ah ts'ree-*HEEM *hah-p'rah-*HEEM *leh-hah-*GEE-*ah l'shahm*
*leef-*NEH *sh'moh-*NEH?

בָּרוּךְ הַבָּא!
Bah-ROOKH hah-BAH!
Welcome!

אֲדוֹן לֵוִי מַגִּיעַ לְבֵית יְדִידוֹ בְּשָׁעָה שְׁמוֹנֶה בְּדִיּוּק.
Ah-DOHN Leh-VEE mah-GEE-ah l'veht y'dee-DOH b'shah-AH sh'moh-NEH
b'dee-YOOK.
Mr. Levy arrives at the house of his friend at eight o'clock **sharp.**

מְצַלְצֵל בְּפַעֲמוֹן הַדֶּלֶת הָרֹאשִׁית.
M'tsahl-TSEHL beh-fah-MOHN hah-DEH-let hah-roh-SHEET.
He rings the front door bell.

נָבוֹן: הָאַח! בָּרוּךְ הַבָּא, יִצְחָק יְקִירִי. אָנָּא הִכָּנֵס!
Nah-VOHN: Heh-AKH! Bah-ROOKH hah-BAH, Yits-HAHK yah-kee-REE.
AH-nah hee-kah-NEHS!
Navon: Oh! Welcome, my dear Isaac. Do come in!

HOW TO SHOW YOUR SURPRISE:

The exclamation !האח (heh-AKH!) is used to express surprise, similar to the English "Oh!"

A USEFUL WORD:

"Please" can be rendered not only by בבקשה (b'vah-kah-SHAH) but also by אנא (AH-nah) when it is used in a sentence, and not as a separate word. אנא (AH-nah) can be abbreviated to נא (nah).

(נכנסים) יכול אתה להשאיר כאן את המעיל והכובע שלך.
(Neekh-nah-SEEM) Yah-HOHL ah-TAH leh-hahsh-EER KAH-ahn ett hah-meh-EEL veh-hah-KOH-vah shell-HAH.
(They enter) You can leave your coat and hat right here.

בוא ואציגך לפני האורחים.
Boh vah-ah-tseeg-HAH leef-NEH hah-oh-r'HEEM.
Come in, and I'll introduce you to the guests.

לוי : תודה רבה. רואה אני, כי יש לך פה מסיבה.
Leh-VEE: Toh-DAH rah-BAH. Roh-EH ah-NEE kee yehsh l'hah poh m'see-BAH.
Levy: Thank you. I see you have a party here.

נבון : אנו הזמנו רק אחדים מידידינו הקרובים.
Nah-VOHN: AH-noo heez-MAH-noo rahk ah-HAH-deem mee-y'dee-DEH-noo hah-k'roh-VEEM.
Navon: We have invited only some of our close friends.

(מוביל את אדון לוי לחדר האורחים, מקום
(Moh-VEEL ett ah-DOHN Leh-VEE lah-hah-DAHR hah-oh-r'HEEM, m'kohm
(He leads Mr. Levy into the living room, where

שהגברת נבון שקועה בשיחה עם גברת אחת ואדון אחד.)
sheh-hah-g'VEH-ret Nah-VOHN sh'koo-AH b'see-HAH im g'VEH-ret ah-HAHT vah-ah-DOHN eh-HAHD.)
Mrs. Navon is absorbed in a conversation with a lady and a gentleman.)

אדון נבון : שרה, יקירתי ! האוכל להפסיקך לרגע ?
Ah-DOHN Nah-VOHN: Sah-RAH, yah-kee-rah-TEE! Hah-oo-HAHL leh-hahf-see-KEHKH l'REH-gah?
Mr. Navon: Sarah, my dear! May I interrupt you for a moment?

NOTE ON POLITENESS:

The verb יכול (*yah*-HOHL) means both "can" and "may". A colloquial interrogative form like "May I?" can be best rendered, in Hebrew, by the use of the future tense. That is why Mr. Navon says האוכל (*Hah-oo*-HAHL) which literally means "shall I be able to...?", but corresponds, in spirit, to a polite "may I...?"

הרשיני להציג לפניך את ידידי הותיק אדון לוי.
*Hahr-*SHEE-*nee leh-hah-*TSEEG *l'fah-*NAH-*yeekh ett y'dee-*DEE
*hah-vah-*TEEK *Ah-*DOHN *Leh-*VEE.
Allow me to introduce to you my old friend Mr. Levy.

אדון לוי : נעים לי להכירך, גברת !
*Ah-*DOHN *Leh-*VEE: *Nah-*EEM *lee leh-hah-kee-*REHKH, *g'veh-*ret!
Mr. Levy: How do you do, Madam?

A SOCIAL NOTE:

The expression נעים לי להכירך (*nah-*EEM *lee leh-hah-kee-*REHKH) has been freely translated by "How do you do?" This standard formula used after a social introduction literally means: "It is pleasant to me to know you, Madam".

גברת נבון: שמחה אני לבואך, אדון לוי,
*g'veh-*ret *Nah-*VOHN: *S'meh-*HAH *ah-*NEE *l'voh-ah-*HAH, *ah-*DOHN *Leh-*VEE,
Mrs. Navon: I am glad to meet you, Mr. Levy,

ותודה רבה לך בעד הפרחים הנחמדים.
*v'toh-*DAH *rah-*BAH *l'hah beh-*AHD *hah-p'rah-*HEEM *hah-nekh-mah-*DEEM.
and thanks very much for the lovely flowers.

מקוה אני, כי תחבב את תל-אביב.
*M'kah-*VAH *ah-*NEE, *kee t'hah-*BEHV *ett Tel-Ah-*VEEV.
I hope you will like Tel-Aviv.

אדון לוי : לא הספקתי עדין לראות הרבה בעיר,
*Ah-*DOHN *Leh-*VEE: *Lo hees-*PAHK-*tee ah-*DAH-*yin leer-*OHT
*hahr-*BEH *bah-*EER,
Mr. Levy: I have not as yet managed to see much of the city,

אבל נתרשמתי מגודל העיר והסגנון הנהדר של הבנינים המודרניים.
*ah-*VAHL *neet-rah-*SHAHM-*tee mee-*GOH-*del hah-*EER veh-hah-seeg-*NOHN
*hah-neh-*DAHR shell hah-been-yah-*NEEM hah-moh-der-nee-*YEEM.
but was quite impressed with the size of the city and the style of the beautiful modern buildings.

אדון נבון : יצחק, בוא נא, ותפיר את ידידינו.

Ah-DOHN Nah-VOHN: Yits-HAHK, boh nah, v'tah-KEER ett y'dee-DEH-noo.

Mr. Navon: Isaac, come, please, and make the acquaintance of
our friends.

פרופסור וגברת כהן, אדון לוי.

Proh-FES-sohr oo-g'VEH-ret Kohn, ah-DOHN Leh-VEE.

Professor and Mrs. Kohn, Mr. Levy.

פרופסור והגברת כהן : נעים לנו להכירך אדון לוי !

*Proh-FES-sohr veh-hah-g'VEH-ret Kohn: Nah-EEM LAH-noo leh-hah-keer-
HAH ah-DOHN Leh-VEE?*

Professor and Mrs. Kohn: How do you do, Mr. Levy?

אדון לוי : נעים לי להכירך, גברת.

Ah-DOHN Leh-VEE: Nah-EEM lee leh-hah-kee-REHKH, g'VEH-ret.

Mr. Levy: How do you do, Madam?

וגאה אני באמת ללחוץ את ידך, פרופסור.

V'geh-EH ah-NEE beh-eh-METT leel-HOHTS ett yah-d'HAH, Proh-FES-sohr.

And I am really proud to shake hands with you, Professor.

זה עתה קראתי את ספרך האחרון על הנושא

Zeh ah-TAH kah-RAH-tee ett seef-r'HAH hah-ah-hah-ROHN ahl hah-noh-SEH

I have just read your last book on the subject of

„יציאת מצרים", וברצוני לברך אותך

"Y'tsee-AHT-Meets-RAH-yim," oo-veer-tsoh-NEE l'vah-REHKH oh-t'HAH

"The Exodus from Egypt," and I wish to congratulate you

על עבודתך זו היוצאת מן הכלל.

ahl ah-voh-daht-HAH zoh hah-yoh-TSEHT meen hah-k'LAHL.

on this outstanding piece of work.

פרופסור : תודה רבה לך אדוני.

Proh-FES-sohr: Toh-DAH rah-BAH l'hah ah-doh-NEE.

Professor: Thank you very much, sir.

הערכה כזו מקורא אמריקאי מחניפה מאד.

*Hah-ah-rah-HAH kah-ZOH mee-koh-REH ah-meh-ree-KAH-ee
makh-nee-FAH meh-OHD.*

Such appreciation from an American reader is very flattering.

הקראת את עבודתי במקור העברי ?

Hah-kah-RAH-tah ett ah-voh-dah-TEE bah-mah-KOHR hah-eev-REE?

Did you read my work in the original Hebrew?

אדון לוי: לא, לדאבוני. יכלתי להשיג רק תרגום.

Ah-DOHN Leh-VEE: Lo, l'dah-ah-voh-NEE. Yah-HOHL-tee leh-hah-SEEG
rahk teer-GOOM.

Mr. Levy: No, to my regret, I could only obtain a translation.

אלא שסבור אני שהיה זה תרגום טוב מאד,

EH-lah sheh-sah-VOOR ah-NEE sheh-hah-YAH zeh teer-GOOM tohv
meh-OHD,

But I think it was a very good translation,

עד כמה שאני יכל לשפט.

ahd KAH-mah sheh-ah-NEE yah-HOHL leesh-POHT.

as far as I can judge.

פרופסור: כן, המתרגם האנגלי שלי ד"ר ליקום,

Proh-FES-sohr: Kehn, hah-m'tahr-GEHM hah-ahn-GLEE sheh-LEE
Dr. LEE-koos,

Professor: Oh, yes, my English translator, Dr. Lekus,

הוא עצמו סופר מצוין והייתי מאושר

hoo ahts-MOH soh-FEHR m'tsoo-YAHN, veh-hah-YEE-tee meh-oo-SHAHR

is an eminent writer himself, and I was happy

למצא מתרגם שכזה.

leem-TSOH m'tahr-GEHM sheh-kah-ZEH.

to find such a translator.

המעונין אתה בחקירת ההיסטוריה, אדוני?

Hah-meh-oon-YAHN ah-TAH bah-hah-kee-RAHT hah-hees-TOHR-yah,
ah-doh-NEE?

Are you interested in historical research, sir?

אדון לוי: הייתי תמיד מעונין

Ah-DOHN Leh-VEE: Hah-YEE-tee tah-MEED meh-oon-YAHN

Mr. Levy: I have always been interested

בה כחובב, והסברתך למאורע ההיסטורי ההוא

bah k'hoh-VEHV, veh-hahs-bah-raht-HAH lah-meh-oh-RAH
hah-hees-TOH-ree hah-HOO

in it as an amateur, and your explanation of that historical event

ענין אותי במיוחד.

een-YEHN oh-TEE beem-yoo-HAHD.

interested me especially.

גברת נבון: רבותי, התכבדו ביין, בבקשה.

G'VEH-ret Nah-VOHN: Rah-boh-TIGH, heet-kah-b'DOO b'YAH-yeen, b'vah-kah-SHAH.

Mrs. Navon: Gentlemen, please help yourself to wine.

אדון לוי, טעם נא מן העוגות האלה.

Ah-DOHN Leh-VEE, teh-AHM nah meen hah-oo-GOHT hah-EH-leh.

Mr. Levy, please taste these cakes.

לוי: תודה לך, גברת. לחיים וחג שמח.

Leh-VEE: Toh-DAH lakh, G'VEH-ret. Leh-hah-YIM v'hahg sah-MEH-akh.

Levy: Thank you, Madam. To your health and a happy holiday.

נבון: גבירותי ורבותי, הכנסו לחדר אחר;

Nah-VOHN: G'vee-roh-TIGH v'rah-boh-TIGH, hee-kah-n'SOO l'HEH-der ah-HEHR;

Navon: Ladies and gentlemen, please enter the other room;

הדור הצעיר שלנו ירקוד עכשו את רקוד

hah-DOHR hah-tsah-EER sheh-LAH-noo yeer-KOHD akh-SHAHV ett ree-KOOD

our young generation will now dance

ה„הורה". הבה נצטרף אליהם.

hah-"HOH-rah". Hah-VAH neets-tah-REHF ah-leh-HEMM.

the "Hora" dance. Let us join them.

לוי: הוי! כמה מעניין! אף פעם לא ראיתי הופעה

Leh-VEE: Hoy! KAH-mah meh-ahn-YEHN! Aff PAH-ahm lo rah-EEH-tee hoh-fah-AH

Levy: Oh! how interesting! I have never seen a performance of

של הרקוד המסורתי.

shell hah-ree-KOOD hah-m'soh-rah-TEE.

this traditional dance.

(כולם עוברים לחדר אחר)

(Koo-LAHM oh-v'REEM lah-HEH-der ah-HEHR)

(They all go to another room)

נבון: ילדים! זה הוא ידידי אדון לוי מאמריקה.

Nah-VOHN: Y'lah-DEEM! Zeh hoo y'dee-DEE Ah-DOHN Leh-VEE meh-Ah-MEH-ree-kah.

Navon: Children! This is my friend, Mr. Levy, from America.

הראו לו את רקוד ה„הורה" האמתי.

Hahr-oo lo ett ree-KOOD hah-"HOH-rah" hah-ah-mee-TEE.

Show him the real "Hora" dance.

אלה ילדי רות ועוזי ובני דודיהם

EH-leh y'lah-DIGH, *Ruth veh-Oo-zee, oo-v'NEH doh-deh-*HEMM

These are my children, Ruth and Uzi, and their cousins

רבקה ואברהם כספי.

*Reev-*KAH *veh-Ahv-rah-*HAHM KAHS-*pee.*

Rebecca and Abraham Caspy.

NOTE ON RELATIVES:

The word בֶּן־דוד (*ben-*DOHD) translated here as "cousin" literally means "son of the uncle". In the preceding sentence you encounter the contracted plural form, linked to the possessive pronoun: בְּנֵי־דודיהם (*b'neh doh-deh-*HEMM) meaning "their cousins".

הבחורה הצעירה והנחמדה הזאת היא בת הפרופסור כהן.

*Hah-bah-hoo-*RAH *hah-tseh-ee-*RAH *veh-hah-nekh-mah-*DAH *hah-*ZOHT *hee baht hah-Proh-*FES-*sohr Kohn.*

This lovely young lady is the daughter of Professor Kohn.

הצעירים: ברוך בואך, אדון לוי!

*Hah-tseh-ee-*REEM: *Bah-*ROOKH *boh-ah-*HAH, *ah-*DOHN *Leh-*VEE!

Young people: You are welcome, Mr. Levy!

אדון לוי: תודה לכם בעד קבלת הפנים הלבבית,

*Ah-*DOHN *Leh-*VEE: *Toh-*DAH *lah-*HEMM *beh-*AHD *kah-bah-*LAHT *hah-pah-*NEEM *hah-l'vah-*VEET,

Mr. Levy: Thank you for the hearty welcome,

ידידי הצעירים. צחוקכם, פניכם המאושרים

*y'dee-*DIGH *hah-tseh-ee-*REEM. *Ts'hohk-*HEMM, *p'neh-*HEMM *hah-meh-oo-shah-*REEM

my young friends. Your smiling, happy faces

עושים גם אותי צעיר יותר. חג שמח לכולכם.

*oh-*SEEM *gahm oh-*TEE *tsah-*EER *yoh-*TEHR. *Hahg sah-*MEH-*akh l'hool-*HEMM.

make me feel younger too. A happy holiday to all of you.

הגברת כהן: אינך צריך רק להרגיש את עצמך צעיר,

*Hah-G'veh-ret Kohn: Ehn-*HAH *tsah-*REEKH *rakh-leh-hahr-*GEESH *ett ahts-meh-*HAH *tsah-*EER,

Mrs. Kohn: You don't have only to feel young,

אדון לוי ; אתה בעצמך איש צעיר באמת.

*ah-*DOHN *Leh-*VEE; *ah-*TAH *beh-ahts-meh-*HAH *eesh tsah-*EER *beh-eh-*METT.

Mr. Levy; you are quite a young man yourself.

לוי : כן אלא שיכול אני עדין להיות אבא

Leh-VEE: *Kehn, eh-*LAH *sheh-yah-*HOHL *ah-*NEE *ah-*DAH-*yin* lee-YOHT.
*ah-*BAH

Levy: Well, but I still could be these

לילדים אלה, גברתי. בכל אופן תודה בעד המחמאה.

*lee-y'lah-*DEEM EH-*leh,* G'veer-TEE. *Bhohl* OH-*fenn toh-*DAH *beh-*AHD
*hah-makh-mah-*AH.

children's father, Madam. Anyway, thanks for the compliment.

הגברת כהן הצעירה : אתה כמובן אינך יכול להיות אבא שלי.

Ÿah-G'VEH-ret KOHN *hah-tseh-ee-*RAH: *Ah-*TAH *k'moo-*VAHN *ehn-*HAH
*yaah-*HOHL *leeh-*YOHT *ah-*BAH *sheh-*LEE.

Miss Kohn: You certainly could not be my father.

אינך מבוגר למדי.

*Ehn-*HAH *m'voo-*GAHR *l'mah-*DIGH.
You are not old enough.

NOTE ON AGE:

The adjective "old" cannot be exactly translated into Hebrew, which provides four different words, embodying four different meanings that same word can have, to wit:

1) זקן   (*zah-*KEHN) "old" in the sense of "aged".

2) מבוגר   (*m'voo-*GAHR) "old" in the sense of "mature", "adult" or "elder" as compared to somebody else.

3) בן   (*ben*) "old" as used in "seven years old", "twenty years old", etc. The word בן (*ben*) literally means "son". For a feminine subject בת (*baht*) must be used, which means "daughter".

4) ישן   (*yah-*SHAHN) means "old" for an object (not a person), like "an old hat, book", etc.

לוי : ובכן, אני מניח שיכולתי להיות דודך, גברת אסתר.

Leh-VEE: *Oo-v'*HEHN, *ah-*NEE *m'*NEE-*akh sheh-yah-*HOHL-*tee leeh-*YOHT
*doh-*DEHKH, g'VEH-ret Ess-TEHR.

Levy: Then, I suppose I could be your uncle, Miss Esther.

נבון : רואה את, אסתר, יש לך כבר "דוד אמריקאי"! חיש מהר.

Nah-VOHN: *Roh-*AH *aht,* Ess-TEHR, *yehsh lakh k'vahr "dohd
Ah-meh-ree-*KAH-*ee"! Heesh mah-*HEHR.

Navon: You see, Esther, you already have got an "American uncle"!
Very quickly.

TWO WORDS — SAME MEANING:

The word חיש (*heesh*) means "fast". So does the word מהר (*mah-*HEHR). Both words used one after the other give extra emphasis to that meaning, and can be freely translated as "very quickly".

הצעירים : (צוחקים) יחי „דודנו"!
*Hah-tseh-ee-*REEM: (*tsoh-hah-*KEEM) *Y'hee* "*dod-*DEH-*noo*"!
Young people: (laughing) Long live our "uncle"!

ואולי הוא רק דודה של אסתר? הידד אסתר!
*Veh-oo-*LIGH *hoo rahk doh-*DAH *shell Ess-*TEHR? *Heh-*DAHD, *Ess-*TEHR!
Or is he only Esther's uncle? Bravo, Esther!

(מסתדרים במעגל לרקוד.)
(*Mees-tahd-*REEM *bah-mah-*GAHL *l'ree-*KOOD.)
(They form a circle to dance.)

אדון נבון : חכו, חכו עד שאשים
*Ah-*DOHN *Nah-*VOHN: *Hah-*KOO, *hah-*KOO, *ahd sheh-ah-*SEEM
Mr. Navon: Wait, wait, till I put a good

על הפטפון תקליט טוב. (מסדר את התקליט, והרקוד מתחיל.)
*ahl hah-*PAH-*teh-fohn tahk-*LEET *tohv*. (*M'sah-*DEHR *ett hah-tahk-*LEET, *veh-hah-ree-*KOOD *maht-*HEEL.)
record on the phonograph. (Sets the record and the dance begins.)

אדון לוי : איזה רקוד חי וחנני!
*Ah-*DOHN *Leh-*VEE: EH-*zeh ree-*KOOD *high veh-hee-nah-*NEE!
Mr. Levy: What a lively and graceful dance!

רואה אני שהילדים האלה הם באמת רקדנים מובהקים.
*Roh-*EH *ah-*NEE *sheh-hah-y'lah-*DEEM *hah-*EH-*leh hehm beh-eh-*METT *rahk-dah-*NEEM *moov-hah-*KEEM.
I see that these young people are really expert dancers.

אדון נבון : שמח אני, כי זה מוצא חן בעיניך
*Ah-*DOHN *Nah-*VOHN: *Sah-*MEH-*akh ah-*NEE, *kee zeh moh-*TSEH *hehn beh-eh-*NEH-*hah,
Mr. Navon: I am glad you like it,

ואנו נדאג לכך כי תלמד את הרקוד הזה לפני שובך לאמריקה.
*veh-*AH-*noo need-*AHG *l'hakk, kee teel-*MAHD *ett hah-ree-*KOOD *hah-*ZEH *leef-*NEH *shoo-v'*HAH *lah-Ah-*MEH-*ree-kah.
and we'll see that you learn this dance before you go back to America.

A USEFUL IDIOM:

The expression ‫זה מוצא חן בעיניך‬ (*zeh moh-*TSEH *hehn beh-eh-*NEH-*hah*) is widely used to say "you like it", "he likes it", etc. Its literal, rather florid meaning is: "it finds grace in your (his, her, etc.) eyes".

‫(אחרי המסיבה)‬

(*Ah-hah-*RAY *hah-m'see-*BAH)

(After the party)

‫אדון לוי : אני מודה לך, גברתי, מאד מאד,‬

*Ah-*DOHN *Leh-*VEE: *Ah-*NEE *moh-*DEH *lakh, gveer-*TEE, *meh-*OHD *meh-*OHD,

Mr. Levy: I thank you very much, Madam,

‫בעד הערב הנעים ביותר.‬

*beh-*AHD *hah-*EH-*rev hah-nah-*EEM *b'yoh-*TEHR.

for a most enjoyable evening.

‫אדון נבון : היה לנו העונג לארח אותך אצלנו.‬

*Ah-*DOHN *Nah-*VOHN: *Hah-*YAH *LAH-noo hah-*OH-neg *leh-ah-*RAY-*akh oh-t'*HAH *ets-*LEH-noo.

Mr. Navon: It was a pleasure for us to have you as our guest.

‫אנו מקוים לראותך במהרה שוב בתוכנו במקום‬

*AH-noo m'kah-*VEEM *leer-oh-t'*HAH *beem-heh-*RAH *shoov b'toh-*HEH-noo, b'mah-*KOHM

We hope to see you soon again among us, where

‫שתהיה תמיד אורח חביב ביותר,‬

*sheh-teeh-*YEH *tah-*MEED *oh-*RAY-*akh hah-*VEEV *b'yoh-*TEHR,

you will always be a most welcome guest,

‫ואל תשכח שאבוא מחר אליך בשעה 9‬

*veh-*AHL *teesh-*KAKH *sheh-ah-*VOH *mah-*HAHR *eh-*LEH-hah b'shah-*AH 9

and don't forget that I will come for you at 9 o'clock

‫לקחת אותך לטיול לירושלים.‬

*lah-*KAH-*haht oh-t'*HAH *l'tee-*YOOL *lee-Yeh-roo-shah-*LAH-*yim.

tomorrow to take you for a drive to Jerusalem.

‫אדון לוי : אהיה מוכן. אתה באמת אדיב מאד.‬

*Ah-*DOHN *Leh-*VEE: *Eh-*YEH *moo-*HAHN. *Ah-*TAH *beh-eh-*METT *ah-*DEEV *meh-*OHD.

Mr. Levy: I shall be ready. You are really very kind.

THINKING IN HEBREW
(Answers on page 294)

1. האחר אדון לוי למסיבת אדון נבון ?

Hah-eh-HEHR ah-DOHN Leh-VEE leem-see-BAHT ah-DOHN Nah-VOHN?

2. מי קבל את פניו ליד הדלת בבואו ?

Mee kee-BEHL ett pah-NAHV l'yahd hah-DEH-let b'voh-OH?

3. בפני מי הוצג אדון לוי אחר־כך ?

Beef-NEH mee hoo-TSAHG ah-DOHN Leh-VEE ah-HAHR-kahkh?

4. מה אומרת הגברת נבון ?

Mah oh-MEH-ret hah-g'VEH-ret Nah-VOHN?

5. מה אומר אדון לוי לפרופסור כהן ?

Mah oh-MEHR ah-DOHN Leh-VEE lee-Proh-FES-sohr Kohn?

6. משום מה גאה אדון לוי לפגש את הפרופסור ?

Mee-SHOOM mah geh-EH ah-DOHN Leh-VEE leef-GOHSH ett hah-Proh-FES-sohr?

7. איך ידע אדון לוי על עבודתו המדעית של הפרופסור ?

Ehkh yah-DAH ah-DOHN Leh-VEE ahl ah-voh-dah-TOH hah-mah-dah-EET shell hah-Proh-FES-sohr?

8. המעדיף אתה לקרא עבודה ספרותית בתרגום, או במקור ?

Hah-mah-ah-DEEF ah-TAH leek-ROH ah-voh-DAH seef-roo-TEET b'teer-GOOM, oh b'mah-KOHR?

9. באיזה נושא מטפל ספרו של הפרופסור ?

Beh-EH-zeh noh-SEH m'tah-PEHL seef-ROH shell hah-Proh-FES-sohr?

10. המוצא אתה ענין בהיסטוריה עברית ?

Hah-moh-TSEH ah-TAH een-YAHN b'hees-TOHR-yah eev-REET?

11. את מי הכיר אדון לוי אחר-כך ?

Ett mee hee-KEER ah-DOHN Leh-VEE ah-HAHR-kahkh?

12. מה בדעתם של הצעירים לעשות ?

Mah b'dah-TAHM shell hah-tseh-ee-REEM lah-ah-SOHT?

13. הראה אדון לוי פעם את הרקוד הזה לפני-כן ?

Hah-rah-AH ah-DOHN Leh-VEE PAH-ahm ett hah-ree-KOOD hah-ZEH leef-NEH-hehn?

14. איך זה מצא חן בעיניו ?

Ehkh zeh mah-TSAH hehn beh-eh-NAHV?

15. ההצליחה המסיבה אצל אדון נבון.

Hah-heets-LEE-hah hah-m'see-BAH EH-tsell ah-DOHN Nah-VOHN?

16. מה יעשו האדונים נבון ולוי למחרת ?

Mah yah-ah-SOO hah-ah-doh-NEEM Nah-VOHN v'Leh-VEE l'mokh-RAHT?

שָׁעוּר 33

טיול לירושלים

Tee-YOOL *lee-yeh-roo-shah-*LAH-*yim*

A trip to Jerusalem

אדון לוי מחכה לפני המלון „נורדאו פלז'ה".
*Ah-*DOHN *Leh-*VEE *m'hah-*KEH *leef-*NEH *hah-mah-*LOHN
"NOHR-*dow* PLAH-*zhah*".
Mr. Levy is waiting in front of the Hotel "Nordau Plaza".

אדון נבון מופיע במכונית שלו קיזר-פריזר החדשה.
*Ah-*DOHN *Nah-*VOHN *moh-*FEE-*ah bah-m'hoh-*NEET *sheh-*LOH
KIGH-*zer* FRAY-*zer hah-hah-dah-*SHAH.
Mr. Navon appears in his new Kaiser-Frazer car.

251

נבון: בּוֹקר טוֹב, יצחק! הִכָּנֵס!

Nah-VOHN: BOH-*ker tohv*, *Yits*-HAHK! *Hee-kah*-NEHS!

Navon: Good morning, Isaac! Get in!

מקוה אני, כּי לא נתתי לך לחכּוֹת הרבּה.

M'kah-VEH *ah*-NEE, *kee lo nah*-TAH-*tee l'hah leh-hah*-KOHT *hahr*-BEH.

I hope I didn't keep you waiting much.

לוי: (בּהִכָּנסוֹ למכוֹנית) לא ולא!

Leh-VEE: (*beh-hee-kahn*-SOH *lah-m'hoh*-NEET) *Lo vah*-LO!

Levy: (Entering the car) Not at all!

DEFINITELY "NO":

The expression לא ולא (*lo vah*-LO) gives the nega-
tion לא (*lo*) a particular stress, similar to "Oh, no",
"not at all", "definitely no", etc.

איזו מכוֹנית יפה יש לך. האם הוּבאה מחוּץ לארץ?

EH-*zoh m'hoh*-NEET *yah*-FAH *yehsh l'hah*. *Hah*-IM *hoov*-AH
mee-HOOTS *lah-ah*-*rets*?

What a fine car you have here. Is it imported?

נבון: לא היא מיוּצרת פּה בּחיפה.

Nah-VOHN: *Lo. Hee m'yoo*-TSEH-*ret poh beh*-HAY-*fah*.

Navon: No. It is made right here in Haifa.

יש לנו כּאן בּית-חרוֹשת.

Yehsh LAH-*noo* KAH-*ahn beht-hah*-ROH-*shet*.

We have a factory here.

NOTE ON TRADE:

The word הוּבאה (*hoov*-AH) literally means "brought",
but is used also for "imported". The words "import"
and "export" are יבוּא (*y'voo*) and יצוּא (*y'tsoo*).
These words are derived from בוֹא (*boh*) "to come"
and יצא (*yah*-TSOH) "to go out".

בּכל זאת, חלקים מוּבאים מאמריקה.

B'hohl zoht, *hah-lah*-KEEM *moo-vah*-EEM *meh-Ah*-MEH-*ree-kah*.

However, parts are imported from America.

לוי: כּנראה יש תּנוּעה גדוֹלה בּמרכּז העיר.

Leh-VEE: *Kah-neer*-EH *yehsh t'noo*-AH *g'doh*-LAH *b'mer*-KAHZ *hah*-EER.

Levy: There seems to be much traffic in the center of the city.

נבון : כֵּן, בשעה זו הולך כל איש לעבודתו.

Nah-VOHN: *Kehn, b'shah-*AH *zoh hoh-*LEHKH *kohl eesh*
*lah-ah-voh-dah-*TOH.

Navon: Yes, at this time everyone is going to his work.

עתה אנו עולים על הדרך הראשית המובילה לירושלים.

*Ah-*TAH *AH-noo oh-*LEEM *ahl hah-*DEH*-rekh hah-roh-*SHEET
*hah-moh-vee-*LAH *lee-Yeh-roo-shah-*LAH*-yim.*

Now we are coming to the highway which leads to Jerusalem.

לוי : זוכר אני את הכביש. זוהי הדרך בה באנו מלוד.

*Leh-*VEE: *Zoh-*HEHR *ah-*NEE *ett hah-k'*VEESH.
*zoh-hee hah-*DEH*-rekh bah* BAH*-noo mee-*LOD.

Levy: I remember the road.
This is the way we came in from Lod.

נבון : כֵּן. זה שדה-התעופה ושם אתה

Nah-VOHN: *Kehn, Zeh s'deh-hah-teh-oo-*FAH, *v'shahm ah-*TAH

Navon: Yes. That is the airport over there where you

רואה את נחיתת האוירון.

*roh-*EH *ett n'hee-*TAHT *hah-ah-vee-*ROHN.

see the plane landing.

לוי : כמה זמן נוסעים לירושלים ?

*Leh-*VEE: KAH*-mah z'mahn noh-seh-*EEM *lee-Yeh-roo-shah-*LAH*-yim?*

Levy: How long does it take to get to Jerusalem?

נבון : אין זה טיול ארוך. זה לוקח רק כשעה וחצי.

Nah-VOHN: *Ehn zeh tee-*YOOL *ah-*ROKH. *Zeh loh-*KAY*-akh rahk k'shah-*AH
*vah-*HEH*-tsee.*

Navon: It isn't a long trip It takes only about an hour and a half.

לוי : איזו תחנת-בנזין מודרנית !

*Leh-*VEE: EH*-zoh takh-*NAHT*-ben-*ZEEN *moh-*DER*-neet!*

Levy: What a fine modern gas station!

נבון : טוב שהזכרתני.

Nah-VOHN: *Tohv sheh-heez-kahr-*TAH*-nee.*

Navon: Good that you reminded me.

צריכים אנו לבנזין בשביל הנסיעה.

*Ts'ree-*HEEM AH*-noo l'ven-*ZEEN *beesh-*VEEL *hah-n'see-*AH.

We need some gasoline for the trip.

(לבעל התחנה) הכנס שנים-עשר גלון בנזין, בבקשה . . .

(*L'*VAH*-ahl hah-takh-*NAH) *Hakh-*NEHS *sh'nehm-ah-*SAHR *gah-*LOHN
*ben-*ZEEN, *b'vah-kah-*SHAH...

(To attendant) Put in twelve gallons of gas, please...

לא, אין לי צורך בשמן, תודה.

Lo, ehn lee TSOH-*rekh* b'SHEH-*men, toh-*DAH.

No, I don't need any oil, thank you.

בעל התחנה : מגיע חמש לירות ושש מאות פרוטה, אדוני.

BAH-*ahl hah-takh-*NAH: *Mah-*GEE-*ah hah-*MEHSH LEE-*roht v'shehsh
meh-*OHT *proo-*TAH, *ah-doh-*NEE.

Attendant: That will be five pounds, six hundred mils, sir.

MONETARY NOTE:

The Israeli pound is divided into 1,000 mils, called
פרוטה (*proo-*TAH) in the singular and פרוטות (*proo-*TOHT) in the plural.

לוי : הנה, הבה ואשלם אנכי, איני רוצה כי תשלם את כל ההוצאות.

*Leh-*VEE: *Hee-*NEH, HAH-*vah vah-ah-shah-*LEHM *ah-noh-*HEE!
*Eh-*NEE *roh-*TSEH *kee t'shah-*LEHM *ett kohl hah-hoh-tsah-*OHT.

Levy: Here, let me pay it!
I don't want you to pay all the expenses.

ANOTHER WORD FOR "I":

The word אנכי (*ah-noh-*HEE) also means "I", like
אני (*ah-*NEE), but is somewhat more emphatic.

נבון : בשום אופן.

*Nah-*VOHN: *B'shoom* OH-*fenn.*

Navon: Under no circumstances.

כל זמן שהנך בישראל הנך אורחי.

*Kohl z'mahn sheh-heen-*HAH *b'Yis-rah-*EHL *heen-*HAH *ohr-*HEE.

As long as you are in Israel, you are my guest.

לוי : נוסעים אנו כשעה.

*Leh-*VEE: *Noh-seh-*EEM AH-*noo k'shah-*AH.

Levy: We have been traveling about an hour.

האם אנו קרובים לירושלים?

*Hah-*IM AH-*noo k'roh-*VEEM *lee-Yeh-roo-shah-*LAH-*yim?*

Are we near to Jerusalem?

נבון : כן, אלה ההרים שאליהם אנו מתקרבים, נקראים :

*Nah-*VOHN: *Kehn,* EH-*leh heh-hah-*REEM, *sheh-ah-leh-*HEMM AH-*noo
meet-kahr-*VEEM *neek-rah-*EEM:

Navon: Yes, those mountains we are approaching are called:

„שער הגיא". עלינו לנסע

"SHAH-*ahr hah*-GHIH". *Ah*-LEH-*noo leen*-SOH-*ah*

"The Gates of the Valley". We have only about

רק כעשרים וחמשה קילומטר, אלא שכל הדרך הררית.

rahk keh-ess-REEM *vah-hah-mee*-SHAH *kee-loh*-MET-*ter*, EH-*lah sheh*-KOHL
hah-DEH-*rekh hah-rah*-REET.

25 kilometers to go, but the whole way is hilly.

לוי : הכביש המתפתל הזה הוא מגוון מאד.

Leh-VEE: *Hah-k'*VEESH *hah-meet-pah*-TEHL *hah*-ZEH *hoo m'goo*-VAHN
meh-OHD.

Levy: This winding road is very picturesque.

נבון : וגם היסטורי ! המקום הזה שם הוא „עמק אילון",

Nah-VOHN: *V'gahm hees*-TOH-*ree*! *Hah-mah*-KOHM *hah*-ZEH
shahm hoo "EH-*mek-Ah-yah*-LOHN",

Navon: And historic too! That spot over there is "Emech Ayallon",

איפה שהעמיד יהושע את השמש, עד שנצח את אויבי ישראל.

eh-FOH *sheh-heh-eh*-MEED *Yeh-hoh-shoo-ah ett hah*-SHEH-*mesh*, *ahd*
sheh-nee-TSAKH *et oy*-VEH *Yis-rah*-EHL.

where Joshua stopped the sun to defeat the enemies of Israel.

נבון : עכשו אנו מתקרבים למוצא. רוצה אני

Nah-VOHN: *Akh*-SHAHV AH-*noo meet-kahr*-VEEM *l'*MOH-*tsah*.
Roh-TSEH *ah*-NEE

Navon: Now we are approaching Moza. I want

לעצור פה, כדי להראות לך את הנוף.

lah-ah-TSOHR *poh k'deh leh-hahr*-OHT *l'hah ett hah*-NOHF.

to stop here to show you the scenery.

לוי : מה רואים כאן ?

Leh-VEE: *Mah roh*-EEM KAH-*ahn?*

Levy: What does one see here?

נבון : מכאן אפשר לראות את ירושלים

Nah-VOHN: *Mee*-KAH-*ahn eff*-SHAHR *leer*-OHT *ett Yeh-roo-shah*-LAH-*yim*

Navon: From here one can see Jerusalem

ממזרח ואת הים ממערב.

mee-meez-RAKH *veh-ett hah*-YAHM *mee-mah-ah*-RAHV.

to the east and the sea to the west.

לוי : פה מקום טוב לעשות צלומים. בבקשה לעצור פה !

Leh-VEE: *Poh mah*-KOHM *tohv lah-ah*-SOHT *tsee-loo*-MEEM. *B'vah-kah*-SHAH
lah-ah-TSOHR *poh!*

Levy: Here is a good place to take some photos. Stop here, please!

A POLITE IMPERATIVE:

You already know how to form the imperative, which normally is a shortened construction closely resembling the stem. Another and a very polite way is to use the infinitive, preceded by בבקשה (*b'vah-kah-*SHAH) as in the foregoing sentence. Examples:

בבקשה לבוא! (*b'vah-kah-*SHAH *leekh-*TOHV) "Please write!"

בבקשה לכתב! (*b'vah-kah-*SHAH *lah-*VOH) "Please come!" The other word for "please", which is אנא (AH-*nah*), should be used only with the regular short imperative. Examples:

אנא, כתב! (AH-*nah k'tohv*) "Please write!"

אנא, בוא! (AH-*nah boh*) "Please come!"

The abbreviation נא (*nah*) of אנא (AH-*nah*) is used *after* the regular short imperative. Examples:

כתב, נא! (*k'tohv, nah*) "Write, please!"

בוא, נא! (*boh, nah*) "Come, please!"

We can also say: תכתב לי, בבקשה (*teekh-*TOHV *lee, b'vah-kah-*SHAH) or נא לכתב לי (*nah leekh-*TOHV *lee*) "Please write to me".

נבון: כמובן, נוכל לעצור פה מאחורי המכוניות האלה.
*Nah-*VOHN: *K'moo-*VAHN, *noo-*HAHL *lah-ah-*TSOHR *poh meh-ah-hoh-*RAY *hah-m'hoh-nee-*YOHT *hah-*EH-*leh*.
Navon: Certainly, we can stop here behind these cars.

לוי: מי הם הצעירים ההם שם?
*Leh-*VEE: *Mee hehm hahts-ee-*REEM *hah-*HEHM *shahm?*
Levy: Who are those young people over there?

למען האמת הנערות יפות ומלאות חיים.
*L'*MAH-*ahn hah-eh-*METT *hahn-ah-*ROHT *yah-*FOHT *oo-m'leh-*OHT *hah-*YEEM.
They are certainly good looking and vivacious.

נבון: נראים הם כמסירים,
*Nah-*VOHN: *Neer-*EEM *hehm keem-sigh-*REEM,
Navon: They look like excursionists,

ואולי הם מאחד הקבוצים הקרובים.
*veh-oo-*LIGH *hehm meh-ah-*HAHD *hah-kee-boo-*TSEEM *hah-k'roh-*VEEM.
perhaps from one of the Kibbutzs nearby.

A NEW WORD:

קבוץ (*Kibbutz*) is a rural settlement of a very well-known type in modern Israel. It is an agricultural community, owning the land jointly cultivated by its members.

לוי: אהה! הייתי רוצה לצלם אותם.

*Leh-*VEE: *Ah-*HAH! *Hah-*YEE-*tee, roh-*TSEH *l'tsah-*LEHM *oh-*TAHM

Levy: Oh! I should like to take a picture of them.

נבון: בסדר, אשאל אותם.

*Nah-*VOHN: *B's*EH-*der, esh-*AHL *oh-*TAHM.

Navon: All right, I'll ask them.

סליחה, המותר לנו לצלם אתכם ?

*S'lee-*HAH, *hah-moo-*TAHR LAH-*noo l'tsah-*LEHM *ett-*HEMM?

Excuse me, could we take a picture of you?

ידידי הוא מאמריקה, ורוצה לקבל תמונה מקבוצתכם.

*Y'dee-*DEE hoo *meh-Ah-*MEH-*ree-kah, v'roh-*TSEH

*l'kah-*BEHL *t'moo-*NAH *mee-k'voo-tsaht-*HEMM.

My friend is from America, and
wishes to take a picture of your group.

בחורה ראשונה: אהה, זה יפה! שמעו חבריא,

*Bah-hoo-*RAH *ree-shoh-*NAH: *Ah-*HAH, zeh *yah-*FEH!

*Sheem-*OO *hahv-*RAH-*yah,

First girl: Oh, that is fine! Listen, you people,

AN IDIOMATIC EXPRESSION:

The word חבריא (*hahv-*RAH-*yah*) comes from the
ancient Aramaic language and is a colloquialism de-
signating a gathering of people that can be used to
say "people" or "folks" when addressing a number of
listeners.

בואו הנה. אדון אחד מאמריקה רוצה לצלם אותנו.

BOH-*oo* HEH-*nah. Ah-*DOHN *eh-*HAHD *meh-Ah-*MEH-*ree-kah*

*roh-*TSEH *l'tsah-*LEHM *oh-*TAH-*noo.

come over here. A gentleman from America
wants to take our picture.

בחורה שניה: טוב! אולי נתקבל כ„כוכבים" לקולנוע.

*Bah-hoo-*RAH *sh'nee-*YAH: *Tohv!* *Oo-*LIGH *neet-kah-*BEHL

*k-"koh-hah-*VEEM" *l'kohl-*NOH-*ah.

Second girl: Good! Maybe we can become movie stars.

בחור צעיר: אל תחלמי על כך. הכוכבים היחידים שתפגשי

*Bah-*HOOR *tsah-*EER: *Ahl takh-l'*MEE *ahl kakh. Hah-koh-hah-*VEEM

*hah-y'hee-*DEEM *sheh-teef-g'*SHEE

A young man: Do not dream about it. The only stars you will meet

יהיו אלה שתראי בקולנוע הערב.

*yee-*YOO *EH-leh sheh-teer-*EE *bah-kohl-*NOH*-ah hah-*EH*-rev.*

will be the ones you will see at the movies tonight.

אבל קדימה. אנו נעמד כאן כשההרים מאחורינו.

*Ah-*VAHL *kah-*DEE*-mah.* AH*-noo nah-ah-*MOHD KAH*-ahn*

*k'sheh-heh-hah-*REEM *meh-ah-hoh-*REH*-noo.*

But come on. We will stand here, with the mountains behind us.

לוי : שם, מצוין. שימו לב ! תודה.

*Leh-*VEE: *Shahm, m'tsoo-*YAHN. SEE*-moo lehv!* Toh-DAH.

Levy: There, excellent. Attention! Thank you.

בחורה ראשונה : אל תשכח להראות לנו העתקה

*Bah-hoo-*RAH *ree-shoh-*NAH: *Ahl teesh-*KAKH *leh-hahr-*OHT

LAH*-noo hah-tah-*KAH

First girl: Don't forget to show us a copy

לאחר שתפתח אותן.

*leh-ah-*HAHR *sheh-t'fah-*TEH*-akh oh-*TAHN.

when you have them developed.

לוי : לא אשכח. מה כתבתכם ?

*Leh-*VEE: *Lo esh-*KAKH. *Mah ktohv-t'*HEMM?

Levy: I won't forget. What is your address?

בחורה ראשונה : שלח אותן אלי :

*Bah-hoo-*RAH *ree-shoh-*NAH: *Sh'lakh oh-*TAHN *eh-*LIGH:

First girl: Send them to me:

רבקה שור, קבוץ מוצא, ליד ירושלים.

*Reev-*KAH *Shohr, Kee-*BOOTS MOH*-tsah, l'yahd Yeh-roo-shah-*LAH*-yim*

Rebecca Shor, Kibbuts Moza, near Jerusalem.

נבון (אל לוי) : לא אמרתי לך כך ?

*Nah-*VOHN *(ell Leh-*VEE): *Lo ah-*MAHR*-tee l'hah kahkh?*

Navon (to Levy): Didn't I tell you so?

הכרתי אותם מיד כשראיתים,

*Hee-*KAHR*-tee oh-*TAHM *mee-*YAHD *k'sheh-reh-ee-*TEEM,

I recognised them immediately when I saw them,

הם נראו כה יפים ובריאים.

*hehm neer-*OO *koh yah-*FEEM *oo-v'ree-*EEM.

they were so good looking and healthy.

THINKING IN HEBREW
(Answers on page 294)

1. ‏לאן נוסעים שני הידידים ?‏
Leh-AHN noh-seh-EEM sh'neh hah-y'dee-DEEM?

2. ‏מה אומר אדון נבון על המכונית שלו ?‏
Mah oh-MEHR ah-DOHN Nah-VOHN ahl hah-m'hoh-NEET sheh-LOH?

3. ‏באיזה כוון הם נוסעים ?‏
Beh-EH-zeh kee-VOON hehm noh-seh-EEM?

4. ‏האוהב אתה לטיל במכונית מחוץ לעיר ?‏
Hah-oh-HEHV ah-TAH l'tah-YEHL beem-hoh-NEET mee-HOOTS lah-EER?

5. ‏מה מוכרח אדון נבון לקנות בדרך ?‏
Mah mookh-RAKH ah-DOHN Nah-VOHN leek-NOHT bah-DEH-rekh?

6. ‏במה נתפרסם „שער-הגיא" ?‏
Bah-MEH neet-pahr-SEHM "SHAH-ahr-hah-GHIGH"?

7. ‏איזה הוא הנוף היפה ביותר בדרך לירושלים ?‏
EH-zeh hoo hah-NOHF hah-yah-FEH b'yoh-TEHR bah-DEH-rekh lee-Yeh-roo-shah-LAH-yim?

8. ‏מדוע נעצרו פה התירים ?‏
Meh-DOO-ah neh-ets-ROO poh hah-tah-yah-REEM?

9. ‏את מי הם פגשו כאן?‏
    Ett mee hehm pah-g'SHOO KAH-ahn?

10. ‏מי הם האנשים האלה?‏
    Mee hehm hah-ah-nah-SHEEM hah-EH-leh?

11. ‏הישלח להם אדון לוי את התמונות?‏
    Hah-yeesh-LAKH lah-HEMM ah-DOHN Leh-VEE ett hah-t'moo-NOHT?

12. ‏איך נראים הצעירים האלה?‏
    Ehkh neer-EEM hah-tseh-ee-REEM hah-EH-leh?

13. ‏איך הוא האקלים בישראל?‏
    Ehkh hoo hah-ahk-LEEM b'Yis-rah-EHL?

14. ‏מהי התוצרת החקלאית הטפוסית בישראל?‏
    MAH-hee hah-toh-TSEH-ret hah-hahk-lah-EET hah-tee-poo-SEET b'Yis-rah-EHL?

15. ‏מהי התוצרת התעשיתית שם?‏
    MAH-hee hah-toh-TSEH-ret hah-tah-ah-see-yah-EET shahm?

16. ‏הגדולה התנועה בדרכים?‏
    Hah-g'doh-LAH hah-t'noo-AH bah-d'rah-HEEM?

ירושלים

*Yeh-roo-shah-*LAH-*yim*

Jerusalem

נבון: הנה אנחנו נכנסים עכשו לירושלים

*Nah-*VOHN: *Hee-*NEH *ah-*NAKH-*noo neekh-nah-*SEEM *akh-*SHAHV
*lee-Yeh-roo-shah-*LAH-*yim*

Navon: Here we are now entering Jerusalem,

הבירה. עכשו אסיע אותך קצת

*hah-bee-*RAH. *Akh-*SHAHV *ah-*SEE-*ah oh-t'*HAH *k'tsaht*

the capital. Now I'll drive you a little

דרך הרחובות הראשיים, בטרם נסור

DEH-*rekh hah-r'hoh-*VOHT *hah-roh-shee-*YEEM, *b'*TEH-*rem* **nah-**SOOR

through the main streets, before we go to

261

למלון לארוחת-הצהרים.

l'mah-LOHN *lah-ah-roo*-HAHT-*hah-tsoh-hoh*-RAH-*yim.*

a hotel for lunch.

לוי : יודע אתה, נמצא אני עדין תחת הרושם

Leh-VEE: *Yoh*-DEH-*ah ah*-TAH, *neem*-TSAH *ah*-NEE *ah*-DAH-*yin*

TAH-*haht hah*-ROH-*shem*

Levy: You know, I am still under the impression

של הנוף שנהניתי ממרומי מוצא.

shell hah-NOHF *sheh-neh-heh*-NEH-*tee mee-m'roh*-MEH MOH-*tsah,*

of the view we enjoyed from the heights of Moza.

נרגש אני באמת להיות בעיר זו,

Neer-GAHSH *ah*-NEE *beh-eh*-METT *lee*-YOHT *beh*-EER *zoh,*

I am really thrilled to be in this city,

שבה כל דבר נראה נצחי.

sheh-BAH *kohl dah*-VAHR *neer*-EH *neets*-HEE.

where everything seems eternal.

נבון : כן, נכון הדבר שהעיר היא עתיקה מאד,

Nah-VOHN: *Kehn, nah*-HOHN *hah-dah*-VAHR *sheh-hah*-EER *hee*

ah-tee-KAH *meh*-OHD,

Navon: Well, it is true that this town is very ancient,

אבל יש בה שכונות חדשות עם בנינים מודרניים.

ah-VAHL *yehsh bah sh'hoo*-NOHT *hah-dah*-SHOHT *im been-yah*-NEEM

moh-der-nee-YEEM.

but there are new districts with modern buildings.

לוי : איזה סגנון אדריכלי משונה בשכונים העתיקים האלה.

Leh-VEE: EH-*zeh seeg*-NOHN *ahd-ree*-HAH-*lee m'shoo*-NEH

bah-shee-koo-NEEM *hah-ah-tee*-KEEM *hah*-EH-*leh.*

Levy: What a strange architectural style in these old dwellings.

זהו באמת סגנון מזרחי, לא כן ?

ZEH-*hoo beh-eh*-MEET *seeg*-NOHN *meez-rah*-HEE, *lo hehn?*

It is really oriental, isn't it?

נבון : ירושלים העתיקה היא, כמובן, עיר

Nah-VOHN: *Yeh-roo-shah*-LAH-*yim hah-ah-tee*-KAH *hee, k'moo*-VAHN, *eer*

Navon: Old Jerusalem is, of course, an oriental

מזרחית, ובכל זאת אתה מוצא בה סמנים
*meez-rah-*HEET, *oo-v'hohl zoht ah-*TAH *moh-*TSEH *bah see-mah-*NEEM
city, and yet you find in it marks of all

מכל התרבויות, ומכל התקופות.
*mee-*KOHL *hah-tahr-boo-*YOHT, *oo-mee-*KOHL *hah-t'koo-*FOHT.
civilizations, and of every age.

לוי: מה נפלא הדבר! נשימתך נעצרת
*Leh-*VEE: *Mah neef-*LAH *hah-dah-*VAHR! *N'shee-mah-t'*HAH *neh-eh-*TSEH*-ret*
Levy: How wonderful! It takes your breath away

לחשוב, כי זהו המקום, שבו בנו
*lah-hah-*SHOHV, *kee zeh-hoo hah-mah-*KOHM, *she-*BOH *bah-*NOO
to think that it is the place where our

אבותינו את בית-המקדש המפואר,
*ah-voh-*TEH*-noo ett beht-hah-meek-*DAHSH *hah-m'foh-*AHR,
forefathers built the glorious temple,

וכי היונים, הרומאים, הערבים, הצלבנים,
*v'hee hah-Y'vah-*NEEM, *hah-Roh-mah-*EEM, *hah-Ahr-*VEEM,
*hahTsahl-vah-*NEEM,
and that Greeks, Romans, Arabs, Crusaders,

הטורקים והבריטים, כולם השתלטו
*hah-Toor-*KEEM *veh-hah-B'*REE*-teem, koo-*LAHM *heesh-tahl-*TOO
Turks and British have all held sway

על העיר הזאת, אך ורק, כדי להחזירה
*ahl hah-*EER *hah-*ZOHT, *akh v'rahk, k'deh leh-hakh-zee-*RAH
over this city, but to return it to

לבניהם של אלה שיסדוה לפני אלפי שנים.
*leev-neh-*HEMM *shell* EH*-leh sheh-yees-*DOO*-hah leef-*NEH *ahl-*FEH
*shah-*NEEM.
the sons of those who founded it thousands of years ago.

נבון: אנו יכולים באמת להיות גאים ואסירי תודה על כך.
*Nah-*VOHN: AH*-noo y'hoh-*LEEM *beh-eh-*METT *lee-*YOHT *geh-*EEM
*vah-ah-see-*REH *toh-*DAH *ahl kahkh.*
Navon: We can indeed be proud and grateful for it.

TWO IMPORTANT IDIOMS:

אסיר תודה (*ah-*SEER *toh-*DAH) means "thankful". It is derived from the word תודה (*toh-*DAH) "thanks" which literally means "recognition" and the word אסיר (*ah-*SEER), which means "bound". So, the literal meaning of the expression is "bound in recognition", or "grateful".

"Unthankful" is expressed by the idiom כפוי טובה (*k'fooy toh-*VAH) which literally means "concealing (a) favor".

לוי : האח! המחזה משתנה שוב. זה נראה

*Leh-*VEE: *Heh-*AKH! *Hah-makh-*ZEH *meesh-tah-*NEH *shoov. Zeh neer-*EH

Levy: My! The scene is changing again. This looks

דומה יותר לעיר מודרנית בארצות המערב.

*doh-*MEH *yoh-*TEHR *leh-*EER *moh-*DER-*neet beh-ahr-*TSOHT *hah-mah-ah-*RAHV.

more like a modern city of the west.

נבון : כן, עכשו הגענו לרחוב בן-יהודה, הנושא

*Nah-*VOHN: *Kehn, akh-*SHAHV *hee-*GAH-*noo leer-*HOHV Ben-Yeh-hoo-*DAH, *hah-noh-*SEH

Navon: Yes, it does, we have now reached Ben-Yehuda street, which

את שמו של אבי הלשון העברית המודרנית.

*ett sh'moh shell ah-*VEE *hah-lah-*SHOHN *hah-Eev-*REET *hah-moh-*DER-*neet.

bears the name of the father of the modern Hebrew language.

הרובע החדש הזה של העיר נבנה על

*Hah-*ROH-*vah heh-hah-*DAHSH *hah-*ZEH shell hah-*EER neev-*NAH *ahl

This new district of the town has been built

ידי החלוצים שלנו.

*y'deh hah-hah-loo-*TSEEM *sheh-*LAH-*noo.

by our pioneers.

לוי : אכן, זוהי עיר בעלת אלף פנים.

*Leh-*VEE: *Ah-*HEHN, *zoh-*hee eer *bah-ah-*LAHT *EH-leff pah-*NEEM.

Levy: It is indeed a city with a thousand faces.

איזה מקום מקסים לחיות בה! החומות העתיקות,

*EH-zeh mah-*KOHM *mahk-*SEEM *leekh-*YOHT *bah! Hah-hoh-*MOHT *hah-ah-tee-*KOHT,

What a fascinating spot to live in! The old walls,

השרידים מבית-המקדש שלנו, מגדל
*hah- ree-*DEEM *mee-beht-hah-meek-*DAHSH *sheh-*LAH-*noo, meeg-*DAHL
the remnants of our temple, the tower

דוד, קברי האבות, ועכשו
*Dah-*VEED, *keev-*REH *hah-ah-*VOHT, *veh-akh-*SHAHV
of David, the catacombs, and now

ירושלים החדשה והמודרנית
*Yeh-roo-shah-*LAH-*yim hah-hah-dah-*SHAH, *veh-hah-moh-*DER-*neet
this new and modern Jerusalem

המזהירה ביפיה! הרחובות האלה נראים כמרכז מסחרי.
*hah-mahz-hee-*RAH *b'yohf-*YAH! *Hah-r'hoh-*VOHT *hah-*EH-*leh neer-*EEM
*k'mer-*KAHZ *mees-hah-*REE.
shining with its beauty! These streets look like a business center.

נבון: זה רחוב יפו, הרחוב המסחרי הראשי.
*Nah-*VOHN: *Zeh r'hohv* YAH-*foh, hah-reh-*HOHV *hah-mees-hah-*REE
*hah-roh-*SHEE.
Navon: It is the Jaffa road, the main business thoroughfare.

זה אמנם מקום של עושר. עליך להבין
*Zeh ohm-*NAHM *mah-*KOHM *shell* OH-*sherr. Ah-*LEH-*hah leh-hah-*VEEN
It is indeed a place of wealth. You must realize

כי אלפי תירים וצלינים מכל הדתות
*kee ahl-*FEH *tah-yah-*REEM *veh-tsahl-yah-*NEEM *mee-*KOHL *hah-dah-*TOHT
that thousands of tourists and pilgrims of every religion

מבקרים שנה שנה את ירושלים.
*m'vahk-*REEM *shah-*NAH *shah-*NAH *ett Yeh-roo-shah-*LAH-*yim.
visit Jerusalem every year.

הזרם המתמיד הזה של תירים הוא
*Hah-*ZEH-*rem hah-maht-*MEED *hah-*ZEH *shell tah-yah-*REEM *hoo
This steady flow of tourists is

מקור לעושר רב.
*mah-*KOHR *leh-*OH-*sherr rahv.*
a source of great wealth.

לוי : רואה אני שדאגו כאן לכל הנוחיות לתירים.

*Leh-*VEE: *Roh-EH ah-*NEE *she-dah-ah-*GOO KAH-*ahn l'hohl hah-noh-*
hee-YOHT *l'tah-yah-*REEM.

Levy: I see that every accommodation has been provided here for the
comfort of the tourists.

הבט על המלון הנהדר הזה.

*Hah-*BEHT *ahl hah-mah-*LOHN *hah-neh-*DAHR *hah-*ZEH.
Look at this magnificent hotel.

נבון: זה מלון „המלך דוד", אחד המפורסמים

*Nah-*VOHN: *Zeh mah-*LOHN *"Hah-*MEH-*lekh Dah-*VEED",
*ah-*HAHD *hah-m'foohr-*

Navon: This is the Hotel "King David", one of the best-known

ביותר בעולם, וסוף טיולנו.

*sah-*MEEM *b'yoh-*TEHR *bah-oh-*LAHM, *v'sohf tee-yoo-*LEH-*noo.*
hotels in the world, and the end of our journey.

אעמיד פה את המכונית, ונכנס לארוחת הצהרים.

*Ah-ah-*MEED *poh ett hah-m'hoh-*NEET, *v'nee-kah-*NEHS *lah-ah-roo-*
HAHT *hah-tsoh-hoh-*RAH-*yim.*

I shall park my car here, and we shall go in for lunch.

לוי : אה ! אתה רוצה לסעוד כאן ארוחת הצהרים !

*Leh-*VEE: OH! *Ah-*TAH *roh-*TSEH *lees-*OHD KAH-*ahn ah-roo-*HAHT-
*hah-tsoh-hoh-*RAH-*yim!*

Levy: Oh! You want us to lunch here!

ואני הייתי רוצה למקום שנלך טפוסי יותר,

*Vah-ah-*NEE *hah-*YEE-*tee ro-*TSEH *sheh-neh-*LEHKH *l'mah-*KOHM
*tee-poo-*SEE *yoh-*TEHR,

And I would like to go to some place more typical,

מאשר למקום מפואר זה.

*meh-ah-*SHERR *l'mah-*KOHM *m'foh-*AHR *zeh.*
rather than to this sumptuous place.

נבון: אם זה הוא מבוקשך, הבה ואראה... טוב,

*Nah-*VOHN: *Im zeh hoo m'voo-kahsh-*HAH, HAH-*vah veh-err-*EH ... *tohv,*
Navon: If such is your wish, let me see... well,

את המכונית יכולים אנו בין־כך ובין־כך

*ett hah-m'hoh-*NEET *y'hoh-*LEEM AH-*noo behn-*KAKH *oo-vehn-*KAKH
we can park the car here anyway

להעמיד פה, ונסור ברגל לאחת

*leh-hah-ah-*MEED *poh, v'nah-*SOOR *bah-*REH-*gell leh-ah-*HAHT
and we will take a walk to

המסעדות הקטנות הקרובות, מקום בו

*hah-mees-ah-*DOHT *hah-k'tah-*NOHT *hah-k'roh-*VOHT, *mah-*KOHM *boh*
a small restaurant near by, where you will be able

תוכל לטעום מאכלים יהודיים טפוסיים.

*too-*HAHL *leet-*OHM *mah-ah-hah-*LEEM *yeh-hoo-dee-*YEEM *tee-poo-see-*YEEⱮ.
to taste typical Jewish dishes.

הייתי מציע זאת לראשונה, לו הייתי יודע

*Hah-*YEE-*tee mah-*TSEE-*ah zoht la-ree-shoh-*NAH, *loo hah-*YEE-*tee*
*yoh-*DEH-*ah*
I would have suggested it in the first place, if I had known

לבטח, כי אתה כה אוהב את האוכל היהודי.

*lah-*VEH-*takh, kee ah-*TAH *koh oh-*HEHV *ett hah-*OH-*hell hah-y'hoo-*DEE.
for sure that you like the Jewish food so much.

NOTE ON THE CONDITIONAL:

The conditional is expressed, in Hebrew, with the aid of the verb היה (*hah-*YOH) "to be" or|and יכול (*yah-*HOHL) "can", used as auxiliaries. We find, accordingly, the following types of construction:

a) **Conditional with "to be" as auxiliary verb.** The auxiliary is used in the past, the main verb in the present tense. Examples:

הייתי כותב (*hah-*YEE-*tee koh-*TEHV) "I would write".
הייתי הולך (*hah-*YEE-*tee hoh-*LEHKH) "I would go".

The use of this form requires a statement of the condition or prerequisite in the subordinate part of the sentence, starting with אילו (EE-*loo*) or its abbreviation (*loo*) "if". Example:

הייתי קורא, אילו (לו) היה לי פנאי.

*Hah-*YEE-*tee koh-*REH, EE-*loo* (*loo*) *hah-*YAH *lee p'nigh.*
I would read, if I had time.

b) **Conditional with "can" as auxiliary verb.** The auxiliary is used in the past tense, the main verb in the infinitive. Example:

יכולתי לכתב (*yah-*HOHL-*tee leekh-*TOHV) "I could write" or "I could have written".

To say "I could" or "I might" we use both auxiliaries, the first one in the past, the other one in the present tense, which gives us the construction הייתי יכול (*hah-*YEE-*tee yah-*HOHL) "I could" or יכול הייתי (*yah-*HOHL *hah-*YEE-*tee*).

To say "I might be able to write" we have to use both auxiliaries as shown above, plus the main verb (to write) in the infinitive. So we say: יכול הייתי לכתב... or הייתי יכול לכתב (hah-YEE-tee yah-HOHL leekh-TOHV) "I might be able to write," or (yah-HOHL hah-YEE-tee leekh-TOHV).

Don't confuse the conditional with the form, הייתי כותב (hah-YEE-tee koh-TEHV), which means "I used to write", etc.

לוי: תודה לך, זה רעיון מצוין. בכל זאת,
Leh-VEE: Toh-DAH l'hah, zeh rah-YOHN m'tsoo-YAHN. B'hohl zoht,
Levy: Thank you, this is an excellent idea. However,

עלינו ללכת תחילה למלון, כדי להזמין
ah-LEH-noo lah-LEH-het t'hee-LAH l'mah-LOHN, k'deh leh-hahz-MEEN
we should go to a hotel first, to reserve

לנו שני חדרים בשביל הלילה, לאחר שאמרת
LAH-noo sh'neh hah-dah-REEM, beesh-VEEL hah-LIGH-lah leh-ah-HAHR
she-ah-MAHR-tah
two rooms for the night, since you said

כי כאן נמצאים כל כך הרבה זרים.
kee KAH-ahn neem-tsah-EEM kohl kakh hahr-BEH zah-REEM
that there are so many foreigners here.

נבון: צדקת, אסור לנו לדחות זאת, כל
Nah-VOHN: Tsah-DAHK-tah, ah-SOOR LAH-noo leed-HOHT zoht, kohl
Navon: Right you are, we should not delay this; perhaps all the

החדרים יכולים להיות אחר-כך תפוסים.
hah-hah-dah-REEM y'hoh-LEEM lee-YOHT ah-HAHR-kakh t'foo-SEEM.
rooms might be taken after that.

לוי: ובכן, נזמין חדרים במלון תחילה,
Leh-VEE: Oo-v'HEHN, nahz-MEEN hah-dah-REEM bah-mah-LOHN t'hee-LAH,
Levy: Well, let us first reserve rooms in the hotel

ואחר-כך נחליט, לאן נלך לסעוד ארוחת-הצהרים.
veh-ah-HAHR-kakh nakh-LEET, leh-AHN neh-LEHKH lees-OHD
ah-roo-HAHT-hah-tsoh-hoh-RAH-yim.
and then we will decide later where to go for lunch.

(ונכנסים למלון.)
(Neekh-nah-SEEM lah-mah-LOHN)
(They go in the hotel.)

THINKING IN HEBREW
(Answers on page 295)

1. ההיית נוסע לישראל, לו היתה לך הזדמנות לכך ?

Heh-hah-YEE-tah noh-SEH-ah l'Yis-rah-EHL, loo hah-y'TAH l'hah heez-dahm-NOOT l'hakh?

2. מה יכול היה לראות תיר, אלו עלה על „מגדל-דוד" ?

Mah yah-HOHL hah-YAH leer-OHT tah-YAHR, EE-loo ah-LAH ahl "Meeg-DAHL-Dah-VEED"?

3. מה עשה על לוי רושם חזק ביותר בבואו לירושלים ?

Meh ah-SAH ahl Leh-VEE ROH-shem hah-ZAHK b'yoh-TEHR b'voh-oh lee-Yeh-roo-shah-LAH-yim?

4. מדוע מוצא אדון לוי, כי ירושלם היא נצחית ?

Mah-DOO-ah moh-TSEH ah-DOHN Leh-VEE, kee Yeh-roo-shah-LAH-yim hee neets-HEET?

5. מי היה אליעזר-בן-יהודה ?

Mee hah-YAH Eh-lee-EH-zer-Ben-Yeh-hoo-DAH?

6. ‏מהם הדברים המיוחדים בירושלים שיש לראותם ?‏

Mah-HEHM *hah-d'vah*-REEM *hah-m'yoo-hah*-DEEM
bee-Yeh-roo-shah-LAH-*yim* *she*-YEHSH *leer-oh*-TAHM?

7. ‏המבקרים הרבה תירים בעיר זו ?‏

Hah-m'vahk-REEM *hahr*-BEH *tah-yah*-REEM *beh*-EER *zoh?*

8. ‏אילו מעלות לתנועה גדולה זו ?‏

EH-*loo* *mah-ah*-LOHT *leet-noo*-AH *g'doh*-LAH *zoh?*

9. ‏כיצד עוזרת המדינה לפתוח התירות ?‏

Keh-TSAHD *oh*-ZEH-*ret* *hah-m'dee*-NAH *l'fee*-TOO-*akh* *hah-tah-yah*-ROOT?

10. ‏מדוע מסרב אדון לוי לסעד במלון ארוחת הצהרים ?‏

Mah-DOO-*ah* *m'sah*-REHV *ah*-DOHN *Leh*-VEE *lees*-OHD *b'mah*-LOHN
ah-roo-HAHT *hah-tsoh-hoh-RAH*-*yim?*

11. ‏מה הם עושים עם המכונית בשעת ארוחת-הצהרים ?‏

Mah *hehm* *oh*-SEEM *im* *hah-m'hoh*-NEET *beesh*-AHT *ah-roo*-HAHT-
hah-tsoh-hoh-RAH-*yim?*

12. ‏למה צריך להזמין חדרים במלון מראש ?‏

LAH-*mah* *tsah*-REEKH *leh-hahz*-MEEN *hah-dah*-REEM *bah-mah*-LOHN
meh-ROHSH?

13. ‏כמה זמן הם עומדים להשאר בירושלים ?‏

KAH-*mah* *z'mahn* *hehm* *oh-m'*DEEM *leh-hee-shah*-EHR *bee*-YEH-*roo*-
shah-LAH-*yim?*

14. ‏המרוצה אדון לוי מסיורו ?‏

Hah-m'roo-TSEH *ah*-DOHN *Leh*-VEE *mee-see-yoo*-ROH?

15. ‏המרוצה אתה בהחלט מהתקדמותך בשפה העברית ?‏

Hah-m'roo-TSEH *ah*-TAH *beh-hekh*-LEHT *meh-heet-kahd-moot*-HAH
bah-sah-FAH *hah-*Eev-REET?

16. ‏התדע מה עליך לעשות ?‏

Hah-teh-DAH *mah* *ah*-LEH-*hah* *lah-ah*-SOHT?

APPENDIX

A FINAL WORD ON VERBS

We have prepared the following more detailed explanation of the Hebrew verbs to facilitate their use by the advanced student.

It is much easier to use them if you understand how they are related to each other. But before discussing this relationship, let us consider what you will have learned about Hebrew verbs so far. (We hope!) You are aware that the basic form of each verb is its stem (*not* its infinitive).

You also know that there are four groups of verbs, which can usually be recognized by the vowels occurring in the *stem*. They are:

VOWEL SEQUENCE

Group I: (ah-oh) like: (*kah*-TOHV)—"write"

Group II: (ah-eh) like: (*kah*-TEHV)—"engrave"

Group III: (ah-eh, but with the prefix "h") like: (*hakh*-TEHV)— "dictate"

Group IV: (heet-ah-eh) like: (*heet-lah*-BEHSH)—"dress oneself"

You also know that all verb stems are based on three consonants only, with a few exceptions, and that the first three groups each have two voices, the active and the passive.

Example: כתב (*kah*-TOHV) "write"

הכתב (*hee-kah*-TEHV) "be written"

The fourth group has no passive voice, since it consists of *reflexive* verbs, like "dress oneself", "wash oneself", etc.

It is important to realize that a Hebrew verb belongs to a definite group, not as a result of blind chance, but according to its meaning.

Thus, verbs expressing a *normal* everyday action usually belong in the first group. Examples: נפל (*nah*-FOHL) "fall", נשא (*nah*-SOH) "carry", etc.

In the second group we find verbs expressing a *strong* action, which is either intense in itself, or demands a stronger or a more protracted effort.

Examples:

כתב (*kah*-TEHV) — "engrave" (the physical effort of engraving on stone)

הלך (*hah*-LEHKH) — "walk around" (walking to and fro is an action protracted over a period of time)

271

דבר   (*dah*-BEHR) — "speak" (apparently, speaking is a more intense form of expressing yourself than writing!

The third group consists mainly of verbs expressing an action *transferred to another person or object.*

Examples:

הכתב   (*hakh*-TEHV) — "dictate"
האכל   (*hah-ah*-HEHL) — "feed"

The fourth group is, as you already know, composed of *reflexive* verbs. We shall now give you, group by group, the basic patterns of conjugation in the present, past and future tenses.

GROUP I (ACTIVE VOICE)

STEM: כתב "write"

PRESENT TENSE

	SINGULAR				PLURAL		
	Masc.		Fem.		Masc.		Fem.
I	כותב	I	כותבת	we	כותבים	we	כותבות
you	"	you	"	you	"	you	"
he	"	she	"	they	"	they	"

PAST TENSE

	SINGULAR				PLURAL		
	Masc.		Fem.		Masc.		Fem.
I	כתבתי	I	כתבתי	we	כתבנו	we	כתבנו
you	כתבת	you	כתבת	you	כתבתם	you	כתבתן
he	כתב	she	כתבה	they	כתבו	they	כתבו

FUTURE TENSE

	SINGULAR				PLURAL		
	Masc.		Fem.		Masc.		Fem.
I	אכתב	I	אכתב	we	נכתב	we	נכתב
you	תכתב	you	תכתבי	you	תכתבו	you	תכתבנה
he	יכתב	she	תכתב	they	יכתבו	they	תכתבנה

IMPERATIVE

sing.	כתב	*sing.*	כתבי
plur.	כתבו	*plur.*	כתבנה

REMARKS: Within the first group, we find some constructions that do not follow the above pattern.

1. The one-syllable verbs take the following forms:

STEM: קום "stand up"

Masc.		Fem.
קם	*PRESENT*	קמה
קמתי	*PAST*	קמתי
אקום	*FUTURE*	אקום
קום	*IMPERATIVE*	קומי

2. The three-syllable verbs ending in the guttural sounds ע ח 'ע take a final syllable characterized by the vowel ַ ע_ח' (ah) in the present, the future and the imperative. Otherwise, they follow the basic pattern above.

Examples:

פּוֹתֵחַ (poh-TAY-akh) "I open"   קוֹרֵעַ (koh-RAY-ah) "I tear"

אֶפְתַּח (ehf-TAHKH) "I shall open"   אֶקְרַע (ehk-RAH) "I shall tear"

3. Verbs beginning with נ'ל'י lose that consonant in the future.

Examples:

נָפַל (nah-FOHL) "fall"   אֶפֹּל (eh-POHL) "I shall fall"

לָקַח (lah-KOH-ahk) "take"   אֶקַּח (ek-KAKH) "I shall take"

יָשַׁב (yah-SHOHV) "sit"   אֵשֵׁב (eh-SHEHV) "I shall sit"

4. As you know (see preface on Alphabet) the letters א'ה'ו'י can be either vowels or consonants. In verbs where one of these letters appears as a vowel, the future and sometimes the past tense show some peculiar formations.

Examples:

יָשַׁנְתִּי (yah-SHAHN-tee) "I slept"   אִישַׁן (ee-SHAHN) "I shall sleep"

In verbs where ה (h) occurs at the end, that letter changes into a י֖ (ee) in the past, and into ה ֶ (eh) in the future tense.

Examples:

קָנָה (kah-NOH) "buy"   קָנִיתִי (kah-NEE-tee) "I bought"

אֶקְנֶה (ehk-NEH) "I shall buy"

5. In verbs where the same consonant occurs twice in the ending of the stem, that consonant occurs only once in all tenses.

סָבַב (sah-VOHV) "surround"   סַב (sahv) "I surround"

סַבּוֹתִי (sah-BOH-tee) "I surrounded"

אָסֹב (ah-SOHV) or אֶסֹב (eh-SOHV) "I shall surround"

GROUP I   (PASSIVE VOICE)

Not all the verbs of the first group have a passive voice. We have intransitive verbs, such as נָפַל (nah-FOHL) "fall", which cannot become passive. The basic pattern of conjugation for the passive voice is given below:

STEM: הִכָּתֵב (hee-kah-TEHV) "be written".

	Masc.		Fem.	
I	נִכְתָּב	PRESENT	I	נִכְתֶּבֶת
I	נִכְתַּבְתִּי	PAST	I	נִכְתַּבְתִּי
I	אֶכָּתֵב	FUTURE	I	אֶכָּתֵב
	הִכָּתֵב	IMPERATIVE		הִכָּתְבִי

The passive voice of one-syllable verbs takes the following forms:

הכון   (*hee*-KOHN) "be prepared"

נכון   (*nah*-HOHN) "I am prepared"

נכונותי   (*n'hoo*-NOH-*tee*) "I was prepared"

אכון   (*eh*-KOHN) "I will be prepared"

In verbs where the same consonant occurs twice at the end, like (*sah*-VOHV) "surround", the stem of the passive voice loses one consonant and we obtain הסב (*hee*-SAHV) "be surrounded". The tenses will be:

נסב   (*nah*-SAHV) "I am surrounded"

נסבותי   (*neh-sah*-BOH-*tee*) "I was surrounded"

אסב   (*ee*-SAHV) "I will be surrounded"

GROUP II   (ACTIVE VOICE)

All the verbs of this and of all the following groups take an initial מ (*m*) in the present tense.

STEM: כתב (*kah*-TEHV) "engrave"

PRESENT TENSE

	Singular				Plural		
	Masc.		Fem.		Masc.		Fem.
I	מכתב	I	מכתבת	we	מכתבים	we	מכתבות
you	"	you	"	you	"	you	"
he	"	she	"	they	"	they	"

PAST TENSE

	Singular				Plural		
	Masc.		Fem.		Masc.		Fem.
I	כתבתי	I	כתבתי	we	כתבנו	we	כתבנו
you	כתבת	you	כתבת	you	כתבתם	you	כתבתן
he	כתב	she	כתבה	they	כתבו	they	כתבו

FUTURE TENSE

	Singular				Plural		
	Masc.		Fem.		Masc.		Fem.
I	אכתב	I	אכתב	we	נכתב	we	נכתב
you	תכתב	you	תכתבי	you	תכתבו	you	תכתבנה
he	יכתב	she	תכתב	they	יכתבו	they	תכתבנה

IMPERATIVE

sing.	כתב		sing.	כתבי
plur.	כתבו		plur.	כתבנה

REMARKS: Verbs of the second group, derived from one-syllable verbs of the first group, such as קומם (*koh*-MEHM) "restore", from קום (*koom*) "stand", take the following forms:

מקומם   (m'koh-MEHM) "I restore"
קוממתי   (koh-MAHM-tee) "I restored"
אקומם   (ah-koh-MEHM) "I will restore"

GROUP II · (PASSIVE VOICE)

STEM: כותב (koo-TAHV) "be engraved"

מכותב	*PRESENT*	מכותבת	
כותבתי	*PAST*	כותבתי	
אכותב	*FUTURE*	אכותב	

GROUP III   (ACTIVE VOICE)

Verbs of this and of the fourth group take an initial ה (h) in the past tense and in the imperative.

STEM: הכתב (hakh-TEHV) "dictate"

PRESENT TENSE

	SINGULAR				PLURAL		
	Masc.		*Fem.*		*Masc.*		*Fem.*
I	מכתיב	I	מכתיבה	we	מכתיבים	we	מכתיבות
you	"	you	"	you	"	you	"
he	"	she	"	they	"	they	"

PAST TENSE

	SINGULAR				PLURAL		
	Masc.		*Fem.*		*Masc.*		*Fem.*
I	הכתבתי	I	הכתבתי	we	הכתבנו	we	הכתבנו
you	הכתבת	you	הכתבת	you	הכתבתם	you	הכתבתן
he	הכתיב	she	הכתיבה	they	הכתיבו	they	הכתיבו

FUTURE TENSE

	SINGULAR				PLURAL		
	Masc.		*Fem.*		*Masc.*		*Fem.*
I	אכתיב	I	אכתיב	we	נכתיב	we	נכתיב
you	תכתיב	you	תכתיבי	you	תכתיבו	you	תכתבנה
he	יכתיב	she	תכתיב	they	יכתיבו	they	"

IMPERATIVE

sing.	הכתב		*sing.*	הכתיבי
plur.	הכתיבו		*plur.*	הכתבנה

REMARKS: Verbs derived from first group one-syllable stems, like השב (hah-SHEHV) "return" (give back from שוב (shoov) "return (come back)", take the following form in the past tense: השיבותי (hah-shee-VOH-tee) "I returned" or "I gave back".

GROUP III   (PASSIVE VOICE)

STEM: הכתב (hokh-TAHV) "be dictated to"

Masc.		Fem.
מכתב	*PRESENT*	מכתבת
הכתבתי	*PAST*	הכתבתי
אכתב	*FUTURE*	אכתב

Verbs of the one-syllable group take the following forms:

Pres.:   מושב (moo-SHAHV) "I am returned"
Past: הושבתי (hoo-SHAHV-tee) "I was returned"
Fut.   אושב (oo-SHAHV) "I will be returned"

GROUP IV

STEM: התלבש (heet-lah-BEHSH): "dress" (oneself)

PRESENT TENSE

	SINGULAR				PLURAL		
	Masc.		Fem.		Masc.		Fem.
I	מתלבש	I	מתלבשת	we	מתלבשים	we	מתלבשות
you	"	you	"	you	"	you	"
he	"	she	"	they	"	they	"

PAST TENSE

	SINGULAR				PLURAL		
	Masc.		Fem.		Masc.		Fem.
I	התלבשתי	I	התלבשתי	we	התלבשנו	we	התלבשנו
you	התלבשת	you	התלבשת	you	התלבשתם	you	התלבשתן
he	התלבש	she	התלבשה	they	התלבשו	they	התלבשו

FUTURE TENSE

	SINGULAR				PLURAL		
	Masc.		Fem.		Masc.		Fem.
I	אתלבש	I	אתלבש	we	נתלבש	we	נתלבש
you	תתלבש	you	תתלבשי	you	תתלבשו	you	תתלבשנה
he	יתלבש	she	תתלבש	they	יתלבשו	they	"

IMPERATIVE

sing	התלבש	sing.	התלבשי
plur.	התלבשו	plur.	התלבשנה

The one-syllable group (example: התקומם (heet-koh-MEHM) "rebel" from קום (koom) "stand" doubles the last consonant (as you have already seen in the second group) and takes the vowel ו (oh) in the middle syllable, instead of the regular — (ah). Examples:

התקומם (heet-koh-MEHM): "he rebelled"
יתקומם (yeet-koh-MEHM): "he will rebel"

NOTE ON THE IMPERATIVE:

Remember that the second and third groups have *no* imperative in their passive voices.

The preceding tables are not exhaustive, but they illustrate the main patterns of Hebrew verb conjugation. It is much easier to learn them if you understand the correlation of the groups and the derivation of one Hebrew verb from another. This sketch demonstrates these relations in the growth of a tree, a living symbol of the rebirth of Israel's ancient language flourishing in a revitalized land.

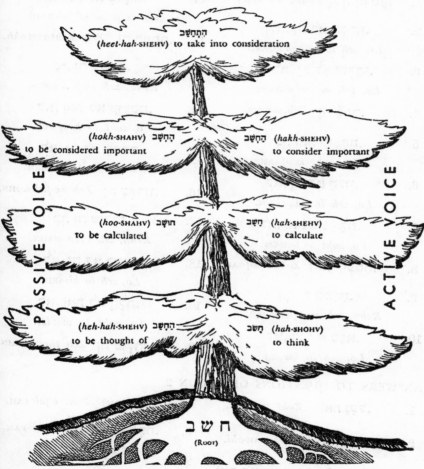

The root from which the stems of the four groups are developed is a combination of three consonants, meaningless in itself but acquiring various meanings, as it becomes incorporated in a verb.

ANSWERS

ANSWERS TO QUESTIONS OF LESSON 1

1. כֵּן, זֶה סֵפֶר. *Kehn, zeh* SEH-*fer.*

2. לֹא, זֶה לֹא עִפָּרוֹן.
*Lo, zeh lo ee-pah-*ROHN.

3. לֹא, זֶה לֹא שׁוּלְחָן.
*Lo, zeh lo shool-*HAHN.

4. זֶה סֵפֶר. *Zeh* SEH-*fer.*

5. כֵּן, זֹאת קוּפְסָה.
*Kehn, zoht koof-*SAH.

6. לֹא, זֶה לֹא חַלּוֹן.
*Lo, zeh lo hah-*LOHN.

7. לֹא, זֹאת לֹא דָלֶת.
Lo, zoht lo DEH-*let.*

8. זֹאת קוּפְסָה. *Zoht koof-*SAH.

9. כֵּן, זֶה מַפְתֵּחַ.
*Kehn, zeh mahf-*TEH-*akh.*

10. לֹא, זֶה לֹא כִּסֵּא.
*Lo, zeh lo kis-*SEH.

11. לֹא, זֹאת לֹא מְנוֹרָה.
*Lo, zoht lo m'noh-*RAH

12. זֶה מַפְתֵּחַ. *Zeh mahf-*TEH-*akh.*

13. כֵּן, זֶה עִפָּרוֹן.
*Kehn, zeh ee-pah-*ROHN.

14. לֹא, זֹאת לֹא קוּפְסָה.
*Lo, zoht lo koof-*SAH.

15. לֹא, זֶה לֹא מַפְתֵּחַ.
*Lo, zeh lo mahf-*TEH-*akh.*

16. זֶה עִפָּרוֹן. *Zeh ee-pah-*ROHN

17. כֵּן, זֶה שׁוּלְחָן.
*Kehn, zeh shool-*HAHN.

18. לֹא, זֶה לֹא כִּסֵּא.
*Lo, zeh lo kis-*SEH.

19. לֹא, זֹאת לֹא דָלֶת.
Lo, zoht lo DEH-*let.*

20. זֶה שׁוּלְחָן. *Zeh shool-*HAHN

ANSWERS TO QUESTIONS OF LESSON 2

1. זֹאת נַעַל. *Zoht* NAH-*ahl.*

2. זֹאת נַעַל. *Zoht* NAH-*ahl.*

3. זֹאת לֹא עֲנִיבָה אַף לֹא מִטְפַּחַת
*Zoht lo ah-nee-*VAH *aff lo meet-*PAH-*haht.*

4. זֹאת כְּפָפָה. *Zoht k'fah-*FAH.

5. זֹאת כְּפָפָה. *Zoht k'fah-*FAH.

6. לֹא, זֶה לֹא עִפָּרוֹן.
*Lo, zeh lo ee-pah-*ROHN.

7. זֶה כּוֹבַע. *Zeh* KOH-*vah.*

278

8.   לֹא, זֹאת לֹא שִׂמְלָה.   10.   לֹא, זֹאת לֹא עֲנִיבָה.
*Lo, zoht lo seem-*LAH.   *Lo, zoht lo ah-nee-*VAH.

9.   זֶה כּוֹבַע.   11.   כֵּן, זֶה כּוֹבַע.
Zeh KOH-*vah.*   *Kehn, zeh* KOH-*vah.*

ANSWERS TO QUESTIONS OF LESSON 3

1.   לֹא, הָעֵט לֹא כָּחוֹל.   9.   זֹאת מְנוֹרָה   *Zoht m'noh-*RAH.
*Lo, hah-*EHT *lo kah-*HOHL.

2.   הָעֵט יָרֹק.   *Hah-*EHT *yah-*ROHK.   10.   הַמְּנוֹרָה כְּחוּלָה.
                                     *Hah-m'noh-*RAH *k'hoo-*LAH.

3.   לֹא, הָעֵט לֹא אָדֹם.   11.   לֹא, הִיא לֹא אֲדוּמָה.
*Lo, hah-*EHT *lo ah-*DOHM.   *Lo, hee lo ah-doo-*MAH.

4.   הָעֵט לֹא לָבָן, אַף לֹא שָׁחוֹר.   12.   לֹא, הִיא לֹא אֲפוּרָה.
*Iah-*EHT *lo lah-*VAHN *aff lo shah-*HOHR.   *Lo, hee lo ah-foo-*RAH.

5.   זֶה עִפָּרוֹן.   *Zeh ee-pah-*ROHN.   13.   כֵּן, זֶה הַסֵּפֶר הָאָדֹם.
                             *Kehn, zeh hah-*SEH-*fer hah-ah-*DOHM.

6.   לֹא, הָעִפָּרוֹן לֹא אָדֹם.   14.   לֹא, זֶה לֹא הַסֵּפֶר הַצָּהֹב.
*Lo, hah-ee-pah-*ROHN *lo ah-*DOHM.   *Lo, zeh lo hah-*SEH-*fer*
                                     *hah-tsah-*HOHV.

7.   לֹא, הָעִפָּרוֹן לֹא שָׁחוֹר.   15.   הַסֵּפֶר אָדֹם.
*Lo, hah-ee-pah-*ROHN *lo shah-*HOHR.   *Hah-*SEH-*fer ah-*DOHM.

8.   הָעִפָּרוֹן צָהֹוב.
*Hah-ee-pah-*ROHN *tsah-*HOHV.

ANSWERS TO QUESTIONS OF LESSON 4

1.   כֵּ ן, הַסֵּפֶר הָאָדֹם אָרוֹךְ.   2.   כֵּן, הוּא רָחָב.
*Kehn, hah-*SEH-*fer hah-ah-*DOHM *ah-*ROKH.   *Kehn, hoo rah-*HAHV.

3.   כֵּן, הוּא גָּדוֹל.   4.   כֵּן, הַסֵּפֶר הַיָּרֹק קָצָר.
*Kehn, hoo gah-*DOHL.   *Kehn, hah-*SEH-*fer hah-yah-*ROHK *kah-*TSAHR.

5.   כֵּן, הוּא צָר.   6.   כֵּן, הוּא קָטָן.
Kehn, hoo tsahr.   *Kehn, hoo kah-*TAHN.

7.   הַשִּׂמְלָה הָאֲרוּכָּה שְׁחוֹרָה.
*Hah-seem-*LAH *hah-ah-roo-*KAH *sh'hoh-*RAH.

8.   הַשִּׂמְלָה הַצְּהוּבָה קְצָרָה.   *Hah-seem-LAH hah-ts'hoo-VAH k'tsah-RAH.*

9.   הַשִּׂמְלָה הַקְּצָרָה צְהוּבָה.   10.   ...יא לֹא שְׁחוֹרָה, אַף לֹא כְּחוּלָה.

Hah-seem-LAH hah-k'tsah-RAH t'shoo-VAH.   Hee lo sh'hoh-RAH, aff lo k'hoo-LAH.

11.   הַחַלּוֹן הָרָחָב כָּחוֹל.   12.   הַחַלּוֹן הָאָדוֹם קָצָר.

Hah-hah-LOHN hah-rah-HAHV kah-HOHL.   Hah-hah-LOHN hah-ah-DOHM kah-TSAHR.

13.   לֹא, הַחַלּוֹן הַכָּחוֹל לֹא קָטָן.   *Lo, hah-hah-LOHN hah-kah-HOHL lo kah-TAHN.*

14.   לֹא, הַסֵּפֶר הַיָּרוֹק לֹא רָחָב; הוּא צָר.

Lo, hah-SEH-fer hah-yah-ROHK lo rah-HAHV; hoo tsahr.

15.   הַסֵּפֶר הַיָּרוֹק צָר.   16.   הַחַלּוֹן הַגָּדוֹל כָּחוֹל.

Hah-SEH-fer hah-yah-ROHK tsahr.   Hah-hah-LOHN hah-gah-DOHL kah-HOHL.

17.   הַסֵּפֶר הַיָּרוֹק קָצָר.

Hah-SEH-fer hah-yah-ROHK kah-TSAHR.

18.   לֹא, הַסֵּפֶר הָאָדוֹם לֹא קָצָר, הוּא אָרוֹךְ.

Lo, hah-SEH-fer hah-ah-DOHM lo kah-tsahr, hoo ah-ROKH.

ANSWERS TO QUESTIONS OF LESSON 5

1.   אֲנִי אָדוֹן . . . . .   (אֲנִי גְּבֶרֶת . . . . .)

Ah-NEE Ah-DOHN. . . . .   (Ah-NEE G'veh-ret. . . . .)

2.   כֵּן, אֲנִי אֲמֶרִיקָאִי.   (כֵּן, אֲנִי אֲמֶרִיקָאִית.)

Kehn ah-NEE Ah-meh-ree-KAH-ee.   (Kehn, ah-NEE Ah-meh-ree-kah-EET.)

3.   לֹא, אֲנִי לֹא מוֹרֶה.   *Lo, ah-NEE lo moh-REH.*

4.   לֹא, אֲנִי לֹא יִשְׂרְאֵלִי.   (לֹא, אֲנִי לֹא יִשְׂרְאֵלִיָּה.)

Lo, ah-NEE lo Yis-reh-eh-LEE.   (Lo, ah-NEE lo Yis-reh-eh-lee-YAH.)

5.   אַתָּה אָדוֹן נָבוֹן, הַמּוֹרֶה.   6.   כֵּן, אַתָּה מוֹרֶה.

Ah-TAH Ah-DOHN Nah-VOHN, hah-moh-REH.   Kehn, ah-TAH moh-REH.

7.   לֹא, אַתָּה לֹא אֲמֶרִיקָאִי, אַתָּה יִשְׂרְאֵלִי.

Lo, ah-TAH lo Ah-meh-ree-KAH-ee, ah-TAH Yis-reh-eh-LEE.

8.   לֹא, אַתָּה לֹא סְפָרַדִי.   9.   הִיא יִשְׂרְאֵלִית.

Lo, ah-TAH lo Sfah-rah-DEE.   Hee Yis-reh-eh-LEET.

10.   לֹא, הוּא לֹא צָרְפָתִי, הוּא אֲמֶרִיקָאִי.

Lo, hoo lo Tsohr-fah-TEE, hoo Ah-meh-ree-KAH-ee.

11. לֹא, הוּא לֹא יִשְׂרְאֵלִי, הוּא אָמֶרִיקָאִי.

Lo, hoo lo Yis-reh-eh-LEE, hoo Ah-meh-ree-KAH-ee.

12. לֹא, אֲנִי לֹא אַנְגְלִי.   לֹא, אֲנִי לֹא אַנְגְלִיָה.

Lo, ah-NEE lo Ahn-GLEE.   (fem.) *Lo, ah-NEE lo Ahn-glee-YAH.*

13. מוֹרִס שֶׁבַּלְיֶה הוּא צָרְפָתִי.   *Maurice Chevalier hoo Tsohr-fah-TEE.*

14. הִיא לֹא צָרְפָתִיָה, אַף לֹא אִיטַלְקִיָה, הִיא יִשְׂרְאֵלִיָה.

Hee lo Tsohr-fah-tee-YAH, aff lo Ee-tahl-kee-YAH, hee Yis-reh-eh-lee-YAH.

15. לֹא, אִידֶן לֹא אָמֶרִיקָאִי, הוּא אַנְגְלִי.

Lo, Eden lo Ah-meh-ree-KAH-ee, hoo Ahn-GLEE.

16. לֹא, מַרְלִין דִיטְרִיך לֹא סְפַרְדִיָה, הִיא גֶרְמַנִיָה.

Lo, Marlene Dietrich lo Sfahr-dee-YAH, hee Ger-mah-nee-YAH.

17. הַכּוֹבַע הַזֶה גָדוֹל.   **18.**   הַצַנָארוֹן הַזֶה רָחָב.

Hah-KOH-vah hah-ZEH gah-DOHL.   *Hah-tsah-vah-ROHN hah-ZEH rah-HAHV.*

19. אֲנִי לֹא מוֹרֶה, אֲנִי תַלְמִיד.

Ah-NEE lo moh-REH, ah-NEE tahl-MEED.

אֲנִי לֹא תַלְמִידָה, אֲנִי מוֹרָה.

(fem.) *Ah-NEE lo tahl-mee-DAH, ah-NEE moh-RAH.*

ANSWERS TO QUESTIONS OF LESSON 6

1. הַסֵפֶר עַל הַשׁוּלְחָן.   **2.**   כֵּן, הַסֵפֶר עַל הַשׁוּלְחָן.

Hah-SEH-fer ahl hah-shool-HAHN.   *Kehn, hah-SEH-fer ahl hah-shool-HAHN.*

3. לֹא, הַסֵפֶר לֹא מִתַּחַת לַשׁוּלְחָן, הוּא עַל הַשׁוּלְחָן.

Lo, hah-SEH-fer lo mee-TAH-haht lah-shool-HAHN, hoo ahl hah-shool-HAHN.

4. הָעֵט בְּתוֹךְ הַקוּפְסָה.   *Hah-EHT b'tokh hah-koof-SAH.*

5. לֹא, הָעֵט לֹא עַל הַסֵפֶר, הוּא בְּתוֹךְ הַקוּפְסָה.

Lo, hah-EHT lo ahl hah-SEH-fer, hoo b'tokh hah-koof-SAH.

6. הַחַלוֹן מֵאַחוֹרֵי הַשׁוּלְחָן.   *Hah-hah-LOHN meh-ah-hoh-REH hah-shool-HAHN.*

7. הַמוֹרָה עַל־יַד הַשׁוּלְחָן.   *Hah-moh-REH ahl-YAHD hah-shool-HAHN.*

8. לֹא, הַמוֹרָה לֹא מִתַּחַת לַשׁוּלְחָן, הוּא עַל־יַד הַשׁוּלְחָן.

o, hah-moh-REH lo mee-TAH-haht lah-shool-HAHN, hoo ahl-YAHD hah-shool-HAHN.

9.   לֹא, הוּא לֹא לִפְנֵי הַשּׁוּלְחָן, הוּא עַל־יַד הַשּׁוּלְחָן.

Lo, hoo lo leef-NEH hah-shool-HAHN, hoo ahl-YAHD hah-shool-HAHN.

10.   הַדֶּלֶת מֵאֲחוֹרָיו.   11.   כֵּן, הַדֶּלֶת בַּקִּיר.

Hah-DEH-let meh-ah-hoh-RAHV.   *Kehn, hah-DEH-let bah-KEER.*

12.   כֵּן, הַנְּיָר בְּתוֹךְ הַסֵּפֶר.   *Kehn, hah-n'YAHR b'tokh hah-SEH-fer.*

13.   הַקּוּפְסָה מִתַּחַת לַשּׁוּלְחָן.   14.   הָעֵט בְּתוֹךְ הַקּוּפְסָה.

Hah-koof-SAH mee-TAH-haht lah-shool-HAHN.   *Hah-EHT b'tokh hah-koof-SAH.*

15.   לֹא, הַמַּפְתֵּחַ לֹא בַּכִּיס, הוּא עַל הַשּׁוּלְחָן.

Lo, hah-mahf-TEH-akh lo bah-KISS, hoo ahl hah-shool-HAHN.

16.   הַסֵּפֶר הַזֶּה גָּדוֹל.   17.   הַכּוֹבַע שֶׁעַל הַכִּסֵּא גָּדוֹל.

Hah-SEH-fer hah-ZEH gah-DOHL.   *Hah-KOH-vah sheh-AHL hah-kis-SEH gah-DOHL.*

18.   תֵּל־אָבִיב לֹא בְּאַנְגְּלִיָה, הִיא בְּיִשְׂרָאֵל.

Tel-Ah-VEEV lo beh-Ahn-glee-YAH, hee b'Yis-rah-EHL.

19.   נְיוּ יוֹרְק בְּאָמֶרִיקָה.   20.   אֲנִי בִּנְיוּ יוֹרְק.

New-YORK beh-Ah-MEH-ree-kah.   *Ah-NEE bee-New-YORK.*

ANSWERS TO QUESTIONS OF LESSON 7

1.   הַמּוֹרָה שָׂם אֶת הַסֵּפֶר עַל הַשּׁוּלְחָן.

Hah-moh-REH sahm ett hah-SEH-fer ahl hah-shool-HAHN.

2.   לֹא, הוּא אֵינוֹ לוֹקֵחַ אֶת הַסֵּפֶר, הוּא שָׂם אֶת הַסֵּפֶר.

Lo, hoo eh-NOH loh-KAY-akh ett hah-SEH-fer, hoo sahm ett hah-SEH-fer.

3.   לֹא, הוּא אֵינוֹ שָׂם אֶת הַסֵּפֶר מִתַּחַת לַשּׁוּלְחָן.

Lo, hoo eh-NOH sahm ett hah-SEH-fer mee-TAH-haht lah-shool-HAHN.

4.   הוּא אֵינוֹ לוֹקֵחַ אֶת הַקּוּפְסָה.   *Hoo eh-NOH loh-KAY-akh ett hah-koof-SAH.*

5.   הוּא אֵינוֹ יוֹשֵׁב, הוּא עוֹמֵד.   *Hoo, eh-NOH yoh-SHEHV, hoo oh-MEHD.*

6.   לֹא, הוּא אֵינוֹ סוֹגֵר אֶת הַחַלּוֹן.   *Lo, hoo eh-NOH soh-GEHR ett hah-hah-LOHN.*

7.   הוּא פּוֹתֵחַ אֶת הַחַלּוֹן.   *Hoo poh-TAY-akh ett hah-hah-LOHN.*

8.   לֹא, הַתַּלְמִידָה אֵינָה פּוֹתַחַת אֶת הַדֶּלֶת.

Lo, hah-tahl-mee-DAH eh-NAH poh-TAH-haht ett hah-DEH-let.

9.   לֹא, הַגְּבֶרֶת בֵּילָה אֵינָה פּוֹתַחַת אֶת הַדֶּלֶת.

Lo, hah-g'VEH-ret BEH-leh eh-NAH poh-TAH-haht ett hah-DEH-let.

0. לֹא, הַמּוֹרָה אֵינוֹ פּוֹתֵחַ אֶת הַקּוּפְסָה.

*Lo, hah-moh-*REH *eh-*NOH *poh-*TAY-akh *ett hah-koof-*SAH.

1. לֹא, הַמּוֹרָה אֵינוֹ הוֹלֵךְ לְנִיוּ יוֹרק, הוּא הוֹלֵךְ לְתֵל-אָבִיב.

*Lo, hah-moh-*REH *eh-*NOH *hoh-*LEHKH *lee-New-*YORK,
*hoo hoh-*LEHKH *l'Tel-Ah-*VEEV.

2. כֵּן, הוּא בָּאֲוִירוֹן. 13. לֹא, הוּא אֵינוֹ הוֹלֵךְ לְפָּרִיז.

*Lo, hoo eh-*NOH *hoh-*LEHKH *l'Pah-*REEZ.   *Kehn, hoo bah-ah-vee-*ROHN.

4. נִיוּ יוֹרק גְּדוֹלָה. 15. לֹא, אֲנִי לֹא בְּהוֹלִיבוּד.

*New-*YORK *g'doh-*LAH.   *Lo, ah-*NEE *lo b'*HOH-*lee-vood.

6. הַמּוֹרָה הוֹלֵךְ לְתֵל-אָבִיב. *Hah-moh-*REH *hoh-*LEHKH *l'Tel-Ah-*VEEV.

ANSWERS TO QUESTIONS OF LESSON 8

1. אֲנִי סוֹפֵר מֵאֶחָד עַד עֲשָׂרָה.

*Ah-*NEE *soh-*FEHR *meh-eh-*HAHD *ahd ah-sah-*RAH.

2. אַתָּה סוֹפֵר: אֶחָד שְׁנַיִם שְׁלוֹשָׁה וְכוּ'.

*Ah-*TAH *soh-*FEHR *eh-*HAHD *sh'*NAH-*yim sh'loh-*SHAH *veh-*HOO.

3. הוּא סוֹפֵר. 4. בַּחֶדֶר הַזֶּה שְׁנֵי כִּסְאוֹת.

*Hoo soh-*FEHR.   *Bah-*HEH-*der hah-*ZEH *sh'neh kis-*OHT.

5. כֵּן, יֵשׁ שָׁם שׁוּלְחָן. 6. עַל הַשּׁוּלְחָן יֵשׁ קוּפְסָה אַחַת.

*Kehn, yehsh shahm shool-*HAHN.   *Ahl hah-shool-*HAHN *yehsh koof-*SAH *ah-*HAHT.

7. שֵׁשׁ פְּעָמִים חָמֵשׁ הֵן שְׁלוֹשִׁים.

*Shehsh peh-ah-*MEEM *hah-*MEHSH *hehn sh'loh-*SHEEM.

8. לֹא, שְׁתֵּי פְּעָמִים שְׁתַּיִם הֵן אַרְבַּע.

*Lo, sh'teh peh-ah-*MEEM *sh'*TAH-*yim hehn ahr-*BAH.

9. שֶׁבַע פְּעָמִים שָׁלוֹשׁ הֵן עֶשְׂרִים וְאַחַת.

SHEH-*vah peh-ah-*MEEM *shah-*LOSH *hehn ess-*REEM *veh-ah-*HAHT.

0. הַנִיוּ-יוֹרק-טַימְס עוֹלָה בַּחֲמִשָּׁה סֶנְטִים.

*Hah-New-York-Times oh-*LEH *bah-hah-mee-*SHAH SEN-*teem.

1. הַסֵּפֶר הַזֶּה עוֹלָה בַּחֲמִשָּׁה דוֹלַרִים.

*Hah-*SEH-*fer hah-*ZEH *oh-*LEH *bah-hah-mee-*SHAH *doh-*LAH-*reem.

2. לֹא, הַסֵּפֶר הַזֶּה אֵינוֹ עוֹלָה בַּעֲשָׂרָה דוֹלַר.

*Lo, hah-*SEH-*fer hah-*ZEH *eh-*NOH *oh-*LEH *bah-ahs-ah-*RAH DOH-*lahr.

13. ‏לֹא, הַשָּׁעוֹן הַזֶה אֵינוֹ עוֹלֶה בְּמֵאָה לִירוֹת.‎

Lo, hah-shah-OHN hah-ZEH eh-NOH oh-LEH b'meh-AH LEE-roht.

14. ‏לֹא, שִׁשָּׁה וּשְׁנַיִם הֵם שְׁמוֹנָה.‎

Lo, shee-SHAH oo-sh'NAH-yim hehm sh'moh-NAH.

ANSWERS TO QUESTIONS OF LESSON 9

1. ‏לַמּוֹרָה עִתּוֹן מִתַּחַת לַזְרוֹעַ.‎

Lah-moh-REH ee-TOHN mee-TAH-haht lah-z'ROH-ah.

2. ‏כֵּן, זֶה עִתּוֹן מִתַּחַת לִזְרוֹעַ הַמּוֹרָה.‎

Kehn, zeh ee-TOHN mee-TAH-haht lee-z'ROH-ah hah-moh-REH.

3. ‏לֹא, אֵין זֶה עִפָּרוֹן בְּכִיס הַמּוֹרָה.‎

Lo, ehn zeh ee-pah-ROHN b'hees hah-moh-REH.

4. ‏הָעִתּוֹן מִתַּחַת לִזְרוֹעַ הַמּוֹרָה.‎

Hah-ee-TOHN mee-TAH-haht lee-z'ROH-ah hah-moh-REH.

5. ‏לֹא, הַסַּרְגֵּל לֹא מִתַּחַת לְרַגְלוֹ הַיְמָנִית שֶׁל הַמּוֹרָה.‎

*Lo, hah-sahr-GEHL lo mee-TAH-haht l'rahg-LOH hah-y'mah-NEET
shell hah-moh-REH.*

6. ‏בְּיַד הַיְמָנִית שֶׁל הַמּוֹרָה עִפָּרוֹן.‎

B'yahd hah-y'mah-NEET shell hah-moh-REH ee-pah-ROHN.

7. ‏כֵּן, בַּקּוּפְסָה שְׁלוֹשָׁה עֶפְרוֹנוֹת.‎

Kehn, bah-koof-SAH sh'loh-SHAH eff-roh-NOHT.

8. ‏עַל הַשֻּׁלְחָן שְׁלוֹשָׁה מַפְתְּחוֹת‎ *Ahl hah-shool-HAHN sh'loh-SHAH mahf-t'HOH*

9. ‏הַסְּפָרִים עַל הַשֻּׁלְחָן.‎ *Hah-s'fah-REEM ahl hah-shool-HAHN.*

10. ‏מִתַּחַת לַשֻּׁלְחָן שְׁנֵי כְּלָבִים.‎

Mee-TAH-haht lah-shool-HAHN sh'neh k'lah-VEEM.

11. ‏כֵּן, עַל הַקִּיר שָׁלוֹשׁ תְּמוּנוֹת.‎ *Kehn, ahl hah-KEER shah-LOSH t'moo-NOH*

12. ‏עַל הַשֻּׁלְחָן אַרְבָּעָה סְפָרִים.‎ *Ahl hah-shool-HAHN ahr-bah-AH s'fah-REEM*

13. ‏כֵּן, לַמּוֹרָה עֶשְׂרִים לִירוֹת בַּכִּיס.‎

Kehn, lah-moh-REH ess-REEM LEE-roht bah-KISS.

14. ‏כֵּן, הַכּוֹבַע עַל הַכִּסֵּא הַקָּטָן.‎

Kehn, hah-KOH-vah ahl hah-kis-SEH hah-kah-TAHN.

ANSWERS TO QUESTIONS OF LESSON 10

1. אֲנִי כּוֹתֵב אֶת הָאוֹת אָלֶף עַל הַנְּיָר.

Ah-NEE *koh*-TEHV *ett hah-*OHT *Ah-lef ahl hah-n'*YAHR.

2. אַתָּה כּוֹתֵב אֶת הַמִּלָּה חוֹפֶשׁ. *Ah*-TAH *koh*-TEHV *ett hah-mee*-LAH HOH-*fesh*.

3. אָדוֹן נָמְזוּ כּוֹתֵב אֶת הָאָלֶף־בֵּית עַל הַלּוּחַ.

Ah-DOHN GAHM-*zoo koh*-TEHV *ett hah-Ah-lef-beht ahl hah-*LOO-*akh*.

4. אֲנִי קוֹרֵא אֶת הַמִּשְׁפָּט: „אֲנִי יִשְׂרְאֵלִי".

Ah-NEE *koh*-REH *ett hah-meesh*-PAHT "*ah*-NEE *Yis-reh-eh*-LEE".

5. בַּמִּשְׁפָּט הַזֶּה תֵּשַׁע אוֹתִיּוֹת.

Bah-meesh-PAHT *hah-*ZEH TEH-*shah oh-tee-*YOHT.

6. כֵּן, אֲנִי קוֹרֵא עִבְרִית. *Kehn, ah*-NEE *koh*-REH *eev-*REET.

7. כֵּן, אָדוֹן בֶּרְלִיץ קוֹרֵא עִבְרִית.

Kehn, ah-DOHN BER-*litz koh*-REH *eev-*REET.

8. כֵּן, הוּא מְדַבֵּר עִבְרִית. *Kehn, hoo m'dah-*BEHR *eev-*REET.

9. כֵּן, אָדוֹן נָבוֹן מְדַבֵּר אַנְגְּלִית.

Kehn, ah-DOHN *Nah-*VOHN *m'dah-*BEHR *ahn-*GLEET.

10. אֲנִי מְדַבֵּר עִבְרִית. *Ah*-NEE *m'dah-*BEHR *eev-*REET.

11. לֹא, הוּא אֵינוֹ מְדַבֵּר צָרְפָתִית.

Lo, hoo eh-NOH *m'dah-*BEHR *tsohr-fah-*TEET.

12. „גֶּנְטְלְמַן" הִיא מִלָּה אַנְגְּלִית. "*Gentleman*" *hee mee-*LAH *ahn-*GLEET.

13. כֵּן, אַתָּה אוֹמֵר אֶת הָאָלֶף־בֵּית.

*Kehn, ah-*TAH *oh-*MEHR *ett hah-Ah-lef-beht*.

14. לֹא, אֲנִי אֵינֶנִּי אוֹמֵר אֶת הָאָלֶף־בֵּית הָרוּסִי.

*Lo, ah-*NEE *eh-*NEN-*nee oh-*MEHR *ett hah-Ah-lef-beht hah-roo-*SEE.

15. הַמּוֹרֶה הָעִבְרִי אוֹמֵר אֶת הָאָלֶף־בֵּית הָעִבְרִי.

*Hah-moh-*REH *hah-eev-*REE *oh-*MEHR *ett hah-Ah-lef-beht hah-eev-*REE.

16. בִּירוּשָׁלַיִם מְדַבְּרִים עִבְרִית.

*Bee-Yeh-roo-shah-*LAH-*yim m'dah-b'*REEM *eev-*REET.

17. כֵּן, בְּמֶקְסִיקוֹ מְדַבְּרִים סְפָרַדִית.

*Kehn, b'Mexico m'dah-b'*REEM *sfah-rah-*DEET.

18. בְּמַדְרִיד אֵין מְדַבְּרִים רוּסִית. *b'*MAHD-*reed ehn m'dah-b'*REEM *roo-*SEET.

NOTE TO STUDENT:
In order to help your fluency in reading Hebrew we have prepared the following answers *only* in Hebrew text, without using phonetics. This will not be too difficult inasmuch as you have already encountered these words in the corresponding lessons and questions.

ANSWERS TO QUESTIONS OF LESSON 11

7. כן, היא קוראת עתון עברי.	1. המורה כותב על הלוח.
8. כן, הוא מדבר עברית.	2. לא, הגברת בילה אינה כותבת.
9. היא קוראת עתון עברי.	3. כן, היא קוראת.
10. כן, אני קורא עברית.	4. המורה כותב את המלה „הקשב" על הלוח.
11. לא, אני אינני מדבר ספרדית.	
12. כן, הוא מדבר צרפתית.	5. הוא כותב בגיר.
13. כן, הוא מדבר אנגלית.	6. לא, הוא אינו כותב את האלף־בית.
14. היא יושבת.	

ANSWERS TO QUESTIONS OF LESSON 12

8. לאלף־בית העברי עשרים ושתים אותיות.	1. למורה כובע על הראש.
	2. לא, לרותי שערות בהירות.
9. למורה עתון בידו.	3. כן, יש לי עפרון.
10. לפתה שלושים תלמידים.	4. כן, לתלמידים יש ספרים.
11. כן, לרוקפלר הרבה כסף.	5. לשולחן ארבע רגלים.
12. כן, לבית־הספר ברליץ הרבה תלמידים.	6. לא, למורה אין שערות רבות.
	7. כן, לרותי יש מטריה.

ANSWERS TO QUESTIONS OF LESSON 13

8. לרותי כסף פחות מכולם.	1. לגברת בילה מאה לירות.
9. לא, לה מעט כסף.	2. לא, לה אין כה הרבה כסף כמו למורה.
10. כן, למורה מעט ספרים.	
11. כן, אני קורא הרבה ספרים עבריים.	3. למורה יותר כסף מאשר לרותי.
12. התלמיד כותב יותר תרגילים.	4. כן, למורה עפרונות על אוזנו.
13. כן, בספר זה הרבה עמודים.	5. כן, למורה יותר עפרונות מאשר לרותי.
14. לא, בניו־יורק־טיימס אין כה הרבה עמודים כמו בספר זה.	6. לא, לה יותר ספרים מאשר למורה.
15. בכיסך ששים ושלוש לירות.	7. למורה כסף יותר מכולם.
16. לי יש עשרים ושמונה לירות.	

ANSWERS TO QUESTIONS OF LESSON 14

1. כן, הוא נותן לה ספר.
2. הוא נותן לה משהו.
3. היא אינה עושה כלום.
4. לא, הן אינן נותנות כובע למורה.
5. אף אחד אינו מדבר לרותי.
6. הוא אינו אומר לה כלום.
7. לא, היא אינה אומרת לאביר כלום.
8. לא, היא אינה נותנת לו כלום.
9. אביר אינו אומר כלום.
10. כן, הם מדברים אל המורה בשעת השעור.
11. כן, הם אומרים לו „שלום" לפני השעור.
12. אחרי השעור אין המורה אומר להם כלום.
13. ביד השמאלית של הגברת בילה יש משהו.
14. אני מספר לך משהו.
15. המורה אינו אומר לה כלום.
16. אף היא אינה אומרת כלום.

ANSWERS TO QUESTIONS OF LESSON 15

1. כן, למורה יש סיגריה בידו.
2. ביד השמאלית של בילה מטפחת.
3. לא, אין בידה הימנית כלום.
4. גם בידה השמאלית אין כלום.
5. לא, אף איש אינו עומד לידו השמאלית של המורה.
6. רותי לפני השולחן.
7. כן, בידה הימנית של בילה ספר.
8. אף איש אינו יושב על הכסא.
9. על השולחן אין כלום.
10. בידו הימנית של המורה סיגריה.
11. אף איש אינו עומד לידו השמאלית של המורה.
12. מתחת לכסא אין כלום.
13. אף איש אינו עומד לפני רותי.
14. אף איש אינו לידה השמאלית של רותי.
15. כן, מישהו עומד מאחורי השולחן, והוא המורה.
16. לא, הוא אינו חובש כובע לראשו.
17. לו אין כלום על ראשו.

ANSWERS TO QUESTIONS OF LESSON 16

1. המורה מריח את הבצל באף.
2. לא, לבצל ריח רע.
3. כן, לשושנה ריח טוב.
4. היא מריחה שושנה.
5. לא, איני רואה את הדברים שמאחורי.
6. כן, אנו רואים את הדברים שלפנינו.
7. לא, אין אנו שומעים מישהו דופק בדלת.
8. כן, אנו אוכלים לחם.
9. כן, אנו רואים אותו בקולנוע.
10. כן, אנו שמים סוכר בקפה.
11. כן, רבים אוכלים לחם לבן.
12. כן, רבים שותים הרבה קוקה קולה.
13. לא, אין אנו שמים חלב בתה.
14. לא, אין אנו שמים סוכר בבשר.
15. אנו חותכים בשר בסכין.

16. לא, אין אנו אוכלים אפונה   18. לא, אין אנו שותים באף.
בספין.   19. אנו שותים בפה.
17. אנו כותבים גם בעט וגם בעפרון

ANSWERS TO QUESTIONS OF LESSON 17

1. אנו חותכים בשר בסכין.   10. כן, אני אוהב גבינה.
2. לא, אין אנו אוכלים בשר בכף.   11. לא, אין אני אוהב תה בלי סוכר.
3. אנו אוכלים מרק בכף.   12. כן, אני אוהב בירה.
4. כן, אני אוהב את ריח השושנה.   13. כן, הן אוהבות פרחים.
5. לא, אין אני אוהב את ריח   14. כן, אני אוהב לדבר עברית.
הגבינה.   15. כן, שפת הים של תל-אביב
6. כן, אני אוהב קפה בסוכר.   יפה מאד.
7. לא, אין אני אוהב מרק בלי מלח.   16. כן, הבגדים בחלונות הראוה של
8. לא, אין אני אוהב את ריח   רחוב בן-יהודה יפים מאד.
השום.   17. הנשר יפה.
9. כן, אני אוהב את טעם תות-   18. כן, השפה העברית יפה.
השדה.   19. כן, אני אוהב לשמוע אותה.

ANSWERS TO QUESTIONS OF LESSON 18

1. כן, רותי נוגעת באפיר.   10. כן, הוא יכול לצאת מהחדר.
2. לא, היא אינה יכולה לנגוע בידו   11. לא, בלי עפרון ובלי עט אין אתה
הימנית של המורה.   יכול לכתב.
3. כן, המורה יכול לנגע בכובעה   12. לא, אין אנו יכולים לראות מה
של רותי.   שמאחורינו.
4. לא, הוא אינו נוגע בה.   13. לא, אין התלמידים יכולים לנגע
5. כן, המנורה נמוכה.   בתקרה.
6. כן, הוא יכול לנגע בה.   14. כן, אני יכול לשבר גפרור.
7. המורה נוגע בידו.   15. לא, אין אני יכול לשבר מפתח
8. כן, הוא מרכיב משקפים.   של הדלת.
9. לא, אין הוא יכול לראות בלי   16. כן, אני יכול לנגע בספרי.
משקפים.

ANSWERS TO QUESTIONS OF LESSON 19

1. כן, רותי רוצה לאכול את התפוח.   4. משום שאינו רוצה.
2. לא, היא אינה יכולה לנגע   5. לא, הוא אינו רוצה לתת אותו
בתפוח.   לה.
3. לא, הוא אינו נותן לה את   6. כן, כדי לצאת מוכרח אני לפתח
התפוח.   את הדלת.

.7 כן, אנו מוכרחים לפקח את עינינו אם אנו רוצים לראות.

.8 כן, זקוק אני לכסף כדי לנסע.

.9 כדי לכתב יש לנו צורך בניר ועפרון או עט.

.10 אם הדלת סגורה, ואני רוצה לצאת, אני מוכרח לפתח אותה.

.11 לא, הוא אינו יכול לראות בלי משקפים.

.12 כדי לקרא אני זקוק לספר.

.13 כדי ללכת לאופרה אנו מוכרחים לקנות כרטיסים.

.14 לא, אין אני יכול לאכל מרק בסכין.

.15 אנו משתמשים בכף כדי לאכל מרק.

.16 כן, אתה זקוק לכסף כדי ללכת לקולנוע.

.17 כן, המלצר מגיש את האוכל לשולחן במסעדה.

.18 אתה משאיר דמי שתיה למלצר על השולחן.

.19 כן, אתה מוכרח לשלם בעד האוכל.

ANSWERS TO QUESTIONS OF LESSON 20

.1 כן, יש שעונים בחדר זה.

.2 השעונים על הקיר ועל השולחן.

.3 יש לי שעון-יד.

.4 את שעון-הכיס אני שם בכיס.

.5 שעוני הוא מזהב.

.6 כן, לשעוני מחוג לשניות.

.7 ביום עשרים וארבע שעות.

.8 בדקה ששים שניות.

.9 לא, שעוני אינו ממהר.

.10 השולחן עשוי מעץ.

.11 אף הכסא עשוי מעץ.

.12 כן, השולחן גדול מהכסא.

.13 לא, התמונה אינה ארופה מהקיר.

.14 לא, החלון אינו גדול כמו הדלת.

.15 כן, המעיל ארוך מהחזיה.

.16 לא, שניהם טובים במדה שוה.

.17 כן, אני מבטא עברית היטב.

.18 כן, אני רואה היטב.

.19 לא, הוא אינו רואה היטב בלי משקפים.

.20 כן, הוא רואה טוב יותר במשקפים.

ANSWERS TO QUESTIONS OF LESSON 21

.1 בשנה שלוש-מאות ששים וחמשה ימים.

.2 השבוע מורכב משבעה ימים.

.3 השנה מתחילה בראשון לינואר.

.4 היא נגמרת בשלושים ואחד בדצמבר.

.5 שמות החדשים האלה הם: ינואר, מרס ומאי.

.6 שמות חדשי השנה הם: ינואר, פברואר... וכו'.

.7 שבת היא היום האחרון בשבוע.

.8 היום יום רביעי בשבוע.

.9 לא, אתמול לא היה יום ראשון.

.10 בשבת אין אני הולך לבית-הספר.

.11 כן, יום ששי יהיה החמשה-עשר בחודש. (לא, יום ששי לא יהיה החמשה-עשר בחודש.)

.12 היום הוא יום ה...

13. יום שני הבא יהיה יום ה...
14. יום שני שעבר היה יום ה...
15. כן מחר יהיה היום האחרון בחודש.

16. אנו עובדים ששה ימים בשבוע.
17. לא, אין אני עובד בשבת.
18. בחמשי באייר חל חג יום העצמאות.

ANSWERS TO QUESTIONS OF LESSON 22

1. עשרים וארבע שעות-היום מחולקות ליום ולילה.
2. ביום אור.
3. לא, עכשו לא חושך.
4. אור היום בא מן השמש.
5. השמש בשמים.
6. המנורה מאירה את החדר בלילה.
7. אנו מדליקים בלילה את החשמל, כדי לראות.
8. בלילה אנו רואים את הירח והכוכבים בשמים.
9. השמש זורחת ממזרח.
10. בחודש מרס זורחת השמש בשעה שש בבוקר.

11. בעונת הקיץ הימים ארופים.
12. כן, בקיץ ארופים הימים מן הלילות.
13. בעונת החורף ארופים הלילות.
14. בלילה אנו מדליקים את האור.
15. בדרך כלל אני הולך לישון בשעה אחת-עשרה.
16. אני קם בשעה שש בבוקר.
17. אני אוכל ארוחת-בוקר בשעה שבע בבוקר.
18. אני מתחיל לעבוד בשעה שמונה.
19. אני גומר את עבודתי בשעה חמש לפנות-ערב.
20. כן, אני אוהב לעבוד.

ANSWERS TO QUESTIONS OF LESSON 23

1. מזג אויר רע השמים אפורים.
2. השמים מכוסים עננים.
3. לא, עתה אין גשמים יורדים.
4. לא, אין אני אוהב לטייל ברחובות בגשם.
5. בגשם אני לוקח אתי מטריה.
6. היום מזג אויר יפה.
7. לא, אין אני יוצא לרחוב במזג אויר רע.
8. כן, בקוטב הצפוני קר.
9. כרגיל יורד שלג בחדשי דצמבר, ינואר ופברואר.

10. לא, לא תמיד יורד שלג בפברואר.
11. לא, לפעמים יורד שלג באפריל.
12. הגשמים באים מן העננים.
13. לא, לא נעים ללכת בחוץ בגשם.
14. בחדשי החורף אנו לובשים בגדים חמים.
15. בדרך כלל מזג האויר בישראל יפה.
16. כדי להתחמם יושב אני ליד התנור.
17. השמש זורחת ביום.

ANSWERS TO QUESTIONS OF LESSON 24

1. תנועת „חבת-ציון" התחילה רשמית בשנת 1885.

2. ד"ר הרצל היה מיסדה של התנועה הציונית.

3. ב"ועידת קטוביץ" נוסדה תנועת "חבת-ציון".
4. לא, יהודה לא הכין את שעורו בהיסטוריה.
5. אחרי ההצגה הלך יוסף למסיבה לבית יהודית.
6. במסיבה פגש את נילי, רבקה, עוזי, גדעון, ועוד ידידים רבים.
7. מתי התחילה רשמית תנועת "חבת-ציון"? שאל המורה את יהודה.
8. לא יהודה לא ידע את התשובה הנכונה.
9. אני קם בשעה שבע בבוקר.
10. אתמול התעוררתי בשעה שש.
11. קמתי בשבע.

12. לפני ארוחת-הבוקר התרחצתי והתלבשתי.
13. לבשתי חליפה אפורה.
14. לא, התרחצתי במים חמים.
15. כן, התלבשתי מהר.
16. כן, אכלתי מוקדם ארוחת-בוקר.
17. כן, שמתי חלב לתוך הקפה.
18. כן, בשבוע האחרון קבלתי שני מכתבים.
19. כן, עניתי עליהם.
20. לא, אתמול לא טילתי.
21. הלכתי לעבודה.
22. כן, שמעתי חמשה קונצרטים בחורף האחרון.
23. כן, צחקתי הרבה בהצגה.

ANSWERS TO QUESTIONS OF LESSON 25

1. המורה ילך הערב הביתה.
2. כן, היא תהיה בבית הלילה.
3. רותי תבוא לגברת בילה לארוחת-הצהרים.
4. כן, הוא יקום מאוחר מחר.
5. הוא לא ילך לבית-הספר מחר, כי מחר תהיה שבת.
6. בשבוע הבא יעבד ששה ימים.
7. ביום שבת ננוח.
8. משה ויצחק ילכו מחר לשפת-הים.
9. כן, הם יזמינו את יהודית ומרים.
10. הם יפגשו בשעה עשר בבוקר.

11. הם יאכלו ארוחת-הצהרים במסעדה.
12. משה יטלפן לנערות.
13. לא, הם לא יקחו אתם אוכל.
14. כן, בקרוב אסע לישראל.
15. אני אסע באוירון.
16. כן, בשבוע הבא נאכל יחד ארוחת-הצהרים.
17. רוצה אני, כי תטלפן אלי ביום שני.
18. מדוע לא, תוכל להזמין אתו ללכת אתנו.
19. נפגש בקפה "תמר".

ANSWERS TO QUESTIONS OF LESSON 26

1. כדי לחיות, על החיות לאכל, לשתות ולנשם.
2. כדי לחיות אנו זקוקים לאכל, לשתות ולנשם.
3. חמשת החושים הם: חוש הראיה, השמיעה, הריח, הטעם

והמשוש.
4. שמות חיות-הבית העיקריות הם: הסוס, הפרה, הכלב והחתול.
5. אנו נושמים באף.
6. הדגים חיים במים.
7. הנחש זוחל על הארץ.

8. היא מיצרת דבש.

9. שמות חיות-השדה העיקריות
הם: האריה, הנמר, הפיל והזאב.

10. לכלב ארבע כפים.

11. לעוף שתי רגלים.

12. ברגליהן הן מהלכות.

13. הם עפים באויר.

14. כן, הם שוחים באוקינוס.

15. לא, אי-אפשר לנו לחיות בלי
לאכל ולנשם.

16. צבע הדם אדום.

17. הלב גורם למחזור הדם.

18. מקום הלב בחזה.

19. כן, מצב בריאותי טוב.

20. לא, אם אוכל הרבה לא אעכל
את האוכל בנקל.

ANSWERS TO QUESTIONS OF LESSON 27

1. המורה שמח, כי יש לו הרבה
כסף.

2. לא, רותי אינה מאושרת.

3. היא בוכה, משום שהפובה
נשברה.

4. כן, היא עצובה.

5. לא בכל הדברים עולה האדם על
החיות.

6. לא, אי-אפשר לדבר נכונה בלי
לחשוב.

7. אני לומד עכשו עברית.

8. כן, למדתי לרקד.

9. כן, יודע אני את שם הנשיא של
ישראל.

10. לא, אינך יודע כמה כוכבים יש
בשמים.

11. לא, אי-אפשר לדעת מה יהיה
מזג האויר בשבוע הבא.

12. כן, הוא יודע את המרחק בין
תל-אביב לירושלים.

13. כן, למדתי אנגלית.

14. עוד אני זוכר אותה.

15. לא, לא שכחתיה.

16. כן, יש לי זכרון טוב.

17. כן, מרוצה אני כשהנני יודע
שמזג האויר יהיה טוב.

18. כן, הנני מרוצה כשאני עוזב את
העיר בקיץ.

19. לא, איני מפחד ללכת בחושך.

ANSWERS TO QUESTIONS OF LESSON 28

1. הנה שמות כמה ארצות הקרובות
לישראל: סוריה, לבנון, טורקיה,
מצרים, עבר-הירדן והאי
קפריסין.

2. אנו נוסעים מישראל לארצות-
הברית באוירון או באניה..

3. מתל-אביב לירושלים נוסעים
במכונית, או ברכבת.

4. לפני צאתי לטיול אני אורז את
מזודתי.

5. לא, לשדה-התעופה אני נוסע
במכונית או בטקסי (מונית).

6. אני אומר לנהג: לשדה-התעופה,
בבקשה.

7. כרטיסי נסיעה ברכבת קונים
בתחנת-רכבת, או במשרדי
נסיעות.

8. הסבל נושא את המזודות לתוך
הקרון.

9. הנסיעה במכונית מתל-אביב
לירושלים לוקחת כשעתים.

מרקחת — רפואות.

10. אני שאול שוטר שיראה לי את הדרך.

12. לחנות כזאת קוראים חנות "כל-בּוֹ".

11. החנויות הן: חנות לספרים; לצרכי-אוכל; לירקות, לפרחים. באטליז מוכרים בשר. בבית-

13. בּעל החנות או הזבּן (הזבּנית).

14. אני נכנם לחנות לכובעים.

ANSWERS TO QUESTIONS OF LESSON 29

10. הוא תוצאה מהשקאה, ופתוח החקלאות האינטנסיבי.

1. הם נוסעים לישראל.

11. לדעתו תל-אביב היא עיר מודר־נית ביותר וגאות כל היהודים.

2. לא, הם אינם נוסעים לא בּרכבת, אף לא בּאניה. הם טסים בּאוירון.

3. אני מעדיף לנסוע בּאוירון.

12. כּן, שדה-התעופה קרוב לתל-אביב.

4. כּי בּאוירון נוסעים מהר.

5. לאחרונה הם נפגשו בּאמריקה.

13. משום שהוא דורך בּפעם הראשונה על אדמת אבות.

6. משום שהיו ידידים טובים, וזה זמן רב שלא התראו.

14. אדון נבון עונה, כּי הוא מבין יפה לרוחו.

7. עם התקרב האוירון לחוף ישראל רואים את החוף הצהוב.

15. כּן, בּרצון הייתי נוסע לישראל.

16. הערים הראשיות בּישראל הן: ירושלים, תל-אביב וחיפה.

8. לפנים היה הנוף כּולו מדבּר.

9. כּיום הכּל מוריק, והחקלאות מפותחת.

ANSWERS TO QUESTIONS OF LESSON 30

היש לך מה להצהיר?

1. היא בּרכה אותם בּמלים: "בּרוכים הבּאים!"

10. על דברים חדשים, מטבּע חוץ, ודברים אחרים מלבד אלה שהם לצרכי עצמו.

2. הם פנו תחילה למשרד-העליה, ואחר-כּך למכם.

11. אדון לוי גמר תחילה, כּי לא היה לו מה להצהיר.

3. שם שואלים אותך את השם, האזרחות, המקצוע, והכּתובת.

12. משום שקנה מצלמה חדשה בּחוץ-לארץ.

4. לא, אדון לוי הוא אזרח אמריקאי.

13. הוא החליפם בּלירות ישראליות.

5. הוא מצא שהעברית של אדון לוי מצוינת.

14. הם נפגשו שוב בּיציאה מן המכם.

6. הוא למד אותה מהוריו, ואחר־כּך בּבית-הספר בּרליץ.

15. לא, הם לקחו מונית.

16. הם הפנו את הנהג תחילה למלון "נורדאוי-פּלז׳ה", בּו ישהה אדון לוי. אחר-כּך יסע אדון נבון לביתו.

7. עדיין לא, אבל מקוה אני לדבּר עברית כּמוהו בּקרוב.

8. א) כּן, הייתי פעם שם. ב) לא, אף פעם לא הייתי שם.

9. בּבקשה לפתח את המזוודות.

ANSWERS TO QUESTIONS OF LESSON 31

8. הוא יאכל אותה במלון.

1. הוא הזמין אותו לביתו לארוחת־ערב.

9. לא, כי שבת מחר, ואשאר בבית.

2. הוא יבוא לביתו של אדון נבון בשעה שמונה בערב.

10. הוא קנה אותם בחנות לפרחים.

3. כן, בביתו תהיה מסיבת־חנוכה בערב.

11. לבן, שחור, אדום, כחול, אפור, צהוב, חום.

4. כן, אערך מסיבה, ואזמין כמה ידידים לביתי.

12. לא, מוכר הפרחים ישלח אותם לפי הכתובת של אדון נבון.

5. הוא ישהה שם כמה שבועות.

13. הם עלו בשש לירות, כולל מס.

6. ילד־המלון יביא את המזודות לחדרו.

14. הם יתקבלו שם לפני שעה שמונה בערב.

7. יתרחץ, יוציא את בגדיו, ויחליף לבושו.

15. משום שאדון לוי יבקר שם. בשמונה, והוא רוצה, כי הפרחים יגיעו שמה לפני בקורו.

ANSWERS TO QUESTIONS OF LESSON 32

8. כמובן, מעדיף אני את המקור על התרגום, אם אני יודע את השפה.

1. לא, הוא בא בדיוק בשעה שמונה כמדובר.

9. הוא מטפל בנושא „יציאת־מצרים".

2. אדון נבון בעצמו קבל את פניו ליד הדלת.

10. כן, אני מעונין מאד בהיסטוריה עברית.

3. הוא הוצג בפני הגברת נבון ופרופסור כהן.

11. אחר־כך הוא הכיר את הצעירים ובתו של הפרופסור.

4. היא אומרת שהיא שמחה להכיר את אדון לוי.

12. הם ירקדו את רקוד ה„הורה".

5. הוא אומר שגאה הוא ללחוץ את ידו.

13. לא, הוא אינו זוכר אם ראה פעם את הרקוד הזה.

6. משום שהוא מעריץ מאד את עבודתו המדעית.

14. זה מצא חן בעיניו מאד מאד.

7. הוא קרא את ספרו בתרגום אנגלי.

15. כן, האורחים בלו יפה את הזמן.

16. למחרת הם יערכו טיול לירושלים.

ANSWERS TO QUESTIONS OF LESSON 33

3. הם נוסעים בכוון דרומי־מזרחי.

1. הם נוסעים לירושלים?

4. כן, ברצון אני יוצא לטיול מחוץ לעיר.

2. הוא אומר שזו לא הובאה מן החוץ, אלא מיוצרת פה בישראל.

.5 בדרך הוא מוכרח לקנות בנזין.

.6 כי זהו „עמק-אילון", איפה שהעמיד יהושע את השמש עד שנצח את אויבי ישראל.

.7 הנוף היפה ביותר הוא מוצא. מכאן אפשר לראות את ירושלים ממזרח, ואת הים ממערב.

.8 הם נעצרו פה כדי לעשות צלומים.

.9 הם פגשו כאן קבוצה של צעירים סימפטיים.

.10 הם באים מקבוץ מוצא.

.11 כן, הוא ישלח אותן אחרי הפתוח.

.12 הם נראים חסונים, יפים, ושזופי-שמש.

.13 האקלים הוא ים-תיכוני, ממוזג ונעים.

.14 התוצרת החקלאית הטפוסית היא: תפוח-הזהב, הזית, הגפן, התאנה והרמון.

.15 התוצרת התעשיתית היא: מכונות, שמן, מלט, מצי פירות, בדים, נעלים וכו'.

.16 כן, עם גדול האוכלוסיה, ופתוח הכבישים, גדלה התנועה בדרכים.

ANSWERS TO QUESTIONS OF LESSON 34

.1 כן, ברצון הייתי נוסע, אלו היו לי אמצעים לכך.

.2 אלו עלה תיר על „מגדל-דוד", היה רואה את כל העיר העתיקה.

.3 הציורויות שבין סגנוני הבניה בעיר העתיקה והעיר המודרנית, עשו עליו רושם חזק ביותר.

.4 משום שהיא אחת הערים העתיקות בעולם, מקום שישבו בו עמים רבים.

.5 הוא היה מחיה השפה העברית המודרנית.

.6 הכותל המערבי, הר הצופים, הר הרצל והעיר העתיקה.

.7 כן, רבים מאד באים מכל הארצות, תירים וצלינים.

.8 היא מביאה עושר ותרבות אוניברסלית.

.9 היא סוללת יותר כבישים

ומפתחת קוי-אור.

.10 כי הוא רוצה לטעם מאכלים יהודיים טפוסיים.

.11 הם מעמידים אותה באחד הרחובות.

.12 כי יכול להיות שלרגל האורחים הרבים הבאים אל העיר, לא יהיה אחר-כך מקום במלון.

.13 הם ישהו שם רק יום אחד, ואחר-כך ישובו לתל-אביב.

.14 כן, הוא מרוצה מאד, ומאושר לדרוך על אדמת עיר הקודש והנצח.

.15 כן, אני מרוצה מאד מהתקדמותי, אלא שהייתי רוצה להמשיך ללמד ולהשתלם עוד בשפה זו.

.16 הדרך הטובה ביותר היא להשתלם בבית-הספר ברליץ.

GLOSSARY

א

father *m.* אָב (אַבָּא)	air *m.* אֲוִיר	one *f.* אַחַת *m.* אֶחָד
ancestors (fathers) *m.* אָבוֹת	airplane *m.* אֲוִירוֹן	eleven *m.* אַחַד-עָשָׂר
to lose אָבַד	motor car *m.* אוֹטוֹ	some; few *m.* אֲחָדִים
loss *f.* אֲבֵדָה	enemy *m.* אוֹיֵב	delay *m.* אִחוּר
watermelon *m.* אֲבַטִּיחַ	food *m.* אוֹכֶל	back אָחוֹר
spring *m.* אָבִיב	population *f.* אוּכְלוֹסִיָה	to be late *v.* אִחֵר
but אֲבָל	perhaps אוּלַי	another; different אַחֵר
limb, organ *m.* אֵבָר	but; however; hall אוּלָם	last *adj.* אַחֲרוֹן
pear *m.* אַגָּס	courage *m.* אֹמֶץ	אַחַר כָּךְ (אַחֲרֵי כֵן)
sir, mister *m.* אָדוֹן	manner; way *m.* אֹפֶן	afterwards
polite; kind אָדִיב	ocean *m.* אוֹקְיָנוֹס	slow אִטִּי
red אָדֹם	light *m.* אוֹר	butcher-shop *m.* אִטְלִיז
man, person *m.* אָדָם	guest, visitor *m.* אוֹרֵחַ	which אֵיזֶה
earth; soil *f.* אֲדָמָה	length *m.* אֹרֶךְ	Italy *f.* אִיטַלְיָה
on the contrary אַדְרַבָּא	happiness *m.* אֹשֶׁר	Italian *adj.* אִיטַלְקִי
architectural אַדְרִיכָלִי	letter *f.* אוֹת	island *m.* אִי
to love; like אָהַב	sign; signal *m.* אוֹת	dissatisfaction *m.* אִי-רָצוֹן
love *f.* אַהֲבָה	me אוֹתִי	impossible אִי-אֶפְשָׁר
or אוֹ	then אָז	how אֵיךְ
about אוֹדוֹת	warning *f.* אַזְהָרָה	which (plur.) אֵילוּ
goose *m.* אַוָּז	citizen *m.* אֶזְרָח	not אֵין
ear *f.* אֹזֶן	citizenship *f.* אֶזְרָחוּת	intelligent *adj.* אִינְטֶלִיגֶנְטִי

296

to entertain, to receive (guests) אָרַח	England f. אַנְגְלִיָה	intensive אִינְטֶנְסִיבִי
long אָרֹךְ	English adj. אַנְגְלִי	where אֵיפֹה
to last אָרַךְ	we אָנוּ (אֲנַחְנוּ)	Europe f. אֵירוֹפָּה
lion m. אַרְיֵה	I אֲנִי (אָנֹכִי)	man m. אִישׁ
bag, purse m. אַרְנָק	ship f. אֳנִיָה	only; but אַךְ
land; country f. אֶרֶץ	men, people m. אֲנָשִׁים	to eat אָכַל
United States f. pl. אַרְצוֹת־הַבְּרִית	forbidden אָסוּר	indeed אָכֵן
woman f. אִשָּׁה	Asia f. אַסְיָה	to אֶל
confirmation approval m. אִשּׁוּר	obliged; grateful אֲסִיר תּוֹדָה	not אַל
to confirm, approve אִשֵּׁר	nose m. אַף	but; only; except אֶלָּא
who; which אֲשֶׁר	also; even אַף	these אֵלֶּה
visa f. אַשְׁרָה	although אַף־עַל־פִּי	if אִלּוּ
(the sign of the accusative) אֶת	never אַף פַּעַם	to me אֵלַי
you (singular) m. אַתָּה	then; consequently אֵפוֹא	thousand אֶלֶף
f. אַתְּ	peas f. אֲפוּנָה	alphabet m. אָלֶף־בֵּית
you (plur.) אַתֶּם	grey אָפוֹר	if; whether אִם
Athens f. אַתּוּנָה	peach m. אֲפַרְסֵק	mother f. אֵם (אִמָּא)
with me אִתִּי	possible אֶפְשָׁר	bath f. אַמְבַּטְיָה
yesterday אֶתְמוֹל	finger f. אֶצְבַּע	brave adj. אַמִּיץ
	near; near by, at אֵצֶל	though; indeed אָמְנָם
ב.	climate m. אַקְלִים	middle m. אֶמְצָעִי
in; at ... בְּ	four m. אַרְבָּעָה	to say אָמַר
in fact, really בֶּאֱמֶת	Argentine f. אַרְגֶנְטִינָה	America f. אָמֶרִיקָה
please בְּבַקָשָׁה	meal f. אֲרוּחָה	truth f. אֱמֶת
garment m. בֶּגֶד	to pack אָרַז	please אָנָא

to seek; request, apply	בַּקֵּשׁ
request f.	בַּקָשָׁה
duck m.	בַּרְוָז
blessed; praised	בָּרוּךְ
welcome	בָּרוּךְ־הַבָּא
clear; certain	בָּרוּר
Brazil f.	בְּרַזִילְיָה
healthy	בָּרִיא
health f.	בְּרִיאוּת
Britain f.	בְּרִיטַנְיָה
pact f.	בְּרִית
to congratulate to bless; to greet;	בֵּרֵךְ
knee f.	בֶּרֶךְ
blessing f.	בְּרָכָה
willingly	בְּרָצוֹן
lightning m.	בָּרָק
in order to, for	בִּשְׁבִיל
while, during	בִּשְׁעַת
meat m.	בָּשָׂר
beef m.	בְּשַׂר־בָּקָר
veal m.	בְּשַׂר־עֵגֶל
chicken m.	בְּשַׂר־עוֹף
roast meat m.	בָּשָׂר צָלוּי
daughter f.	בַּת
inside; within	בְּתוֹךְ
as	בְּתוֹר

synagogue m.	בֵּית־כְּנֶסֶת
hospital m.	בֵּית־חוֹלִים
to weep; cry	בָּכה
weeping m.	בְּכִי (בְּכִיָה)
nevertheless	בְּכָל־זֹאת
not	בַּל
to spend time	בִּלָּה
without	בְּלִי
but, except	בִּלְתִּי
with instrum.	בַּמֶּה
soon; speedily	בִּמְהֵרָה
son m.	בֵּן
cousin	בֶּן־דוֹד (בַּת־דוֹד)
to build	בָּנה
gasoline m.	בֶּנְזִין
construction f.	בְּנִיָה
building m.	בִּנְיָן
bank m.	בַּנְק
for; through	בְּעַד
husband; possessor m.	בַּעַל
approximately; about	בְּעֶרֶךְ
onion m.	בָּצָל
bottle m.	בַּקְבּוּק
visit m.	בִּקוּר
to visit	בַּקֵּר
ox m.	בָּקָר

linen, cloth m.	בַּד
examination, check f.	בְּדִיקָה
I intend to	בְּדַעְתִּי
to check	בָּדַק
clear	בָּהִיר
to come	בּוֹא
doll f.	בּוּבָּה
morning m.	בּוֹקֶר
young man m.	בָּחוּר
girl f.	בַּחוּרָה
disgust, repugnance f.	בְּחִילָה
to pronounce	בִּטֵּא
expression m.	בִּטוּי
sure adj.	בָּטוּחַ
surely	בֶּטַח
especially; mostly	בְּיוֹתַר
between; among	בֵּין
anyway	בֵּין־כָּךְ
to understand	בִּין
understanding f.	בִּינָה
capital city f.	בִּירָה
beer f.	בִּירָה
house m.	בַּיִת
school m.	בֵּית־סֵפֶר
drug-store m.	בֵּית־מִרְקַחַת

ג.

נָאֶה proud

נַאֲוָה pride f.

נָבֹהַ high

גְּבִינָה cheese f.

גְּבֶרֶת lady, Mrs., Miss

גָּדוֹל great; large

גִּדּוּל growth m.

גּוֹבַה height f.

גּוֹדֶל size m.

גּוּף body m.

גַּז gas m.

גֶּזֶר carrot m.

גִּיר chalk m.

גָּלִיל Galilee m.

גַּם also; too

גָּמַר to finish

גֶּמֶר end m.

גָּמָל camel m.

גָּנַב to steal

גַּנָּב thief m.

גֶּפֶן vinetree f.

גַּפְרוּר match m.

גֶּרֶב sock m.

גָּרַם to cause; effect

נָרְמַנְיָה Germany f.

גֶּשֶׁם rain m.

ד.

דָּאָבוֹן sorrow, regret m.

דָּאַן to worry

דְּאָגָה anxiety, worry f.

דְּבוֹרָה bee f.

דִּבּוּר speaking; speech m.

דִּבֵּר to speak

דָּבָר thing; word m.

דְּבַשׁ honey m.

דָּג fish m.

דּוּבְדְּבָנִים cherries (plur.) m.

דֻּגְמָא example, sample m.

דּוֹד uncle m.

דּוֹדָה aunt f.

דּוֹפֶק pulse m.

דָּחַק to press

דַּי enough

דִּיּוּק precision m.

דִּיֵּק to be exact v.

דָּלַק to burn

דֶּלֶק fuel m.

דֶּלֶת door f.

דָּם blood m.

דָּמָה to liken; compare

דִּמְיוֹן likeness; imagination m.

דְּמֵי־שְׁתִיָּה tip m.

דֵּעָה opinion f.

דָּפַק to beat, to knock

דַּקָּה minute f.

דָּרוֹם south m.

דָּרַךְ to tread

דֶּרֶךְ way; road f.

(בְּ)דֶרֶךְ־כְּלָל generally

דַּרְכּוֹן passport m.

ה.

הַ the

הֲ interrogative particle

הָאָח! oh!

הָאַר to light

הֵבָא to bring

הִבְדִּל to separate; distinguish

הַבְדָּלָה separation f.

הָבָה let's

הַבֵּט to look

הַבְטֵחַ to promise, to assure

הַבְטָחָה promise f.

הָבֵן to understand

הַגִּיעַ to reach; arrive

הַדְלֵק to light

they f. / m.	הֵן / הֵם
check, cheque f.	הַמְחָאָה
to take off (airplane)	הַמְרִיא
to continue	הַמְשֵׁךְ
to wait	הַמְתֵּן
waiting f.	הַמְתָּנָה
pleasure; enjoyment f.	הֲנָאָה
here	הֵנָּה
to put	הָנִיחַ
here I am	הִנְנִי
to explain	הַסְבֵּר
explanation f.	הַסְבָּרָה
to carry (by vehicle)	הַסַּע
to supply	הַסְפֵּק
supply f.	הַסְפָּקָה
to take away	הָסֵר
organization f.	הִסְתַּדְרוּת
to prefer	הַעֲדֵף
to be absent	הֵעָדֵר
to disappear	הֵעָלֵם
to place	הַעֲמֵד
placing f.	הַעֲמָדָה
to stop	הַעֲצֵר
to evaluate, appreciate	הַעֲרֵךְ
evaluation, appreciation f.	הַעֲרָכָה
to recollect	הִזָּכֵר
to invite	הַזְמֵן
invitation f.	הַזְמָנָה
to damage	הַזֵּק
to decide	הַחְלֵט
decision f.	הַחְלָטָה
to change	הַחְלֵף
change f.	הַחְלָפָה
to flatter	הַחֲנֵף
to be	הָיָה
well	הֵיטֵב
to be burned	הִכָּוָה
to prepare	הָכֵן
preparation f.	הֲכָנָה
to enter	הִכָּנֵס
to bring in, put in	הַכְנֵס
bringing in; income f.	הַכְנָסָה
to recognize, to know	הַכֵּר
to force	הַכְרֵחַ
necessity m.	הֶכְרֵחַ
to dictate	הַכְתֵּב
dictation f.	הַכְתָּבָה
to fight	הִלָּחֵם
to go; walk	הָלַךְ
going; walking f.	הֲלִיכָה
lighting f.	הַדְלָקָה
to enjoy	הֵהָנֵה
he, she f. / m.	הִיא / הוּא
since, because	הוֹאִיל
transportation f.	הוֹבָלָה
India f.	הוֹדוּ
to find out to inquire,	הִוָּדַע
to inform	הוֹדִיעַ
announcement f.	הוֹדָעָה
present tense m.	הֹוֶה
alas!	הוֹי
to realize	הִוָּכַח
to prove	הוֹכִיחַ
proof f.	הוֹכָחָה
to be born	הִוָּלֵד
to appear	הוֹפִיעַ
appearance f.	הוֹפָעָה
to spend; to take out	הוֹצֵא
expense; publication f.	הוֹצָאָה
"Hora" (dance)	"הוֹרָה
parents (pl.) m.	הוֹרִים
to meet, have the opportunity	הִזְדַּמֵּן
opportunity f.	הִזְדַּמְּנוּת
to be careful	הִזָּהֵר
to warn	הַזְהֵר

to take care	הַשְׁגַּח
care, supervision f.	הַשְׁגָּחָה
to exterminate	הַשְׁמֵד
extermination f.	הַשְׁמָדָה
to be careful	הִשָּׁמֵר
this year	הַשָּׁנָה
irrigation, watering f.	הַשְׁקָאָה
to irrigate, water	הַשְׁקָה
to tan (sun)	הִשְׁתַּזֵּף
to dominate	הִשְׁתַּלֵּט
to improve	הִשְׁתַּלֵּם
to use	הִשְׁתַּמֵּשׁ
to change	הִשְׁתַּנֶּה
to stretch (oneself)	הִשְׂתָּרֵעַ
to correspond	הִתְאֵם
accordance f.	הַתְאָמָה
to be formed	הִתְהַוָּה
to begin	הִתְחֵל
beginning f.	הַתְחָלָה
to get warm	הִתְחַמֵּם
to help oneself	הִתְכַּבֵּד
to dress oneself	הִתְלַבֵּשׁ
to move	הִתְנוֹעֵעַ
to wake up	הִתְעוֹרֵר
to be delayed, to stop	הִתְעַכֵּב
to take interest	הִתְעַנְיֵן

preface f.	הַקְדָּמָה
to charm; fascinate	הַקְסֵם
to surround	הַקֵּף
to be called	הִקָּרֵא
to listen	הַקְשֵׁב
listening f.	הַקְשָׁבָה
mountain m.	הַר
to be seen	הֵרָאֵה
to show	הַרְאֵה
much; many	הַרְבֵּה
to feel	הַרְגֵּשׁ
feeling f.	הַרְגָּשָׁה
smell f.	הֲרָחָה
to smell	הָרִיחַ
to get wet	הַרְטֵב
to assemble, to wear (eyeglasses)	הַרְכֵּב
assembly f.	הַרְכָּבָה
lecture f.	הַרְצָאָה
to lecture	הַרְצֵה
mountainous	הֲרָרִי
to leave	הַשְׁאֵר
to remain	הִשָּׁאֵר
to swear	הִשָּׁבַע
to sell	הִשָּׁבֵר
to reach, obtain	הַשֵּׂג
accomplishment m.	הֶשֵּׂג

to admire	הַעֲרֵץ
admiration f.	הַעֲרָצָה
to copy	הַעְתֵּק
copy f.	הַעְתָּקָה
to be stricken	הִפָּגֵעַ
to turn over	הָפֹךְ
to amaze	הַפְלֵא
to direct	הַפְנֵה
loss; damage m.	הֶפְסֵד
to stop; interrupt	הַפְסֵק
interruption f.	הַפְסָקָה
to disturb	הַפְרֵעַ
disturbance f.	הַפְרָעָה
to present; introduce; perform	הַצֵּג
introduction; show f.	הַצָּגָה
to declare	הַצְהֵר
declaration f.	הַצְהָרָה
to catch cold	הִצְטַנֵּן
to need	הִצְטָרֵךְ
to join	הִצְטָרֵף
to propose	הַצִּעַ
to save, to rescue	הַצֵּל
luck; success f.	הַצְלָחָה
to succeed	הַצְלִיחַ
proposal f.	הַצָּעָה
to come early	הַקְדֵּם

amateur *m.*	חוֹבֵב
circle *m.*	חוּג
month *m.*	חוֹדֶשׁ
sick *m.*	חוֹלֶה
brown	חוּם
heat *m.*	חוֹם
city wall *f.*	חוֹמָה
coast; shore *m.*	חוֹף
freedom; vacation *m.*	חוֹפֶשׁ
outside; except	חוּץ
abroad	חוּץ־לָאָרֶץ
winter *m.*	חוֹרֶף
sense *m.*	חוּשׁ
darkness *m.*	חוֹשֶׁךְ
chest *m.*	חָזֶה
waistcoat *f.*	חֲזִיָּה
strong	חָזָק
to return	חָזַר
to live	חָיָה
animal *f.*	חַיָּה
life *pl. m.*	חַיִּים
palate *m.*	חֵיךְ
soldier *m.*	חַיָּל
quickly; swiftly	חִישׁ
to wait	חִכָּה
to fall upon, be due on	חָל

to crawl	זָחַל
olive *m.*	זַיִת
to remember	זָכַר
memory *m.*	זִכָּרוֹן
time *m.*	זְמָן
in need of	זָקוּק
old *m.*	זָקֵן
wreath *m.*	זֵר
stranger *m.*	זָר
to speed up; accelerate	זֵרֵז
to shine	זָרַח
to flow	זָרַם
stream; flood *m.*	זֶרֶם
to sow	זָרַע
seed *m.*	זֶרַע

ח.

to love; like	חָבַב
love *f.*	חִבָּה
lovely	חָבִיב
parcel *f.*	חֲבִילָה
friend *m.*	חָבֵר
friend *f.*	חֲבֵרָה
to put on (a hat); bind up	חָבַשׁ
feast *m.*	חַג
room *m.*	חֶדֶר
new	חָדָשׁ

to grieve	הִתְעַצֵּב
to wonder	הִתְפַּלֵּא
to advance	הִתְקַדֵּם
advance; progress *f.*	הִתְקַדְּמוּת
to approach	הִתְקָרֵב
to meet	הִתְרָאָה
to be excited	הִתְרַגֵּשׁ
to wash oneslef	הִתְרַחֵץ
to be impressed	הִתְרַשֵּׁם

ו.

and	וְ (וּ)
so, therefore	וּבְכֵן
certain; sure	וַדַּאי
etc.	וְכוּ' (וְכוּלֵיהּ)
young of an animal *m.*	וָלָד
convention *f.*	וְעִידָה
of long standing *m.*	וָתִיק

ז.

wolf *m.*	זְאֵב
fly *m.*	זְבוּב
salesman *m.*	זַבָּן
this one *f.* זֹאת *m.*	זֶה
gold *m.*	זָהָב
this is	זֶהוּ
cheap	זוֹל

to treat, take care of	טִפֵּל	desire, wish; thing m.	חֵפֶץ	milk m.	חָלָב
taxi m.	טַקְסִי	midnight f.	חֲצוֹת	to get ill	חָלָה
before	טֶרֶם	half m.	חֲצִי	dream m.	חֲלוֹם
		agriculture f.	חַקְלָאוּת	window m.	חַלּוֹן
import m.	יְבוּא	farmer	חַקְלַאי	pioneer m.	חָלוּץ
dry	יָבֵשׁ	investigation f. research; inquiry	חֲקִירָה	God forbid!	חָלִילָה
land f.	יַבָּשָׁה	to investigate	חָקַר	suit of clothes f.	חֲלִיפָה
hand f.	יָד	to think	חָשַׁב	exchange pl.	חֲלִיפִין
friend m.	יָדִיד	arithmetic, bill, check m.	חֶשְׁבּוֹן	to pass	חָלַף
knowledge, information; news f.	יְדִיעָה	electricity m.	חַשְׁמַל	to divide; share	חָלַק
to know	יָדַע	cat m.	חָתוּל	part m.	חֵלֶק
Jew m.	יְהוּדִי	signature f.	חֲתִימָה	warm; hot	חַם
day m.	יוֹם	to cut	חָתַךְ	sour	חָמוּץ
Greece f.	יָוָן	to sign	חָתַם	donkey m.	חֲמוֹר
dove f.	יוֹנָה			sour soup, borsht f.	חֲמִיצָה
beauty m.	יוֹפִי	**ט.**		five f. חֲמֵשׁ m.	חֲמִשָּׁה
more	יוֹתֵר	good	טוֹב	fifth	חֲמִישִׁי
together	יַחַד	to fly	טוּס	grace, charm m.	חֵן
individual	יָחִיד	Turkey f.	טוּרְקְיָה	flattery f.	חֲנוּפָה
relation; attitude m.	יַחַס	trip, stroll m.	טִיוּל	shop f.	חֲנוּת
wine m.	יַיִן	to travel, to stroll	טַיַּל	to protect	חוּס
can v.	יָכֹל	to telephone	טִלְפֵּן	God forbid!	חַס וְחָלִילָה
to bear (children)	יָלַד	tasty	טָעִים	lettuce f.	חַסָּה
child f. יַלְדָּה m.	יֶלֶד	to taste	טָעַם	strong, powerful, sturdy	חָסֹן
native m.	יְלִיד	taste m.	טַעַם	deficiency, defect m.	חִסָּרוֹן
		type, character m.	טִפּוּס	to desire; wish	חָפֵץ

to go לֵךְ

sea m. ם

right m. מִין

24 hours f. מָמָה

to found סֹד

foundation m. סוֹד

jasmine m. סָמִין

forest m. עַר

fair; beautiful; good פֶה

Japan f. פֶּן

to go out צֵא

export m. צוּא

exit f. צִיאָה

to produce צֵר

dear m. קִיר

expensive קָר

to go down; descend רֵד

moon m. רֵחַ

green רוֹק

vegetables pl. m. רָקוֹת

there is שׁ

to sit שֵׁב

session, conference f. שִׁיבָה

to sleep שָׁן

old שָׁן

Israel f. שְׂרָאֵל

---

mosquito m. יַתּוּשׁ

possibly יִתָּכֵן

remainder m. יֶתֶר

כ.

like; as כ ...

to have pain; ache כָּאַב

pain m. כְּאֵב

here כָּאן

whenever; when, as כַּאֲשֶׁר

to extinguish כָּבָה

heavy adj. liver m. כָּבֵד

road m. כְּבִישׁ

already כְּבָר

to conquer, occupy (milit.) כָּבַשׁ

in order to כְּדֵי

so כֹּה

hat m. כּוֹבַע

to burn כָּוָה

direction m. כִּוּוּן

burn f. כְּוִיָה

star m. כּוֹכָב

glass f. כּוֹס

shirt f. כֻּתּוֹנֶת

wall m. כּוֹתֶל

blue כָּחֹל

---

that, because כִּי

today, at present כַּיּוֹם

how כֵּיצַד

so כָּךְ

after all כִּכְלוֹת־הַכֹּל

all, whole, every כֹּל

department store כָּל־בּוֹ

dog m. כֶּלֶב

nothing כְּלוּם

tool, utensil m. כְּלִי

general rule m. כְּלָל

to include כָּלַל

general; common כְּלָלִי

anemone f. כַּלָנִית

how much; some כַּמָה

like כְּמוֹ

of course; naturally כַּמּוּבָן

like him כָּמוֹהוּ

almost כִּמְעַט

yes כֵּן

entrance f. כְּנִיסָה

wing f. כָּנָף

apparently כַּנִּרְאָה

chair m. כִּסֵּא

to cover כָּסָה

silver, money m. כֶּסֶף

to learn	לָמַד	heart *m.*	לֵב	ugliness *m.*	כִּעוּר
to teach	לִמֵּד	hearty; cordial	לְבָבִי	anger *m.*	כַּעַס
teaching, learning *m.*	לִמּוּד	clothing *m.*	לְבוּשׁ	spoon (s) paw (s) *f.*	כַּף כַּפּוֹת
sufficiently	לְמַדַּי	to put on (clothes), wear	לָבַשׁ	palm (s) of the hand *f.*	כַּף כַּפַּיִם
whatever	לְמַה	white	לָבָן	ungrateful	כְּפוּי טוֹבָה
why	לָמָּה	underwear *m.*	לְבָנִים	as; like; according to	כְּפִי
lemon *m.*	לִימוֹן	Lebanon *f.*	לְבָנוֹן	glove *f.*	כְּפָפָה
lemonade *f.*	לִימוֹנַדָה	to my regret	לְדַאֲבוֹנִי	village *m.*	כְּפָר
on the next day	לְמָחֳרָת	flame *f.*	לֶהָבָה	as usually	כָּרָגִיל
to whom	לְמִי	to them	לָהֶם	cabbage *m.*	כְּרוּב
upward	לְמַעֲלָה	on the contrary	לְהֶפֶךְ	ticket *m.*	כַּרְטִיס
to us	לָנוּ	good bye, see you again	לְהִתְרָאוֹת	shark *m.*	כָּרִישׁ
according to	לְפִי	if	לוּ	to write	כָּתַב
toward evening	לִפְנוֹת־עֶרֶב	calendar, blackboard *m.*	לוּחַ	writing *m.*	כְּתָב
before me	לְפָנַי	cheek; jaw *f.*	לֶחִי	class, party *f.*	כִּתָּה
before; in front	לִפְנֵי	To your health!	לְחַיִּים!	address *f.*	כְּתוֹבֶת
formerly	לְפָנִים	bread *m.*	לֶחֶם	shoulder *f.*	כָּתֵף
sometimes	לִפְעָמִים	to press	לָחַץ		
to take	לָקַח	near by	לְיַד	**ל.**	
because of;	לְרֶגֶל	night *m.*	לַיְלָה	to . . .	ל
tongue; language *f.*	לָשׁוֹן	lilac *m.*	לִילָךְ	not, no	לֹא
into	לְ תוֹךְ	Israeli pound *f.*	לִירָה	national	לְאוּמִי
		to that	לְכָךְ	nationality *f.*	לְאוּמִיּוּת
מ.		to soil	לַכְלֵךְ	finally	לָאַחֲרוֹנָה
from . . .	מ	therefore	לָכֵן	slowly	לְאַט
very	מְאֹד	without	לְלֹא	where to	לְאָן

to revive; restore to life	מְחַיֶּה
price *m.*	מְחִיר
sickness *f.*	מַחֲלָה
department; class *f.*	מַחְלָקָה
flattery; compliment *f.*	מַחְמָאָה
tomorrow	מָחָר
thought *f.*	מַחֲשָׁבָה
coin *m.*	מַטְבֵּעַ
bed *f.*	מִטָּה
load, cargo *f.*	מִטְעָן
handkerchief *f.*	מִטְפַּחַת
aim, purpose *f.*	מַטָּרָה
umbrella *f.*	מִטְרִיָה
who	מִי
who is (he)	מִיהוּ
special	מְיוּחָד
mile *m.*	מִיל
juice *m.*	מִיץ
any one	מִישֶׁהוּ
water *pl. m.*	מַיִם
kind; gender, sex *m.*	מִין
machine *f.*	מְכוֹנָה
automobile; motor car *f.*	מְכוֹנִית
covered	מְכוּסֶה
distinguished	מוּבְהָק

sure, assured	מוּבְטָח
museum *m.*	מוּזֵיאוֹן
brain *m.*	מוֹחַ
better	מוּטָב
ready, prepared	מוּכָן
compelled	מוּכְרָח
expert *m.*	מוּמְחֶה
taxi *f.*	מוֹנִית
Moscow *f.*	מוֹסְקְבָה
early	מוּקְדָם
teacher *m.*	מוֹרֶה
teacher *f.*	מוֹרָה
permitted; allowed	מוּתָּר
to pour	מָזַג
temperament *m*	מֶזֶג
weather *m.*	מֶזֶג־הָאֲוִיר
suitcase *f.*	מִזְוָדָה
speedy	מְזוֹרָז
luck *m.*	מַזָּל
fork *m.*	מַזְלֵג
east *m.*	מִזְרָח
eastern	מִזְרָחִי
hand of clock *m.*	מָחוֹג
divided	מְחוּלָק
show *m.*	מַחֲזֶה
cycle, circulation *m.*	מַחֲזוֹר

hundred *f.*	מֵאָה
late	מְאוּחָר
event *m.*	מְאוֹרָע
happy	מְאוּשָׁר
where from	מֵאַיִן
food; meal, dish *m.*	מַאֲכָל
host *m.*	מְאָרֵחַ
adult *m.*	מְבוּגָר
to be sought	מְבוּקָשׁ
pronunciation *m.*	מִבְטָא
connoisseur *m.*	מֵבִין
telegram *m.*	מִבְרָק
towel *f.*	מַגֶּבֶת
tower *m.*	מִגְדָּל
waiter *m.*	מַגִּישׁ
tray *m.*	מַגָּשׁ
desert *m.*	מִדְבָּר
spoken of	מְדוּבָּר
dimension; measure *f.*	מִדָּה
why	מַדּוּעַ
state *f.*	מְדִינָה
science *m.*	מַדָּע
scientific	מַדָּעִי
what	מָה
speed *f.*	מְהִירוּת
quickly	מַהֵר

A

key m.	מַפְתֵּחַ	tax m.	מַס	ugly	מְכוֹעָר
to find	מָצָא	party f.	מְסִבָּה	customs m.	מֶכֶס
position, situation, condition m.	מַצָּב	dangerous	מְסוּכָּן	to sell	מָכַר
frequent	מָצוּי	tradition f.	מָסוֹרֶת	acquaintance m.	מַכָּר
excellent	מְצוּיָן	trade, commerce m.	מִסְחָר	letter m.	מִכְתָּב
forehead m.	מֵצַח	journey, trip m.	מַסָע	full	מָלֵא
camera f.	מַצְלֵמָה	restaurant f.	מִסְעָדָה	work f.	מְלָאכָה
Egypt f.	מִצְרַיִם	number m.	מִסְפָּר	artificial	מְלָאכוּתִי
temple m.	מִקְדָשׁ	circle m.	מַעְגָּל	besides	מִלְבַד
place, spot m.	מָקוֹם	interesting	מְעַנְיֵן	word f.	מִלָה
source m.	מָקוֹר	little; few	מְעַט	hotel m.	מָלוֹן
hyphen m.	מַקָּף	coat m.	מְעִיל	dictionary; glossary m.	מִלוֹן
profession, occupation m.	מִקְצוֹעַ	from above	מֵעַל	melon m.	מֶלוֹן
refrigerator m.	מְקָרֵר	advantage f.	מַעֲלָה	salt m.	מֶלַח
bitter	מַר	west m.	מַעֲרָב	war f.	מִלְחָמָה
master; sir, Mr. m.	מַר	western	מַעֲרָבִי	cement m.	מֶלֶט
sight; view m.	מַרְאֶה	deed; story m.	מַעֲשֶׂה	king m.	מֶלֶךְ
from the start; over again	מֵרֹאשׁ	hence	מֵעַתָּה	waiter m.	מֶלְצָר
satisfied	מְרוּצָה	a day and a night	מֵעֵת-לָעֵת	temperate	מְמוּזָּג
distance m.	מֶרְחָק	backward	מְפַגֵּר	candy pl. m.	מַמְתָּקִים
center m.	מֶרְכָּז	geographical map; table cloth f.	מַפָּה	from	מִן
soup m.	מָרָק	glorified	מְפוֹאָר	to count	מָנָה
mixture (drug) f.	מִרְקַחַת	famous	מְפוּרְסָם	leader m.	מַנְהִיג
load m.	מַשָּׂא	developed	מְפוּתָּח	rest f.	מְנוּחָה
something	מַשֶּׁהוּ	napkin f.	מַפִּית	lamp f.	מְנוֹרָה
different; strange	מְשׁוּנֶה	because	מִפְּנֵי	to avoid, to prevent	מָנַע

hawk m. נֵץ

eternity m. נֶצַח

to conquer, נִצַּח
to win

eternal נִצְחִי

victory m. נִצָּחוֹן

point; period f. נְקוּדָה

easy נָקֵל

sausage m. נַקְנִיק

excited נִרְגָּשׁ

to carry נָשָׂא

to blow נָשַׁב

president m. נָשִׂיא

women pl. נָשִׁים

breath f. נְשִׁימָה

to breathe נָשַׁם

soul f. נְשָׁמָה

to drop; fall off נָשַׁר

eagle m. נֶשֶׁר

to give נָתַן

to be received, נִתְקַבֵּל
admitted

ס.

cause f. סִבָּה

to deem סָבוּר

around סָבִיב

porter m. סַבָּל

comfort f. נוֹחִיוּת

to wander נוֹעַ

view m. נוֹף

feather f. נוֹצָה

normal נוֹרְמָלִי

subject m. נוֹשֵׂא

to drip נָזַל

damage m. נֶזֶק

desirable, lovely נֶחְמָד

snake m. נָחָשׁ

descend (plane) נָחַת

landing (plane) f. נְחִיתָה

paper m. נְיָר

right נָכוֹן

low נָמוּךְ

tiger m. נָמֵר

to test, try נִסָּה

test, experience m. נִסָּיוֹן

journey; trip f. נְסִיעָה

to journey, travel נָסַע

pleasant נָעִים

to lock נָעַל

shoe f. נַעַל

boy m. נַעַר

girl f. נַעֲרָה

wonderful נִפְלָא

police f. שְׁטָרָה

silk m. שִׁי

to pull שֹׁךְ

during שֶׁךְ

apricot m. שְׁמֵשׁ

family f. שִׁפְחָה

sentence m. שֶׁפֶט

drink m. שְׁקָה

eye-glasses pl. שְׁקָפַיִם

office m. שְׁרָד

to touch שֵׁשׁ

dead ח

when תֵּי

metal f. תָּכֶת

studious תָּמִיד

נ.

please

prophecy f. וּאָה

south;
south country m.

to touch עַ

to approach

rare יר

driver m. ג

splendid דָר

comfortable, ח
convenient

cart; wagon f.	עֲגָלָה
till; up to	עַד
delicate	עָדִין
still; yet	עֲדַיִן
cake f.	עוּגָה
more	עוֹד
world m.	עוֹלָם
pleasure m.	עוֹנֶג
fowl m.	עוֹף
to fly	עוּף
skin; leather m.	עוֹר
to wake	עוּר
neck (back of) m.	עוֹרֶף
riches; wealth m.	עוֹשֶׁר
to leave	עָזַב
to help	עָזַר
pen m.	עֵט
to wrap	עָטַף
eye f.	עַיִן
tired	עָיֵף
main object m.	עִיקָר
city; town f.	עִיר
spider m.	עַכָּבִישׁ
mouse m.	עַכְבָּר
hindrance m.	עִכּוּב
to digest	עִכֵּל

fin m.	סְנַפִּיר
to dine	סָעַד
story m.	סִפּוּר
ship f.	סְפִינָה
cup m.	סֵפֶל
to count	סָפֹר
book m.	סֵפֶר
Spain f.	סְפָרַד
literature f.	סִפְרוּת
review f.	סְקִירָה
to refuse	סָרַב
refusal m.	סֵרוּב
ruler m.	סַרְגֵּל
ribbon; film m.	סֶרֶט
autumn m.	סְתָו

ע.

to work	עָבַד
work f.	עֲבוֹדָה
past m.	עָבָר
to pass over, cross	עָבֹר
side m.	עֵבֶר
Transjordan	עֵבֶר-הַיַּרְדֵּן,
Hebrew f.	עִבְרִית
tomato f.	עַגְבָנִיָה
calf m.	עֵגֶל

style m.	סִגְנוֹן
to shut; close	סָגֹר
cigarette f.	סִגַרְיָה
order m.	סֵדֶר
merchant, businessman m.	סוֹחֵר
sugar m.	סוּכָּר
horse m.	סוּס
end m.	סוֹף
writer m.	סוֹפֵר
goods, merchandise f.	סְחוֹרָה
finishing, completion m.	סִיּוּם
visit; tour m.	סִיּוּר
to finish	סַיֵּם
to visit, to tour	סַיֵּר
sum m.	סַךְ
total sum m.	סַךְ-הַכֹּל
amount m.	סְכוּם
knife f.	סַכִּין
danger f.	סַכָּנָה
basket m.	סַל
pardon f.	סְלִיחָה
to pave	סָלַל
beet m.	סֶלֶק
sugarbeet m.	סֶלֶק-סוּכָּר
mark m.	סִמָּן

mouth *m.* פֶּה	myself (בְּ)עַצְמִי	now עַכְשָׁו
here פֹּה	independence *f.* עַצְמָאוּת	on עַל
to fear פָּחַד	to stop עָצַר	near by עַל־יַד
fear *m.* פַּחַד	principal עֶקְרוֹנִי	leaf *m.* עָלֶה
less פָּחוֹת	evening *m.* עֶרֶב	to go up; cost; to excel עָלָה
raspberry *m.* פֶּטֶל	Arabia *f.* עֲרָב	immigration *f.* עֲלִיָה
mushroom *f.* פִּטְרִיָה	to arrange; to lay the table עָרַךְ	I have to; I must עָלַי
elephant *m.* פִּיל	value *m.* עֵרֶךְ	people (nation) *m.* עַם
steel *f.* פְּלָדָה	to do עָשָׂה	with עִם
leisure *m.* פְּנַאי	done עָשׂוּי	to stand עָמַד
to turn; turn toward פָּנָה	tenth עֲשִׂירִי	page in book; column *m.* עַמּוּד
face *m.* *pl.* פָּנִים	smoke *m.* עָשָׁן	deep עָמֹק
comma *m.* פְּסִיק	*m.* עֲשָׂרָה ten	valley *m.* עֵמֶק
statue, sculpture *m.* פֶּסֶל	*f.* עֶשֶׂר	grapes *pl.* עֲנָבִים
once *f.* פַּעַם	time *f.* עֵת	to answer עָנָה
bell *m.* פַּעֲמוֹן	now עַתָּה	tie *f.* עֲנִיבָה
to wound פָּצַע	newspaper *m.* עִתּוֹן	matter; interest *m.* עִנְיָן
wound *m.* פֶּצַע	future *m.* עָתִיד	cloud *m.* עָנָן
to open (eyes) פָּקַח	ancient עַתִּיק	branch (of tree) *m.* עָנָף
clever person *m.* פִּקֵּחַ		to be busy עָסַק
officer; employee *m.* פָּקִיד	**פ.**	business; occupation *m.* עֵסֶק
wild *m.* פָּרָא	glory *m.* פְּאָר	pencil *m.* עִפָּרוֹן
cow *f.* פָּרָה	be backward; to lag behind פִּגֵּר	tree *m.* עֵץ
fur *f.* פַּרְוָה	delay *m.* פִּגּוּר	sad עָצוּב
small coin *f.* פְּרוּטָה	meeting *f.* פְּגִישָׁה	thing, bone *f.* עֶצֶם
fruits *m.* *pl* פֵּרוֹת	to meet פָּגַשׁ	to shut (eyes) עָצַם

France *f.* צָרְפַת

hunt, hunting *m.* צַיִד

flower *m.* פֶּרַח

French צָרְפָתִי

mark, note *m.* צִיוּן

Paris *f.* פָּרִיז

to point out צַיֵן

publicity *m.* פִּרְסוּם

ק.

coolness *f.* צִינָה

to make famous, advertise פִּרְסֵם

agricultural group in Israel *m.* קִבּוּץ

painting *m.* צִיוּר

butterfly *m.* פַּרְפָּר

a small farming community *f.* קְבוּצָה

figurative, imaginative צִיוּרִי

to take off (clothes), to spread פָּשַׁט

to receive קִבֵּל

picturesqueness *f.* צִיוּרִיוּת

development *m.* פִּתּוּחַ

reception *f.* קַבָּלַת-פָּנִים

shadow *m.* צֵל

to develop פִּתַּח

grave *m.* קֶבֶר

cross *m.* צְלָב

to open פָּתַח

forward קָדִימָה

crusaders צַלְבָּנִים

doorway; entrance *m.* פֶּתַח

holy קָדוֹשׁ

photography; picture *m.* צִלּוּם

line *m.* קַו

dish, plate *f.* צַלַחַת

צ.

before קוֹדֶם

pilgrims *m.* צַלְיָנִים

color *m.* צֶבַע

holiness *m.* קוֹדֶשׁ

to photograph צִלֵּם

tulip *m.* צִבְעוֹנִי

to hope קִוָּה

to ring צִלְצֵל

justice *m.* צֶדֶק

pole *m.* קוֹטֶב

radish *f.* צְנוֹנִית

yellow צָהֹב

talking picture *m.* קוֹלְנוֹעַ

young *m.* צָעִיר

noon *pl.* צָהֳרַיִם

to stand up קוּם

to cry צָעַק

neck *m.* צַוָּאר

monkey *m.* קוֹף

to annoy; trouble צָעַר

collar *m.* צַוָּארוֹן

cashier, teller *m.* קוּפַּאי

trouble; pain *m.* צַעַר

to hunt צוּד

box; cashier's window *f.* קוּפָּה

to look צָפָה

cold צוֹנֵן

box *f.* קוּפְסָה

expected; foreseen צָפוּי

scouts *pl.* צוֹפִים

cold *m.* קוֹר

north *m.* צָפוֹן

Mt. Scopus הַר הַצוֹפִים

course *m.* קוּרְס

frog *f.* צְפַרְדֵּעַ

form *f.* צוּרָה

small קָטָן

narrow צַר

need *m.* צוֹרֶךְ

stomach *f.* קֵבָה

necessary צָרִיךְ

to laugh צָחַק

Russia f.	רוּסְיָה
physician m.	רוֹפֵא
to run	רוּץ
impression m.	רוֹשֶׁם
to note	רָשַׁם
wide	רָחָב
street m.	רְחוֹב
to wash	רָחַץ
far	רָחוֹק
wet	רָטוֹב
lung f.	רֵיאָה
smell, odor m.	רֵיחַ
soft	רַךְ
to ride	רָכַב
train f.	רַכֶּבֶת
pomegranate m.	רִמּוֹן
bad	רַע
hunger m.	רָעָב
idea, concept m.	רַעְיוֹן
noise m.	רַעַשׁ
to heal	רָפָא
medicine f.	רְפוּאָה
to wish	רָצָה
wish, will m.	רָצוֹן
floor f.	רִצְפָּה
only	רַק

ornament m.	קִשּׁוּט
to decorate	קִשֵּׁט
scales pl.	קַשְׂקַשִּׂים

ר.

to see	רָאָה
show window m.	חַלּוֹן רַאֲוָה
suitable; worthy	רָאוּי
sight f.	רְאִיָּה
moving picture m.	רָאִינוֹעַ
head; chief; leader, top m.	רֹאשׁ
first	רִאשׁוֹן
first in rank; chief	רָאשִׁי
master, rabbi m.	רַב
much	רַב
jam f.	רִבָּה
gentlemen	רַבּוֹתַי
fourth	רְבִיעִי
a quarter m.	רֶבַע
usual	רָגִיל
foot; leg f.	רֶגֶל
a while m.	רֶגַע
city district m.	רוֹבַע
wind; direction (geog.) m.	רוּחַ
Rome f.	רוֹמָא
romantic	רוֹמַנְטִי

existence m.	קִיּוּם
to fulfill, maintain	קִיֵּם
summer m.	קַיִץ
wall m.	קִיר
easy, light (not heavy)	קַל
to absorb	קָלַט
Canada f.	קָנָדָה
to buy	קָנָה
purchase f.	קְנִיָּה
magic m.	קֶסֶם
dish f.	קְעָרָה
coffee m.	קָפֶה
to jump	קָפַץ
Cyprus f.	קִפְּרִיסִין
chopped meat f.	קְצִיצָה
short	קָצָר
a little, some	קְצָת
cold	קַר
to read; call	קְרָא
near; relative	קָרוֹב
railroad car m.	קָרוֹן
ice m.	קֶרַח
reading; call f.	קְרִיאָה
cool	קָרִיר
to tear	קָרַע
hard	קָשֶׁה

to rejoice	שָׂמַח
joy f.	שִׂמְחָה
blanket f.	שְׂמִיכָה
heaven; sky m. pl.	שָׁמַיִם
dress f.	שִׂמְלָה
oil m.	שֶׁמֶן
to hear	שָׁמַע
to watch, guard	שָׁמַר
sun m.	שֶׁמֶשׁ
to serve, officiate	שָׁמֵשׁ
tooth f.	שֵׁן
Shanghai f.	שַׁנְחַי
year f.	שָׁנָה
sleep f.	שֵׁנָה
to change	שִׁנָה
change m.	שִׁנּוּי
second f. שְׁנִיָּה m.	שֵׁנִי
second (1/60 of a minute) f.	שְׁנִיָּה
two f. שְׁתַּיִם m.	שְׁנַיִם
teeth f.	שְׁנַיִם
twelve m.	שְׁנֵים־עָשָׂר
hour f.	שָׁעָה
watch m.	שָׁעוֹן
pocketwatch m.	שְׁעוֹן־כִּיס
lock watch m.	שְׁעוֹן־קִיר
bean f.	שְׁעוּעִית

rose f.	שׁוֹשַׁנָּה
to swim	שָׂחָה
black	שָׁחוֹר
conversation f.	שִׂיחָה
to put	שִׂים
to lie	שָׁכַב
district (city) f.	שְׁכוּנָה
to forget	שָׁכַח
to improve	שַׁכְלֵל
shoulder m.	שְׁכֶם
of	שֶׁל
snow m.	שֶׁלֶג
to send	שָׁלַח
peace; greetings m.	שָׁלוֹם
three m. שְׁלוֹשָׁה f.	שָׁלֹשׁ
third	שְׁלִישִׁי
messenger, envoy m.	שָׁלִיחַ
to pay	שִׁלֵּם
there	שָׁם
name m.	שֵׁם
left m.	שְׂמֹאל
eight m. שְׁמוֹנָה f.	שְׁמוֹנָה
rumor f.	שְׁמוּעָה
eighth	שְׁמִינִי

to dance	רָקַד
dancer m.	רַקְדָן
dance m.	רִקּוּד
official	רִשְׁמִי

שׁ.

that; which . . .	שֶׁ
to ask	שָׁאַל
question f.	שְׁאֵלָה
to inhale; breathe in	שָׁאַף
week m.	שָׁבוּעַ
oath f.	שְׁבוּעָה
seven m.	שִׁבְעָה
seven f.	שֶׁבַע
to break	שָׁבַר
Sabbath f.	שַׁבָּת
field m.	שָׂדֶה
airport m.	שְׂדֵה־תְּעוּפָה
to stay	שָׁהָה
again; to return	שׁוּב
equal	שָׁוֶה
policeman m.	שׁוֹטֵר
table m.	שֻׁלְחָן
garlic m.	שׁוּם
nothing	שׁוּם דָּבָר
different	שׁוֹנֶה

always תָּמִיד	within תּוֹךְ	lesson m. שִׁעוּר
movement, traffic f. תְּנוּעָה	worm f. תּוֹלַעַת	gate m. שַׁעַר
to go astray תָּעָה	use; benefit, advantage f. תּוֹעֶלֶת	hair m. שֵׂעָר
aviation f. תְּעוּפָה	phenomenon f. תּוֹפָעָה	language; lip f. שָׂפָה
industry f. תַּעֲשִׂיָּה	result f. תּוֹצָאָה	seashore beach f. שְׂפַת־הַיָּם
apple m. תַּפּוּחַ	production f. תּוֹצֶרֶת	to judge שָׁפַט
orange m. תַּפּוּחַ־זָהָב	turn; row; line m. תּוֹר	to spill שָׁפַךְ
potato m. תַּפּוּחַ־אֲדָמָה	strawberry f. תּוּת־הַשָּׂדֶה	quietness, silence m. שֶׁקֶט
to occupy, catch תָּפַס	feeling f. תְּחוּשָׁה	sinking, setting (of sun) f. שְׁקִיעָה
duty; task m. תַּפְקִיד	at first תְּחִילָה	to sink; set שָׁקַע
menu m. תַּפְרִיט	station f. תַּחֲנָה	remnant m. שָׂרִיד
hope f. תִּקְוָה	under תַּחַת	to rule שָׂרַר
epoch; period, season f. תְּקוּפָה	saucer f. תַּחְתִּית	service m. שֵׁרוּת
phonograph record m. תַּקְלִיט	appetite m. תֵּיאָבוֹן	to serve שֵׁרַת
ceiling f. תִּקְרָה	theater m. תֵּיאַטְרוֹן	six f. שֵׁשׁ m. שִׁשָּׁה
culture f. תַּרְבּוּת	middle, center תִּיכוֹן	sixth שִׁשִּׁי
translation m. תִּרְגּוּם	Mediterranean Sea m. יָם־הַתִּיכוֹן	to drink שָׁתָה
exercise m. תַּרְגִּיל	briefcase, file m. תִּיק	
rooster m. תַּרְנְגֹל	tourist m. תַּיָּר	ת.
turkey m. תַּרְנְגֹל־הֹודוּ	tourism f. תַּיָּרוּת	fig f. תְּאֵנָה
answer f. תְּשׁוּבָה	often תְּכוּפוֹת	to describe תֵּאֵר
payment m. תַּשְׁלוּם	plan, program f. תָּכְנִית	date m. תַּאֲרִיךְ
m. תִּשְׁעָה nine	to hang תָּלָה	tea m. תֵּה
f. תֵּשַׁע	pupil m. תַּלְמִיד	would you kindly תּוֹאִיל
ninth תְּשִׁיעִי	picture f. תְּמוּנָה	thanks f. תּוֹדָה

NOTE ON HEBREW HANDWRITING:
You already know the printed Hebrew letters. Here are
the handwritten ones. Remember that Hebrew has *no*
capital letters. The handwritten *final* letters are given
at the end of the alphabet.

EXAMPLES OF
HEBREW HANDWRITING

ברוכים הבאים לישראל,

גבירותי ורבותי !

(You will find this in print on page 223, lines 1 and 2.)

אתה מדבר עברית מצוין.

(You will find this in print on page 225, line 4.)

הבשקאור לפתח התקלאות

האינסיבי או לפאות.

(You will find this in print on page 218, line 8)

ובכן ועתה אני יצא לספר, לקרא

לכתב עברית.

(See if you can decipher this yourself!)